The Economic Impact of Counterfeiting and Piracy

OECD

ORGANISATION FOR ECONOMIC CO-OPERATION AND DEVELOPMENT

The OECD is a unique forum where the governments of 30 democracies work together to address the economic, social and environmental challenges of globalisation. The OECD is also at the forefront of efforts to understand and to help governments respond to new developments and concerns, such as corporate governance, the information economy and the challenges of an ageing population. The Organisation provides a setting where governments can compare policy experiences, seek answers to common problems, identify good practice and work to co-ordinate domestic and international policies.

The OECD member countries are: Australia, Austria, Belgium, Canada, the Czech Republic, Denmark, Finland, France, Germany, Greece, Hungary, Iceland, Ireland, Italy, Japan, Korea, Luxembourg, Mexico, the Netherlands, New Zealand, Norway, Poland, Portugal, the Slovak Republic, Spain, Sweden, Switzerland, Turkey, the United Kingdom and the United States. The Commission of the European Communities takes part in the work of the OECD.

OECD Publishing disseminates widely the results of the Organisation's statistics gathering and research on economic, social and environmental issues, as well as the conventions, guidelines and standards agreed by its members.

This work is published on the responsibility of the Secretary-General of the OECD. The opinions expressed and arguments employed herein do not necessarily reflect the official views of the Organisation or of the governments of its member countries.

Corrigenda to OECD publications may be found on line at: *www.oecd.org/publishing/corrigenda*.

© OECD 2008

Foreword

This report, covering counterfeiting and piracy resulting in the production of tangible goods, is Phase I of a three-phase project examining the Economic Impact of Counterfeiting and Piracy. Phase II will cover digital piracy, while Phase III will cover all other forms of counterfeiting.

The report was prepared by the Structural Policy Division of the OECD Directorate for Science, Technology and Industry. Overall direction was provided by Wolfgang Hübner. The main authors were Peter Avery, Fabienne Cerri, Linda Haie-Fayle, Karsten Bjerring Olsen, Danny Scorpecci and Piotr Stryszowski. Significant contributions were also made by Alexandra Excoffier, Jakob von Ganske, Shigeki Kamiyama, Young-Nien Li, Fabrizio Pagani, Christina Sampogna, Hagbong Sim, Yuing-Chun Tsai and Jeoung Yeol Yu.

The study was carried out under the guidance of an expert Informal Advisory Group composed of OECD member governments and industry representatives, and the study team wishes to acknowledge the valuable assistance provided by that Advisory Group.

The report was presented to the OECD Committee on Industry, Innovation and Entrepreneurship, which agreed to its public release. The study was undertaken with the support of governments, industry and international organisations such as the World Trade Organization (WTO), the World Intellectual Property Organization, (WIPO), the World Customs Organization (WCO) and Interpol, and the authors express their gratitude for the inputs provided by all participants.

Table of Contents

EXECUTIVE SUMMARY

Magnitude and effects of counterfeiting and piracy necessitate strong action

Analysis carried out in this report indicates that international trade in counterfeit and pirated products could have been up to USD 200 billion in 2005. This total does not include domestically produced and consumed counterfeit and pirated products and the significant volume of pirated digital products being distributed via the Internet. If these items were added, the total magnitude of counterfeiting and piracy worldwide could well be several hundred billion dollars more.

Counterfeiting and piracy are illicit businesses in which criminal networks thrive. The report shows that the items that they and other counterfeiters and pirates produce and distribute are often substandard and can even be dangerous, posing health and safety risks that range from mild to life-threatening. Economy-wide, counterfeiting and piracy undermine innovation, which is key to economic growth.

The magnitude and effects of counterfeiting and piracy are of such significance that they compel strong and sustained action from governments, business and consumers. More effective enforcement is critical in this regard, as is the need to build public support to combat the counterfeiting and piracy. Increased co-operation between governments, and with industry, would be beneficial, as would better data collection.

Key findings and recommendations

The report suggests ways to develop information and analysis, and calls on governments to consider strengthening legal and regulatory frameworks, enhance enforcement and deepen the evaluation of policies, programmes and practices.

Market analysis – critical to developing an effective response

The market for counterfeit and pirated products can be divided into two important sub-markets. In the *primary market*, consumers purchase counterfeit and pirated products believing they have purchased genuine articles. The products are often sub-standard and carry health and safety risks that range from mild to life-threatening. In the *secondary market*, consumers looking for what they believe to be bargains knowingly buy counterfeit and pirated products. The policies and measures to combat counterfeiting and piracy in the two markets differ; it is therefore important to know how much of a threat each poses when considering product-specific strategies.

Main elements of the report

- Analyses the structure of the markets for counterfeit and pirated products; the analysis highlights the importance of distinguishing those consumers who knowingly purchase counterfeit or pirated products, from those who are deceived.

- Assesses the scope of products being counterfeited and pirated.

- Examines the principal factors driving production and consumption.

- Estimates the potential magnitude of counterfeited and pirated goods in international trade, based on a new econometric model.

- Establishes and applies a 17-point framework for assessing the effects of counterfeiting and piracy economy-wide, as well as on rights holders, consumers and governments.

- Presents a framework for assessing the effectiveness of the policies and related initiatives being pursued to combat counterfeiting and piracy.

- Describes and evaluates the main national and international initiatives being taken by governments and business to combat counterfeiting and piracy.

- Examines in detail the situation in the audio-visual, automotive, electrical components, food and drink, pharmaceutical and tobacco sectors.

- Outlines ways that information and analysis on counterfeiting and piracy could be strengthened; and

- Suggests areas where policies and practices to combat counterfeiting and piracy could be strengthened.

The study identifies a number of factors that are important to understanding why some products are counterfeited or pirated more frequently than others, and why counterfeiting and piracy are more common in certain parts of the world than others. The factors provide a framework for assessing the *propensity* of a product to be counterfeited or pirated, which can be used to guide quantitative research. They can also be used to suggest areas where government and industry should focus efforts to combat the illicit operations. The propensity framework is applied to the analysis of the six industry sector case studies included in the report.

Magnitude and scope – larger than the national GDPs of 150 economies and affecting nearly all product sectors

This study shows that counterfeit and pirated products are being produced and consumed in virtually all economies, with Asia emerging as the single largest-producing region. In recent years, there has been an alarming expansion of the types of products being infringed, from luxury items (such as deluxe watches and designer clothing), to items that have an impact on personal health and safety (such as pharmaceutical products, food and drink, medical equipment, personal care items, toys, tobacco and automotive parts).

With respect to magnitude, the study notes that promising work has been done in a number of sectors to measure the extent of counterfeiting and piracy, but that much more can and should be done. The situation of each industry is unique, therefore techniques for carrying out such analysis need to be tailored to the sectors concerned.

To date, no rigorous quantitative analysis has been carried out to measure the overall magnitude of counterfeiting and piracy. This report notes the difficulties that would need to be addressed before such an estimate could be made, and then presents a methodology for estimating the role of counterfeiting and piracy in international trade, which is only a part, albeit an important one, of the total picture.

An analysis of international trade data (landed customs value basis[1]) was carried out using the methodology; it suggests that up to USD 200 billion of internationally traded products could have been counterfeit or pirated in 2005. This amount is larger than the national GDPs of about 150 economies[2]. The figure does not, however, include counterfeit and pirated products that are produced and consumed domestically, nor does it include non-tangible pirated digital products being distributed via the Internet. If these items were added, the total magnitude of counterfeiting and piracy worldwide could well be several hundred billion dollars more.

Effects – broad and profound

The report presents and applies a framework for assessing the effects of counterfeiting and piracy. Included in the analysis are assessments of the: *1)* general socio-economic effects (on innovation and growth, criminal activities, environment, employment, foreign direct investment, and trade); *2)* effects on rights holders (on sales volume and prices, brand value and firm reputation, royalties, firm-level investment, costs and the scope of operations); *3)* effects on consumers (health and safety risks and consumer utility); and *4)* effects on government (tax revenues, expenditures and corruption).

The analysis shows that criminal networks and organised crime thrive via counterfeiting and piracy activities. The items that counterfeiters and pirates produce are often substandard, sometimes endangering the lives of those who purchase them. These illicit activities steal market share from legitimate businesses and undermine innovation, with negative implications for economic growth. Bribery associated with counterfeiting and piracy weakens the effectiveness of public institutions at the expense of society at large. Moreover, the savings that consumers may achieve by knowingly purchasing lower-priced counterfeit or pirated products need to be considered in a broader context. Depending on the product, consumers can be worse off. In some cases, consumers seeking to save money may be exposing themselves to health and safety risks when the products concerned are substandard. Governments are also directly affected: tax revenues are foregone and costs are incurred in combating the problem, and public institutions are weakened when criminal networks use corruption to facilitate their counterfeiting and piracy activities.

Policies and measures

The report presents an eight-point framework for assessing the effectiveness of policies and measures to combat counterfeiting and piracy, and describes the situation for 15 different economies/regions (Brazil, Canada, China, European Union, France, India, Israel, Italy, Japan, Korea, Russia, Switzerland, Chinese Taipei, United Kingdom, United

---

1. Customs value is the value of merchandise assigned by customs officials; in most instances this is the same as the transaction value appearing on accompanying invoices. Landed customs value includes the insurance and freight charges incurred in transporting goods from the economy of origin to the economy of importation. Further information on valuation is available from the UN Comtrade Database (http://comtrade.un.org/).

2. Based on World Bank data for the year 2005.

States). The analysis indicates that the economies examined appear to have mechanisms in place to combat counterfeiting and piracy and that, in most cases, these mechanisms meet the basic obligations contained in the World Trade Organization's Agreement on Trade Related Aspects of Intellectual Property (*i.e.* TRIPS). Within this framework, there has been a general tendency for economies to strengthen civil and criminal sanctions in recent years. In practice, however, enforcement is still viewed by many as inadequate.

Improving efforts to combat counterfeiting and piracy

At the national governmental level, two of the principal challenges in combating counterfeiting and piracy are: *1)* to find ways to enhance enforcement; and *2)* to raise awareness of counterfeiting and piracy issues. More needs to be done to detect and undermine counterfeiting and piracy at the point where infringement originates. Actions are also required to keep the Internet from becoming an even more prominent distribution channel for counterfeit and pirated products. Multilaterally, ways to strengthen the existing framework and practices could be explored. Suggestions mentioned in this regard include strengthening civil and criminal remedies to more effectively redress the harm caused to rights holders, expanding border measures and increasing information disclosure. Furthermore, at the governmental level, co-operation with industry and among governments could be strengthened. Finally, development of effective policies and practices would benefit from more regular assessment, through peer review and related examinations.

While the OECD study has been able to provide insights into the situation, the report also notes that the information base needs to be strengthened. Governments, business and other interested stakeholders could do a far better job collecting and analysing information that is essential for designing and implementing effective strategies for combating counterfeiting and piracy. The report identifies a number of ways that this could be done, including: *1)* establishing a common approach for collecting enforcement data; *2)* developing a reporting framework to document the health and safety effects of counterfeit and pirated product; *3)* making more extensive use of surveys to provide insights into the markets for counterfeit and pirated products; and *4)* increasing co-operation between governments and business.

Improved information would enable more far-reaching analyses to be carried out on the magnitude and effects of counterfeiting and piracy on economies. In turn, this would provide governments and other stakeholders with a firmer basis for developing more informed and effective policies and programmes to combat the illicit practices.

Part I

OVERALL ASSESSMENT OF COUNTERFEITING AND PIRACY

Part I

Chapter 1

INTRODUCTION

1.1. Background

Protection of intellectual property rights (IPR) is an issue of high importance and increasing priority for governments. Its importance reflects the growing recognition of the key role that intellectual property (IP) plays in promoting innovation and growth on the one hand, and, on the other, increasing concern with the adverse effects that counterfeiting and piracy are having on economies and society as a whole.

The broadening scope and magnitude of counterfeiting and piracy is a key issue in this regard. Infringing products are no longer limited to falsely branded items such as fashion clothing, luxury watches and designer sunglasses, but now include a growing number of common food and drink, pharmaceutical, chemical, electronic and household products. These products, which are often substandard, can pose significant health and safety risks to consumers. Moreover, it appears that fake products, which have traditionally been sold largely on open markets, are finding their way at an increasing pace into legitimate distribution systems, and thus onto the shelves of established shops. Organised criminal groups are seen as playing an increasingly important role in this regard, benefiting significantly from highly profitable counterfeiting and piracy operations. Finally, the growth in the use of the Internet as a platform for selling products has provided a new outlet that counterfeiters and pirates have been quick to exploit.

Priority has therefore been given to enhancing international co-operation to reduce commerce in counterfeit and pirated products. The increasing priority is reflected in the efforts that governments and the business community have made in recent years to improve the effectiveness of IP policies and programmes worldwide. These include national actions, sectoral initiatives, and co-operation in multilateral efforts.

On the multilateral front, the World Intellectual Property Organization (WIPO), World Customs Organization (WCO) and Interpol have been working closely with the business community to identify new strategies to combat counterfeiting and piracy, and together they have organised several global and regional congresses since 2004 to address emerging issues. In addition, the World Trade Organization (WTO) provides a forum for the discussion of issues related to IP protection under the Agreement on Trade-Related Aspects of Intellectual Property Rights (TRIPS) that was agreed to during the Uruguay Round.

These issues have also been addressed plurilaterally in the context of the G8 summit meetings held in 2005 and 2006. The G8 countries recognised that innovation processes are increasingly threatened by IPR violations and reaffirmed their commitment to combating counterfeiting and piracy (G8, 2006).

1.2. OECD project

The initiatives that are being taken by governments and business to enhance efforts to combat counterfeiting and piracy have been hampered by a lack of information on the magnitude and scope of the problem worldwide. The clandestine nature of infringing activities and consequent difficulties in developing statistical information have been key factors in this regard.

To improve the situation, governments, with the support of the business community, turned to the OECD and requested it to carry out a comprehensive assessment of the problem, building on a report on counterfeiting issued in 1998 (OECD, 1998) (see Annex 1.A1 for the terms of reference). The assessment is to be completed in three phases, of which this is the first[1]. In this phase, infringements of trademarks, copyrights, patents and design rights are being examined, to the extent that they involve physical (*i.e.* non-digital) products. This means that intangible products such as digital files exchanged over the Internet or by other electronic means are not covered by this first phase. The work is being financed jointly by governments and the business community.

The Phase I assessment has been structured to include: *1)* an analysis of trends and developments, and an assessment of the effects of counterfeiting and piracy on rights holders, consumers and society at large (including governments); *2)* exploration of techniques that can be used to improve measurement of the volume and scope of counterfeiting and piracy worldwide; *3)* a description and assessment of the polices and measures being used to combat counterfeiting and piracy in OECD and non-OECD economies, at both the national and multilateral levels; and *4)* a series of industry sectoral assessments that illustrate the various forms that counterfeiting and piracy can take, and the different types of effects that counterfeit and pirated products can have on affected parties.

The research was carried out in co-operation with individuals, firms, organisations and governmental agencies that have expertise and experience in IP areas. Information was collected from various sources, including surveys distributed to governments -- one general country/economy survey (see Annex 1.A2) and one customs-specific survey (see Annex 1.A4) -- and to industry (see Annex 1.A3). The general country/economy survey was sent to the 30 OECD member countries and to six non-member economies. The customs survey was sent to all 169 WCO members. The industry surveys were made generally available and were widely distributed by associations. Twenty responses were received to the general country/economy survey, 70 responses to the customs-specific survey and approximately 80 responses to the industry survey. Furthermore, in support of the work, two expert meetings were organised to explore ways to improve measurement techniques.

---

1.   Phase II will focus on digital piracy while Phase III will focus on other types of IPR infringement. Work on each of these phases will proceed once the scope for each has been decided and funding has been secured.

1.3. Definitions and parameters of report

Counterfeiting and piracy are terms used to describe a range of illicit activities linked to intellectual property rights (IPR) infringement. The mandate for the OECD project confines work to the infringement of IP rights described in the WTO Agreement on Trade-Related Aspects of Intellectual Property Rights (TRIPS).[2] As indicated above, the first phase of the project covers four types of infringements: trademarks, copyrights, patents and design rights (to the extent that they involve tangible products).

1.3.1. Trademarks

A trademark is a distinctive sign that identifies certain goods or services as those produced or provided by a specific person or enterprise. Under the TRIPS Agreement, this includes any sign, or any combination of signs, capable of distinguishing the goods or services of one undertaking from those of other undertakings. Such signs may include, in particular, words including personal names, letters, numerals, figurative elements and combinations of colours, as well as any combination of such signs.

The trademark confers exclusive rights to the rights holder, who can prevent third parties from unauthorised use of signs for goods or services that are identical or similar to those in respect to the registered trademark, if there is a risk of confusion (Article 16.1 TRIPS). Trademark protection is also subject to limited exceptions, such as fair use of descriptive terms, provided that certain conditions are met. Those are addressed in Article 17 TRIPS. While the period of protection varies, the initial term of registration shall be of no less than seven years pursuant to Article 18 TRIPS. The registration may be renewed indefinitely, on payment of additional fees.

In a number of jurisdictions, trademarks do not need to be registered in order to be protected. Even in these instances, registration does, however, offer a number of advantages. Under the Madrid Protocol, for example, once a trademark has been registered or applied for in a jurisdiction, an application can be made to have the trademark registered simultaneously in multiple jurisdictions, through an international application process overseen by WIPO, in co-operation with national authorities.

1.3.2. Copyright and related rights

Copyright describes the rights given to authors for their creative works. The kind of works that may be covered by copyright include: literary works, such as novels, poems, plays, reference works, newspapers and computer programs; databases; films, musical compositions, phonograms, performances, broadcasts and choreography; artistic works such as paintings, drawings, photographs and sculpture; architecture; and advertisements, maps and technical drawings. The rights do not cover ideas, procedures, methods of operation or mathematical concepts as such. Unlike trademarks, creative works do not have to be registered in order to be protected; a copyright applies from the moment of

---

2. Substandard, adulterated or mislabelled pharmaceutical products that do not violate a trademark or patent are thus beyond the scope of the study, as are, for example, replacement automotive oil filters and head lamps that are made by firms other than the original equipment manufacturer (provided the replacement parts do not violate a patent or trademark).

creation of the literary and artistic work. Formal registration may, however, provide additional protection.

Copyright provides the author with exclusive rights to prevent third parties from using the creation without his authorisation. Acts that require the authorisation of the rights holder include reproduction of the work in various forms, such as printed publications or sound recordings, the distribution of copies, the public performance of the work, its broadcasting or other communication to the public, its translation into other languages and its adaptation, such as a novel into a screenplay. Under Article 6*bis* of the Berne Convention, the author is also granted certain moral rights, such as the right to claim authorship and to object to any modification of the work that would be prejudicial to his honour or reputation; this is not mandatory under the TRIPS Agreement. Limitations and exceptions to the exclusive rights are provided in the Berne Convention and Article 13 TRIPS.

Related rights aim at protecting the interests of performers, producers of sound recordings and broadcasting organisations. Like authors, they benefit from certain exclusive rights that are detailed in Article 14 TRIPS.

Copyright protection is time-bound. Under TRIPS, protection should correspond at least to the natural life of the creator plus 50 years after his death, or, if the author is not a natural person, to not less than 50 years from the end of the calendar year of authorised publication or of the creation of the work, failing an authorised publication within 50 years from the making of the work. Under the 1996 WIPO treaties, the economic rights of authors are valid for at least 50 years after the author's death. The term of protection for phonogram producers and performers in recorded music has to be at least 50 years from fixation or from the time that the performance took place. Broadcasting organisations are benefiting from at least 20 years of protection counted from the end of the calendar year in which the broadcast took place. Some countries with a developed IP-based industry have now extended the term of protection to longer periods. There is a trend for countries to adopt longer terms than the minima required by TRIPS and the WIPO Treaties, *e.g.* a term of the life of the author plus 70 years, or at least 70 years from first publication if the author is not a natural person, and provide 70 years or more for sound recordings.

1.3.3. Patents

Patents are generally available for any inventions, whether products or processes, in all fields of technology, provided that they are new, involve an inventive step and are capable of industrial application. The criteria that are applied to determine patentability tend to vary among countries, as do the technical requirements that must be fulfilled in order for a patent to be granted.

A patent enables the patent holder to exclude unauthorised parties from making, using, offering for sale, selling or importing a protected product as well as a product obtained by a patented process, and from using a patented process. According to Article 30 TRIPS, Members may provide limited exceptions to the exclusive rights conferred by a patent, provided that such exceptions do not unreasonably conflict with the normal exploitation of the patent and do not unreasonably prejudice the legitimate interests of the patent owner, taking into account the legitimate interests of third parties. Compulsory licensing and government use without the authorisation of the rights holder are also allowed, but they are subject to conditions aimed at protecting the legitimate interests of the rights holder. Under the TRIPS Agreement, the patent right is offered for a period of at least 20 years from the date of filing an application for a patent.

In exchange for the offering of this period of exclusivity, the information disclosed in the patent application must be laid open and be made publicly available, so as to stimulate further research and innovation.

Patent rights are geographically bound, which means that a party must apply for a patent in every jurisdiction in which it wishes to protect, and possibly market, its new product or process. In order to alleviate some of the burden of multiple applications for patents throughout the world, a more centralised application procedure through the Patent Co-operation Treaty (PCT) process is available.

1.3.4. Industrial designs

Under the TRIPS Agreement, industrial design is defined as the ornamental or aesthetic aspect of an article. The design may consist of three-dimensional features, such as the shape or surface of an article, or of two-dimensional features, such as patterns, lines or colour. Industrial designs are applied to a wide variety of products of industry and handicraft, including technical and medical instruments, watches, jewellery. An industrial design usually does not protect any technical features of the article to which it is applied.

Based on the exclusive rights conferred, the right holder can prevent third parties from making, selling or importing articles bearing or embodying a protected design without his authorisation. In other words, design protection does not exclude other manufacturers from producing or dealing in similar products with the same utilitarian functions, as long as those products do not embody or reproduce the design in question. Pursuant to Article 26.2 TRIPS, limited exceptions may be provided for, subject to certain conditions.

In most countries, an industrial design must be registered in order to be protected. As a general rule, in order to be registered, the design must be "new" or "original". Different countries have varying definitions of such terms, as well as variations in the registration process itself. Generally, "new" means that no identical or very similar design is known to have existed before. Once a design is registered, a registration certificate is issued. The TRIPS Agreement requires that the duration of protection be at least 10 years. Protection in multiple jurisdictions can be obtained by registering an industrial design through the WIPO, under the Hague Agreement.

Depending on the particular national law and the kind of design, an industrial design may also be protected as a work of art under copyright law. In some countries, industrial design and copyright protection can exist concurrently. However, in other countries, they are mutually exclusive: once the owner chooses one kind of protection, the other type may no longer be invoked.

References

G8 (2006), "Combating IPR Piracy and Counterfeiting", Saint Petersburg, Russia, http://en.g8russia.ru, accessed July 2006.

OECD (1998), "The Economic Impact of Counterfeiting", www.oecd.org.

Annex 1.A1.

PROJECT MANDATE[5]

Background

Counterfeiting and piracy are longstanding problems that appear to be growing in scope and magnitude. These practices can have negative effects on the sales and profits of affected firms, while raising economic, health, safety and security effects for governments and consumers. The emergence of the Internet has significantly increased the distribution channels for counterfeit and pirated goods, and raised jurisdictional problems in combating such practices.

There has recently been an upsurge in private sector mobilisation to raise awareness of this issue. Some OECD member governments are also placing renewed emphasis on combating counterfeiting and piracy.

The OECD is being asked to carry out the project described in this document in light of *1)* its previous work on the subject; and *2)* its research and analytical capabilities.

The activity is foreseen in the draft Programme of Work and Budget (PWB) 2005/2006 under output 1.2.1. The work proposal template is provided in the Annex of that document. The project would be funded through voluntary contributions and would be carried out only in so far as such voluntary contributions are received.

Given the preliminary nature of the discussion that the Committee on Industry and Business Environment had on the proposal, it is considered appropriate to submit the matter to Council directly.

Objective

The objective of the proposed project will be to improve factual understanding and awareness of the harmful effects that infringements of intellectual property rights, as described and defined in the WTO TRIPS Agreement, have on governments, business and consumers in member countries and non-member economies. Given time and resource constraints, it is proposed that the project be carried out in three phases, which would be separately funded. Each of these phases will be reflected in separate reports to be supplemented by an overall final report covering all three phases.

The first Phase will focus on counterfeit and pirated products (*i.e.* tangible products that infringe trademarks or copyrights) as well as patent and design infringements. As indicated below, an analytical report will be prepared that will include a series of sectoral

---

5.   The dates and timetable cited in the project mandate have in the meantime been subject to change.

assessments that illustrate the different types of effects that the illicit practices can have on economies. In addition to the report, regional workshops and a Global Forum will be held to provide further opportunities to examine and discuss issues.

The second Phase will examine the impact of piracy of digital content. To properly scope the work on piracy of digital content, the Secretariat will organise a technical meeting with experts from member governments to develop the parameters of the work for consideration by the Committee on Industry and Business Environment, or its successor, during the third quarter of 2005, while work on Phase I is already progressing. Following this scoping work, Phase II will be undertaken provided that adequate funding is available.

The reports on Phases I and II of the study will be submitted to the Council in 2006. Phase III of the study on infringements of other intellectual property rights not examined so far will be launched in the second half of 2006 and presented to Council in 2007. In order to properly scope the work to be done in Phase III, the Secretariat will organise a technical meeting with experts from member governments to develop the parameters of the work, for consideration by the Committee on Industry and Business Environment, or its successor. Following this scoping work, Phase III will proceed provided that adequate funding is available. Phase III will be conducted in a manner that does not prejudice discussions taking place in other international *fora*.

Upon completion of the whole project, the Council will consider, if justified by the conclusions of the study, whether further work should be undertaken to encourage governments in member countries and non-member economies to develop more effective policies to combat counterfeiting and piracy. The further work envisaged would be dependent on the availability of adequate funding.

The first phase of the project will seek to:

Enhance factual understanding of the problem

The last rigorous analysis of counterfeiting and piracy from a global perspective dates back to 1998 (OECD, *Economic Impact of Counterfeiting*). This work will be updated and expanded through a new analysis that will develop factual information on the scope, volume, trends and impacts of piracy and counterfeiting that is comparable across industries and countries. The study will be fact-finding in nature, and include:

- *An analysis of trends and developments*. The changing volume and scope of counterfeiting and piracy will be examined, as will its role in international trade. Changes in the types of products being counterfeited, and the regions where counterfeiting and piracy are taking place will be highlighted.

- The factors driving counterfeiting and piracy will be identified and discussed, as will the role of new technologies in facilitating counterfeiting and piracy activities.

- *An assessment of the effects on firms, consumers and government*. A methodological framework for assessing the effects of counterfeiting and piracy on stakeholders will be elaborated. In addition to economic factors, health, safety and security factors will be highlighted. The assessment will include special attention to the adverse effects that the practices can have on those countries where counterfeiting and piracy are most pronounced.

- *A series of sectoral assessments*. A number of sectoral case studies will be conducted, illustrating the various forms of counterfeiting and piracy, and the different types of effects on producers, consumers and governments. The products to be studied will include those with significant safety, health and/or social implications (in addition to economic ones), such as pharmaceuticals, food and drink, consumer products, spare parts and car accessories, aircraft components, toys and electronic equipment (*e.g.* mobile phones, batteries). Other consumer products with important economic, employment and innovation implications will also be covered, such as software (some with security/safety implications), electrical and optical equipment, chemicals, music recordings, motion pictures, books (especially school text books), sportswear, luxury goods and fashion clothes and perfumes. Selection will also take into account the availability of information.

- *A description and assessment of policies and measures used to combat counterfeiting and piracy.* National and multilateral policies and measures taken by governments, business and other stakeholders to combat counterfeiting and piracy will be described and assessed, with particular attention to those policies and measures which have been found to be particularly effective. To the extent possible, the policies and measures taken in key non-OECD economies will be included.

Raise awareness of the problem

The study will be a key part of a broader initiative that will, as indicated above, include a series of regional workshops. The workshops will be aimed at developing factual information on counterfeiting and piracy trends in different regions as well as understanding trends in related policy-making. They should provide a platform for increased familiarity among key public, as well as private, sector players in OECD and non-OECD economies participating in this activity. Regional workshops in Brazil, China, India and Russia, as well as a Global Forum on Phase I, are envisaged to be held in 2006. A second Global Forum will be organised in 2007.

Methodology and timetable

The project will be overseen by the Committee on Industry and Business Environment, or its successor. Other OECD bodies will, however, be kept apprised of the work. TUAC and BIAC will be involved with the project as will the Consumers International, and co-ordination will be pursued with other international bodies active in the counterfeiting/piracy area (such as WTO, WCO, WIPO and Interpol).

In order to adhere to the tight timeframes envisioned, an informal advisory group will be created, with the participation of representatives from all member countries and organisations that have an interest in the project. The project will be carried out and completed in accordance with the usual OECD rules and procedures regarding the proper evaluation and monitoring of projects.

With respect to timeframes, the report on the first phase will be completed in mid-2006 and that on the second phase by the end of 2006. The report on the third Phase is expected to be ready as soon as possible in 2007, followed soon after by the completion of the overall final report. The reports will be made publicly available. The regional workshops will be organised during 2006. A Global Forum on Phase 1 will be targeted for the second half of 2006. A second Global Forum will be organised in 2007 to mark the conclusion of the whole project.

Annex 1.A2

COUNTRY/ECONOMY SURVEY

On 28 April 2005, the OECD Council agreed to carry out a project on counterfeiting and piracy [see DSTI/IND(2005)1]. Work on Phase I of the project has since been initiated [see DSTI/IND(2005)2]. This Phase will include a review of the situation in economies and an assessment of the efforts that governments and other authorities are making to combat counterfeiting and piracy. Information and data that are crucial for the review will be developed primarily through the attached questionnaire. A related questionnaire is being sent to industries affected by counterfeiting and piracy.

Please note that the questionnaire concerns Phase I of the project. This Phase covers infringements of trademarks, copyrights, patents and design rights[6], when the infringements involve tangible products. Intangible, digital products that are not embodied in a tangible medium (such as a CD or a DVD) will be covered in Phase II.

In addition to completing the questionnaire, submission of reports or studies related to the project would be welcome.

If you have any questions regarding the survey or the project please contact:

| Mrs. Linda Haie-Fayle
e-mail : Linda.Haie-Fayle@oecd.org
Tel: 33 1 45 24 91 33

or

Mr. Peter Avery
e-mail: Peter.Avery@oecd.org
Tel: 33 1 45 24 93 63 | OECD
Structural Policy Division
Directorate for Science, Technology
and Industry
2 rue André-Pascal
75775 Paris Cedex 16

Fax: 33 1 44 30 62 57 |

Replies to the questionnaire are requested by no later than **15 September 2005** and should be sent preferably by e-mail to: counterfeit@oecd.org or by mail to the address above.

---

6.   Definitions of these terms are as defined in the WTO Agreement on Trade-Related Aspects of Intellectual Property Rights (TRIPS).

OECD COUNTERFEITING AND PIRACY PROJECT
Country/Economy Questionnaire

COUNTRY/ECONOMY:

CONTACT PERSON:

Telephone/Fax:

E-mail:

Note: The term *counterfeiting and piracy* in this questionnaire covers infringements of trademarks, copyrights (and related rights), patents and design rights. It relates to tangible products only [*i.e.* intangible digital products which are not embodied in a tangible medium (such as a CD or a DVD) are not covered; these products will be examined in a subsequent phase of the project]. In responding to questions, please address trademark, copyright, patent and design issues separately (to the extent possible).

Q1 How have the magnitude and scope of infringements of trademarks, copyrights, patent and design rights (*i.e.* counterfeiting and piracy) changed in your economy in recent years (*e.g.* over the last 5 years)?

A description of the techniques and sources of information you have used to estimate the magnitude and scope would be appreciated.

Points that could be covered:

- With respect to your domestic economy, the extent to which counterfeiting and piracy is taking place within your borders and the nature of the counterfeiting and piracy activities:
  - Principal types of products being counterfeited and pirated in your economy;
  - Indication of how the magnitude and scope have changed in recent years;
  - How operations for counterfeiting and pirating products are organised (*i.e.* from the acquisition of protected inputs to the manufacture of products) and financed;
  - Description of how counterfeit and pirated products are being moved from production centres or other locations into domestic and foreign markets, and who benefits from the illicit commerce;
  - Role of organised crime in production and distribution of products;
- Exports of counterfeit and pirated products from your country/economy:
  - Principal exports markets and the principal products being exported;
- Imports of counterfeit and pirated products:
  - Principal import sources and the principal products being imported;
  - Principal means that are used to penetrate your market;
  - Role of organised crime in facilitating imports;
- How the volume of trade in counterfeit and pirated products (*i.e.* the level of imports and exports) has changed in recent years in your economy;
- Principal factors that explain the changes in the scope and magnitude of counterfeiting and piracy worldwide and in your economy.

Q2	What have been the principal effects of counterfeit and pirated products on your economy?
	This would include the health, safety and the economic effects on producers, holders of the IPR rights, consumers/purchasers, workers and society at large, including governments. Effects on governments and society at large would include international trade, foreign investment, tax revenues and law enforcement.
	A description of the techniques that were used to measure the effects would be appreciated.
Q3	Please describe the principal policies and programmes being used in your economy to combat counterfeiting and piracy, and otherwise protect the intellectual property rights concerned. How have these policies and programmes changed in recent years?
	Areas covered could include *(i)* the legal framework for combating counterfeiting and piracy, *(ii)* enforcement (internal and border measures) through criminal, civil and administrative systems, *(iii)* training and technical assistance, *(iv)* public awareness initiatives, and *(v)* international co-operation and co-ordination.
	In providing a response, please avoid a simple cataloguing of laws and related instruments. A more qualitative description would be preferred.
	Points that could be covered:
	– Judicial and other means available for domestic rights holders, foreign rights holders and governments to combat infringements;
	– Financial and other costs associated with industry and government efforts to combat infringements;
	– Scope and severity of criminal, civil and administrative penalties for infringements, and the extent to which these penalties are applied
Q4	Taken as a whole, how effective have the policies and programmes (including public/private partnerships) been in combating counterfeiting and piracy, *(i)* within your domestic economy and *(ii)* at borders and *(iii)* internationally?
	Points that could be covered:
	– Identification of policies and programmes that have been the most effective in reducing counterfeiting and piracy;
	– Ways that policies and programmes need to be strengthened;
	– Ways that international co-operation and co-ordination to combat counterfeiting and piracy need to be improved at the national and multilateral levels
Q5	What additional points would you like to make concerning counterfeiting and piracy?

Annex 1.A3

INDUSTRY SURVEY

In response to rising concerns in government and the business community, the OECD has launched a project that will assess the effects of counterfeiting and piracy on economies. The objective of the project is to improve factual understanding and awareness of the effects that infringements of intellectual property rights, as described and defined in the WTO Agreement on Trade-Related Aspects of Intellectual Property Rights (TRIPS) have on governments, business and consumers in OECD member countries and non-member economies.

The project will be conducted in co-operation with organisations that are active in counterfeiting/piracy, including the World Trade Organization, the World Customs Organization, the World Intellectual Property Organization, Interpol and relevant non-governmental organisations (NGOs). Liaison with the business community and labour will be co-ordinated through the OECD Business and Industry Advisory Committee (www.biac.org) and the OECD Trade Union Advisory Committee (www.tuac.org).

As indicated in the project description contained in the Annex, the project is being conducted in three phases. The first phase will cover infringements of trademarks, copyrights, patents and design rights, when the infringements involve tangible products. Intangible, digital products which are not embodied in a tangible medium (such as a CD or a DVD) will be covered in the second phase of the project.

In support of the project, industries are being invited to provide information on their respective situations. The attached questionnaire, which is voluntary, has been developed to help facilitate the process. Please fill it out as completely as possible (*i.e.* do not be concerned if you are not in position to respond fully to each question). In responding, please indicate *i)* which industry is covered by the questionnaire and *ii)* the name (including e-mail address and phone number) of a contact if we have follow-up enquiries. Submission of industry studies and reports related to the study would also be welcome.

The information collected in the questionnaires will be used to assist the research team in developing insights into counterfeiting and piracy in different sectors. If you do not wish your firm or association to be named in the report as the source for the information contained in the questionnaire, you can indicate so by placing a checkmark in the first box of the questionnaire in the area provided. All such requests not to be mentioned will be honoured.

Please note that a related questionnaire is being sent to governments.

If you have any questions regarding the survey or the project please contact:

Mrs. Linda Haie-Fayle e-mail : Linda.Haie-Fayle@oecd.org Tel: 33 1 45 24 91 33 or Mr. Peter Avery e-mail: Peter.Avery@oecd.org Tel: 33 1 45 24 93 63	OECD Structural Policy Division Directorate for Science, Technology and Industry 2 rue André-Pascal 75775 Paris Cedex 16 Fax: 33 1 44 30 62 57

Replies to the questionnaire are requested by no later than **15 September 2005** and should be sent preferably by e-mail to: counterfeit@oecd.org or by mail to the address above.

INDUSTRY QUESTIONNAIRE

NAME OF COMPANY/ASSOCIATION:

COUNTRY:

CONTACT PERSON:

Telephone/Fax:

E-mail:

If you do not wish your company/association to be named in the report as the source for the information contained in this questionnaire, please check here: ☐

Note: The term *counterfeiting and piracy* in this questionnaire covers infringements of trademarks, copyrights (and related rights), patents and design rights. It relates to tangible products only [*i.e.* intangible digital products which are not embodied in a tangible medium (such as a CD or a DVD) are not covered; these products will be examined in a subsequent phase of the project]. In responding to questions, please address trademark, copyright, patent and design issues separately (to the extent possible).

Q1	What products made by your industry are most affected by infringements of trademarks, copyrights, patents and design rights (*i.e.* counterfeiting and piracy)? How have the magnitude and scope of the infringements involving these products changed in recent years (*e.g.* focussing on the last 5 years)?
	
	A description of the techniques and sources of information you have used to estimate the magnitude and scope would be appreciated.
	
	Points that could be covered:
	
	• Extent to which counterfeiting and piracy of your industry's products is taking place:
	    – Principal types of products being counterfeited and pirated;
	    – Indication of how the magnitude and scope of the counterfeiting and piracy of your industry's products have changed in recent years;
	    – Identification of the principal areas where your industry's products are being counterfeited and pirated (*i.e.* the economies or regions of the world where the practices are most problematic);

	– How operations for counterfeiting and pirating products are organised (*i.e.* from the acquisition of protected inputs to the manufacture of products) and financed;
	– Description of how counterfeit and pirated products are being moved from production centres or other locations into domestic and foreign markets and who benefits from the illicit commerce;
	– Role of organised crime in production and distribution of products;
	• International trade in counterfeit and pirated products in your industry sector:
	– Identification of the economies that are the major exporters and importers of the counterfeit and pirated products;
	– Principal counterfeit and pirated products traded;
	• Principal factors that explain the changes in the scope and magnitude of counterfeiting and piracy in your industry sector.
Q2	What have been the principal effects of the counterfeiting and piracy in your industry sector?
	This would include the health, safety and economic effects on your industry (including workers), consumers/purchasers and governments.
	A description of the techniques you have used to measure the effects would be appreciated.
	The effects on industry could cover how counterfeiting and piracy have affected:
	• Overall business strategies;
	• Investment in domestic and foreign production facilities;
	• Industry innovation and creation/development of products;
	• Product development;
	• Marketing strategies;
	• Product costs and pricing;
	• Workers; and
	• International trade.
Q3	What measures has your industry taken to combat the counterfeiting and piracy of its products? How effective have these measures been? What are the principal remaining challenges?
	Points that could be covered:
	• Discussion of technologies that have been most effective in helping to defend trademarks and copyrights and, to the extent applicable, patent and design rights;
	• Industry and firm-level initiatives that have been taken to protect trademarks, copyrights, patents and design rights;
	• Costs associated with these measures.

Q4	How effective have government policies and programmes (including public/private partnerships) been in combating counterfeiting and piracy in your domestic economy and foreign economies? This would include enforcement activities, legal frameworks, public awareness initiatives and international co-operation and co-ordination. Points that could be covered: <ul><li>Identification of the policies and programmes that have, in your view, been the most effective in reducing counterfeiting and piracy in your industry;</li><li>Industry experience in combating infringements worldwide (success rates, challenges faced by your industry in using existing policies, programmes and laws, etc.);</li><li>Legal and related costs associated with defending rights;</li><li>Obstacles in defending rights;</li><li>Ways in which policies and programmes need to be strengthened worldwide</li></ul>
Q5	What additional points would you like to make concerning counterfeiting and piracy in your industry?

Annex 1.A4

CUSTOMS SURVEY

Background

The OECD, which is an intergovernmental organisation (see www.oecd.org), is conducting a study on the magnitude, scope and effects of counterfeiting and piracy on producers, consumers and governments. The study will focus specifically on trademark, copyright, patent and design violations. Further information on the project can be accessed on the Internet at www.oecd.org/sti/counterfeiting.

The OECD research team has met with customs officials to discuss how information on customs seizures could be used in the study. Whilst acknowledging there were significant limitations, it was agreed that such information could be highly useful and that the knowledge and experience of customs officials could provide informed insights that could clarify a number of points, and that this could best be done through a survey.

The WCO has agreed to distribute this questionnaire to customs organisations as part of its work on counterfeiting and piracy.

Your co-operation in responding to the survey, which is voluntary, would be greatly appreciated.

We understand that there is no standardised way of collecting data that can be used by customs authorities, and we would welcome receiving the data in whatever format is available to you. However, we would be grateful for any advice you can give us on possible limitations of specific characteristics of your data that we should take into consideration when analysing it.

In addition to statistical information, please note that we are requesting customs officials to make estimates and judgements in a number of areas. We recognise the limitations of this approach, and the difficulties that it may pose, but we believe that your judgements in most instances will represent the best information available.

In addition to completing the questionnaire, submission of reports or studies related to the project would be welcome.

If you have any questions regarding the survey or the project please contact:

Mrs. Linda Haie-Fayle e-mail : Linda.Haie-Fayle@oecd.org Tel: 33 1 45 24 91 33 or Mr. Peter Avery e-mail: Peter.Avery@oecd.org Tel: 33 1 45 24 93 63	OECD Structural Policy Division Directorate for Science, Technology and Industry 2 rue André-Pascal 75775 Paris Cedex 16 Fax: 33 1 44 30 62 57

QUESTIONNAIRE

Replies to this questionnaire are requested by no later than **17 February 2006**. The replies should be sent preferably by email to: counterfeit@oecd.org. Alternatively, completed questionnaires could be faxed to the OECD at (33 1) 44 30 62 57, or be sent by mail to the attention of Ms. Haie-Fayle, at the OECD address indicated above.

1. What is the reporting country/economy?

2. Who could be contacted for any follow-up questions?

   (a) Name of contact person:

   (b) E-mail of contact person:

   (c) Telephone number of contact person:

3(a). The research team is interested in compiling a **detailed** list of *(i)* the specific counterfeit and pirated products that have been seized in recent years (at any time during 1999-2005), and *(ii)* the countries from which the seized products originated. The level of detail would preferably be comparable to the Harmonized System (HS) classification, at the **six-digit** level. Information on the type of infringement and the HS classification would also be appreciated. An example follows:

Product: Countries:

Type of infringement: HS item number:

Automotive gear boxes   Country A, Country B   Trademark   8708.40

Information on the products seized should be provided, even if other information (on countries, type of infringement and HS item number) are not available.

3(b). If available, information on the quantity and value of the individual products seized would also be appreciated. This would preferably be provided on a country-by-country basis. Such information could be for a recent year or, if possible, for a series of years. The information could be provided in whatever format is readily available.

4(a). To the extent possible, please provide data on the **number** and estimated **value** of seizures of counterfeit and pirated goods for the following years. Please report the "**Total**" number and value of seizures, even if data on the different types of seizures are not available. If data are not available, please indicate by entering "NA". If data for all years (1999-2005) are not available, please provide information for those years where such data are available.

Types	1999	2000	2001	2002	2003	2004	2005
	Number of seizures						
Trademark							
Copyright							
Patent							
Design							
Total							
	Estimated value of seizures						
Trademark							
Copyright							
Patent							
Design							
Total							

4(b). What currency is the value of seizures expressed in?

4(c). Please indicate whether the total value you report is in denominations of thousands, millions, or otherwise.

4(d). What is the method used to compute the value of seized goods (*e.g.* value of "legitimate" articles, market value of counterfeited and pirated items, etc.)?

4(e). If data on the total number of seizures are incomplete or unavailable, please provide your views (based on your observations and experience) on how the number of seizures of counterfeit and pirated goods seems to have changed between 1999 and 2005:

The overall number of seizures has (check one and complete, as appropriate):

     □ **increased**, by about _____% between 1999 and 2005;
      (Note: percent can be expressed as a single number, or a range.)

     or

     □ **decreased**, by about _____% between 1999 and 2005;

     or

     □ remained **about the same** between 1999 and 2005.

5. Changes in the number of seizures between 1999 and 2005 reflect *(i)* changes in counterfeiting and piracy activity, *(ii)* improved detection methods, *(iii)* changes in the laws governing infringements, and *(iv)* other factors, or a combination thereof.

Based on your observations and experience, how much do you estimate the number of seizures changed between 1999 and 2005, due only to changes in counterfeiting and piracy activity (check one and complete, as appropriate)?

     □ **increased,** by approximately _____%.
      (Note: percent can be expressed as a single number, or a range.)

     or

     □ **decreased,** by approximately _____%.

     or

     □ no change.

6. How has the range (or types) of counterfeit and pirated products that have been seized during the past 5 years changed? (Check one)

     The range of counterfeit and pirated products being seized:

     □ has become more limited.

     □ is basically the same.

     □ has been expanding steadily.

     □ has been expanding rapidly.

7(a). What are the principal ways that your customs officials detect counterfeit and pirated goods? Please indicate frequency by checking the appropriate box.

	Rarely	Sometimes	Often	Very often
Targeting (through profiling and related techniques)	☐	☐	☐	☐
Special alerts (or "tip-offs") received by customs officials that specific imports shipments are believed to contain infringing goods	☐	☐	☐	☐
Random examinations	☐	☐	☐	☐
Other (please specify):	☐	☐	☐	☐

7(b). Additional information on the targeting techniques being used to detect counterfeit and pirated goods would be welcome (use additional sheets, as required.

8. Based on your experience, do you have any rough idea of the percentage of imported counterfeit and pirated goods that are being intercepted at your borders (either overall or in specific product categories)?

Yes ☐   No ☐

9. Please provide any comments on *(i)* the information that has been provided in the questionnaire, or *(ii)* other comments related to the project.

Chapter 2

THE MARKETS FOR COUNTERFEIT AND PIRATED GOODS

2.1. Summary

In this chapter, we: *1)* describe how the markets for legitimate and infringing products operate and interact; *2)* identify the key factors that drive demand and supply of counterfeit and pirated products; and *3)* indicate how economy wide institutional factors influence the location of where counterfeit and pirated products are produced and consumed. In so doing, this chapter presents a framework for analysing and under-standing the phenomenon.

With respect to the operation of markets, the analysis draws a distinction between primary markets, which are defined as markets in which rights holders compete with counterfeiters and pirates who sell their products deceptively to consumers, portraying their products as legitimate items; and secondary markets, in which consumers willingly purchase infringing products from counterfeiters and pirates, generally at reduced prices, knowing that the products are not legitimate. The two-market approach is used to analyse markets involving trademark and copyright infringements; it is seen as ill-suited for assessing patent and design infringement, due to the significantly different nature of the infringements and the resulting different effects that they have on markets.

Concerning the supply side, the decision of a party to become a counterfeiter or pirate of a product is driven by a separate but related set of drivers, which apply regardless of whether the infringer targets the primary or secondary market. These supply drivers are related to: market opportunities; the technological and distribution challenges associated with an undertaking; and the risks involved (Table 2.1). The demand for infringing products is driven by three types of drivers, related to: the product in question; the individual consumer characteristics; and the institutional environment in which the consumer operates. Note that the demand drivers are relevant only for the secondary market, where purchasers knowingly choose to buy counterfeit and pirated items.

In order to distinguish between the description of the markets for counterfeiting and piracy and a dynamic analysis of the effects of counterfeiting, a static economic analysis is presented in this chapter. A dynamic approach that will additionally present the effects of counterfeiting and piracy is introduced in Chapter 5.

Table 2.1. Summary table of drivers for counterfeit and pirate activities

Counterfeit or pirate supply Driving factors	Knowing demand for counterfeit or pirated products Driving factors
Market characteristics	**Product characteristics**
High unit profitability	Low prices
Large potential market size	Acceptable perceived quality
Genuine brand power	Ability to conceal status
Production, distribution and technology	**Consumer characteristics**
Moderate need for investments	No health concerns
Moderate technology requirements	No safety concerns
Unproblematic distribution and sales	Personal budget constraint
High ability to conceal operation	Low regard for IPR
Easy to deceive consumers	
Institutional characteristics	**Institutional characteristics**
Low risk of discovery	Low risk of discovery and prosecution
Legal and regulatory framework	Weak or no penalties
Weak enforcement	Availability and ease of acquisition
Penalties	Socio-economic factors

The drivers provide an analytical framework that can be applied to specific products to assess the propensity for counterfeiting and piracy in those product areas from an *a priori* (*i.e.* non-empirical) perspective (see Chapter 3). They can also be used to develop general demand and supply functions for counterfeit and pirated products.

2.2. Market structure

2.2.1. Market actors

The markets in which genuine and counterfeit products compete are made up of producers (*i.e.* rights holders and counterfeiters and pirates) and consumers.

2.2.2. Rights holders

Rights holders are those individuals and entities that hold the rights of usage of trademarks, copyrights and neighbouring rights, patents and design rights. Rights holders thus represent the legitimate suppliers of products to markets.

2.2.2.1. Holders of trademarks

Trademarks are officially registered and privately owned names, symbols or other devices by which the product carrying the trademark can be exclusively identified. Holders of trademarks tend to be firms, although any individual in principle could hold one. The trademarks are used by consumers to authenticate the origin, standard and quality of the product associated with them. In this sense, they function as information tools that enable consumers to easily and efficiently choose products expected to meet certain standards and levels of satisfaction.

The value of a trademark is influenced by a number of variables, including the investment of the rights holders in production standards, product development and marketing efforts. It also depends on past consumer experience with the products associated with the brand name. These properties give trademark owners a monopolistic market power from which they may derive higher value from their sales, compared with unmarked products.

The value of a trademark can be defined as the discounted stream of expected future income attributable to the trademark, less the costs of sustaining it. Trademark values are hence derived from sales and price, but are not easily estimated because of their evolving and intangible nature. It is clear, however, that their value can be immense (Table 2.2).

Table 2.2. Estimated brand values, 2006

Rank	Brand	Value (billion USD)
1	Coca-Cola	67
2	Microsoft	60
3	IBM	56
4	GE	49
5	Intel	32
6	Nokia	30
7	Toyota	28
8	Disney	28
9	McDonald's	28
10	Mercedes-Benz	22
11	Citigroup	21
12	Marlboro	21
13	Hewlett-Packard	20
14	American Express	20
15	BMW	20
16	Gillette	20
17	Louis Vuitton	18
18	Cisco	18
19	Honda	17
20	Samsung	16

Note: The estimates are produced annually by Interbrand for the journal *Business Week* and assess the brand values based on a variety of issues, *i.e.* strategic brand management, marketing budget allocation, portfolio management, brand extensions, mergers and acquisitions, licensing, investor relations, etc.

Source: Interbrand, *Business Week* (2006).

2.2.2.2. Holders of copyrights, patents and design rights

Copyrights, patents and design rights are intended to promote investment in new products and processes. While copyrights tend to focus on creative works (music, movies, literature), patents are concerned more with technological and scientific innovations (inventions, technical ideas and designs). The objective of all three types of protection, however, is to protect the capital, inspiration and efforts of the originator by providing the party concerned with rights over the use of the copyright, patent or design. This provides a type of monopoly as it sharply limits competition, permitting rights holders with the means to recover development costs and to earn a return on their investment. Moreover, the intellectual property rights greatly facilitate the sharing of information and knowledge, as they provide incentives to the rights holders to present their creations on the market.

2.2.3. Counterfeiters and pirates

Parties that engage in counterfeiting or piracy exploit without authority the economic value associated with the ownership and rights of a trademark, copyright, patent or design right. Infringing parties can be individuals or groups who engage in the illicit practice for either personal or commercial benefit. While trademark infringement, for instance, is typically motivated by commercial interests, copyrights (such as the unauthorised reproduction of software and music) are also often breached for personal benefit.

Trademark infringement is in most instances a deliberate act by the infringing party. The same goes for most breaches of copyrights, although some copyright infringement can also be unintentional. The technical nature of patent infringement and the subjective nature of design infringement can also result in unintentional breaches, with issues often having to be resolved through legal proceedings; the difficulty in knowing whether a patent or design right exists in a given jurisdiction can also contribute to unintentional breaches.

Parties that engage in counterfeiting or piracy free-ride on the creative and economic efforts incurred by legitimate rights holders in the development of new products and processes and the establishment of markets.

2.2.4. Consumers

Consumers include parties that acquire items for their own use, as well as parties that acquire items used as inputs in production of other items, or for maintenance. From an IPR perspective, there are three types of consumers: *1)* those interested in acquiring a legitimate product; *2)* those that will, under certain conditions, willingly and knowingly purchase a counterfeit or pirated product; and *3)* those that are uninterested in, or indifferent about, the IPR status of a product.

Indifference is probably greatest among consumers in the case of patent and design infringements, as these infringements are not apparent and, as mentioned above, are highly legalistic and technical in nature.

2.2.5. Market characteristics

In the absence of counterfeiting and piracy, markets for IPR-protected products are characterised by rights holders who exercise their monopoly power to maximise profits. Economic theory indicates that this is done by determining the price and level of production at which marginal revenues equal marginal costs; given the demand faced by the rights holder (Figure 2.1).

Figure 2.1. Determining the price of genuine goods

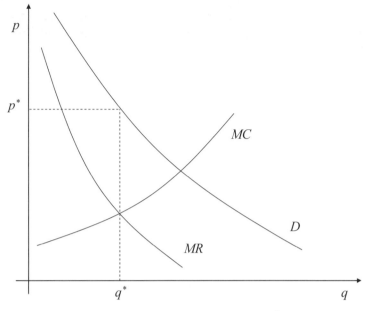

Note: Demand is depicted by a downward sloping curve denoted D. The price p^* is set where the marginal revenue equals the marginal costs ($MR=MC$) resulting in a market size of q^*.

While the price set by the rights holders may be affected by competition in related markets, the entrance of counterfeit and pirate suppliers introduces direct competition into the rights holder's protected market. It should be emphasised that this form of competition comes from the violation of law and is an illegal activity.

In the case of patent and design infringement, the new competition either comes from additional production of a protected item, or through unauthorised exploitation of a protected technology. The latter can either limit sales of the rights holder of the technology, or undercut advantages the rights holder might otherwise have enjoyed in producing particular goods.

In the case of trademark and copyright infringement, the competition effectively carves the market into two interrelated submarkets, a *primary market* where genuine and deceiving infringements are traded, and a *secondary market* where fake products are purchased knowingly by consumers.

- *Primary market.* Consumers who demand goods of genuine, non-infringing origin establish a market that is referred to in this report as the primary market. The only way that counterfeiters and pirates can penetrate this market is to deceive consumers into believing that their products are authentic (see Box 2.1). When this happens, the primary market is essentially divided into two constituent parts; namely a deceptive part and the remaining genuine part. The size of the primary market depends on the price level that is set by the rights holder, and on the degree to which the secondary market overlaps the primary market (discussed below).

- *Secondary market.* Under certain conditions, consumers are often willing to purchase products they know are not legitimate. They might be reluctant to do so in the case of a pharmaceutical item, but could be quite interested in a pirated CD. For most products, their willingness to purchase an item that is not legitimate is likely to increase as the discount from the rights holder's price increases. For example, there is likely to be virtually no demand for counterfeit and pirated products if these are priced at the same level as legitimate products; but demand could be significant at greatly reduced prices (Figure 2.2).

Figure 2.2. Entry of infringed goods on the secondary market

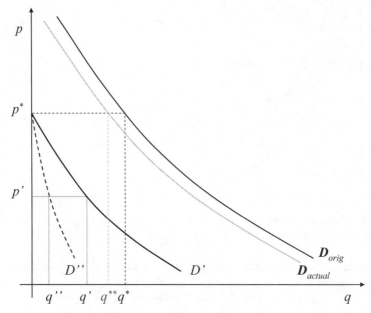

Note: $\boldsymbol{D}_{orig}$ indicates the demand curve for an IPR protected product faced by the legitimate rights holder in the absence of counterfeiting and piracy (the primary market). Counterfeiters and pirates enter with supplies of non-deceptive infringements in the secondary market where total demand is indicated by D'. The line D'' denotes the subset of individuals in the secondary market (D') who would demand the original goods (stay in the primary market) if the lower-priced fake was not available. Sales of infringements to this group reduce the actual demand that the rights holder faces to $\boldsymbol{D}_{actual}$.

The diagram above depicts a static-market situation in which the rights holder establishes a price for a product, p^*, expecting to sell a certain volume, q^*. If infringing products are sold at the same price as the genuine, consumers will in most cases not acquire these knowingly, as there is no apparent incentive. However, at the price of p' for fakes, a number of q' units will be sold in the secondary market. Depending on the rate of substitutability that exists between genuine and non-deceiving infringements, a portion of these, say q'', will come at the direct expense of the rights holder, and thus effectively reduce legitimate sales by q'', corresponding to q^{**} in the figure ($q'' = q^* - q^{**}$). The remaining quantity sold in the secondary market, *i.e.* the difference between q'' and q', would, on the other hand, have no direct effect on legitimate sales, as it represents sales to parties unwilling to pay the higher price p^* for the genuine product had the fake not been available. Of course, in addition to the sales lost to counterfeiters and pirates on the secondary market, the rights holder would also lose sales to counterfeiters and pirates who had successfully deceived consumers into buying their product, thinking they had purchased a legitimate, genuine item. This situation, however, is not depicted in the graph.

The foregoing underscores the need to distinguish between fake products that deceive consumers and those that are openly sold as fakes to consumers. As seen, the markets for deceptive and non-deceptive products have significantly different characteristics (Box 2.1).

Box 2.1. Deceptive vs. non-deceptive products

From the perspective of demand, a counterfeit or pirated good that successfully deceives a consumer is considered identical to the genuine item it infringes. In such cases, deceptive infringements and genuine goods are perfect substitutes, and they will retain this characteristic until such time as the consumer discovers he has been deceived (which may never happen). The genuine and infringing products therefore compete head-on in the primary market.

An infringing product that does not deceive is evidently bought on entirely different principles as one that does. When consumers can identify the counterfeit or pirated nature of a product, it enables them to compare the infringing product with its genuine counterpart and base their choice of acquisition on a wide range of factors, including potential cost savings and perceived differences in quality between the genuine and infringing product. Moreover, since influences stemming from cultural aspects, such as differences in moral considerations and perceptions of social image, are of importance to the demand for non-deceptive infringements, the size and characteristics of these markets are also likely to differ across countries. As infringing products are identifiable in secondary markets, these products are not necessarily perfect substitutes from the consumer perspective, and substitution rates are generally lower.

Grossman and Shapiro (1998*a* and 1998*b*) were among the first to develop market analysis along these lines. In this connection, however, it must be emphasised that whether an infringement is marketed deceptively is *not* a property of the actual infringing good; rather it is determined by the individual consumer's *perception*. Hence, while a particular counterfeit item may succeed in deceiving some consumers, and lead them to acquire a fake product unknowingly, the deception may not necessarily apply to all consumers, some of whom could knowingly buy the fake (on the secondary market). The central question, therefore, becomes the degree to which the particular type of infringe-ment invokes false perceptions of genuineness in consumers. This perspective differs from how the concept of deception and non-deception has traditionally been viewed, since it implies that deceptive and secondary markets coexist for any given type of infringement, and that these markets are interrelated.

Determining the degree to which infringing products deceive consumers is further-more crucial when dealing with the impact of counterfeiting and piracy. Both deceptive and non-deceptive sales tap into the primary market, but in different ways. Since deceptive infringements compete directly (and as perfect substitutes) with genuine goods, deceptive product sales effectively reduce sales of the rights holder on a one-for-one basis. This is generally not the case in the secondary market.

2.3. Factors driving production and consumption of counterfeit and pirated products

The scope and magnitude of counterfeiting and piracy are largely defined by the factors that motivate actors to produce/consume counterfeit and pirated products, and the institutional environment (*i.e.* legal, regulatory, economic and cultural) in which the counterfeiting and piracy production and/or consumption take place.

High profit margins, for example, can provide a strong incentive for manufacturing counterfeit luxury products (*e.g.* designer clothing and up-scale watches), while relatively low prices may entice image-conscious consumers, unwilling to pay full prices for genuine articles, to knowingly buy falsely branded items.

Concerning the institutional environment, the legislation and regulations that protect IPR, combined with the effectiveness of how these rights are enforced, are key determinants of where counterfeiting and piracy take place, as are public attitudes about IPR. Since these factors are likely to differ significantly across countries, so does the extent to which these activities occur. On the consumption side, income levels are also likely to play a significant role as they determine the budget constraint of a single consumer.

This section of the report examines the factors that drive production and consumption of counterfeit and pirated products. In this regard, it is emphasised that while product and individual characteristics influence the decision to consume, or produce, counterfeit items directly, institutional factors also play a critical role. A further, more formal elaboration of how the markets operate is presented in Annex 2.A1.

2.3.1. Supply drivers

As in any business, parties that engage in commercial counterfeiting or piracy do so to make a profit. They, therefore, face the same market challenges as those faced by legitimate businesses. Hence, concerns about production costs, distribution channels and consumer behaviour are as real for infringers as they are for legitimate producers. Those who engage in non-commercial activities, on the other hand, are likely to do so for a variety of reasons, some of which may have no economic underpinnings.

The essential principle behind commercial counterfeiting and piracy is free-riding on the economic value associated with intellectual property rights ownership. Because of this, the products targeted for infringement tend to be those for which legitimate markets or brands are already well-developed. If markets or brands are immature, the costs and risks of supplying infringing goods can be high, while incentives are low.

Counterfeiters and pirates can enjoy large competitive advantages over legitimate rights holders because they usually do not incur the research and development costs of rights holders. The advantages are particularly high for products with high IP content and low manufacturing costs (such as certain copyrighted products and pharmaceuticals). They do, however, face significant challenges, as they face risks of prosecution if their operations are detected, and there may be considerable difficulties in producing and distributing products.

2.3.2. Factors affecting production and supply

The decision of a party to engage in production of counterfeit or pirate goods involves, first of all, a determination of what will be counterfeited or pirated, and in the case of trademark and copyright-infringing products, whether the primary or secondary market will be targeted, or both. The decision of what to produce and which markets to target is driven by factors related to: *1)* the characteristics of the market; *2)* technological and logistical considerations; and *3)* the institutional environment (Table 2.3). These factors may differ according to the type of infringement involved, as well as across economies.

Table 2.3. Factors driving supply of infringements

Driving factor	Condition favoring counterfeiting and piracy	Category
Market characteristics		
Unit profitability	High unit profitability	
Market size	Large potential market(s)	Market potential
Genuine brand power	High level of brand recognition or popularity	
Production, distribution and technology		
Production investments	Simple, low cost equipment	
Technology requirements	Not sophisticated, easy to acquire	
Logistics	Simple and cheap logistics	
Marketing and sale of products	Easy to establish/infiltrate distribution channels	Market exploitation
Ability to conceal operation	Easy to hide illicit operations	
Ability to deceive	Easy to deceive consumers	
Institutional characteristics		
Risk of discovery	Low risk of detection	
Legal and regulatory framework	Weak laws	
Enforcement	Weak enforcement	Market risks
Penalties	Weak sanctions	

2.3.3. Market characteristics

Interest in counterfeiting or pirating a product depends in large part on the size of the market(s) that potentially can be exploited, and the unit profitability of the infringing item.

2.3.3.1. Unit profitability

The higher the potential unit profitability of counterfeiting and piracy, the higher is the incentive for infringers to enter the market. Unit profitability is determined by the price of the product relative to its cost of production (*i.e.* potential return on sales). In the case of trademark and copyright infringements, the profitability will of course depend on whether the infringing party targets the primary or secondary market. In the case of patent infringement, an added dimension is the effect that the use of a protected technology could have on the efficiency (and, eventually, profitability) of a firm.

In the case of trademark and copyright infringement, the highest unit profits for counterfeiters and pirates generally involve the sale of products on a primary market, where consumers are deceived into thinking that they have bought genuine items. In this case, premium prices can be charged for low-cost alternatives; the sectoral write-up on pharmaceuticals (Part III) illustrates the considerable sums that can be earned in such a situation. Secondary markets generally provide interesting opportunities through the large-scale supply of low-priced infringements that do not attempt to deceive consumers; branded clothing and luxury items, as well as pirated software, music and motion pictures are cases in point.

2.3.3.2. Size of markets

The larger the size of a market for a particular product, the larger is the incentive, everything else being equal, to exploit the associated markets for infringements. This follows from the expectation that a larger customer base associated with the market carries the potential for a larger customer base for infringing goods.

In the case of trademarks and copyrights, there are likely to be practical limits on the extent to which counterfeit and pirated products can penetrate primary markets, particularly if the infringing products are of noticeably lower quality. Penetration beyond such a limit might lead to lower profits stemming from the loss of ability to deceive (invoked by the market size), leading to lower sales, higher risks, etc.

As explained earlier, the size of the secondary market for a product is derived from total demand for a product. It can be quite small, as is generally the case for pharmaceuticals, or so large that it exceeds the size of the primary market. Thus, for counterfeiters and pirates, the secondary market does not suffer from the same limitations as the primary market does, because there is no deliberate intent by suppliers to deceive.

2.3.3.3. Brand power

Closely linked to profitability and market size is the attention that the public pays to a brand. Generally, the more power a brand has among consumers, the greater the incentive to infringe that trademark.

As discussed earlier, brands are used by rights holders to differentiate their products from those of their competitors. The brands generally evoke consumer expectations with respect to product quality, functionality, exclusivity, attractiveness and/or the brands may be valued for the image they project. Products infringing on high-powered brands may be more profitable relative to less-known, or less-regarded brands, due to larger market size or the higher price premium that the brand holder might command over comparable products. The sector write-up on tobacco (see Part III) illustrates this point; while cigarettes are comparably priced, counterfeiting efforts have focused on Marlboro, which is the leading brand (see Table 2.2).

While it can be argued that brand power is inseparable from the "core" drivers of unit profitability and market size, brands nevertheless hold another aspect. This stems from the fact that high-powered brands are usually better recognised by consumers than are the actual products on which the brands appear. The brand itself may thus be used by infringing parties to sell products that have little or no resemblance to any of the genuine items produced by the brand owner; *i.e.* the brand carries with it the image and recognition that boost the attractiveness of an otherwise unrelated product.

2.3.4. Production, distribution and technology

To exploit the market potential, the production and distribution of counterfeit and pirated goods must also be economically and technically feasible.

2.3.4.1. Production investments and technology requirements

Counterfeiting and piracy that require advanced and costly production equipment is seen as limiting the number of parties that would engage in infringing activities. For example, as discussed in the automotive sector write-up (see Part III), automobiles or products of similar complexity are difficult targets for counterfeiters, even if they can utilise cheap labour and substandard parts for production. This follows, since the production requires special and costly equipment. On the other hand, the counterfeiting of automobile parts is more feasible, and has been pursued. The sector write-up on audio-visual products provides another example (see Part III). Today, the ease by which one can pirate music CDs or motion picture DVDs make these products easy targets for infringing parties; this is in sharp contrast to the situation that existed previously, when costly equipment was needed to make high-quality copies.

Patents, which are often the result of significant investment in research and development, can sometimes be of a highly technical and complex nature, and would therefore be unlikely targets for infringers, according to the scheme above. However, in order to secure the exclusive rights, patent applicants are in most instances required to reveal considerable amounts of detailed information about the patent, which essentially also reduces the cost and difficulty of infringing it.

It should be noted that in many cases, the act of counterfeiting or piracy may not involve production. It may, for example, simply entail falsely labelling or packaging an item that otherwise did not violate an IP. This would include, for example, marking a generic replacement brake part for an automobile to falsely indicate that the article was as an OEM (Original Equipment Manufacturer) branded item, or adding, without authorisation, a trademarked sticker to a product indicating that the product conformed to an industry standard. As discussed later in the report (Chapter 3), free-trade ports have served as locations where items that have been imported legitimately from one country are repackaged in ways that violate IPRs, and then are exported to third countries.

2.3.4.2. Logistics

Logistics is of particular relevance with respect to goods that infringe trademarks and copyrights.

The management of both inbound and outbound materials, parts, supplies and finished goods constitutes another aspect that affects the likelihood and extent to which a product is infringed. It is reasonable to assume, for instance, that the costlier and more complex the logistical management structure for bringing illicit goods to the market, the lower the likely level of infringing activity. As indicated in the food and beverage sector report (see Part III), this explains why counterfeiting activities are relatively limited.

Concerning handling and transportation of infringements, it is noteworthy to mention that while the associated costs of these processes may correlate positively with the complexity of the product being infringed, this relationship does not always hold. For instance, products of a simple character may cause significant cost concerns for infringing parties if these, for example, are of odd sizes or fragile. Another aspect linked with the logistic processes of the infringer is the risk incurred. For instance, the economic cost of transport and handling is one thing, while the risk of detection, prosecution and penalty is quite another. The two aspects are obviously linked and must be taken into account as such.

2.3.4.3. Marketing and sales of products

The sales challenges pertain in particular to trademark- and copyright-infringing goods.

The easier it is to establish channels through which counterfeit and pirated products can be distributed and sold (or the lower the efforts required to penetrate existing ones), the greater the scope for parties to engage in an IP-infringing business. The challenges associated with distribution differ considerably across products. Infringing items produced without the intent to deceive consumers may be sold easily and in large quantities through street vendors, open markets or the Internet. However, finding ways to infiltrate established channels of distribution to market fake products deceptively to consumers can constitute a major hurdle for counterfeiters and pirates.

The structure of distribution channels is also a factor. A multi-level distribution situation system provides greater opportunities for infringers to infiltrate the system. For instance, providing infringements in a context where the targeted product is sold directly by a manufacturer to consumers could prove very difficult. Such a case could be illustrated by factory outlet stores, where products are provided and sold by the rights holder. On the other hand, as discussed in the tobacco sector report, the successive breaking up of bulk shipments into smaller consignments makes it easier to introduce counterfeit products into distribution chains.

Figure 2.3 depicts different channels through which counterfeiters and pirates distribute their products. It indicates the relative difficulties counterfeiters and pirates would have in deceiving consumers, and the ease of infiltrating of a given distribution network.

Generally, the more secure the distribution network targeted by infringing parties, the higher is the requirement of the products they supply. As such, it is also more likely for counterfeit and pirated products to be of a highly deceptive nature if they are distributed through, say, branded shops and chains, or intermediate producers (producers of goods used in further manufacturing), which have stricter quality controls than, say, street vendors. Indeed, if a given infringing product is distributed through branded shops, consumers will not be aware of its illicit nature. In fact, it could be the case that even the retailers are not aware that a given product is counterfeited. This could happen if the infiltration occurred, for example, at an early stage of distribution (which seems relatively difficult to execute).

Figure 2.3. Distribution channels of infringements

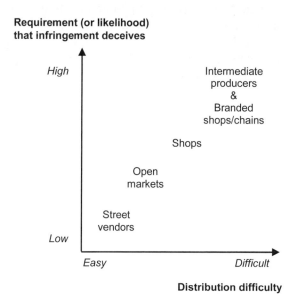

The Internet, which is a virtual marketplace, is not included in Figure 2.3. On the one hand, it is extremely easy for counterfeiters and pirates to establish sales links of both deceptive and non-deceptive products using the Internet, *i.e.* through e-mail, on-line auctions and related sales sites. On the other hand, there are technologies and services available for monitoring certain activities, which may limit sales of infringing products.

2.3.4.4. Ability to conceal operations

The ability to conceal operations is of particular relevance to trademark and copyright infringement.

Given the illicit nature of counterfeit and pirated production, distribution and sales, there is always a risk that infringers will be detected, prosecuted and penalised for their actions. Hence, in order to operate on the counterfeit and pirate markets, infringers must exert efforts to conceal their operations to reduce the risk. Everything else being equal, this implies a greater incentive to target genuine products, for which production, distri-bution and sales of infringements are easy to conceal. For instance, the ease by which one can produce pirated music CDs and remain undetected makes this form of infringement activity likelier than the production of counterfeit automobiles, which is much harder to conceal.

2.3.4.5. Ability to deceive

The ability to deceive consumers into believing that an item is not counterfeit is particularly important in the case of trademark infringement.

As mentioned earlier, in order to sell products on the primary market, counterfeiters need to deceive consumers into believing that the products they are selling are genuine. Hence, the more difficult it is to deceive consumers, the less appealing it will be for counterfeiters to cultivate an infringement activity that targets the primary market.

The success of deception with an infringing product depends on three aspects: *1)* the characteristics of the product itself; *2)* the packaging; and *3)* the manner in which the product is sold. If the product, or the packaging of an infringing product, does not live up to what is expected of the genuine good, consumers will be able to discern it. At times, even if both content and packaging perfectly resemble those associated with the genuine item, a sales point that invokes suspicion, such as the sale of an expensive branded watch in an open-market environment, can introduce doubt about authenticity.

2.3.5. Institutional characteristics

Although the production of counterfeit and pirated products virtually takes place in all economies worldwide, the extent to which it occurs varies significantly among economies. The differences can in large part be explained by examining a number of institutional factors, including a wide range of legal, cultural, political and social characteristics that either impede or facilitate trade in counterfeit and pirated products.

2.3.5.1. Legal and regulatory framework

The legal and regulatory frameworks combating counterfeiting and piracy are key institutional factors since they can have significant impacts on the behaviour of counterfeiters and pirates. Legal systems provide rights holders with instruments to take action against parties that infringe on what is legally protected, and to claim compensation for the losses suffered as a result of the infringement. Strong frameworks can deter illicit activity, while weak frameworks would effectively be viewed as permissive.

2.3.5.2. Enforcement and the risk of discovery

Laws and regulations can affect the level of counterfeiting and piracy, but only to the extent that they are enforced. If the resources devoted to enforcement are inadequate, or if intellectual property rights are not otherwise enforced by the public authority, the value of the laws and regulations for the rights holders is diminished.

The level of corruption deserves mentioning in this regard since its influence may undermine enforcement through many different channels: illicit production facilities may go undetected if authorities choose to ignore them; distribution channels may be breached if fake goods are allowed to be mixed with genuine articles at various stages of distribution; or complaints may never be acted on if authorities effectively shelve cases. Even the strictest law could therefore potentially be without influence on a party's decision to counterfeit/pirate, or not.

From the perspective of infringers, the main concern relative to enforcement is the risk of getting caught, since there is a range of possible negative consequences if this occurs. The ability to conceal operations is obviously one of the factors influencing the risk level, but there are important institutional aspects as well. Different types of counterfeits and pirated items may be more sought after by public authorities and are thus riskier business than others. Moreover, the overall level and effectiveness of enforcement is an important factor affecting the risk. The risk of discovery, and costs that may be incurred to avoid same, must however be seen relative to the potential consequences that infringers may face. For instance, if the consequences are small, the risk of discovery may have little practical impact on the counterfeiting and piracy activity.

2.3.5.3. Penalties

Penalties reflect the consequences that infringing parties may suffer if they are discovered. In this regard, the impact of enforcement on the supply of infringements may vary considerably according to the criminal frame, that is, the severity of the sanctions. There is a significant difference, for instance, between a minor fine that effectively can be absorbed as a cost of doing business, and a prison sentence. In many countries, IP crime is addressed largely through *civil proceedings* under which a private party sues a counterfeiter, or a pirate, to recover damages. The consequences are far lighter than would be the case under *criminal proceedings*, under which government prosecution can result in fines and/or incarceration.

2.3.6. Demand drivers

What drives demand for counterfeit and pirated products? In the case of patent and design-infringing products, consumers are (as pointed out earlier) likely to be indifferent about, or unaware of, the infringing nature of such products. Demand is thus likely to be subject to the same drivers as those for the non-infringing articles.

The markets for trademark and copyright infringing products, however, differ. In the case of the primary market, demand for infringements does not, by definition, exist; and hence, no specific drivers other than those driving demand for genuine products are relevant (*i.e.* deceptive infringements are acquired on the same grounds as genuine products). This is in sharp contrast to the secondary market, where consumers *knowingly choose* to purchase a fake product. Such consumption takes place for a variety of reasons. A fake product may, for example, satisfy the consumer in ways that are similar to products of genuine origin, but at a lower cost. In cases of trademark-infringing products, for instance, image-conscious consumers may be able to achieve a comparable level of pleasure or satisfaction by buying a high-quality replica watch, as would be achieved with a genuine branded article. With respect to copyright infringement, consumers may in many instances acquire a product that enjoys a quality as high as those of genuine copies.

Counterfeit and pirated goods are, however, usually not perfect substitutes for, and are often of lower quality than, their original counterparts. Hence, the choice whether to acquire a fake product or not is based on the difference between the value consumers can expect to derive from the genuine product considering its price, and that which they expect to derive from the infringing product, given its price. As such, even a low-quality infringing product may be subject to substantial demand if the price difference between the genuine product and the infringement is sufficiently large.

2.3.7. Factors affecting demand and consumption

The factors that drive knowing demand for counterfeit and pirated goods can be grouped into three principal categories based on the characteristics of: *1)* the product in question; *2)* the individual consumer; and *3)* the institutional environment in which the individual consumer operates (Table 2.4). Evaluating these factors for specific products can provide insights into the size and location of potential demand.

The relative importance of each of the factors varies by product, and thus has to be evaluated on a case-by-case basis.

Table 2.4. Drivers of demand for non-deceptive infringements

Driving factor	Condition favoring counterfeiting and piracy	Category
Market characteristics		
Price	Low price; big difference in price to genuine item	
Quality and nature of product	High quality; small difference in quality to genuine item	Product
Ability to conceal status	Easy to conceal infringing nature of the product	
Consumer characteristics		
Health concerns	No or low health impact	
Safety concerns	No or low potential safety impact	
Personal income	High budget concerns by consumers	Consumer
Personal values	Low regard for IPR and related laws	
Institutional characteristics		
Risk of discovery	Low risk of discovery	
Risk of prosecution	Low risk of prosecution	
Penalties	Weak sanctions	Institutions
Availability and ease of acquisition	Easy access and availability of products	
Socio-economic factors	Lack of concern for IPR, etc.	

2.3.8. Product characteristics

The extent to which consumers demand a particular type of infringement depends in large part on the characteristics of the product concerned, *i.e.* its price, quality and functionality. The ability to conceal the infringing character of the product may also be important.

2.3.8.1. Price

One of the key factors influencing a consumer's decision to purchase a counterfeit or pirated product is the price of the infringing good relative to the price of the legitimate item. As discussed earlier, demand for an infringing article is likely to be negligible when priced the same as the genuine article, and it would grow as the disparity favouring the infringing product increased.

2.3.8.2. Quality and nature of product

The satisfaction that consumers expect to derive from a given product influences the types of infringements consumers are willing to consume. Satisfaction generally relates to an item's functionality, its effect on physical well-being and/or the image it projects. The therapeutic effect of medicine, for instance, is the primary property of the product, and motivates consumption through its expected treatment effect. For clothes, the motivating factors tend to be a combination of functionality and style, as well as the image, if any, that the brand reflects. Generally speaking, the higher the anticipated quality of an infringement is, the higher the demand.

For consumers who knowingly buy counterfeit and pirated goods, it is well known that infringing products usually are of lower quality than their genuine counterparts. The satisfaction that consumers expect to derive from an infringing product is for this reason often lower than what is expected of genuine products, and therefore the failure of infringements to live fully up to the genuine standard is also more readily accepted. In turn, this is also what enables demand for infringements through lower prices, for example, and what separates the secondary market from the primary. However, the demand for infringements is likely to be affected by the consequences of its potential failure, which in turn depend on the wants and needs it is supposed to satisfy, and thus affect the power exerted by both the price and quality drivers. Two aspects of particular importance in this regard concern the potential negative health and safety effects of infringements. These are discussed below.

2.3.8.3. Ability to conceal status

The ability of the consumer to conceal the counterfeit or pirated nature of a product may be important for certain products, and may therefore affect the purchasing decision of a party. The need to conceal may range from reasons related to vanity (*i.e.* not wanting to be identified as the user of a falsely branded luxury item) to legal reasons (not wanting to be subject to prosecution for possession of an infringing item).

2.3.9. Consumer characteristics

The conscious choice to acquire a counterfeit or pirated product is affected by at least three types of factors associated with the individual consumer. The first concerns the consumer's general economic situation and budgetary constraints. The second concerns the nature of any health and safety risks that may be assumed if a fake product is purchased and used. The third is the consumer's attitude about counterfeit and pirated goods.

2.3.9.1. Concern for health and safety aspects

Health and safety concerns obviously figure prominently in consumers' decisions on whether or not to purchase a counterfeited or pirated product. The concerns are likely to vary considerably among products, helping to explain why the secondary market for some items (like pharmaceuticals) is small, while the market for others (like movies and music) is relatively large.

It is important to emphasise that concerns related to health and safety spring from the consumer's general awareness of the potential affects that consumption may have. Since this awareness may differ from consumer to consumer, and indeed is likely to do so across countries, one can also expect cross-country differences in the conscious demand for potential dangerous infringements such as toys, consumer electronics and even pharmaceuticals.

2.3.9.2. Personal income

The personal income of consumers establishes limits on their ability to purchase goods. In some instances, income levels could well be a decisive factor in a consumer's decision to purchase a counterfeit or pirated good. A counterfeit or pirated product that provided an affordable alternative to a genuine product (and was of sufficient quality given price and personal income) could, for example, strongly influence a consumer – particularly if the purchase of the genuine article was not a viable option.

The level of personal income also directs consumption in specific ways. Low-income groups, for instance, typically spend larger parts of their budget on food, beverages and clothing compared to high-income groups, who spend relatively more on transportation, communications and medical/health care (Houthakker, 1957). Demand and consumption of counterfeit and pirated items are thus likely to differ according to income levels. Hence, the tendency to believe that consumption of infringements falls given an increase in income must be taken with care. A higher income may invoke a general shift in consumption patterns and thereby simply motivate consumption of different types of infringements instead of eliminating them.

2.3.9.3. Personal values

An individual's attitudes towards crime and theft could influence the extent and nature of any knowing acquisition of counterfeit or pirated products. Knowing that the production and distribution of certain products are dominated by criminal networks that are profiteering from the operations could be dissuasive; at the same time, consumers might treat different types of infringements in different product areas quite differently. Unauthorised use of a protected trademark of a sports team on a cap, for example, might not be considered in the same way as the pirating of a movie.

2.3.10. Institutional characteristics

The institutional environment in which infringement activities unfold is important because of its direct influence on the demand and consumption of the illicit products as affected, for example, by legal systems. But it is also important for understanding where secondary markets for counterfeit and pirated products are likely to be the strongest.

2.3.10.1. Risk of discovery, prosecution and penalties

The risk of discovery, prosecution and penalty with respect to the conscious consumption of counterfeit or pirated goods is low for most product categories. As such, although these aspects carry the potential for limiting demand and are thereby of importance, they are of little significance in most instances.

An exception to the above is the growing risk of penalisation due to copyright piracy. Music, movie and software associations have increased the number of lawsuits and targeted not only heavy suppliers of copyright material, but also consumers. Increased media coverage of piracy and the rights holders' anti-piracy efforts have also increased the perceived risk for consumers engaging in the purchase of pirated products. Concerning other products, the risk typically occurs only when moving the product across national borders.

2.3.10.2. Availability and ease of acquisition

Due to their illicit nature, counterfeit and pirated products are generally not freely available. The extent to which they can be purchased often depends on the way they are distributed and sold, which can differ significantly among products.

The terms and conditions under which products can be purchased can have profound effects on the level of consumption. If a product is not widely available through numerous commercial outlets, this may significantly reduce the demand because of the high non-monetary cost of acquisition. Even if consumers have both the interest and willingness to acquire a given good, their ability to do so will remain limited as long as the availability of the goods is either low or somehow restricted. Such limitations could come from rights holders' strategy but also from market access restrictions (*e.g.* due to import regulations). The opportunities to purchase vary among countries and methods of distribution; they are greatest where markets are not highly regulated (*e.g.* where open markets are common), and where Internet access, which provides a means to acquire fake products, is greatest. The ease or comfort by which counterfeit and pirated items can be acquired may also boost demand.

Counterfeit items such as fake branded clothes, watches, sunglasses, perfumes, etc., are for instance often sold at open markets or street vendors. Installations like these, which in certain places enjoy high degrees of acceptance from both consumers and authorities, greatly facilitate demand for illicit products by their mere existence. In places where counterfeit and pirated products cannot be marketed easily or effectively, the searching costs are likely to be high and limit demand.

2.3.10.3. Socio-economic factors

The satisfaction that individual agents expect to derive from consuming counterfeit and pirated goods can also be influenced by social and cultural values. These institutional factors exert their influence through different channels related either to markets and their regulations, or consumer behaviour itself, and are as such not emanating from the individuals' own characteristics.

Levels of economic development, general patterns of consumption, the educational systems and the like, could motivate and direct demand of infringements in specific ways, and could therefore also offer explanatory power with respect to cross-country differences in consumption levels. For instance, general patterns of counterfeit and pirated consumption that are specific to individual countries could perhaps be related to the income levels of those countries. This would be in line with the above discussion on personal income and could facilitate an understanding of differences in demand for specific categories of infringing goods across countries.

It could also be argued that differences in educational levels are likely to cause cross-country differences in the general awareness of counterfeit and pirated products (see Box 2.2). A lack in awareness through insufficient education levels mainly induces (strictly speaking) deceptive demand for counterfeits.

A particular case of the lack of awareness concerns the health and safety aspects. In this case, it is possible that consumers may willingly purchase a potentially hazardous infringed product if they are unaware of the potential negative implications related to its consumption. Thus, this lack of awareness on the part of consumers can facilitate a conscious demand for infringements that could be hazardous to consumers' health and safety, such as toys, consumer electronics and pharmaceuticals.

Box 2.2. Consumer awareness

Consumer awareness of counterfeit and pirated products is related to the availability of, and access to, relevant information, and the individual consumer's capacity to comprehend this information. If there are no indications on the infringing nature of a product, in one form or another, consumers are also less likely even to suspect it – even if they have the capacity to comprehend the information, had it been available. Conversely, even if high-quality information is available to consumers, incapacity to comprehend it will keep them unaware and unable to factor the information into their purchasing behaviour.

It should be noted that information here not only refers to the context of infringement sales, *i.e.* suspicious circumstances, but also the degree to which publicly available information facilitates awareness of counterfeit and pirated products. Informational or educational infrastructures, for instance, may fail to facilitate consumer awareness and thereby increase the potential size and profitability of markets for deceptive infringements. This is especially important with respect to developing economies, where access to publicly available information and adequate educational structures may be lacking. Here, despite a relatively low purchasing power, there is large potential for selling low-priced deceptive infringements and thereby gaining a profit.

2.3.10.4. Operation of drivers

Information on how demand drivers actually operate in different sectors can be obtained by studying consumer behaviour. Surveys can be helpful in this regard. One conducted in the United Kingdom, for example, asked parties to indicate their motivations for buying, or not buying, particular counterfeit/pirated products (Tables 2.5 and 2.6). What is particularly notable is the difference in the relative importance of quality, affordability and value as a motivating factor for buying different counterfeit/pirated products, and the difference in the relative importance of health and safety concerns in deciding *not* to buy different counterfeit/pirated products. Further work along these lines would assist in further elaborating the demand propensity framework described in this Chapter.

Table 2.5. Motivation for purchasing counterfeit/pirated goods

Product	Cheaper	Acceptable quality	Could not afford otherwise	More for my money	Children want them
DVDs	97	43	30	27	16
Music	91	57	23	41	7
Computer games	94	24	6	24	12
Business software	100	29	29	29	0
Fashion	72	70	38	45	5
Alcohol and cigarettes	100	29	12	53	0
Toys	33	33	0	33	0

Note: Answers in percent. Multiple answers are possible, so answers do not sum to 100%.

Source: Bryce and Rutter, 2005.

Table 2.6. Motivation for not purchasing counterfeit/pirated goods

Product	Waste of money	Poor quality	Prefer real thing	Children prefer real thing	Links with organised crime	Might be harmful
DVDs	19	44	45	3	56	7
Music	17	44	45	3	55	8
Computer games	16	33	35	3	47	8
Business software	15	24	35	1	39	11
Fashion	19	40	49	3	39	6
Alcohol and cigarettes	21	23	41	1	51	41
Toys	15	35	34	8	33	44

Note: Answers in percent. Multiple answers are possible, so answers do not sum to 100%.

Source: Bryce and Rutter, 2005.

References

Bryce, J. and J. Rutter (2005), "Fake Nation?", www.allianceagainstiptheft.co.uk.

Depken, C. A. and L. C. Simmons (2004), "Social Construct and the Propensity for Software Piracy", *Applied Economic Letters,* Vol. 11.

Grossman, G. and Shapiro, C. (1998*a*), "Counterfeit-Product Trade", *American Economic Review*, Vol. 78, Issue 1.

Grossman G. and Shapiro C. (1998*b*), "Foreign Counterfeiting of Status Goods", *Quarterly Journal of Economics*, Vol. 103, Issue 1.

Houthakker, Hendrik S. (1957), "An International Comparison of Household Expenditure Patterns, Commemorating the Century of Engel's Law," *Econometrica* 25.

Husted, B. W. (2000), "The Impact of National Culture on Software Piracy", *Journal of Business Ethics*, Vol. 26.

Interbrand (2006), "Best Global Brands 2006", a ranking by Brand Value, Interbrand, *BusinessWeek.*

Marron, D. B. and Steel, D. G. (2000), "Which Countries Protect Intellectual Property? The Case of Software Piracy", *Economic Inquiry*, Vol. 38, No. 2

Annex 2.A1

QUANTIFYING SUPPLY AND DEMAND OF COUNTERFEIT AND PIRATED PRODUCTS

This annex outlines a more formal approach for determining demand and supply for counterfeit and pirated products.

Demand

Assume that i is a representative agent in an economy, who derives some satisfaction from consuming a given good k. The value of satisfaction that agent i derives, depends on the quality of the good (higher quality of the good implies higher satisfaction derived from consumption). Denote the value of individual's i satisfaction by $v_i(k)$.

Goods offered on the market differ with respect to the ease of assessment of their quality by consumers. The assessment of quality is the consumer's estimation of the performance of a given product in certain areas that are of particular importance for the consumer. The judgement must be made before the act of purchase. Easy assessment allows for identifying to what extend the needs that a given consumer expects to fulfil by consumption of a given good would be actually fulfilled.

The quality of some types of products cannot be assessed at the moment of purchase. The effects of consumption of goods, such as pharmaceuticals, food products, cosmetics etc. can usually be observed some time after the purchase. Consumers also expect some effect based on sources other than their self-assessment, *i.e.* following from brand reputation, reviews and recommendations, but they cannot judge ex-ante if the expected effects can be realised. Compared to pharmaceuticals and cosmetics, the quality of other types of products, such as music recordings or apparel, can be tested relatively easily. Nevertheless, there is virtually no case when agents can perfectly evaluate the performance of a given good by themselves. Instead, agents can only expect a certain quality and have a certain expected satisfaction denoted by $E[v_i(k)]$. Here, $E[.]$ represents the function of expectations about the true quality of a given product. The function of expectations' formation reflects the awareness of a consumer about the possible performances of a given good k.

In order to obtain good k, however, the agent must exert some level of effort prior to buying the good, such as searching for and locating the item. Denote this non-monetary cost $c_i(k)$. Then, if the price of good k is given by $p(k)$, agent i's expected utility of consuming good k equals:

$$u_i(k) = E([v_i(k)]) - c_i(k) - p(k)$$

The agent will purchase good k if the expected utility is higher than any other known alternative or no-purchase at all, denoted by $A_i(k)$.[7]

Agents differ with respect to the satisfaction that they expect to derive from the consumption of good k, their valuations of alternatives or no purchases at all, as well as with the effort they are willing to put into obtaining the good. These differences depend both on the agents' individual characteristics, such as personal taste, income[8], values and their concerns regarding, for instance, health and safety, etc. Ordering agents with respect to their expected satisfaction minus the non-monetary costs, with the convention that lower i corresponds to higher values of satisfaction, allows for finding an expression for the demand of k. As such, demand is given by the sum of all agents for whom the expected satisfaction, minus the non-monetary cost of purchase, is larger than the economic value of a no-purchase.

$$D(p(k)) = \int (E[v_i(k)] - c_i(k) - A_i(k) - p(k)) \, di$$

Supply

Assume that j is a firm (investor) that operates in a given sector. At time t, firm j invests a given amount $I_{j,t}$ which eventually will result in the creation of intellectual property. Having established the intellectual property rights at time $t+1$, firm j is given the exclusive right to supply good k in its sector. As the sole producer in its sector, firm j sets the price $p^*_j(k)$ that maximises profits (equation A2.1 below), either in the unconstraint way (by picking the price level at which the marginal revenues equal marginal costs) or subject to all potential constraints (*e.g.* threat of competitors from other sectors, actions of antitrust authority).

As long as j remains the only rights holder, its profits are given by:

$$(A2.1) \qquad \pi_j = p^*_j(k) q_j(k) - c_j(q(k), k)$$

where $p_j(k)$ is the price of k, $q_j(k)$ is the quantity of supply on the market, and $c_j(\cdot)$ is the cost of production and distribution. Notice that the quantity supplied $q_j(k)$ equals the demand for k as derived above in the section on demand $D(p(k))$.

To determine if j decides to invest at time t, notice that he/she does so as long as the discounted expected profits are larger than the required investments.[9]

$$f\{\pi_j, R\} > I_t$$

where R is the interest rate and $f\{\cdot\}$ is the function that discounts the prospect of future profit to its present value. The discounting function depends primarily on the interest rate R that is used as the primary input to assess the monetary discount of a future income

---

7. In most cases this is valued as zero; in some cases, *e.g.* when k is a cure for terminal illness, the value of no-purchase at all may approach minus infinity, $E([v_i(0)] = -\infty$.

8. This reflects the notion of agent's i budget constraint.

9. Here all other markets are assumed to be in equilibrium. Otherwise the potential alternatives need to be included.

stream. Apart from interest rate, function f depends on other factors, such as the degree of risk aversion or the industry-specific probability of success in research.

Infringement

Counterfeiting and piracy introduce an additional constraint for the rights holder in the sense of competition. In the case of patent and design infringements, new competition comes either from additional production of a protected item, or through unauthorised exploitation of a protected technology. The latter can either limit sales for the rights holder of the technology, or undercut advantages the rights holder might otherwise have enjoyed in producing particular goods.

To better understand the motives that push agents into counterfeit activities consider the following stylised scenario. Assume that l is an agent that considers engaging in the illicit production and supply of counterfeit or pirated product k' (all variables related to counterfeit products are denoted with a prime hereafter). The non-rival nature of intellectual property greatly facilitates the process of copying, and in many cases, when the IP takes form of a trademark, copyright or design, there is virtually no fixed cost of the theft. Concerning patents, the mechanism of patenting (*i.e.* making all the techno-logical aspects publicly known) significantly reduces the costs of copying. This shifts the focus from the fixed costs to other costs related to the counterfeit or pirate supply of good k.

The relevant costs for potential suppliers of infringements to consider can be broken down into the costs of production, c_P; costs of distribution, c_D; and the expected risk of discovery and related penalty, $s_f(\cdot)$. Clearly, the costs of production, distribution and the expected value of penalty depend on the quantities of the counterfeit supply. The cost of production depends on the quality of the product offered by counterfeiters and pirates. The cost of distribution depends on the type of market in which the infringing goods are supplied. The infiltration of the primary market is usually more difficult than supplying the secondary market, since it requires efforts and resources to get access to the legitimate distribution channels. It is therefore assumed that counterfeiters need to spend a fixed cost of $c_{prim} > 0$ in order to supply their products to the primary market.

Before the infringing good, k', enters the market, the infringing party j decides on its quality and which market (primary or secondary) to use as a main target.

The higher-quality of the infringing product implies higher costs to be paid by the counterfeiter l. As such, the decision to produce high-quality infringing products should be motivated by the prospect of high enough revenues. The revenues of the counterfeiter/pirate depend crucially on the price that l is able to charge for the infringing product.

Concerning the primary market, the price that deceived consumers pay for the good is equal to the price charged by the rights holder $p^*_j(k)$. A more complicated situation occurs on the secondary market, where consumers willingly buy infringing products. To find the price that the infringing party l charges for its products, the demand for the counterfeit products needs to be established.

To determine the demand function for the infringing products, notice first that agent i's willingness to pay is determined by the expected satisfaction minus the non-monetary costs of purchasing the good (including moral concerns, risk of detection and so on) and the alternative of no-purchase at all. Second, and as in the case with any other good, no agent will knowingly demand an infringing product if its price is higher than what the agent is willing to pay. Agent i will therefore only demand the counterfeit product k' if the following two conditions are met.

$$(A2.2) \qquad E[v_i(k')] - c_i(k') - p(k') > E[v_i(k)] - c_i(k) - p(k)$$

$$(A2.3) \qquad E[v_i(k')] - c_i(k') - p(k') > A_i(k)$$

The demand for the infringing product k' as a function of its price is then determined as the sum over all agents for whom the two conditions above hold. For the purpose of generality, the demand for the infringing product k' follows from the equation A2.2 and is represented as a function of both prices:

$$D(p(k')) = \int \left(E[v_i(k')] - c_i(k') - (E[v_i(k)] - c_i(k)) \right) di - (p(k') - p(k))$$

The demand function, which is downward sloping in $p(k')$, is located strictly below the demand for the genuine good.[10] This implies that for equal prices, demand for the genuine good is higher than for infringing goods, and that for equal quantities sold, the market-clearing price for infringements is lower than for genuine goods. The demand for fakes furthermore depends on the price of the genuine product. A higher price of the genuine product implies a higher demand for fakes, whereas a larger difference in willingness to pay (caused by lower quality/satisfaction with the fake products or increased efforts required to obtain infringements) lowers demand for fakes.

If l is the sole supplier of counterfeit product k' (which might happen if, for example, the counterfeit production is controlled by organised criminal networks) then l maximises profits similarly to the producer of the legitimate good. Under this scenario, profits are maximised with respect to price. In the case where more than one producer is involved in supplying goods that infringe on the IP of k, the competitive pressure between counterfeit producers leads to a lower market price of k' and a higher quantity supplied. In the extreme case when there are many non-co-operating suppliers, the market for counterfeit product k' is nearly perfectly competitive (*i.e.* Bertrand competition) and the competition reduces the profits of the counterfeiters to zero. This implies that the market price of k' equals the marginal cost of counterfeit production and distribution. In all intermediate scenarios with imperfect competition and positive profits for counterfeiters, the price lies between these two prices.

Determination of the principal market of infringement[11]

The profits of counterfeiter/pirate l depend on l's market entry mode. In case of successful deception on the primary market[12], the counterfeit/pirate profits are given by:

$$\pi'_{prim,l} = p_l^*(k)q'_{prim,l} - c_{P,l}(q',k') - c_{prim} - c_{D,l}(q',k') - s_l(q',k')$$

If l enters the secondary market, the counterfeit/pirate profits are given by:

$$\pi'_{s,l} = p_{s,l}(k')D_l(p(k')) - c_{P,l}(D_l(.),k') - c_{D,l}(D_l(.),k') - s_l(D_l(.),k')$$

---

10. This follows straightforwardly from the assumption that $E([v_i(k)]) - c_i(k) > E([v_i(k')]) - c_i(k')$ for all i.

11. Where necessary, subscripts *prim* and *s* are used to denote variables related to the primary/secondary markets, respectively.

12. Hence, the quantity supplied on the market is equal to: $q'_j = \arg \max \left(\pi'_j \right)$.

A comparison between the two expected profit streams indicates which market will be targeted by the counterfeiting party j. The factors in favour of primary market infringement are presented below.[13]

- Difference in revenues [$p_j^*(k)q'_{prim,j} - p_{s,j}(k')D_j(p(k'))$]. Large revenues in the primary market, relative to the small revenues in the secondary market, encourage counterfeiters to deceive consumers. High revenues in the primary market are stimulated by a number of factors, including:

  o Rights holder's price [$p_j^*(k)$]. A high monopolistic price increases the expected revenues of a counterfeiter.

  o High prospect of supply of infringing goods [$q'_{prim,j}$]. High volumes of infringing goods on the primary market significantly increase the stream of the counterfeiter's revenues.

  o Low prices in the secondary market [$p_j(k')$]. High competition between counterfeiters results in low prices in the secondary market. This in turn lowers the opportunity cost of deception.

  o Low demand in the secondary market [$D_j(p(k'))$]. Low demand for counterfeit products implies lower revenues in the secondary market, hence lower opportunity cost.

  o High valuation of the alternative [A_i]. High valuation of no-purchase at all reduces the expected utility from the knowingly purchased consumption of a counterfeit product (see condition A2.3). In turn, it decreases expected demand in the secondary market, and reduces the incentive for a counterfeiter to target this market.

- Low costs of entry for the primary market [$-c_{prim}$]. A low cost of entry for the primary market increases the expected profits and creates an additional incentive for counterfeiters to enter this market.

---

13.   The factors in favour of secondary market infringement are inverses of the factors in favour of primary market infringement.

Chapter 3

CURRENT CONDITIONS IN COUNTERFEITING AND PIRACY

3.1. Summary

This chapter presents information on what is currently known about counterfeiting and piracy in different economies and in different product areas. The information has been drawn together from a variety of sources, including analysis that was carried out by governments, industry and research organisations, and information developed through two government surveys and an industry survey that were conducted by the OECD. Issues covered include the:

1. Scope and magnitude of counterfeiting and piracy activities.

2. Areas where the counterfeiting and piracy are taking place.

3. Distribution channels for counterfeit and pirated products.

4. Consuming areas.

5. Economies where counterfeit and pirated products are being sold.

6. Role of criminal networks and organised crime.

With respect to scope and magnitude, available information provides only a crude indication of how widespread counterfeiting and piracy might be. What is not known overwhelms what is known. This became readily apparent when reviewing the information provided in the responses to the OECD country/economy, industry and customs-specific questionnaires[14]. For the most part, neither governments nor industry were in a position to provide solid assessments of their respective situations. One of the key problems is that data have not been systematically collected and evaluated by either of the stakeholders. In many instances, the assessments that parties have made rely excessively on fragmentary and anecdotal information; where data are lacking, unsubstantiated opinions are often treated as facts.

One exception concerns copyright-based sectors. The software, music and film industries have invested considerable time and effort in developing frameworks for evaluating the magnitude, scope and effects of piracy, using surveys, investigative work and inferential analyses as bases. Greater transparency and debate on their methodologies

---

4. The general country/economy survey was sent to the 30 OECD member countries and to six non-member economies. The customs survey was sent to all 169 WCO members. The industry surveys were made generally available and were widely distributed by associations. Nineteen responses were received to the general country/economy survey, 70 responses to the customs-specific survey and approximately 80 responses to the industry survey.

could help to develop more robust models that would advance work on measurement techniques, both overall and in their respective sectors.

Principal conclusions are as follows:

- *Scope and magnitude.* The *scope* of products being counterfeited and pirated is broad and expanding; a notable shift is occurring from luxury to common products; the health and safety risks associated with substandard counterfeit products is a growing concern. Little is known about the overall *magnitude* of the problem as activities are clandestine and fake/pirated products are increasingly difficult to detect.

- *Areas where counterfeiting and piracy are taking place.* While counterfeiting and piracy are taking place in virtually all economies, activities are strongest in Asia, with China emerging as the economy where activities appear to be most widespread.

- *Distribution channels for counterfeit and pirated products.* Counterfeit and pirated products, previously distributed largely through informal markets, are increasingly infiltrating legitimate supply chains, with products now appearing in the shelves of established retail shops. The Internet has provided counterfeiters/pirates with a new and powerful means to sell their products via auction sites, stand-alone e-commerce sites and email solicitations.

- *With respect to trans-border transactions.* Counterfeiters/pirates are constantly altering their tactics to avoid detection; this, combined with the volume of trade passing through ports, poses significant challenges to customs authorities. Free-ports have emerged as an important lieu for processing counterfeit/pirated products.

- *Economies where counterfeit and pirated products are being sold.* Counterfeit and pirated products are being consumed in virtually all economies, but consumption patterns vary for different products. Analyses of specific sectors indicate, for example, that the Middle East represents an important market for automotive parts, while Africa is a major destination for counterfeit pharmaceuticals. Counterfeit cigarettes, on the other hand, are appearing in a broader range of markets.

- *Role of criminal networks and organised crime.* There is clear evidence that criminal networks are playing a significant role in counterfeiting and piracy, and that organised crime figures prominently in this regard. The high profitability of many counterfeiting and piracy operations and low risk of detection and prosecution have provided an attractive environment for the illegal activities. The networks sometimes resort to extortion and bribery of public officials to facilitate their operations, thereby weakening the effectiveness of public institutions at the expense of society at large.

As shown in Table 3.1, the views of governments tend to support these conclusions.

Table 3.1. Views on trends and developments in counterfeiting and piracy, by economy

Economy	Expansion from luxury to common consumer goods	Increase in volumes of infringing goods	Increase in goods that represent a threat to public health and security	Growth of illegal activity on the Internet	Organised crime is a factor
Australia	●	●	●	●	
Canada	●	●	●	●	●
France	●	●	●	●	●
Germany	●	●	●		
Hungary	●	●		●	●
Israel*					
Japan		●		●	
Korea		●			
Mexico*					
Netherlands		●	●		
New Zealand	●	●		●	
Poland*	●			●	●
Portugal	●	●			○
Russia	●	●	●		●
Spain	●	●			
Sweden	●	●	●		
Switzerland		●		●	
Chinese Taipei	●			●	
European Union	●	●	●		●

Notes:

○ Suspected.

* Israel and Mexico provided a general response but not for this section.

Source: OECD (2005b).

3.2. Scope

The scope of infringement concerns the range of products that have been subject to trademark, copyright, patent and design infringement. Concrete evidence of what has been infringed in these areas is available from a variety of sources, including customs and other enforcement activities, investigations carried out by industry and research organisa-tions and legal proceedings. In the case of trademark and copyright infringement, the volume of information available is relatively large from each of the sources mentioned.

In the case of patent and design rights, however, infringement information is less readily available. Not all customs agencies, for example, record data on patent infringe-ments at the border, as these products are not generally seized -- they are simply denied entry. Moreover, industry and research organisations do not appear to have carried out studies of patent infringement from a sectoral aspect. This leaves legal proceedings as virtually the only source for developing sector-specific information; collecting informa-tion from such proceedings would, however, be a daunting and resource-intensive under-taking.

The OECD survey of industry provides indications of the types of infringements that are of greatest concern to different industry sectors. Trademark violations were highlighted in most industry sectors, except for books, motion pictures, sound recordings and textiles, where design and copyright infringements were mentioned more frequently (see Annex Table 3.A1). Patents were mentioned as a concern in a number of sectors, but usually not as frequently as other infringements.

In terms of the range of products being infringed, information developed during the course of the study indicates that the scope of products being counterfeited and pirated is broad. Table 3.2 summarises some of this information. It should be kept in mind that the items mentioned in the table are only illustrative in nature; it is far from exhaustive.

Table 3.2. Examples of products subject to IP infringement

Industry sector	Examples of products subject to IP infringement
Apparel, footwear and designer clothing	T-shirts, hats, jerseys, trousers, athletic footwear, caps, socks, boots
Audio-visual, literary and related copyrighted work	Music, motion pictures, TV programmes, (CDs DVDs), software, books, computer/video games
Automotive	Sco-oters, engines, engine parts, body panels, air bags, windscreens, tires, bearings, shock absorbers, suspension and steering components, automatic belt tensioners, spark plugs, disc brake pads, clutch plates, oil, filters, oil pumps, water pumps, chassis parts, engine components, lighting products, belts, hoses, wiper blades, grilles, gasket materials, rings, interior trim, brake fluid, sealing products, wheels, hubs, anti-freeze, windshield wiper fluid
Chemicals/pesticides	Insecticides, herbicides, fungicides, non-stick coatings, pioneer hi-breed corn seeds
Consumer electronics	Computer components (monitors, casing, hard drives), computer equipment, webcams, remote control devices, mobile phones, TVs, CD and DVD players, loudspeakers, cameras, headsets, USB adaptors, shavers, hair dryers, irons, mixers, blenders, pressure co-okers, kettles, deep fryers, lighting appliances, smoke detectors, clocks
Electrical components	Components used in power distribution and transformers, switchgears, motors and generators, gas, and hydraulic turbines and turbine generator sets, relays, contacts, timers, circuit breakers, fuses, switchgears, distribution boards and wiring accessories, batteries
Food and drink	Fruit (kiwis), conserved vegetables, milk powder, butter, ghee, baby food, instant coffee, alcohol, drinks, candy/sweets
Personal accessories	Watches, jewellery, glasses, luggage, handbags, leather articles
Pharmaceuticals	Medicines used for treating cancer, HIV, malaria, osteoporosis, diabetes, hypertension, cholesterol, cardiovascular disease, obesity, infectious diseases, Alzheimer, prostrate disease, erectile dysfunction, asthma and fungal infections; antibiotics, anti-psychotic products, steroids, anti-inflammatory tablets, pain killers, cough medicines, hormones, and vitamins; treatments for hair and weight loss.
Tobacco	Cigarettes, cigars, and snuff
Toiletry and other household products	Home and personal care products, including shampoos, detergents, fine fragrances, perfumes, feminine protection pads, skin care products, deodorants, toothpaste, dental care products, shaving systems, razor blades; shoe polish; non-prescription medicine
Other	Toys, games, furniture, sporting goods (such as basket balls and golf clubs), stickers, dyed and printed exotic fabrics, belt buckles, decals, flags, lighters, tabletops, flowers, plant cuttings, qualification certificates, abrasive tools, sanitary products (bath tubs, wash basins, toilets), tableware (plates, bowls, cups)

Sources: OECD (2005*a*, 2005*b*) and related research.

Further information on scope emerged from the customs survey, in which officials reported on seizures/interceptions of infringing items. The value of the customs information rests in its detail. Thirteen respondents[15] were able to report information on the basis of Harmonised System nomenclature, on a six-digit basis.[16] Altogether, the economies identified 744 separate commodity items where infringement occurred, which represents 14% of the more than 5 200 HS items.[17]

The infringements covered 19 of the 21 product groupings that together define the full range of products that are commercially traded (Table 3.3).

Table 3.3. IP-infringing products seized by customs authorities in recent years

	General HS commodity groupings	Items infringed (6-digit HS)
1	Live animals; animal products (incl. meat, fish and dairy products)	1
2	Vegetable products (incl. fruit, live plants, cut flowers, coffee, tea, grain)	1
3	Animal or vegetable fats and oils, prepared edible fats and waxes	0
4	Prepared foodstuffs; beverages, spirits and vinegar; tobacco and tobacco substitutes	15
5	Mineral products	0
6	Chemicals and related industries (incl. perfume and pharmaceutical products)	32
7	Plastic and rubber, and related articles	23
8	Raw hides, skins, leather and furs; travel goods; related articles	27
9	Wood & wood products; straw articles; basketware and wickerwork	6
10	Pulp and paper products (incl. books, newspapers, etc.)	39
11	Textiles and textile articles (incl. apparel and clothing)	224
12	Footwear, headgear, umbrellas, walking sticks, riding crops; artificial flowers	37
13	Stone, plaster, cement, ceramic and glass products	13
14	Natural or cultured pearls; precious or semi-precious stones; imitation jewellery; coins	10
15	Metals and metal products (including hand tools and cutlery)	42
16	Machinery and electrical equipment (incl. TVs, electronic equipment, software, CDs and DVDs)	128
17	Transportation equipment (incl. parts)	11
18	Optical and photo equipment; precision instruments; clocks and watches; musical instruments	57
19	Arms and ammunition	5
20	Misc. manufactured articles (incl. furniture, toys, games and sports equipment)	71
21	Works of art, collector's pieces and antiques	2
	Total	**744**

Source: OECD (2006).

15. The respondents were Andorra, Canada, Chile, Fiji, Gabon, Mauritius, Moldova, Panama, Romania, Spain, Chinese Taipei, Thailand and the United States.

16. The economies reported data using the Harmonized Commodity Description and Coding System (HS). The system is a multipurpose international product nomenclature developed by the World Customs Organization. It comprises over 5 200 commodity items, each identified by a six-digit code. The system is used by more than 190 countries and economies as a basis for their Customs tariffs and for the collection of international trade statistics. Over 98% of the merchandise in international trade is classified in terms of the HS.

17. The most comprehensive list was submitted by the United States, which identified more than 600 items; in other economies, the number was less than 100.

The largest number of product groups seized/intercepted were textiles (30% of the total), followed by machinery and electrical equipment (17%). However, what is striking in a closer examination of the data is the number of products being counterfeited and pirated that could pose health and safety risks to unwitting consumers.

It should be noted that the customs data, while detailed, have important limitations. The most notable is that the data only reflect information on infringing items that have been detected in international trade; also, as noted above, for some economies, such as the United States, the data only capture violations of copyrights and trademarks. The actual overall scope is without doubt broader.

Not only is the scope broad, it appears to be expanding. As indicated above, many respondents to the economy survey noted that counterfeiters/pirates had broadened their activities from a focus on luxury goods to common consumer goods.

The survey of customs officials provides further support for this. As shown in Table 3.4, more than half of respondents believe the scope of infringing products being traded expanded during the past five years, with 26% indicating that expansion has been rapid. Those seeing a rapid expansion include the United States, which already has documented a large scope. Only four economies report that the scope narrowed.

Table 3.4. Scope of products subject to IPR border infringement during the past five years

The range of counterfeit and pirated products seized during the past five years has been:			
Expanding rapidly (13)	**Expanding steadily (16)**	**Unchanged (17)**	**More limited (4)**
Cyprus[18]	Argentina	Andorra	Angola
EC	Canada	Australia	Panama
Ghana	Croatia	Bermuda	Slovak Republic
Hungary	Fiji	Bulgaria	Zimbabwe
Japan	Gabon	Chile	
Korea	Germany	China	
Kuwait	Israel	Estonia	
Latvia	Mali	Hong Kong, China	
Luxembourg	Norway	Indonesia	
Malta	Poland	Moldova	
Romania	Russia	Mongolia	
Thailand	Senegal	Namibia	
United States	Serbia	Portugal	
	Slovenia	Spain	
	South Africa	Sudan	
	Switzerland	Chinese Taipei	
		Turkey	

Source: OECD (2006).

---

18. Footnote by Turkey:
    The information in this document with reference to "Cyprus" relates to the southern part of the island. There is no single authority representing both Turkish and Greek Cypriot people on the island. Turkey recognises the Turkish Republic of Northern Cyprus (TRNC). Until a lasting and equitable solution is found within the context of the United Nations, Turkey shall preserve its position concerning the "Cyprus issue".
    Footnote by all the European Union Member States of the OECD and the European Commission:
    The Republic of Cyprus is recognised by all members of the United Nations with the exception of Turkey. The information in this document relates to the area under the effective control of the Government of the Republic of Cyprus.

Additional information on scope tends to be anecdotal in nature. The ICC's Business Action to Stop Counterfeiting and Piracy (BASCAP) initiative has been active on this front in collecting information on incidents, on a systematic basis (see www.bascap.com/news/index.html).

3.3. Magnitude

The overall degree to which products are being counterfeited and pirated is unknown and there do not appear to be any methodologies that could be employed to develop an acceptable overall estimate. However, insights can be gained through an examination of various types of information, including data on enforcement and information developed through surveys. This information has significant limitations, however, and falls far short of what is needed to develop a robust overall estimate. Work carried out on individual sectors has yielded a clearer picture for the sectors concerned; refinement of the measurement techniques used and expansion of efforts into other product areas could eventually help to develop a more complete picture of the overall situation. How these ideas could be taken forward is addressed further in Chapter 6.

3.3.1. Overall magnitude

Only one assessment appears to have been made on the overall magnitude of counterfeiting and piracy worldwide. In 1997, the Counterfeiting Intelligence Bureau of the International Chamber of Commerce published a document that indicated that the overall cost of counterfeiting in the world was about 5% to 7% of world trade. This represented an increase from an estimated 2% to 4% at the end of the 1980s (International Chamber of Commerce, 1997).

The metrics underlying the ICC estimates are not clear. Some have interpreted the figure to mean that counterfeit products traded internationally account for 5% to 7% of total traded goods; others have indicated that the figure relates total counterfeit production (which would include production for domestic consumption as well as export) to world trade. Nor is it clear what types of IPR infringements are included in the estimate. In its narrowest sense, counterfeiting refers strictly to trademark violations. If piracy is included, this would include patent, copyright and other forms of IP infringement. Finally, the ICC report indicates that the estimates reflect judgments that are not supported by clear data.

Insights into magnitude can, however, be gained through an examination of various types of information, including data on enforcement and information developed through surveys.

3.3.2. OECD surveys

The OECD survey of governments, while yielding no specific information on overall magnitudes, reflected a common view that the scope of counterfeit and piracy products is broadening (Table 3.4 above). Information provided by customs officials provides further insights, but the information has limitations as it only pertains to counterfeit and pirated items that enter into international trade.

The customs data show that the value of interceptions/seizures from 35 economies totalled USD 769 million in 2005, which represented 0.01% of total imports for the economies concerned (see Table 3.5 below and Annex Table 3.A2).[19] Anecdotal evidence alone suggests that the actual level of counterfeiting and piracy in international trade is far higher than this figure. The low rate of detection reflects the relative ease with which the character of counterfeit/pirate trade can be disguised, and, as discussed later in this chapter, given with the limited ability of customs officials to physically screen the high volume of freight moving through ports.

Table 3.5. Value of seizures by economy (in USD), 1999-2006

Reporting economy	2006	2005	2004	2003	2002	2001	2000	199
Andorra		295	1,283	1,457	12,882	1,215		32,92
Argentina		45,000						
Bulgaria		3,775,208						
Canada		17,260,470						
Chile		111,060	580,615	104,112				
China		12,364,000	10,169,748	8,212,229	11,552,030	9,892,715	6,848,774	11,114,19
Croatia		405,478	94,638					
Cyprus (a)		545,253	413,704	198,470	207,496	163,360	322,297	175,33
Czech Republic		13,873,564			12,120,833	2,696,409	1,394,711	
Fiji		20,632	2,736			205,465		
Germany		249,671,792	236,561,793	298,753,773	64,986,923	157,111,060	181,931,253	43,417,23
Ghana		399	126	300				
Hong Kong, China		57,007,498	74,437,655	62,844,180	69,909,195	60,333,608	43,333,703	67,832,81
Hungary		15,796,394	1,540,449					
Korea		135,164,773	151,805,641	380,525,541	156,069,558	174,834,463	103,000,670	
Kuwait		5,024,869						
Latvia		8,673,050	291,222	112,407	5,420,714	150,702	199,126	
Lebanon		1,787,528	10,105,771	6,264,790				
Mali		774,586	54,819	80,868	43,550	40,306	204,269	61,56
Malta		42,681,438	24,026,488	154,856	3,068,665	966,933		
Mauritius		366,744						
Mongolia		7,645						
Norway		812,404	1,572,844	1,122,752	287,121	166,453		
Panama		4,817,941	3,680,855					
Peru		5,456,000						
Portugal		8,498,626	4,175,111	2,251,550	3,606,309			
Senegal		44,343						
Serbia		1,022,626	344,565					
Slovak Republic		31,151	786,850	267,158	40,468			
Slovenia		7,500,735						
South Africa		65,755,613	41,740,654	51,718,817				
Switzerland		7,812,556	3,846,364	2,996,194	2,550,380	2,611,475	10,869,625	4,736,38
Thailand		1,288,743	2,925,621	195,403				
Chinese Taipei		6,986,761	11,306,959					
United States	150,000,000	93,234,510	138,767,885	94,019,227	98,990,341	57,438,680	45,327,526	
Total value		**768,619,684**						
Number of reporters	*1*	*35*	*25*	*19*	*15*	*14*	*10*	*7*

(a) See footnote 18, Table 3.4.

Note: See Annex Table 3.A2 for valuation principles.

Source: OECD (2006).

---

19. The response rate to the Customs questionnaire was not high from larger economies, which limited the usefulness of the results. As for the data itself, sizeable fluctuations from year to year in many economies made it difficult to observe any trends or patterns; moreover, in many cases the level of interceptions/seizures reported, when compared to other economies, raised questions about the consistency and comparability of the information. With regard to comparability, it should be noted that the basis for reporting interception values varied among respondents. Some reported on the basis of declared customs value while others reported market value or legitimate item value.

3.3.3. Other surveys

Other insights into overall magnitude are available through consumer surveys that have been carried out by governments, industry and other interested parties. Such surveys can help to develop information on conditions in the secondary market (where consumers knowingly purchase counterfeit and pirated products), but they would be far less useful with respect to the primary market (where consumers are deceived into purchasing a fake product, and may never realise that they had been deceived).

Caution must, of course, be exercised in interpreting the results of surveys, as participants may not necessarily report fully or truthfully on their activities, particularly if these activities involve unlawful deeds. While these limitations need to be kept in mind, the value of surveys in suggesting patterns and changes over time should not be underestimated.

Highlights from several consumer surveys, which tend to be economy based, follow. The surveys show similar patterns with respect to counterfeit or pirated products that consumers most commonly buy knowingly on secondary markets. With respect to the degree of reported counterfeit/pirated purchases, Hong Kong, China and UK respondents were roughly similar (34% to 40%); US respondents, which were asked a narrower question, reported a lower number of counterfeit/pirate consumers (13%) and Brazilian respondents reported a relatively high number (60%).

3.3.3.1. Hong Kong, China

Hong Kong, China has been using consumer surveys extensively to examine counterfeit/pirate buying practices since 1999. The annual surveys reveal a marked shift in reported frequency of buying pirated and counterfeit products over time, with more than half of respondents in the most recent survey reporting that they do not buy counterfeit or pirated goods, suggesting that the problem may be diminishing in magnitude (see Table 3.6). The surveys indicate that music and videos are by far the most common counterfeit/pirated product purchased, followed by software and clothing and accessories far behind (see Table 3.7).

Table 3.6. Hong Kong, China: Survey on frequency of buying pirated or counterfeit goods

(% of respondents)

	1999	2000	2001	2002	2003	2004	2005
Often	3.3	2.7	1.7	1.2	2.8	0.9	0.7
Sometimes	21.4	23.3	19.0	17.0	17.5	16.6	14.3
Seldom	34.6	35.9	32.8	30.9	30.2	27.3	25.5
Never	36.8	36.5	46.1	49.1	47.8	55.2	58.4
Other	3.9	1.6	0.5	1.8	1.7	-	1.1
Sample size	1 004	1 004	1 018	1 006	1 231	1 214	1 206

Source: Hong Kong Intellectual Property Department (2005).

Table 3.7. Hong Kong, China: Counterfeit or pirated products purchased most often

(% of respondents who reported purchases of counterfeit or pirated products)

Sector	2004	2005
Music or movie	63.0	63.8
Computer software	15.2	14.1
Clothing and accessories	7.7	12.3
Games	8.1	6.7
Books	1.9	2.1
Watches	1.2	0.5
Stationery	1.4	0.2
Accessories	-	0.2
Cigarettes	0.8	-
Packaged food	0.4	-
Toys	0.3	-
Sample size	488	544

Source: Hong Kong Intellectual Property Department (2005).

3.3.3.2. United States

Surveys carried out in the United States by the Gallup Organization indicate that 13% to 14% of survey respondents personally purchased, copied or downloaded products in 2004 and 2005 that they knew, or suspected, were not genuine (Gallup, 2005 and 2006). As is the case with Hong Kong, China the most common infringing articles purchased were music, movies and software, followed by clothing (Table 3.6 above). The types of products infrequently purchased also mirrored Hong Kong, China's experience (see Table 3.7 above).

In addition to the types of products purchased, the Gallup survey also provides information on the intensity and frequency of purchases in the various product areas (see Table 3.8 below); these variables are important inputs for any analysis to be carried out on magnitude. The data show, for example, that the intensity and frequency of infringing activities is highest in music where many units were acquired and where the number of times that purchases were made during the past 12 months was also relatively high. Caution needs to be exercised, however, as the sample size in most product areas is relatively small (*i.e.* involving less than 20 of the 1 012 persons surveyed).

Table 3.8. United States: Types, intensity and frequency of counterfeit or pirated products purchased by consumers, 2006

Sector	% buying infringing product	Respondents who reported purchases of counterfeit or pirated products during the past 12 months				
		% buying infringing product	Number of units purchased on most recent occasion		Number of occasions (in last 12 months)	
			Mean	Median	Mean	Median
Songs, music CDs or audiocassettes	6.5	47	20.7	2	14.7	4
Movies, such as VHS, VCDs or DVDs	5.1	37	6.6	1	10.5	2
Computer operating systems or applications	4.1	30	3.6	1	2.0	1.5
Brand name clothing, designer bags and footwear	3.3	24	4.4	2	2.1	1
Perfume or cosmetics	2.2	16	1.7	1	1.5	1
Toys	1.7	12	2.9	2	2.8	2
Jewellery	1.5	11	2.2	1	2.0	1
Food	1.3	9	9.0	2	1.7	2
Video games	1.2	9	3.6	1	5.8	3.5
Alcoholic beverages, soft drinks or mineral water	1.2	9	3.9	2.5	15.1	5
Pharmaceutical or medicines, not generics	1.0	7	3.4	2	4.0	2
Tobacco	0.9	7	4.5	2	10.7	2
Tools or auto parts	0.8	6	2.6	1	1.7	1.5
Brand name watches	0.6	4	1.2	1	2.0	1

Source: Gallup (2006).

3.3.3.3. *England and Northern Ireland*

In England and Northern Ireland, a joint project between government, academia and industry surveyed more than 2 000 people in 2005 to obtain knowledge about end-users' attitudes towards, motivations for, and consumption of counterfeit and pirated goods (Bryce and Rutter, 2005). The survey indicated that 34% of UK respondents had knowingly purchased counterfeit or pirated products at one time or another while 56% had never knowingly purchased an infringing product and indicated that they would not do so in the future. Some 7% indicated that while they had never knowingly purchased an infringing product, they might do so in the future; 3% of respondents were unsure about purchases. The totals were somewhat smaller for Northern Ireland, where 25% of respondents indicated that they had purchased infringing items.

As was the case with surveys in other countries, music, films and clothing were the most common articles purchased (see Table 3.9).

Table 3.9. United Kingdom: Types of counterfeit or pirated products purchased by survey respondents during the last 12 months

Sector	% of total respondents	Percent of those who purchased counterfeit or pirated products
United Kingdom		
DVDs	16	47
Music CDs	16	47
Fashion items	16	47
Digital games	7	21
Northern Ireland		
Music CDs	12	48
Fashion items	11	44
DVDs	10	40
Alcohol and cigarettes	5	20
Computer games	4	16
Business software	2	8
Toys	1	4

Source: Bryce and Rutter (2005).

3.3.3.4. Brazil

In connection with a study measuring demand for fakes, copies and unlicensed goods among Brazilian consumers (Machado, 2005), the Instituto Brasileiro de Opinião Pública e Estatística (IBOPE) surveyed 602 inhabitants of the city of São Paulo. Products covered included clothing, footwear, watches, handbags, eyeglasses, perfume, and video games. This indicated that 60% of the respondents had acquired a counterfeit or pirated product at one time or another.

Some 25% of the respondents reported having bought counterfeit toys within the last year, while less than 10% reported having bought handbags, pens, perfumes and office supplies (Figure 3.1). With respect to acquired quantities, or consumption intensity, the average number of purchased items was highest for office supplies (10); in contrast, purchases of tennis shoes, watches, eyeglasses, handbags and perfume averaged two items.

In a separate national survey, IBOPE found that some 29% of respondents indicated that they had purchased counterfeit clothing within a specified 12-month period, while some 16% indicated they had purchased counterfeit footwear.

Figure 3.1. Consumption frequency and intensity of counterfeit goods

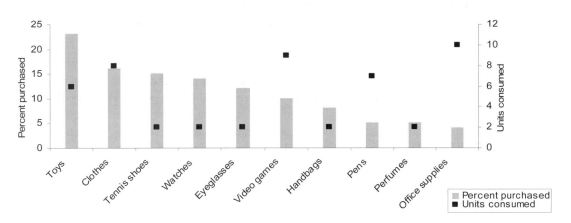

Note: "Percent purchased" refers to the percentage of respondents who purchased the indicated goods, while "units consumed" refers to the average number of articles that was purchased.

Source: Based on Machado (2005).

3.3.4. Sectoral assessments

A number of industry sectors have developed methodologies and carried out research and analysis aimed at estimating the magnitude of piracy, both on a global basis, and in individual economies. The sectors concerned are those that have been heavily impacted by copyright infringement (Table 3.10).

Table 3.10. Industry estimates of piracy, by sector

Sector	Source	Year	Global piracy estimate
Movies	Motion Pictures Association	2005	57% (1)
Music	International Federation of Phonographic Industry	2005	37% (2)
Software	Business Software Alliance/IDC	2005	35% (3)

1. Purchase or receipt of a pirated movie on a VHS, DVD or VCD, as a share of total market (*i.e.* industry plus pirate); figures for MPA members only (*i.e.* Buena Vista International, Inc., Paramount Pictures Corporation, Sony Pictures Releasing International Corporation, Twentieth Century Fox International Corporation, Universal International Films, Inc., and Warner Bros. Pictures International).

2. Sales of pirated music CDs as a share of total sales (*i.e.* industry plus pirate).

3. Number of pirated software units as a share of the total number of software united installed.

Sources: Motion Pictures Association 2006, International Federation of Phonographic Industry, 2006 and Business Software Alliance, 2006.

The assessments are based on a number of different approaches that have been developed to take the specific characteristics of the sectors concerned into account. Movie piracy, for example, largely occurs on the secondary market, where consumers buy a product, knowing that it is pirated. Industry efforts have therefore focused on developing information on the extent to which this occurs in different economies, using consumer surveys, focus groups and the like as principal inputs.

Music industry efforts are more variegated; they are based on: *1)* estimates received from national groups of sound recording producers; *2)* estimates received from external consultants employed by the International Federation of Phonographic Industry (IFPI); and *3)* seizure information extrapolated from IFPI's enforcement teams and data from the national groups.

The software industry's approach is far different. Total annual demand for software is estimated in different economies, based on: *1)* surveys and related research into software use; and *2)* the number of PCs in use. Legitimate software shipments are then estimated and subtracted from total demand to arrive at an estimate of pirated units. The entertainment software industry, estimates for which are not available on a global basis, uses a similar approach.

Assessing the methodologies employed, which would require far more information on the techniques used, is beyond the scope of this report. A general observation would be that information available on the methodologies is not sufficient to make any statements about the robustness of the results. More transparency would help to address this concern, and could provide an important basis for advancing work on measurement, both overall and in the sectors concerned.

3.4. Areas where counterfeiting and piracy are taking place

Information developed during the study suggests that counterfeiting and piracy are taking place in virtually all economies. This proposition is supported by an analysis of data provided to the OECD by customs officials. Reporting economies identified some 149 sources of counterfeit and pirated products, including 27 of the OECD's 30 member countries of which only Iceland, Ireland and Sweden were not mentioned. The sources mentioned include those economies where the counterfeiting or piracy actually took place, as well as economies that served as intermediate shipping points for infringing products.

While there are many sources, data from respondents to the customs survey[20] indicate that the five-largest sources generally accounted for more than 80% of total interceptions. Asia was the leading origin of the intercepted products, with China figuring prominently, appearing on 19 out of 20 of the lists (claiming the number one or two spot in 17 of the 20 listings) (Table 3.11). Hong Kong (China) and Thailand were on half as many lists.

A similar pattern emerges when looked at from the perspective of industry sectors. Information provided by industry in 12 sectors mentions China as a source in each. Russia (8), India, Thailand (7), Chinese Taipei, Turkey, Ukraine (6), Poland, (5), and Italy, Mexico, Pakistan (4) are also highlighted in four or more industry segments.

---

20.   Data on seizures are based on the experience of the following economies: Andorra, Angola, Australia, Cyprus (see footnote 18), Estonia, Fiji, Gabon, Germany, Ghana, Korea, Latvia, Mauritius, Netherlands, Portugal, Romania, Spain, Thailand, United States and the European Union.

Table 3.11. Source of seizures of counterfeit and pirated products in recent years, by economy

Economy reporting seizures	Origin of seized items and share of total seizures (of known sources)
Andorra	Malaysia (57%), Korea (25)%, Mauritius (11)%, Morocco (4)%, China (2)%
Angola (a)	Morocco (43)%, UAE* (14)%, Thailand (14)%, China (14)%, South Africa (7)%, Congo (7)%
Australia (a)	China (26)%, Malaysia (20)%, Thailand (15)%, Indonesia (14)%, Hong Kong, China (8)%
Cyprus (b)	China (49)%, Philippines (13)%, Hong Kong, China (11)%, UAE[1] (6)%, Korea (5)%
Estonia (a)	China (41)%, Russian Federation (29)%, Bulgaria (8)%, UAE[1] (6)%, Turkey (6)%
Fiji (a)	India (96)%, China (4)%
Gabon (a)	China (100)%
Germany	China (46)%, Hong Kong, China (5)%, Vietnam (4)%, Chinese Taipei (13)%, Thailand (4)%
Ghana	Nigeria (100)%
Korea	China (94)%, Hong Kong, China (2)%, Belgium (1)%, Chinese Taipei (1)%, Vietnam (1)%
Latvia	China (56)%, Korea (26)%, Chinese Taipei (10)%, Thailand (7)%, Latvia (<1)%
Mauritius	China (92)%, Thailand (4)%, Indonesia (2)%, India (2)%
Netherlands (c)	China (48)%, Hong Kong, China (10)%, Turkey (3)%, Nigeria (3)%, Chinese Taipei (28)%
New Zealand (a)	China (52)%, Thailand (19)%, Korea (5)%, Hong Kong, China (4)%, Indonesia (3)%
Portugal	China (68)%, Korea (11)%, Malaysia (7)%, Portugal (4)%, Brazil (3)%
Romania	China (38)%, Iran (24)%, Moldova (16)%, Turkey (12)%, UAE[1] (7)%
Spain	China (58)%, Thailand (9)%, United States (8)%, UAE (5)%, Hong Kong, China (4)%
Thailand	China (100)%
United States	China (69)%, Hong Kong, China (6)%, UAE[1] (2)%, India (2)%, Pakistan (2)%
European Union (d,e)	China (38)%, Thailand (10)%, Hong Kong, China (8)%, Turkey (7)%, Malaysia (4)%, United States (4)%

a) Based on number of seizures.

b) See footnote 18.

c) Based on top 10 sources.

d) A number of EU member states provided data; this is reported separately, above.

e) Calculations based on total seizures, including those from unknown sources.

* United Arab Emirates.

Note: Except as noted, percentages represent the share of total seizures where sources are known; some respondents reported a significant level of seizures where the source was unknown. The data are based on reported values, except as noted.

Source: European Commission, 2006b; OECD, 2005b; OECD, 2006; and United States Department of Homeland Security, 2006.

Figure 3.2. Economies listed as sources of counterfeit and pirated products:
Number of times listed by industry sectors

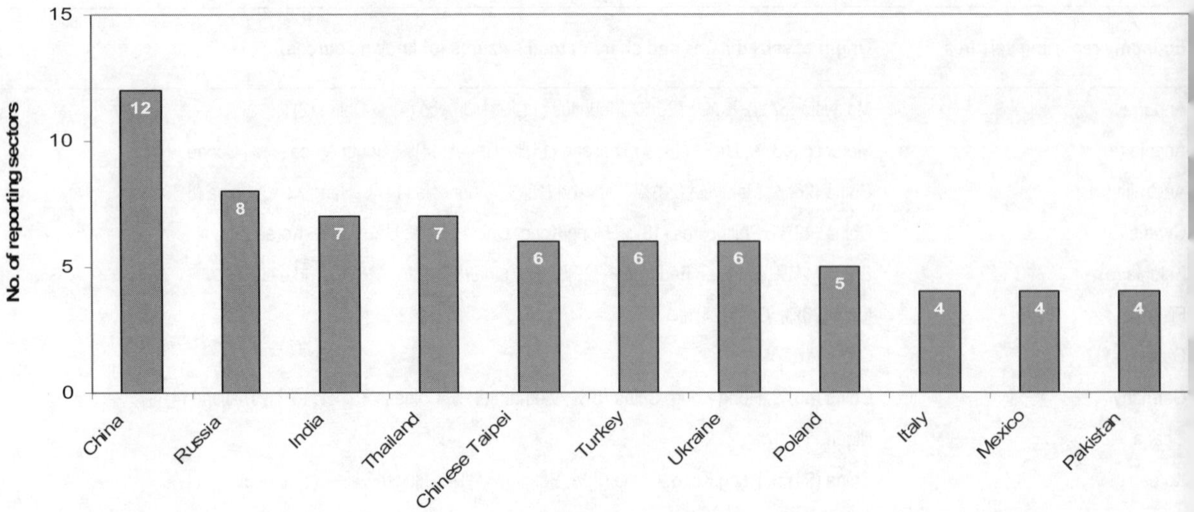

Source: OECD, 2005(*a*).

As discussed in a number of the industry sector write-ups in this report, identifying the locations where infringement is taking place is often not straightforward. The automotive parts sector analysis, for example, indicates that unbranded parts have been made and exported without infringing an IPR from China to the Middle East, where they were repackaged and labelled in ways that infringed trademarks. In another case involving tobacco products, law enforcement officials uncovered an operation in which unbranded cigars produced in the Caribbean area were legitimately exported to the United States, where they were falsely packaged and resold as premium, branded products; the scale of the operation was significant as cigar bands, boxes, cellophane and other materials capable of packaging 30 to 50 million counterfeit cigars were found (El Buen Habano, 2006). Similar, localised counterfeiting has also occurred in the case of apparel, where infringing labels have been affixed to imported garments that have been acquired legitimately (with no infringement apparent) from garment producers and distributors.

Similarly, it is not known to what extent producers are aware that their product lines are being infiltrated, nor is it easy to pinpoint exactly where trademark infringement takes place. Indications are, however, that larger companies are more aware of infringements than small and medium-sized business enterprises. The US Chamber of Commerce recently attempted to identify small local manufacturers that had noticed an increasing tendency for their products to be counterfeited. In some cases, companies had carried out market surveys that showed that their market share had increased but that their sales had not gone up. This suggested that a third party (probably a counterfeiter) had benefited. The Chamber also conducted informal surveys of many of its small and medium-sized focus groups; it showed that the vast majority of SMEs in the US did not know whether their products had been counterfeited or pirated[21].

---

21.   According to discussions with the US Chamber of Commerce.

3.5. Consuming areas

It is apparent that counterfeit and pirated products are being sold in virtually all economies. As mentioned earlier, the levels appear to be higher (relatively speaking) in economies where informal, open-air markets predominate (*i.e.* in developing economies).

But there are also significant differences among products. The sector analyses contained in this report, for example, indicate that the Middle East is a principal market for counterfeit *automotive parts*, but that significant volumes of counterfeits are also consumed in Europe, North America and elsewhere. Consumption of counterfeit *tobacco* products seems more widespread, with developing economies in Latin America, Africa and Asia seeming to have relatively high levels. Effective controls on the distribution of *pharmaceutical* products have sharply limited the distribution of counterfeit products in many economies, but there are exceptions, with particularly serious problems reported in Africa, where substandard counterfeit medicines are contributing to health problems. Counterfeit *electrical components, food and beverages* and *toiletries and household products* are similarly appearing in markets worldwide, with Africa, Asia and Latin America frequently mentioned as key regional markets. Piracy of *music, movies* and *software* appears to be significant in all economies, with particularly high levels estimated for most developing economies.

3.6. Distribution channels

3.6.1. Commercial outlets

Counterfeit and pirated products are distributed through various channels, including *1)* established retail shops; *2)* informal markets and trade fairs; and, increasingly, *3)* through Internet-driven virtual markets. The difficulty in penetrating these markets differs significantly. As discussed in Chapter 2, it is far more difficult to penetrate closely controlled supply chains that link manufacturers to retailers than it is to introduce infringing products into informal markets.

3.6.2. Established retail shops

Established shops tend to be the most difficult as the retailers concerned would, by willingly stocking infringing articles, risk declines in clientele and increased chances of legal action if their illicit behaviour were revealed. However, while more difficult to penetrate, research suggests that the sale of counterfeit and pirated products in established shops is rising. This is noted, for example, in the country review of Canada. There is also indication that this is the case in the United States. The Gallup Poll of consumers conducted in 2006 revealed that legitimate shops or retailers were a principal or an important source for a number of counterfeit and pirated products, including:

- Fashion clothing, designer bags and footwear.

- Toys.

- Pharmaceuticals.

- Beverages.

- Tobacco.

- Jewellery.

- Perfume.

3.6.3. Informal markets and trade fairs

The informal markets, that tend to be more common in developing economies, on the other hand, are far easier to penetrate as distribution is likely to be more decentralised and less regulated, providing greater, lower-risk opportunities for marketing infringing products. Such markets include mobile vendors, bars, clubs and car boot sales, as well as open, street markets. The products sold in the different types of informal markets vary. CDs/DVDs and clothing and personal accessories, for example, are commonly sold on street markets, whereas other more sophisticated products are sold at fairs.

The counterfeit/pirated products sold on informal markets are often difficult to trace back to their sources. One respondent to the industry questionnaire described how CDs and DVDS were sold by persons who were recruited and employed on an *ad hoc* basis, while the parties behind the operation remained out of sight. In some instances, minors were reportedly recruited in order to avoid prosecution if caught (OECD, 2005*a*).

Trade Fairs, where many international business transactions occur, are also relatively easy to penetrate. Trade fair organisers, exhibitors and attendees do not always have the required IPR knowledge that enables them to make informed decisions to avoid infringements. In the case of exhibitors, they might not be adequately aware of their rights and responsibilities at a trade fair, or, if they discover their products are being counterfeit, may not have the resources to seek legal or administrative redress at short notice or in a foreign jurisdiction. Counterfeiters take advantage of the brief duration of many trade shows and the concentration of an industry sector's participants.

Infringements at trade fairs have been reported, for example, in the electronic components sector where counterfeit of electrical components is carried out by registered companies that exhibit "their" products in fairs. It has been reported that these parts were often produced in Guangzhou and were found to be sold at the Guangzhou export commodities fair (also known as the Canton Fair).

3.6.4. Internet

The situation with respect to virtual markets is nuanced. On the one hand, the Internet provides a powerful platform for counterfeiters and pirates to engage large numbers of potential consumers in a highly cost-effective manner. On the other hand, the transparency of most virtual markets provides opportunities for stakeholders to identify and, ultimately, take action against infringements; as discussed below, while this has occurred in a number of instances, it is a difficult process.

The Internet has become an increasingly important vehicle for selling merchandise, with some predicting that the volume of sales will grow from 20% to 30% per year over the next several years (eMarketer, 2006 and IDC, 2005). In addition to rising volume, the range of products being sold is also increasing, and now includes major appliances, branded clothing and jewellery. Consumers and manufacturers have clearly benefited from e-commerce, as have counterfeiters and pirates. For the latter, this can be used cleverly to deceive unsuspecting consumers into buying fake merchandise, while providing a highly effective vehicle for counterfeiters/pirates to expand sales on secondary markets (where consumers knowingly seek out and buy counterfeit/pirated products at reduced prices).

The online environment is attractive to counterfeiters/pirates for a number of reasons:

- *Anonymity.* The ease with which counterfeiters and pirates can conceal their true identity sharply limits the risk of detection.

- *Flexibility.* It is possible for a counterfeiter/pirate located anywhere in the world to establish online merchant sites quickly. Such sites can also be taken down easily or, if necessary, moved to jurisdictions where IPR legislations and/or enforcement are weak.

- *Size of market.* The number of ecommerce sites and volume of listings are huge, making it difficult for rights holders and enforcement agencies to identify and move against infringing counterfeiters/pirates. With respect to auction sites alone, the firm eBay recorded 596 million new listings in the second quarter of 2006 (eBay, 2006). The possibility of marketing a small number of infringing products multiple times can further undermine enforcement efforts.

- *Market reach.* The Internet provides sellers with a means to reach a global audience at low cost, around the clock. For counterfeiters and pirates, who have traditionally thrived in small scale informal markets, this represents a major opportunity to expand sales.

- *Deception.* Utilising readily available software and images on the Internet, counterfeiters/pirates can easily create sophisticated and professional looking websites that are highly effective in deceiving buyers. Misleading or contrived ratings of consumer experiences with Internet vendors can further complicate matters by creating a false sense of security among purchasers. Finally, the infringing products may be sold alongside legitimate articles, which can facilitate deception.

There are basically three ways that the Internet is being used to facilitate counterfeiting/piracy: *1)* auction sites; *2)* more traditional business sites which offer products from a single seller at set prices that show up as a sponsored link in search sites; and *3)* unsolicited commercial email known as spam.

Auction sites, which in many respects resemble informal, open markets, have proven to be a popular venue for counterfeiters/pirates. The firm eBay acknowledges that there has been tremendous growth in the amount of infringing articles available on its site, but that the overall level of confirmed cases was a relatively low 0.01% of total listings. They have moved to curb sale of infringing items through the development of a programme called Verified Rights Owner (VeRO). Under this initiative, brand name owners can have deceptive listings removed the auction site by filing a notice of infringement.

A number of rights holders, however, remain concerned. Despite moving aggressively to remove infringing products, the firm Tiffany found that fake products continued to be offered regularly for sale. Of 186 items it purchased on an auction site in 2004, only 5% turned out to be genuine (Bobelian, 2004*)*. Louis Vuitton and Christian Dior have similarly claimed that the vast majority of items sold on one auction site were counterfeit.

E-commerce sites that are organised along the lines of traditional stores provide another venue for counterfeit/pirated goods. These sites include those operated by businesses that also maintain storefronts, as well as those operated by manufacturers of branded/copyrighted products and those operated by parties whose sole business is based on selling a variety of products via the Internet. The latter have attracted a high level of interest as they often offer branded products at discounted prices; their weak point is that often little is known about their operations, which introduces a higher risk that consumer expectation will not be fulfilled. It is these latter sites that are being used most extensively by parties selling counterfeit/pirated items.

Finally, the sale of counterfeit/pirated products is also being promoted by e-mail solicitations. Such solicitations can be used effectively to generate awareness of the availability of counterfeit/pirated products to audiences that may be interested in knowingly purchasing infringing items. They can also be used to lure unsuspecting consumers to sites designed to deceive purchasers into buying infringing products.

Perhaps most alarming is the apparent success that vendors of counterfeit pharmaceutical products have had in selling their fake products over the Internet. As the write-up on the pharmaceutical sector in this report indicates, the success appears to be particularly high in the case of life-style drugs, like Viagra, where consumers are either terribly naïve or are willing to take risks that could potentially endanger their health in order to acquire low-cost products through Internet pharmacies, about whom they have no knowledge.

3.6.5. Logistics

Another aspect of distribution is the logistics required to move items from production centres to customers; such movement incurs risks of detection and prosecution. In this regard, trans-border movements seem to provide the risks for counterfeiters and pirates, given the surveillance by customs authorities. The stakes can be high. Customs officials in Hamburg made what is believed to be a record seizure in 2006, when 117 containers containing counterfeit merchandise with a genuine brand equivalent value of over USD 490 million was intercepted (World Trademark Law report, 2006).

That said, the overall risk is relatively low, due in large part to the sheer volume of freight that passes through ports. The number of containers arriving in the 20 busiest world ports in 2005 ranged from an average of 10 000+ per day in the case of Laem Chabang (Thailand), to over 63 000 per day in the case of Singapore (UNCTAD, 2006). Even selective x-raying of suspicious cargoes is a time-consuming exercise that would enable only a small fraction of such a large number of containers to be screened,[22] and there is no guarantee that the x-raying would detect infringing products.

Moreover, counterfeiters/pirates further reduce risk of detection through evasive actions. One involves describing infringing items on customs forms in sufficiently vague ways that do not arouse suspicion. Another is to smuggle infringing articles into an economy, either by avoiding customs controls, or by not properly declaring infringing items. With respect to the latter, for example, smugglers of counterfeit cigarettes produced in the Far East tried to deceive customs officials in the United Kingdom by concealing the cigarettes in a container of rice noodles and by hiding the cigarettes in consignments of pottery and ceramic items (HM Revenue and Customs, 2006). Other techniques being used include: *1)* breaking shipments into smaller lots, some of which are then shipped by express air carriers (which seem to be viewed as entailing less risk); 2) exporting unfinished goods that are then labelled and packaged elsewhere; and *3)* "origin-laundering", which involves moving goods through a number of ports (possibly altering documentation in the process) to obscure their origin. Free-trade areas are often used as part of origin-laundering activities.

---

22. Assuming an x-ray process takes 10 minutes, around the clock examination would allow only 144 containers to be screened per machine, per day.

Research on sectors provides further insights into the logistical aspects of distributing counterfeit/pirated products. In the case of toiletry and household products, one firm estimated that about 90% of counterfeited goods over the past year were produced in China. Orders for the fake products were reportedly placed by representatives of Chinese import and export companies, which had contacts with distributors around the world. Similar patterns were observed in the automotive sector and the apparel and footwear sector, except that in the latter there was a growing trend towards direct sales of items to distributors and through the Internet.

In the electrical components sector, the majority of counterfeit products are also said to be manufactured in China and are typically either shipped or transported by air directly to importers in different economies and which then sell the products through local distributors. Intermediary transit points are used to enable counterfeiters to conceal distribution channels by changing delivery companies or splitting shipments into smaller parts, which are then shipped to different economies using different delivery services and modes of transportation.

In the pharmaceutical sector, brokers or middle men are often used to connect buyers and sellers through a series of transactions in order to develop mutual trust. These transactions start out small, with samples exchanged; once a working relationship is established, large orders follow. Counterfeit pharmaceuticals often feed into retail supply chains via e-commerce.

In the audiovisual sector, small-scale commercial production carried out by relatively small units is often made to order and destined for local markets, such as street markets. Large- scale commercial production involves mass production factories run by well-funded and organised groups with extensive distribution networks.

In the case of the tobacco industry, counterfeit items produced in China are reportedly manufactured to order, with orders placed by traders who finance and control the distribution and sale of product in targeted markets.

3.6.5.1. Free-trade areas

Free-trade zones and free ports are areas that governments designate as lying outside the customs jurisdiction of the economies concerned. They were developed as a means to stimulate economic activity by providing international traders with a location where they could store and manipulate goods in transit, without being subject to customs duties and most other customs procedures that would otherwise apply to imported merchandise. The areas range in size from single warehouses to massive complexes comprising hundreds of businesses, as well as whole harbours. Permitted activities include the storing, assembling, packaging and manufacturing of goods, principally for export. Disclosure requirements are generally minimal (Daudpota, 2006).

The lack of controls has made the free-trade areas attractive locations for parties engaging in trade of counterfeit/pirated products. The traders use the areas in three different ways:

- Parties import counterfeit goods into the areas and store them in warehouses, from which the items are subsequently re-exported. Passing the merchandise through the areas allows the parties concerned to "sanitise" shipments and documents in ways that disguise their original point of manufacture or departure; they also allow the parties to essentially establish distribution centres for counterfeit goods, with little or no risk of IPR-related enforcement actions being taken.

- Parties import unfinished goods and further process them in the free trade areas, often adding counterfeit trademarks and/or repackaging or re-labelling goods, prior to the items being exported as finished counterfeit goods to other countries.

- Finally, free trade areas have been used to manufacture counterfeit goods.

Traders are constantly altering shipping routes to avoid detection. Many counterfeit goods originating in China pass through Hong Kong, China, which is an important transhipment point for goods destined for Southeast Asia and points beyond. Also, often the counterfeit goods are then shipped to Dubai (UAE) where they are stored in large warehouses for transshipment in smaller orders to points in the Middle East, North Africa and Europe.

Reports on the situation indicate that the use of free-trade areas as transhipment points for counterfeit/pirated merchandise is widespread, with a high concentration in Asian, Middle Eastern and South American economies. The sector assessment on automotive parts describes the important role that Dubai is playing in facilitating trade in counterfeit parts. In the case of footwear, customs officials in Malta recently seized 134 000 pairs of counterfeit footwear that originated in the Far East and were to be transhipped to other countries (MaltaMedia News, 2006). Other counterfeit items recently seized (in Malta) include 13.7 million cigarettes that originated in the Far East and were destined for North Africa. Within Europe, Ukraine, Lithuania, Estonia and Latvia are cited as transhipment points for CDs, DVDs and software originating from Dubai; the products are reportedly shipped into other European countries via sea links with Finland and other Scandinavian countries (United States Trade Representative, 2005 and Euromoney, 2001).

Transhipment of counterfeit items through Hong Kong, China, which maintains the world's largest free-trade zone, remains a serious problem. The economy has one of the largest container ports in the world, and handles high volumes of traded items. While imports and exports of counterfeit goods are prohibited, goods in transit are specifically excluded from the prohibition, which means that they cannot be intercepted.

Panama's Colon Free Zone is another key transhipment conduit for counterfeit products. While laws empower customs officials to intercept counterfeit products, the volume of containers passing through the country (1.9 million per year, 80% of which represent transhipments), complicate enforcement efforts.

However, increasing attention is being paid by authorities to the problems occurring in free-trade areas. For example, the Gulf Co-operation Council, whose members include Bahrain, Kuwait, Oman, Qatar, Saudi Arabia and the United Arab Emirates have agreed to exclude IPR infringing products from free zones and duty-free shops. While customs authorities have been proactive on this front, the high volume of trade entering into the zones reportedly makes policing difficult. In the case of the United Arab Emirates, counterfeiters/pirates have responded by breaking down shipments so that products come in one consignment and label/packaging materials in another (Daudpota, 2006).

The World Customs Organization has also been active on this front, developing guidelines on controlling free zones, goods in transit/transhipment and obligations of service providers in relation to intellectual property rights infringements. The guidelines call on governments to implement national legislation that clearly specifies that products infringing customs IP cannot be stored or imported into free zones (World Customs Organization, 2005).

3.7. Criminal networks and organised crime[23]

As indicated earlier in this chapter, over a third of the respondents to the OECD economy survey indicate a link, or a suspected link, between counterfeiting/piracy activities and organised crime. A review of industry surveys indicates a similar view; almost all respondents either provided examples of organised crime involvement, or cited suspicions. Counterfeiting and piracy activities are attractive areas for criminal networks for a number of reasons. Profitability can be high, while the risk of prosecution and incarceration is low in most economies, as is the level of any fines that might be applied. The risks are sometimes even further diminished through the bribery and corruption of the authorities responsible for enforcing laws and regulations. Large amounts of money are apparently being made in counterfeiting/piracy, with some of the proceeds being used to fund more sophisticated counterfeiting/piracy operations (EC, 2006*a*).

The scope of organised crime activities in counterfeiting/piracy is reportedly broad, covering a range of sectors. The groups involved are based in many areas of the world and include Asian "triads" (which are involved in heroin trafficking, prostitution, gambling, extortion, money laundering, and alien smuggling) as well as mafias based in Europe and the Americas (OECD, 2005*a* and Bolz, 1992). One of the favourite targets of the crime groups has been pirated CDs and DVDs, where, as the audio-visual sector assessment in this report indicates, profit margins are large. Table 3.12 provides information on some of the documented instances of organised crime involvement.

Table 3.12. Examples of links of organised crime to counterfeiting and piracy

Group	Activity
Asian triads	Sale of pirated DVDs in London
Irish groups	Children's toys, batteries, power tools and veterinary drugs in Northern Ireland
Israeli group with Russian origins	Sale of counterfeit products in Japan
Italian and Eastern European gangs	Importation of pirated CDs into Italy
Russian mafia	Sales of pirated CDs in London

Sources: OECD 2005*a*, OCTF 2006, SOCA, UNIFAB.

Information on the overall extent of organised crime involvement is, however, difficult to document. Still, insights can be gained through government and industry assessments and initiatives. Many countries such as Canada, the United Kingdom and the United States have investigated intellectual property crime in their countries.

---

23.   Organised crime has been defined internationally as a group of three or more persons who work together over a period of time to commit one or more serious crimes in order to obtain a financial or other material benefit (United Nations, 2006). Serious crimes are further defined to include those resulting in incarceration of at least four years, or a more serious penalty. Thus, while counterfeiting and piracy are illegal activities, they would not in most instances be considered serious crimes.

The Royal Canadian Mounted Police, through the Project SHAM, found that operations were becoming more sophisticated with criminal and terrorist organisations participating in IP crime. The RCMP has since devoted increased resources to tackle the problem and launched a national awareness campaign highlighting the dangers and economic costs associated with counterfeit products as well as its connection to organised crime.

The United Kingdom recognised that IP crime was increasingly well-organised and unveiled the country's first IP crime strategy. The UK Serious Organised Crime Agency (SOCA) recently developed a specific programme to tackle IP crime and the Organised Crime Task Force (OCTF) in Northern Ireland made intellectual property crime one of their key priorities.

The US Commissioner of Customs indicated in 1999, for example, that their investigations had showed that organised crime groups were heavily involved in trademark counterfeiting and copyright piracy, with the proceeds often used subsequently to finance more violent crimes (International Anti Counterfeiting Coalition, 2005). In 2004 the White House introduced the Strategy Targeting Organized Piracy (STOP!), a comprehensive initiative aimed at breaking up the criminal networks that traffic in fakes and stop trade in pirated and counterfeit goods at borders.

Further insights are also available in the economy and sector assessments included in this report. The Brazil assessment, for example, indicates a strong presence of organised crime in Latin America, as does the China assessment. In the food and drinks sector, the high profits associated with producing and selling untaxed alcohol have attracted organised crime, which is actively involved in producing and smuggling products. In the tobacco sector, the transport and distribution networks for major smuggling operations are highly organised, secure and difficult to detect, often because of the participation of organised crime in the movement and sale (but rarely in the production) of the counterfeit products.

In the audiovisual sector, organised crime has been linked to human trafficking, where Chinese pirates force the people they smuggle into Europe to work as distributors of pirate products to pay off their transport costs (OECD, 2005a). This is supported in a recent report by the UK Serious Organised Crime Agency (SOCA), where it is said that mainland Chinese organised crime groups are heavily involved in the distribution of counterfeit DVDs and exploit illegal immigrants or asylum seekers to sell them on the streets in the UK (SOCA, 2006).

Further assessments have been undertaken by anti-counterfeiting industry associations, such as the French Union des Fabricants (UNIFAB), which reports regularly on the interrelation between counterfeiting and organised crime, notably in the audiovisual and apparel and footwear sectors, and the International Anti Counterfeiting Coalition (IACC), which produced a White Paper reporting links between counterfeiting and piracy with organised criminal syndicates and terrorist organisations.

Furthermore, according to discussions with government officials, there is also a link between criminal networks involved in piracy and counterfeiting and corruption of government officials. Through bribery, extortion and even drawing officials into the criminal network, organised crime groups can reduce disruption of their distribution channels and the risk of punishment for their unlawful activities.

In addition to the established link between counterfeiting and piracy and organised crime, Interpol has highlighted a disturbing relationship of counterfeiting and piracy with terrorist financing, with IP crime said to be becoming the preferred method of financing for a number of terrorist groups (Interpol, 2003). The links take two basic forms:

- *Direct involvement*, where the terrorist group is implicated in the production or sale of counterfeit goods and remits a significant portion of those funds for the activities of the group. Terrorist organisations with direct involvement include groups that resemble or behave like organised crime.

- *Indirect involvement*, where sympathisers involved in IP crime provide financial support to terrorist groups via third parties.

The Interpol report cites a number of examples. In Northern Ireland, paramilitary groups are involved in IP crime, including the trafficking of counterfeit cigarettes. Their involvement takes the form of control of the markets where counterfeit products are sold. In Kosovo, there is reportedly a long-standing relationship between criminal organisations and local ethnic-Albanian extremist groups that are involved in the sale of a range of counterfeit consumer products, including CDs, DVDs, clothes, shoes, cigarettes and computer software. In South America, counterfeit goods produced in Europe are reportedly sent to a free-trade zone by a group of Lebanese criminals sympathetic to Hizbollah. The goods are then smuggled into a third country, to avoid import taxes, where they are then sold. Alleged connections to Al-Qaeda have been made in the case of a shipment of counterfeit shampoos, creams, cologne and perfume from Dubai to Copenhagen, Denmark.

Interpol launched in January 2007, in partnership with the US Chamber of Commerce, an initiative to help law enforcement agencies fight IP crime by creating a global database of criminal counterfeiting and piracy intelligence, and co-ordinating investigations in multiple regions of the world based on trend analyses derived from the database. It has also established an Intellectual Property Crime Action Group (IIPCAG) with representatives from the police, customs, inter-governmental organisations and private sector associations. The group aims to facilitate international law enforcement action against IP crime, to raise awareness and to improve co-ordination amongst police, customs and the private sector.

References

Bobelian, Michael (2004), "Tiffany and eBay clash over sales of fake goods", *New York Law Journal*, August.

Bolz, Jennifer (1992), "Chinese Organized Crime and Illegal Alien Trafficking: Humans as a Commodity", U.S. Senate Committee on Governmental Affairs; "Asian Organized Crime: The New International Criminal", Hearings before the Permanent Subcommittee on Investigations, http://usinfo.state.gov/eap/Archive_Index/Chinese_Organized_Crime_and_Illegal_Ali en_Trafficking_Humans_as_a_Commodity.html, accessed December 2006.

Bryce, Jo and Jason Rutter (2005), "Fake nation?", www.allianceagainstiptheft.co.uk.

Business Software Alliance (2006), *Third annual BSA and IDC global software piracy study*, www.bsa.org, May.

Daudpota, Faisal (2006), "The report on the role of free trade zones and free ports in unchecked cross-border movement of counterfeit and pirated goods", unpublished.

eBay (2006), "eBay Inc. announces second quarter 2006 financial results", www.ebay.com.

El Buen Habano (2006), "Cigar makers burned by fakes", www.elbuenhabano.com, 28 May.

eMarketer (2006), "US Retail E-Commerce", www.eMarket.com, April.

Euromoney Institutional Investor (2001), "Emerging markets: Eastern Europe enforcement issues remain high on agenda", *Managing Intellectual Property*, March.

European Commission (2006*a*) "A Serious Problem for Everyone", http://ec.europa.eu/taxation_customs/customs/customs_controls/counterfeit_piracy/co mbating/indexen.htm.

European Commission (2006*b*), "Counterfeiting and piracy statistics", at Internet http://ec.europa.eu/taxation_customs/customs/customs_controls/counterfeit_piracy/sta tistics/index_en.htm.

IDC (2005), *Internet Commerce Market Model (ICMM)*, Volume 10.1, October.

Gallup Organization (2005), *US consumer attitudes and behaviours toward counterfeiting*, January.

Gallup Organization (2006), *US consumer attitudes and behaviours on counterfeiting*, May.

HM Revenue and Customs (2006), *New responses to new challenges: Reinforcing the tackling tobacco smuggling strategy*, at Internet www.hm-treasury.gov.uk/media/1E1/67/bud06_tobacco_273.pdf, March.

Hong Kong Intellectual Property Department (2005), *Annual survey of public awareness of intellectual property rights*, at Internet www.ipd.gov.hk/eng/promotion_edu/annual_survey.htm. (last accessed 6 December 2006)

IACC (2005), "The Negative Consequences of International Intellectual Property Theft", *White Paper*.

International Anti-Counterfeiting Coalition (2005), "The Negative Consequences of International Intellectual property Theft: Economic harm, threats to the public health and safety, and links to organized crime and terrorist organizations," *White Paper*.

International Federation of Phonographic Industry (2006), *The recording industry 2006: Piracy report*, www.ifpi.org

International Chamber of Commerce (1997), *Countering counterfeiting: A guide to protecting & enforcing intellectual property rights*, Paris.

Interpol (2003), *The links between intellectual property crime and terrorist financing*, www.interpol.int/public/FinancialCrime/IntellectualProperty/Default.asp

Machado, S. M. (2005), *The Impact of Counterfeiting and Piracy on São Paulo City and Brazil*, US Chamber – IPR Initiatives, Brazil-U.S. Business Council (U.S. Section).

MaltaMedia news(2006), "Customs seize counterfeit footwear", at Internet www.maltamedia.com/news/2005/ln/article_8752.shtml, 23 January.

Motion Picture Association (2006), *The Cost of Movie Piracy,* an analysis prepared by the L.E.K consultancy for the MPA, available at: www.mpaa.org/press_releases/leksummarympa.pdf

OECD (2005*a*), Responses to OECD industry surveys, unpublished.

OECD (2005*b)*, Responses to OECD economy surveys, unpublished.

OECD (2006), Responses to OECD customs survey, unpublished.

Organised Crime Task Force (OCTF), *Organised Crime in North Ireland Annual Report and Threat Assessment 2006*.

RCMP (2004), *A Strategic Intelligence Assessment of Intellectual Property Crime in Canada,* Project SHAM.

SOCA (2006), "The UK threat assessment of organised crime 2006/2007", www.soca.gov.uk

UNCTAD (2006), "Review of maritime transport – 2006", www.unctad.org.

Union des Fabricants (UNIFAB) 2004, *Counterfeiting and Organised Crime Report*, 2nd Edition.

United States Department of Homeland Security (2006), "Response to OECD customs survey", unpublished.

United States Department of Homeland Security (2006), "FY 2005 IPR Seizure Statistics", www.cbp.gov/xp/cgov/import/commercial_enforcement/ipr/seizure/, March.

United States Trade Representative (2005), *2005 Special 301 report*, www.ustr.gov.

World Customs Organization (2005), *Guidelines on controlling free zones in relation to intellectual property rights infringements*, www.wcoipr.org, 12 January.

World Trademark Law Report (2006), *World Trademark Law Report*, 1 December.

Annex 3.A1

TABLES AND FIGURES

Table 3.A1. Sector concerns with IP infringement, by type of infringement, 2005

Sector	Number of responses[1]	% of responses mentioning specific IPR infringement concerns			
		Trademark	Patent	Copyright	Design
Automotive	7	100	14	0	43
Books	1	0	0	100	0
Chemicals/pesticides	2	100	50	50	50
Computer software	2	100	0	100	50
Electronic devices and equipment	9	89	22	22	56
Food and drink	7	86	0	14	14
Luxury goods, perfumes, fashion clothes	3	100	0	0	33
Motion pictures and other video content	4	25	25	100	0
Music	5	0	0	100	0
Pharmaceuticals	7	86	57	0	0
PC and video games	1	100	0	100	0
Sportswear and articles	3	100	0	0	0
Textile items	3	33	0	0	67
Tobacco	3	100	33	33	33
Toiletry and household products	5	100	0	0	0
Tools	1	100	0	0	100
Toys	2	100	50	50	100
Writing implements	1	100	100	0	100

1. Responses include individual companies as well as associations as follows:

Automotive: 2 associations, 5 companies
Books: 1 publisher
Chemicals/pesticides: 1 association, 1 company
Computer software: 1 association, 1 company
Electronic devices and equipment: 3 associations, 6 companies
Food and drink: 1 association, 6 companies
Luxury goods: 1 association, 2 companies
Motion pictures: 2 associations, 2 companies
Music: 5 associations

Pharmaceuticals: 2 associations, 5 companies
PC and video games: 1 association
Sportswear and articles: 2 associations, 1 company
Textile items: 2 associations, 1 company
Tobacco: 3 companies
Toiletry and household products: 5 companies
Tools: 1 company
Toys: 2 associations
Writing implements: 1 company

Source: OECD (2005a).

Table 3.A2. Seizure valuation principles, by economy

Reporting economy	Valuation principle
Andorra	Declared (customs)
Argentina	Legitimate item value
Bulgaria	Legitimate item value given by rights holders
Canada	Fair market*
Chile	Fair market
China	Declared (value of counterfeit/pirate good)
Croatia	Legitimate item value
Cyprus [a]	Declared (customs)
Czech Republic	Invoice value
Fiji	Value (customs)
Germany	Market value of counterfeit/pirated goods
Ghana	Legitimate item value
Hong Kong, China	Legitimate item value, *i.e.* declared (customs)
Hungary	Market value of items
Korea	Official expert and right holder knowledge
Kuwait	Legitimate item value
Latvia	Legitimate item value
Lebanon	Legitimate item value (2005), declared value (2004)
Mali	Market value of counterfeit/pirated goods
Malta	Market value of counterfeit/pirated goods (67%) otherwise legitimate item value
Mauritius	Market value
Mongolia	Declared value at import
Norway	Market value
Panama	Legitimate item value
Peru	Legitimate item value
Portugal	The value was found in the database of Customs (SIVEP: referential values of similar goods
Senegal	Legitimate item value or owner of the good
Serbia	Market value of counterfeited goods
Slovak Republic	Real or estimated tax-free value of product
Slovenia	Real or estimated tax-free value of the product
South Africa	Legitimate item value or owner of the good
Switzerland	Legitimate item value
Thailand	Market value of counterfeit and pirated items
Chinese Taipei	Declared
United States	Cost of the counterfeit merchandise plus the cost of shipping and importing them into the United States

a) See footnote 18 in Chapter 3.
*Canada also reports declared values. In 2005, these amounted to USD 1 410 893.
Source: OECD (2006).

Chapter 4

ESTIMATING THE MAGNITUDE OF COUNTERFEITING AND PIRACY

One of the principal objectives of this report is to explore methodologies and techniques that could be employed to improve measurement of the magnitude of counterfeiting and piracy in economies, both overall and in specific sectors.

This chapter presents potential ways to further develop one approach in particular (see Box 4.1): that which is based on the information available on international trade in regard to counterfeit and pirated goods[24]. It is emphasised that this approach does not account for counterfeit and pirated products that are produced and consumed within economies. This is a significant limitation, as domestic trade in some products and in some economies is considerable. In spite of this, the approach is seen as being one of the better foundations for providing analysis on the infringement phenomenon on a global scale. Ways of expanding the analysis to include domestic markets are promising but are beyond the scope of current work.

The analysis presented in this chapter was carried out using data provided by customs officials on interceptions/seizures. Unfortunately, these data had significant shortcomings as the number of governments providing information was limited, and the completeness of the responses varied considerably. The conclusions reached can therefore be viewed only as a crude indicator of the role of counterfeit and pirated products in international trade.

Box 4.1. The quest for new and improved measurement techniques

In support of its work on counterfeiting and piracy, the OECD, together with WIPO, organised a meeting in October 2005, in which experts from government, industry and academia participated. A second session took place in January 2006. The group concluded that techniques for estimating counterfeiting and piracy levels could be developed on an industry specific basis, but the techniques would have to be based on the characteristics of the industry concerned; no one approach would work for all. The task was seen as far more complicated in the case of global estimates. Among the techniques examined in this regard were: *1)* adapting the measurement techniques used for measuring the size of underground economies; *2)* applying notional propensities to consume counterfeit and pirated products to the items comprising national consumer expenditures; and *3)* exploring what might be done to exploit information available on international trade in counterfeit and pirated products. The expert group expressed interest in the third option, given data availability and estimation potential.

---

2.   Chapter 6 provides an assessment of the techniques that could be employed to develop sector-specific estimates.

The analysis itself is based on an examination of the degree to which different products are detected as counterfeit or pirated in international trade, and the degree to which different economies are detected as sources of these products. Taking a number of known biases into account, this information is then used to estimate a set of relative counterfeiting/piracy propensities. This provides the foundation on which a ceiling of the phenomenon's magnitude is approximated. This analysis, which, it should be emphasised, would be greatly strengthened by improved data on interceptions/seizures, suggests international trade in counterfeit and pirated goods could account for up to USD 200 billion in 2005.[25] This estimate does not tell the whole story. The figure does not include counterfeit and pirated products that are produced and consumed domestically, nor does it include the significant volume of pirated digital products that are being distributed via the Internet. If these items were added, the total magnitude could well be several hundred billion dollars higher.

4.1. Establishing relative propensities

The analytical framework of this analysis builds on the general principles presented in Chapter 2; namely that there are different propensities to produce and consume different types of counterfeit and pirated goods. Apparel and watches, for example, are counterfeited much more intensively than food products and DVD players, due to production and distribution advantages and associated profits. Estimating the counterfeiting intensities (or propensities) is useful for indicating the magnitude of counterfeiting and pirated goods using existing data. Indeed, although the illicit products cannot be directly identified, they are already reflected in many available data sources.

Like all other goods, counterfeit and pirated goods are subject to substantial international trade and are thus reflected in international trade statistics. Similarly, since many infringing goods are sold through legitimate distribution chains, they are consequently reflected in, for example, retail trade statistics. Even fakes that are primarily sold in open markets or by street vendors, and therefore could escape being recorded, could possibly be reflected in statistics on consumer expenditures.

The principal attractions of focusing on international trade, here termed as the "trade approach", are twofold. First, the number of reporting economies covered by international trade statistics is significant and permits analysis of bilateral trade flows at a detailed level. This ensures broad and consistent economy-coverage for the analysis. Secondly, since all internationally traded products undergo some form of processing by customs, including investigation of articles in potential violation of intellectual property rights, national customs agencies are in a position to collect data on counterfeit and pirated goods in a systematic manner.

On the other hand, however, narrowing the focus to counterfeiting and piracy in international trade limits the analysis by omitting those infringing goods that never leave the economy of production. Pure domestic markets for counterfeit and pirated products, which could be of substantial sizes, are therefore not accounted for. Tangible counterfeit and pirated goods that are traded internationally via the Internet are nonetheless covered, in so far as these goods are inspected by customs.

---

23.   It should be noted that the USD 200 billion is not comparable to the figure cited in Chapter 3, which, in addition to traded goods, is believed to include counterfeit and pirated products that are produced and consumed domestically.

4.1.1. Methodology overview

The trade approach has three steps: *1)* identification of those goods that have been detected in international trade as counterfeit or pirated (*i.e.* sensitive goods); *2)* identification of the economies from which the infringing products were shipped; and *3)* estimation of propensities.

- *Identification of sensitive goods*: All goods that have been subject to counterfeiting/piracy and international trade are first identified. These goods are referred to as *sensitive goods*. The total level of trade in these products (including both genuine and infringing articles) is then calculated. Comparing this to total world trade illustrates the relative importance of international trade in those goods that have been subject to infringement.

- *Identifying source economies*: The second step is to identify all economies that have been identified as a source of imports of counterfeit or pirated goods. Such economies are referred to as *source economies,* from which the known geographical aspect of counterfeiting and piracy in international trade is derived. This permits the base of sensitive trade to be refined, by focussing on imports from known sources.

- *Estimating propensities*: The final step involves the estimation of the propensities to which different product types from known sources are counterfeit and/or pirated. This calculation is based on analyses of the interception/seizure statistics provided by customs authorities.

It is emphasised that the framework outlined above does *not* result in a direct estimate of the counterfeiting and piracy magnitude in world trade. Instead, it provides a set of factors describing the relative intensity of international trade in different types of counterfeit and pirated goods by which a ceiling of the trade in infringing goods is approximated.

4.1.2. Data foundation

The trade approach is based on two sources of information; international trade statistics; and, as mentioned above, customs seizures of infringing products. The trade statistics are based on the UN Comtrade database (landed customs value)[26], while the customs seizures are based on data provided to the OECD, through a questionnaire distributed to customs authorities by the World Customs Organization (see Annex 4.A1 for details). Because data on imports generally are believed to be more accurate than data on exports, and because imports also constitute the main focus of customs with respect to investigating and inspecting goods in violation of IPR, the trade approach focuses on imports.

---

26. International statistics are collected from the United Nations Statistics Division (UNSD)-OECD Joint Trade Data Collection and Processing System in the form of the UN Comtrade database. With 124 (March, 2007) reporting economies and 243 partner economies (133 economies in addition to reporting economies), the database covers the largest part of world trade and is considered the most comprehensive trade database available. Products are usually registered on a six-digit Harmonised System basis, making the level of detail of the database quite high. The presented data is based on landed customs value, which is the value of merchandise assigned by customs officials. In most instances, this is the same as the transaction value appearing on accompanying invoices. Landed customs value includes the insurance and freight charges incurred in transporting goods from the economy of origin to the economy of importation.

4.1.2.1. Seizure data

While data on customs seizures are not suitable for direct magnitude measurement, they constitute a valuable source of information with respect to indirect analysis, in so far as they capture the effect of the interplay between the product, market and institutional characteristics that drive counterfeiting and piracy in international trade. The current analysis assumes that seizure statistics are indicatory of: *1)* the relative intensities to which different types of infringing goods actually appear in international trade; as well as *2)* the extent to which infringing goods originate from different trading partners.

These assumptions, however, need to be qualified. Interceptions by Customs authorities are influenced by profiling schemes resulting in a bias in the data; moreover, the authorities may be unaware of a range of products susceptible to infringement and therefore not detect these at all; finally, some products may simply be easier to detect than others, which could further bias interceptions.[27] While techniques can be used (and have been used in this analysis) to adjust data for these biases, such adjustments can only partially address the shortcomings. Moreover, it should be noted that the differences in the way seizures are registered across economies complicates the compilation of comparative data on which an analysis of counterfeit and pirate activities can be based.

4.1.3. Step 1: Identification of sensitive goods

Seizure data provided by customs authorities for this study varied significantly. Although some respondents provided very detailed data, listings were not comparable, detail levels differed significantly and information was simply not provided by a large number of economies. Because of data limitations, a sensitive good was therefore broadly defined for the purposes of this analysis as a category of goods. If any of the reporting customs authorities registered an infringing item belonging to a category, the whole category was treated as "sensitive".

The categories used are the 96 product chapters comprising the Harmonised System (HS) at the 2-digit level[28]. Since not all items in a category necessarily have been subject to counterfeiting or piracy, this approach would tend to overstate the scope. On the other hand, categories where counterfeit or pirated trade has occurred, but has not been detected, would not be included in the scope of sensitive trade and would tend to understate the situation.

4.1.3.1. Range of sensitive goods

Based on available statistics from 53 respondents over the period 1999 to 2005, customs detected articles in violation of intellectual property rights in 64 of the 96 HS chapters (67%). Given the broad product coverage of the HS chapters, and the broad definition of sensitive goods, this is likely to significantly overstate the actual scope. The highly detailed data provided by the United States, for example, registered infringing products in 59 of the 96 chapters (61%). At a more refined level, however, these seizures involved only 678 of the 3 650 (19%) 6-digit product items contained by the 59 chapters.

---

27. Bias may also arise from differences in the intensity to which imports from economies within customs unions are screened for infringing goods, as opposed to imports from economies outside such unions. Given the generality of the model, the impact of such a bias is nevertheless bound to be small.

28. The Harmonized System is an international commodity classification system. See Chapter 3 for further information.

In most cases, 6-digit HS codes were unfortunately not provided by respondents; however, a total of 744 categories were identified for those that did -- only slightly more than 14% of the total number of 6-digit categories (for all 96 HS chapters).

4.1.3.2. Seizure intensities

While the scope of goods that are sensitive to infringement undoubtedly is broad, Chapter 2 suggested that the intensity of counterfeiting and piracy activities differs greatly across different types of goods. This is supported by several of the sector studies, and is furthermore supported by seizure statistics. Calculating the percentages of seized goods in different HS chapters shows that the interceptions are concentrated in a small number of chapters. This is illustrated in Table 4.1, which shows the average of seizure frequencies across goods covered by sensitive HS chapters, weighted by the share of total sensitive imports (total trade in the 64 HS chapters) of the reporting economy.

Table 4.1. Seizure percentages of goods, by HS chapters (2-digit-level)

No.	HS	Description of HS chapter	Seizure pct.	World trade million USD	pct
1	61,62	Articles of apparel and clothing accessories	30.6	247,851	2.8
2	85	Electrical machinery & equip. & parts, telecommunication equip., sound recorders, television recorders	26.8	1,264,702	14.3
3	42	Articles of leather, saddlery & harness, travel goods, handbags, articles of gut	7.9	34,777	0.4
4	64	Footwear, gaiters, & the like	5.4	64,153	0.7
5	24	Tobacco & manufactured tobacco substitutes	5.4	24,346	0.3
6	91	Clocks & watches & parts thereof	4.0	22,974	0.3
7	95	Toys, games & sports equip., parts & accessories	3.7	70,264	0.8
8	90	Optical, photographic, cinematographic, measuring, checking, precision, medical or surgical instruments & accessories	1.9	293,642	3.3
9	48	Paper & paperboard, articles of paper pulp	1.6	128,237	1.5
10	94	Furniture, bedding, cushions, lamps & lightning fittings, illuminated signs, nameplates & the like,...	1.5	119,531	1.4
11	71	Pearls, stones, prec. metals, imitation jewelry, coins	1.3	165,441	1.9
12	96	Miscellaneous manufactured articles	1.2	17,567	0.2
13	65	Headgear & other parts	1.2	4,738	0.1
14	84	Nuclear reactors, boilers, machinery & mechanical appliances, computers	1.2	1,212,512	13.7
15	33	Oils & resinoids, perfumery, cosmetics or toilet preparations	1.0	49,240	0.6
		Top 5 product headings	**76.1**	**1,635,828**	**18.5**
		All product headings above	**94.6**	**3,719,972**	**42.1**

Note: Number of reporting economies totalled 17: Andorra; Australia; Hong Kong (China); Croatia; Cyprus (see footnote 18 in Chapter 3); Czech Republic; Fiji; Hungary; Latvia; Mauritius; Portugal; Romania; South Africa; Spain; Thailand; TFYR of Macedonia; United States. Intensities have been calculated in terms of values, cases, and number of distinct HS codes on the 6-digit level, wherever data were available. Percentages are given by a weighted average, with weights being the reporting economy's share of sensitive imports.

Source: OECD-WCO Customs survey and UNSD-OECD Comtrade Database.

While most of the chapters are self-explanatory as to what products they cover, several require elaboration. Infringing articles belonging to the chapter "Electrical machinery & equipment, etc.", for example, are among the top most seized. The chapter includes a diverse range of products, including motors, generators, batteries, audio equipment and CDs and DVDs (including audio-visual products and software). Because of the broad coverage, it is useful to disaggregate seizures into more detailed categories, where possible, to get a clearer view of the specific types of goods customs have seized. Using the 4-digit HS level suggests that about 94% of all interceptions involve records, tapes and other recoded sound media, including software (HS code 8524)[29]. Electric

---

29.   While HS code 8524 accounts for a high percentage of Chapter 85 seizures, it accounts for only about 2% of total Chapter 85 trade.

apparatus for line telephony, telephone sets, and parts (HS code 8517) cover about 3%, with all other items accounting for 1%, or less, of the total.

HS chapter 90 covers a wide range of instruments and accessories related to optics, photography, cinematography, precision and checking measurement, as well as to medic and surgery. However, the vast majority of seizures recorded by customs (98%) were sunglasses.

The examples of HS chapters 85 and 90 above illustrate that although seizures already are fairly concentrated at the 2-digit level, this concentration appears to be stronger at more detailed levels.

4.1.3.3. Total trade in sensitive goods

Total sensitive trade (*i.e.* the level of imports recorded in the 64 HS chapters where infringements were detected) in 2004 amounted to USD 6.59 trillion, or about 75% of world merchandise trade. Narrowing the focus to the top five HS chapters, which according to Table 4.1 accounted for 76% of all counterfeit and pirate seizures, total registered trade was USD 1.63 trillion, or about 18.5% of world trade. In accordance with the discussion above, this suggests that there are large differences in the intensity, or propensity, with which different types of internationally traded goods are being infringed. The propensity aspect is thus of major importance when assessing the magnitude of counterfeiting and piracy; this is addressed in more detail below.

4.1.4. Step 2: Identification of source economies

A source economy is an economy detected and registered by any reporting customs agency as a source of any item that has been intercepted in violation of an IPR, whatever the amount or value concerned. Hence, a source economy refers to both those economies where actual production of infringing goods is taking place, as well as those economies that function as ports of transit, through which infringing goods pass. As for the identification of sensitive goods, identification of source economies may not be complete as customs authorities may not have detected infringing imports from all suppliers. Any omissions are, however, likely to be of little consequence as the 145 economies that were identified as sources accounted for 95% of world merchandise trade in 2004.

4.1.4.1. Range of source economies

Of the 72 responses received from customs authorities, only 24 provided information on source economies. A number of European economies were added, using indicatory, yet incomplete, statistics obtained from the European Commission's TAXUD database. Detailed responses from Australia, Germany, New Zealand, and the United States, among others, nevertheless facilitated the construction of a rather broad list of different geographical source locations, including, as indicated above, some 145 distinct economies.

Some economies are, of course, more important sources of infringing goods than others; either because they are heavy producers, because they function as important ports of transit, or both. A preliminary indication of this is obtained by examining the frequency, volume and/or value of counterfeit and pirated imports for each reporting economy. Data from 19 economies were used to carry out this analysis. As not all reporting economies carry the same weight in international trade, the data were weighted according to the reporting economy's share of total imports across the 19 reporting economies. The figures and ranking of economies must be treated with care as available data only provide a crude indication of the actual situation. The top sources are therefore presented according to their geographical location.[30] It should also be noted that many source locations were registered as "unknown" by customs and that the importance of registered source economies therefore could be misrepresented.

Table 4.2. Import seizures of counterfeit and pirated goods from top 20 sources

Source economies are listed according to their geographical region

Region of top 20 source economies	Number of source economies in region	Seizures Pct. of total	Registered imports from sources Million USD	Pct. of world imports
Asia (excl. Middla East)	12	69.7	1,926,990	21.8
Middle East	2	4.1	120,137	1.4
Africa	2	1.8	40,983	0.5
Europe	2	1.7	631,449	7.2
North America	1	1.1	805,486	9.1
South America	1	0.8	190,030	2.2
Top sources	**20**	**79.2**	**3,715,075**	**42.1**

Note: Reporting economies totalled 19 including: Andorra; Angola; Australia; Cyprus (see footnote 18 in Chapter 3); Denmark; Estonia; France; Germany; Japan; Latvia; Mauritius; Netherlands, New Zealand; Portugal; Korea, Romania; Spain; United Kingdom; United States. Source economy percentages are calculated as weighted averages of seizure percentages with weights determined by the total import shares of the reporting economies.

Source: OECD-WCO Customs survey and UNSD-OECD Comtrade Database.

The data indicate that the vast majority of goods seized by customs are fairly concentrated, with the 20 largest sources accounting for about 80% of all seizures. The five largest sources, which are all located in Asia, account for nearly 58% of all seizures.

4.1.4.2. Trade in sensitive products from source economies

Imports of sensitive goods from identified source economies totalled USD 6.3 trillion in 2004, which represented about 71% of total trade (Figure 4.1). The current *potential* magnitude of counterfeiting and piracy in international trade is thus substantial. Focusing on imports from top five source economies, these totalled USD 1.3 trillion of which USD 1.2 trillion was trade in sensitive goods (about 14% of world trade). Limiting the focus to the most intensely seized product categories, originating from the 20 largest source economies, total registered imports totalled USD 2 trillion, or about 23% of world trade.

---

30.   Information on seizures drawn from table 4.2 differ from the more general description of seizures presented in Chapter 3 (*i.e.* Table 3.5). There are several reasons for this; *1)* reporting economies with only a few registered observations have been omitted here; *2)* other economies have been included based on TAXUD data; *3)* seizure percentages are in most cases calculated on a more detailed level; and *4)* the seizure percentages have been weighted according to the reporting economy's importance in international trade.

Figure 4.1. Total trade, trade in sensitive goods, and trade in sensitive goods from source economies.

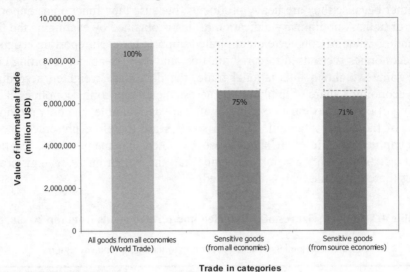

The rightmost bar constitutes the trade-base on which the propensity analysis dealt with in the following section will focus. A small provision is also made, however, to account for counterfeiting and piracy activities with respect to un-identified source economies and product categories.

4.1.5. Step 3: Estimating propensities

The broad range of products subject to counterfeiting and piracy, and the large number of economies involved in exporting these products provide indications of the significance of counterfeiting and piracy in international trade. Developing product- and economy-specific propensities can provide further precision.

4.1.5.1. Propensity framework

The core idea underlying the propensity framework is as follows: if the propensity to which different types of infringing goods are imported from different source economies can be established, then these propensities can be applied to existing statistics on international trade to arrive at an estimate of the overall magnitude of counterfeiting and piracy. In this context, propensities therefore refer to the likelihood that a particular type of counterfeit or pirated goods is imported from a particular trading partner.

Estimating propensities is, of course, a difficult undertaking in and of itself. As pointed out in Chapter 2, propensities are influenced by a series of product and institutional drivers that interact in different ways across different product areas in different economies. In the current analysis, propensities to import infringing goods from different trading partners are developed using seizure data as a basis (Box 4.2).

Box 4.2. Propensities

Statistics on customs seizures provide information on the relative importance of the imports of different types of infringing goods, and their origins. Such statistics may therefore also provide insights that could be useful for estimating propensities of counterfeiting and piracy activities in international trade. However, to be complete, customs agents would have to intercept the full range of infringing products being infringed, and do so in a way that would reflect actual import proportions across source economies. To be robust, such information would have to be provided from a significant number of economies.

In the current analysis, the data provided by customs agencies have a number of shortcomings. On the one hand, some customs authorities provided very detailed data on the specific types of goods intercepted, but not on the source economies of these goods. On the other hand, other customs provided detailed data on the sources from which the infringing goods were imported, but not on the types of goods that were seized. While some responding economies provided the full range of information needed to carry out the propensity analysis, these were few in numbers and generally involved relatively small economies. Thus, in order to draw on as much information as possible, products and source economies are treated separately.[31]

To increase the amount of available data, the analysis makes use of seizure statistics recorded in different ways; *i.e.* in the form of values, cases of interceptions, number of seized items or the number of HS subheadings at the 6-digit level. While this may suggest an underlying analytical inconsistency, it is emphasised that: *1)* seizures are normalised with respect to each reporting economy such that differences in registration principles across economies do not hinder comparability; and that *2)* the correlation coefficients between seizures percentages calculated on different bases are very high anyway (see Annex 4.A1).

The usage of data is also maximised by applying a generalised approach, in which the propensities for products to be counterfeit and for economies to be sources of counterfeit goods are analysed separately. This has the effect of increasing the data coverage of both products and source economies significantly, which increases the robustness of the overall estimation results. Unfortunately, it also reduces the detail of the analysis, meaning that counterfeit trade patterns specific to individual reporting economies, with respect to both product types and trading partners, are not simultaneously accounted for; this introduces bias into the results. On balance, given the large scope of the analysis, the advantages of increasing data coverage were viewed as outweighing the biases.

4.1.5.2. Propensity of importing infringing goods

Everything else being equal, one would expect the seizure percentage of a product infringement to correspond to the relative volume of that particular product type in international trade; if, for example, the volume of traded t-shirts were higher than that of cigarettes, one would expect the number of seized counterfeit t-shirts to be higher compared to that of cigarettes. Recalling the seizure percentages given in Table 4.1, clothing and apparel accounted for 30.6% of all seizures, while tobacco accounted for only 5.4%. However, in relation to the total amount of trade occurring in these product categories, the percentage of seized cigarettes is about 18 times higher than tobacco

---

[1].   See Part I, Chapter 6 of this study for recommendations on improving collection and reporting of data on counterfeiting and piracy.

products' share of world trade (0.3%), whereas clothing and apparel is only 11 times higher than its share (2.8%). Therefore, in relation to what is actually being internationally traded, counterfeit cigarettes are traded more intensively than counterfeit clothing and apparel articles; cigarettes thus have a higher counterfeiting propensity in international trade compared to clothing and apparel.[32]

4.1.5.2.1. Counterfeit propensity factors: products

To obtain a more meaningful measure of seizure intensities, and the propensity to which different types of infringing products are imported, the seizure percentages of infringing goods are related to the import shares of the corresponding 2-digit HS product heading. This is done on an economy-by-economy basis, thus accounting for each reporting economy's product-specific trade flows across its trading partners. A general ranking is then established (see Annex 4.A2). This is reflected in Figure 4.2, which graphs the 64 sensitive product categories according to their general counterfeiting factor.

Figure 4.2. General counterfeiting factors

Ratio between the product's share of seizures and trade

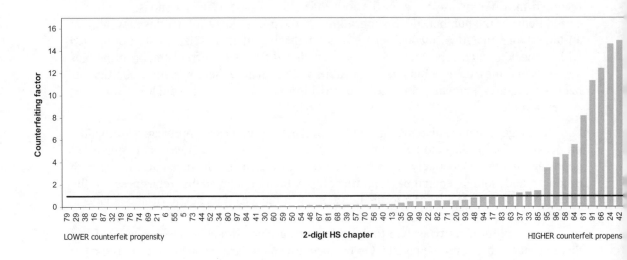

Note: The general counterfeiting factors are constructed from a weighted average of the seizure percentages relative to trade calculated for each reporting economy. Weights are determined according to the economy's share of total trade in sensitive goods. A counterfeiting factor of 1 (the black line) implies that the share of seized counterfeit goods contained in the HS chapter concerned corresponds to that chapter's share of world trade. A counterfeiting factor above 1 thus implies that the infringement intensity is high compared to the amount of trade that occurs in that category, whereas the infringement intensity is low if the factor is below 1.

---

32.   The industry specific counterfeiting propensities are analysed in Part I, Chapter 2 as supply and demand drivers.

Infringement activities appear to be most intensive with respect to products covered by chapter 65 (headgear and other parts) relative to their share of total trade. In fact, the general seizure percentage accounted for by infringing goods in this category is about 16 times larger than the category's share of world trade. Following is: chapter 42 (articles of leather, […], travel goods, handbags, etc.); 24 (tobacco and tobacco substitutes); 66 (umbrellas, sun umbrellas, walking-sticks, whips, riding-crops and parts); 91 (clocks and watches); 61 and 62 (clothing and apparel); and 64 (footwear and gaiters). The black line corresponds to a general counterfeiting factor of 1, *i.e.* indicating a seizure percentage that corresponds to the product category's share of world trade.

4.1.5.2.2. General trade-related index of counterfeiting: products

To gauge the magnitude of counterfeiting and piracy in world trade, the counterfeiting factor described above can be applied to statistics on international trade. Doing so, however, requires a number of assumptions. The construction of a General Trade-Related Index of Counterfeiting for products, denoted GTRIC-p, is an attempt in this direction.

GTRIC-p is meant to capture the relative propensity to which products in international trade are counterfeit and/or pirated relative to total trade in those products, while addressing a number of known biases (see Annex 4.A2 for details). The index is depicted as the black line in the following figure (Figure 4.3). As GTRIC-p essentially is a point estimate of the relative counterfeiting propensity for products, here referred to as the baseline index, the surrounding area illustrates the zone in which the "true" index is likely to fall (at a 95% confidence level).

Figure 4.3. Relative propensity index for importing counterfeit goods across sensitive product categories (GTRIC-p)

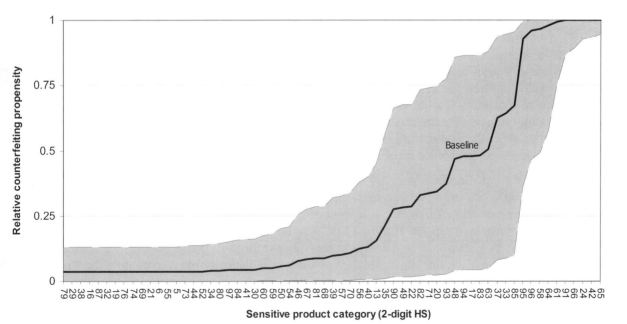

Note: The bold line shows the baseline, or expected, GTRIC (products) with the surrounding area indicating the 95% confidence interval of the index. The full list of GTRIC-p values, and the construction of the index, is described in Annex 4.A2.

GTRIC-p is formed on a 2-digit HS basis and establishes the relative likelihood for products in one chapter to be counterfeit relative to another. Within any one chapter, there could be considerable variation among products and the relative counterfeiting propensities must therefore be seen as averages for the hundreds of goods covered by each HS chapter. As such, the index indicates, for example, that products contained in HS chapter 65 (headgear) are 155% more likely, on average (and relative to total trade in these goods), to be counterfeit than products contained in HS chapter 33 (oils, perfumery, cosmetics, etc). Thus, if the absolute magnitude of product infringements occurring in one HS category were known, GTRIC-p could then be used to generate an overall estimate. Such an estimate, however, would not make any reference to the geographical aspects of counterfeiting and piracy, such as economy-specific trade flows.

The broad product coverage may give rise to potential misrepresentation issues. Some HS chapters, for instance, may exhibit high counterfeiting propensities when they really should be lower, and the other way around. Such misrepresentations, which may also be caused by biases in seizure statistics, could lead to a general distortion of the relative counterfeiting propensities. The construction of GTRIC-p therefore applies a technique that smoothes the differences in relative counterfeiting propensities between HS Chapters. Relative to the HS chapter with highest infringement intensity, this basically means that all other product chapters become more prone to infringement. Finally, potential distortion by outliers are addressed by assuming that the counterfeiting propensities are normally distributed[33] (see Annex 4.A2).

4.1.5.3. Propensity of source economies

4.1.5.3.1. General trade-related index of counterfeiting: source economies

Similar propensities can be calculated for source economies. This is done for all reporting economies by dividing the seizure percentages of source economies by the economies' respective import share of the reporting economy's total imports (across the 145 known source economies). From this, similar as for the product categories above, a General Trade-Related Index of Counterfeiting for economies (GTRIC-e) is established, which indicates the relative propensity of importing infringing goods from different source economies (Figure 4.4) (see Annex 4.A3). As with GTRIC-p, because GTRIC-e is a point estimate of the relative counterfeiting propensity for economies, also referred to as the baseline, the surrounding area illustrates the zone in which the "true" index is likely to fall (at a 95% confidence level).

The black line in Figure 4.4 shows the relative *baseline* propensities of importing infringing goods from one trading partner as opposed to another. It indicates, for example, that the trade-related likelihood of importing counterfeit and pirated goods from Hong Kong, China, is 3% higher than that of China. However, the likelihood of importing such goods from China is almost 800% higher than from the United States. The area that surrounds the black line illustrates the zone that is statistically likely to capture the "true" index (at a 95% confidence interval).

---

33.   GTRIC-p is assumed to follow a left-truncated normal distribution. See Annex 4.A2 for details.

Figure 4.4. Relative propensity index for importing counterfeit goods from source economies (GTRIC-e)

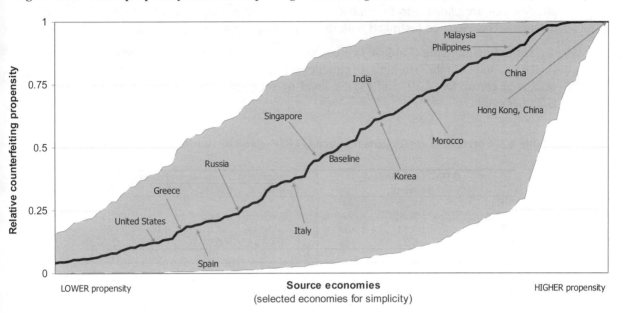

Note: The bold line shows the baseline, or expected, GTRIC (economies) with the surrounding area indicating the 95% confidence interval of the index. For illustration purposes, the graph only depicts the location of selected economies. The full list of the GTRIC-e values, and the construction of the index, is described in Annex 4.A3.

As with GTRIC-p, the ranking of economies could be biased. Certain source economies, for example, are targeted by Customs agencies, which would tend to inflate their ranking. The index therefore applies the same smoothing technique as for products, thus applying relatively higher counterfeiting propensities to less frequently encountered source economies. Potential distortions caused by outliers are furthermore addressed by assuming that the counterfeiting propensities are normally distributed.[34]

4.1.5.3.2. Properties of GTRIC-e

Since GTRIC-e approximates the relative propensities of economies to be sources of counterfeit and pirated imports, it is useful to compare it with other economy-specific indicators potentially related to counterfeiting and piracy. This may first of all help to shed some light on the relationship between GTRIC-e and other macroeconomic variables, and eventually help to provide a better understanding of counterfeiting and piracy in general.

Assuming that domestic production of infringing goods is positively correlated with exports of the illicit goods (*i.e.* large producers also tend to be large exporters) and that GTRIC-e accurately depicts actual counterfeiting and piracy export intensities across different economies, one would expect the index to be influenced, in part, by the strength and efficiency of public institutions. In this regard one would, for example, expect GTRIC-e to be negatively correlated with the strength of legislation and enforcement of

---

34. GTRIC-e is assumed to follow a left-truncated normal distribution. See Annex 4.A3 for details.

IPR[35], and positively correlated with levels of corruption. Moreover, as counterfeiting and piracy often are claimed to be related to the level of economic development, GTRIC-e would also be expected be linked with the level of economic development.

The following table (Table 4.3) presents correlation coefficients between the baseline GTRIC-e and: (1) the strength of intellectual property rights, IPR; (2) an index of perceived corruption, CPI; and (3) the level of economic development here proxied by GDP per capita.

Table 4.3. Correlation coefficients between GTRIC-e and institutional/economic indicators

| | GTRIC (economies) | | Institutional/economic indicators | | | |
	Baseline	*n*	IPR (a)	IPR (b)	CPI	GDP
IPR (a)	-0.28	*54*	1.00			
IPR (b)	-0.30	*77*	0.49	1.00		
CPI	0.31	*103*	-0.69	-0.61	1.00	
GDP	-0.33	*114*	0.73	0.61	-0.90	1.00
			n	*63*	*103*	*123*	*134*

Note: IPR is meant to measure the strength of intellectual property rights: IPR (a) is based on Rapp and Rozek (1990) and IPR (b) is based on the newer Ostergard (2000), which also captures enforcement. CPI is (-1) times the corruption perception indicator measured by Transparency International (2005), and GDP per capita is based on UNSD. The number of economies on which the correlation coefficients have been calculated is given by *n*.

The correlation coefficients between GTRIC-e and the institutional/economic indicators -- IPR (a) and (b), CPI and GDP -- all have the expected signs but are not as strong as expected. From the table, counterfeiting and piracy activities nevertheless appear to be lower in high-income economies, as well as in economies with strong intellectual property rights and where levels of corruption are low.

A simple regression (OLS) analysis of GTRIC-e and GDP per capita indicates a particularly strong relationship, as the following table shows (Table 4.4). To a certain extent, these results support the argument that the relationship between counterfeiting and piracy activities and economic development can be illustrated by an inverted U-shape.

Table 4.4. Relationship between GTRIC-e and GDP per capita

Dependent variable: GTRIC-e	Coefficient	Standard deviation	95% confidence	
GDP per capita	0.04410 ***	0.00677	0.03069	0.05751
GDP per capita (squared)	-0.00084 ***	0.00020	-0.00124	-0.00044
Observations	115			
R-squared	0.322			
Adj. R-squared	0.310			

Note: *** indicates a significance level of 1%. GDP per capita is measured in thousands. No constant was included assuming that no counterfeiting and piracy takes place when GDP per capita equals zero.

---

35.   For a short discussion on the relationship between the strength of IPR regimes and counterfeiting and piracy activities, see Chapter 5, Box 5.1.

An explanation for the inverted U-shape could be that low-income economies generally lack the capital and technological capacity for producing a wide range of products, thus also limiting the capability for producing infringing goods. As economies develop and grow richer, so do the productive and technological capabilities that also affect the possibility for higher scale infringement activities. Institutional developments, however, tend to lag behind economic development – including IPR-related legislation and enforcement practices – which creates favourable conditions for infringement activities. But as economies grow richer and become more knowledge-based, higher emphasis is placed on the role played by IPR, and legislation and enforcement in these areas are tightened. From the regression coefficients given in Table 4.4, this shift is expected when an economy's GDP per capita reaches an amount of about USD 25 000 (Figure 4.5).

Figure 4.5. Predicted relationship between the baseline counterfeit propensity and GDP per capita

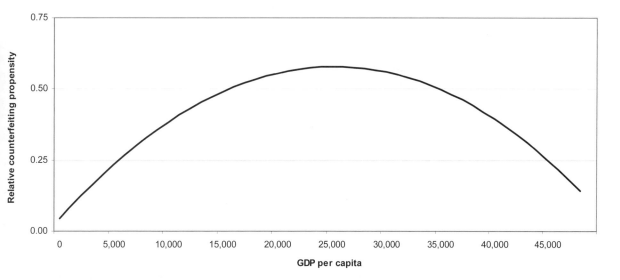

Note: Despite its generalised construction and its underlying assumptions, the GTRIC-e index appears to capture important and valid elements of general counterfeiting and piracy activities across the different economies that it covers.

4.1.5.3.3. Magnitude estimates based on source-economy propensities

Similar to the case of product categories, GTRIC-e can be used to approximate the overall magnitude of counterfeiting and piracy in world trade; here from the perspective of source-economies rather than sensitive goods. This nevertheless entails that knowledge of the counterfeiting/piracy magnitude in one economy can be generated. Estimates based solely on GTRIC-e also do not take product-specific trade flows into account.

4.1.5.4. General propensity for importing infringing goods

The product- and economy-based application of the relative propensity indices (GTRIC-p and GTRIC-e, respectively) serve as foundations for indicating the magnitude of counterfeiting and piracy in world trade. However, as indicated above, they have limitations and more precise information about the international trade in counterfeit and pirated goods can be gained by combining the two indices.

In this regard, it is important to emphasise that the index resulting from the combination of GTRIC-p and GTRIC-e does not account for differences in infringement intensities across different types of goods that may exist between economies (see Box 4.3). For instance, imports of certain counterfeit and pirated goods could be particularly large from some trading partners and small for others. An index taking such "infringement specialisation", or concentration, into account is certainly desirable and not impossible to construct[36]; but it would require detailed seizure data (see Annex 4.A1). The combined index, here denoted GTRIC, is therefore a generalised index that crudely approximates the relative propensities to which particular product types, being imported from specific trading partners, are counterfeit and/or pirated (see Annex 4.A4).

Box 4.3. Generalisation of GTRIC

Generalisation of GTRIC leads to upward bias of infringing goods in world trade

Because the construction of GTRIC is based on independent analyses of product seizures and source economies, the index assumes a generalised structure for all trade in counterfeit and pirated goods. This essentially means that while the model allows for the propensity of importing counterfeit and pirated goods to be higher or lower depending on the infringement-intensity of source economies (as given by GTRIC-e), the relative structure of these traded-infringing goods (given by GTRIC-p) is identical regardless of the source economy.

As some economies may be larger sources of certain counterfeit and pirated goods than others, this constitutes a bias of GTRIC. The bias is, from an average perspective, likely to overstate the general importance played by counterfeiting and piracy in world trade. This follows from the fact that *all* economies that have been detected by customs are assumed to export counterfeit goods across *all* sensitive product categories; *i.e.* according to the generalised counterfeiting propensity given by GTRIC-p. While this could understate the export of specific counterfeit goods from certain economies, especially if the products concerned are contained in categories with relatively low propensities, the overall export of counterfeit goods, which is assumed to occur across all other sensitive product categories, is, on average, likely to more than outweigh this. If, in the extreme case, some economies are heavy counterfeit exporters of several low-propensity products, as well as of those considered to be high, the understatements would tend to be outweighed by the large number of economies for which counterfeit exports are over-estimated.

The index itself can be represented as a matrix table where source economies are listed across the rows and where the 2-digit HS chapters are listed across the columns (see Annex 4.A4). Each element of the matrix, *i.e.* the value of GRTIC, denotes the relative propensity of a given source economy to export infringing products covered by a given HS chapter. It is emphasised that these propensities are relative to each other and that GTRIC itself thereby does not provide information about the absolute magnitude of counterfeiting and piracy in world trade. Instead, the index should be considered as a tool that can be used to work towards better appraisals of the problem.

---

36.   An example of such an index is the Aggregated Trade-Related Index of Counterfeiting (ATRIC), which is introduced in Chapter 5. This index, however, is based on data for a very limited number of economies and is not appropriate for conducting analysis on the magnitude of counterfeiting and piracy in world trade.

4.2. Using propensities to measure counterfeiting and piracy in international trade

While GTRIC does not give a direct measure of the overall magnitude of counte-feiting and piracy in world trade, it establishes relationships that can be useful in this regard. Specifically, overall estimates (reflecting all products and all economies) could be generated by evaluating GTRIC based on inputs in the form of specific counterfeit export rates of any product category and from any source economy. Unfortunately, such export rates, which in the following are referred to as modelling fix-points, are not readily available.

GTRIC can nevertheless be used to approximate a "ceiling" for international trade in counterfeit and pirated goods. This approach is based on establishing an upper fix-point limit; that is, an upper limit of counterfeit exports (in percentages) of those products from those economies where counterfeiting and piracy were most pronounced.[37] In terms of the model, the fix-point generally refers to counterfeit apparel, leather articles and tobacco products exported from developing Asian economies. A relatively high level of counter-feit and pirated exports of 20% of such goods was initially assigned, based on which the implications for other product chapters and economies were assessed.

Attention focused in particular on the implications for products contained in the HS chapter 85, which not only comprises a large share of world trade (more than 14%), but also includes a variety of goods for which there is substantial trade, where notional counterfeiting propensities are believed to be low, and where there is little evidence of widespread counterfeiting and piracy in international trade. Examples of such products include electronic integrated circuits, transmission and radar equipment, wires and cables, television receivers, TV cameras and parts hereof, which, as a group, amount to more than 50% of all trade in chapter 85.[38]

A fix-point of 20% would mean that an average of 20% of wearing apparel, leather articles and tobacco products, exported from infringement-intensive economies, would be counterfeit. At the GTRIC baseline, this would imply that counterfeit exports of goods contained in chapter 85 would average between 12% and 13% from economies such as China, Hong Kong (China), Philippines, Chinese Taipei. Counterfeit exports of such goods from Italy and Spain would average about 5% and 3%, respectively.

As the relatively high rates of counterfeit exports appeared excessive, both on a notional basis and based on other evidence, the fix-point of 20% was considered improbable. Additional simulations were carried out at 15%, 10% and 5%.

---

37. The fix-point enables the estimation of an absolute propensity to export counterfeit goods across HS chapters for all economies. In essence, the propensity is determined by multiplying the fix-point with the product of the counterfeit propensity for goods (as given by GTRIC-p in Figure 4.3) and the counterfeit propensity for the economy concerned (as given by GTRIC-e in Figure 4.4). For example, in the case of Hong Kong, China, which has a GTRIC-e value of nearly 1, the counterfeit export percentages for this economy would be given by GTRIC-p exactly as it appears in Figure 4.3, with the left axis multiplied by the fix-point (*i.e.* 20% instead of 1 if the fix-point were 20%).

8. Examples of products included in chapter 85 are: parts of electric motors, electric transformers, electro-magnets, batteries, electromechanical tools and domestic appliances, shavers, windshield wipers, lamps, water heaters, microphones, loudspeakers, amplifiers, video recording and reproducing instruments, records, tapes and other recorded sound media, computer software, television receivers, monitors, transmission and radar instruments, semi-conductors, electronic circuits and more.

Given a fix-point of 5%, more credible rates of counterfeit export percentages are approached. For trade in goods covered by HS chapter 85, for instance, this would yield average rates of counterfeit exports of about 3% for Asian developing economies, and between 0.1 and 1.2% for Western economies. These rates, it should be noted, represent an average for all products contained in chapter 85; within the chapter, rates for individual items could be far higher (or lower). High rates of counterfeit exports of those goods for which there is most evidence can thus be sustained.

With respect to the implications given by the model, 5% could be a reasonable fix-point for establishing the magnitude for trade in counterfeit and pirated goods; however, it could be higher. As the approach taken by this exercise is to establish a credible "ceiling", while addressing the many information deficiencies surrounding the subject, a fix-point of 10% was therefore considered.

With 10% as the fix-point, counterfeit goods contained in HS chapter 85 from China, Hong Kong (China), Chinese Taipei and the Philippines would all reach the vicinity of 6% (evaluated at the baseline GTRIC).

Considering the specific export composition of goods covered by HS chapter 85 for these economies, which shows very large exports of products that are believed to have low notional propensities to counterfeiting, suggests that a fix-point of 10% is a high estimate. The implied counterfeit exports rates for China and Hong Kong (China), for example, could cover most of both economies' total exports of CDs, DVDs (both recorded and unrecorded), software, telephone sets, microphones, loudspeakers, amplifiers and batteries, and still leave room for non-negligible exports of counterfeit goods in other categories under HS chapter 85.

Table 4.5 illustrates average (baseline) counterfeit export rates of goods contained in HS chapter 85 given the different fix-points considered.

Table 4.5. Exports and estimated (baseline) counterfeit exports of HS chapter 85

Source economy	Registered exports of HS-85 (in % of total exports)	Average (baseline) counterfeit exports (in % of trade in HS-85)		
		Fix-point		
		20%	10%	5%
China	25.1	13.1	6.6	3.3
France	8.6	1.0	0.5	0.2
Germany	10.6	0.6	0.3	0.1
Hong Kong, China	29.0	13.4	6.7	3.4
Italy	6.7	4.9	2.5	1.2
Philippines	56.8	12.2	6.1	3.0
Singapore	32.7	6.1	3.0	1.5
Spain	6.3	2.6	1.3	0.6
Chinese Taipei	38.4	11.5	5.7	2.9
United Kingdom	9.3	1.5	0.7	0.4
United States	14.7	1.6	0.8	0.4

Note: The table illustrates the exports (in percent of totals) of goods contained in HS chapter 85, and what would be the average rate of counterfeit exports (in percent of trade in chapter 85) given fix-points of 5%, 10% and 20%. Counterfeit export rates are given for both baseline and upper limit assumptions.

Source: OECD and UNSD-OECD Comtrade Database.

From a more general perspective, a fix-point of 10% implies that about 5% of all goods exported from Hong Kong, China and China would be counterfeit. Similarly, counterfeit exports from Chinese Taipei and the Philippines would average between% 3 and 4% of all goods. The full range of (baseline) average counterfeit export rates across all HS chapters, as implied by a 10% fix-point, is illustrated for a number of economies in Figure 4.6.

Figure 4.6. Average (baseline) counterfeit exports across HS chapters, selected economies

Estimates based on a fix-point of 10%

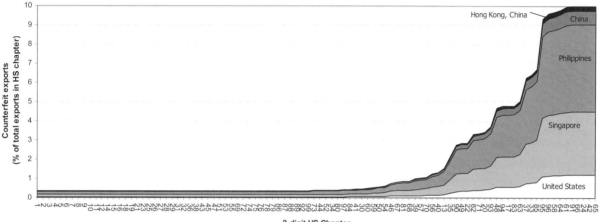

Note: Baseline counterfeit export percentages across HS codes from: Hong Kong, China; China; Philippines; Singapore; and the United States. These economies have been chosen for illustration purposes only.

Given a fix-point of 10%, the overall ceiling of counterfeit and pirated goods in world trade would in 2005 amount to about USD 100 billion. This estimate is nevertheless derived from GTRIC at its baseline and does not address the statistical variability of the index. While taking this statistical uncertainty into account implies that the ceiling could be lower, it also suggests that the ceiling of counterfeit and pirated goods in international trade in 2005 could have been as high as USD 200 billion (see Annex 4.A4).

The ceiling of counterfeit and pirated goods in world trade, as approximated by GTRIC, is consistent with generally low counterfeit interception rates by customs. Based on data provided in response to the OECD/WCO customs survey, for instance, if counterfeit and pirated products accounted for USD 200 billion in world trade, it would mean that customs officials, on average, only intercepted 0.5% of all infringing goods crossing borders.

The relationship between different rates of interception and what would be the corresponding magnitude of counterfeit and pirated goods in world trade is depicted in Figure 4.7. The figure also shows the associated fix-point from which the ceiling of counterfeiting and piracy, evaluated at the upper boundary of confidence, would follow.

Figure 4.7. Magnitude and interception rates of counterfeit and pirated goods

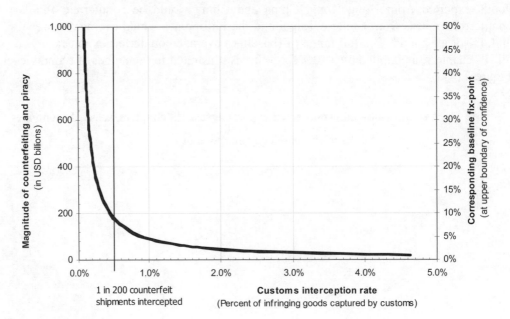

Note: Calculations of the relationship between the ceiling of counterfeit and pirated goods in world trade and interception rates are based on the finding that Customs, on average, capture about 0.01% of all imports (see Chapter 3). The figure also depicts the baseline fix-point that is associated with the magnitude estimate at the model's upper boundary of confidence.

4.2.1. Estimating the global magnitude of counterfeiting and piracy

The estimate of the magnitude of counterfeiting and piracy based on international trade does not tell the whole story. It does not include counterfeit and pirated products that are produced and consumed domestically, nor does it include the significant volume of pirated digital products that are being traded via the Internet. If these items were added, the total magnitude could well be several hundreds of billions more than the USD 200 billion cited above.

Addressing the full scale of counterfeiting and piracy, including both domestic and international markets, more precisely is not currently possible, due in large part to data constraints. Contrary to international markets, where customs agencies function as a valuable source of information on actual infringement activities, information is not sufficiently available on counterfeiting/piracy activities in domestic markets.

If additional data were available, the propensity framework presented in Chapter 2, which was applied to international trade in the analysis above, could be used to develop better indications of the total size of counterfeiting and piracy, based on national expenditure statistics. Further development of propensities would nevertheless have to be carried out to facilitate such an analysis.

References

Hald, A. (1952), *Statistical Theory with Engineering Applications*, John Wiley and Sons, New York.

Ostergard, Robert L. (2000), "The Measurement of Intellectual Property Rights Protection", *Journal of International Business Studies*, Vol. 31, No. 2: 349-360.

Rapp, R. and Rozek, R. (1990), "Benefits and Costs of Intellectual Property Protection in Developing Countries", *Journal of World Trade*, Vol. 24, Issue 5.

Transparency International (2005), *Annual Report 2005*, Transparency International.

Annex 4.A1

COLLECTION AND ASSESSMENT OF DATA

Data development

The general lack of data with respect to counterfeiting and piracy activities necessitates that more information on the phenomenon be developed. One of the most promising sources of information in this regard currently concerns seizure statistics as registered by customs authorities around the globe. Apart from being collected on a systematic basis, in most cases these data also constitute the only official data that exist on infringement activities. Hence, despite their apparent shortcomings, they currently constitute the best foundation for measurement analyses as far as counterfeiting and piracy issues in a global context are concerned.

Survey of customs

To build the foundation on which the magnitude of counterfeiting and piracy in world trade could be analysed, the OECD conducted a survey in co-operation with the WCO via a questionnaire that was sent to national customs authorities in all 169 WCO member states. A total number of 70 responses (41%) were received. Customs agencies were specifically asked to submit detailed statistics on interceptions of infringements, recorded at any time during the period 1999 to 2005, and in any format available. They were furthermore asked to provide information on the volume of seizures, the estimated seizure values, as well as information on the trading partners (economies) from which the infringing products had originated (for the Customs questionnaire, see Annex Part I, Chapter 1, Annex 1.A4).

Responses

Answers to the survey ranged from being limited in their usefulness for developing information on infringement activities to being very detailed and thus of great value with respect to the analysis. Of the 70 responses received, only 45 economies, of which 20 were OECD member economies, provided information detailed enough to allow a more elaborate assessment of the counterfeiting and piracy activity. The number of data records submitted varied largely across economies.

The above could reflect that some agencies answered with less effort and interest than others. However, it is likelier to be a sign of differing obligations concerning the identification of imports in violation of IPR across nations, *i.e.* due to differences in budgetary means as well as priorities. For instance, while IPR is of significant concern in many western economies, other economies may find that the trafficking of drugs, weapons and human beings constitute far bigger problems, thus forcing them to direct all their investigation resources there.

In addition to the 11 EU member states (only three from EU-15) providing detailed statistics on seizures, information from remaining member states has been drawn to the extent possible from officially available statistics through TAXUD. However, these data are not very detailed.

Data description

The data received from customs was in many cases categorised according to the Harmonized System (HS) categorisation index. If this was not the case, such categorisation was made by the OECD. The Harmonized System is a commodity classification system in which articles are grouped largely according to the nature of the materials of which they are made, as has been traditional in customs nomenclatures. The HS contains 5 224 subheadings (on the 6-digit level), which cover all articles in world trade, and therefore provides for a fairly detailed way of representing and analysing the scope of infringements. These subheadings are organised into 1 244 headings (on the 4-digit level) ordered in 96 chapters (2-digit level), which again are arranged in 21 sections (on the 1-digit level).

The original intention was to code all product types seized by customs according to the 6-digit HS level; however, in order to *1)* maximise the utilisation of available information, that is, increase the number of records in the database; and to *2)* ensure data comparability across economies at the same time, the compilation of the statistics received from customs was in turn presented on a 2-digit HS level. This resulted in a database of counterfeit and pirated-product seizures containing 41 722 records of intercepted infringing products. However, given the reporting structure of the different customs agencies, the database is highly unbalanced; *i.e.* some report single seizure incidents per economy of origin for each submitted record, while for others, a record represents the total number of incidents per economy of origin. Some cover from 1999 to 2005, while others only cover a single year, and so on.

The data points in the database include: reporting economy; partner economy; type of good intercepted and its 2-digit HS code; volumes seized (if available); and estimated values (if available). It is emphasised that the data only cover infringements seized by customs. The data are therefore focused on international trade and do not account for infringements that are both produced and consumed within an economy.

Data assessment

Due to the large variety of ways that counterfeiting and piracy related activities are investigated and registered by customs, the data differ with respect to four main issues: *1)* the level of detail of the products' description and/or HS code; *2)* the number of items seized; *3)* the number of cases registered; and *4)* the way seized goods are valued. In some instances, customs provided statistics on seizures in terms of incidents, some in terms of values, some in terms of volumes -- and some only provided information on products and economies of origin without any reference to either incidents, values or volumes. In other instances, products are grouped together in broad categories while they are clearly specified in others, and at great detail. Source economies are usually registered but cannot always be applied to product types, cases or items.

In conclusion, cross-economy comparisons of seizures, their frequencies, quantities and values, as well as from where they originate, are impeded and this poses a challenging problem for the analysis. Despite these shortcomings, and in the light of serious information deficiencies with respect to counterfeiting and piracy activities in general, the statistics compiled on customs seizures constitute both a unique -- and one of the most promising -- means for assessing the problem on a global scale currently.

Note on data usage

In general, the data imbalances necessitated a choice between data consistency (*i.e.* using the same base for the calculation) and the amount of information used. Opting for data consistency would imply that the analysis would have to be based on a very small sample of economies. The choice for using all possible information was therefore made in order to increase overall robustness.

Thus, to increase the number of reporting economies to determine the scope and calculate the relevance of counterfeiting and piracy with respect to both products and their sources, seizure percentages were based on four different bases, depending on the information available for the responding economy. These bases included: *1)* values of infringing articles; *2)* cases of interceptions; *3)* number of seized items; and *4)* number of HS subheadings on the 6-digit level. Because of the greater potential for biases with respect to options 3 and 4 above, these were avoided and only used in three cases -- the third option was used twice, and the fourth option once. In these cases, expanding the economy-coverage was considered as overweighing potential biases. It should be empha-sised, however, that the correlation coefficients between seizure percentages calculated on different bases turned out to be very high (see Table 4.A2.1), hence indicating a high comparability between the different base measures and the weaker strength of potential biases with respect to this aspect of the analysis.

Table 4.A2.1. Correlation coefficients between different calculations of seizure percentages

	Values	Cases	HS 6	Items
Products				
Values	1.00			
Cases	0.96	1.00		
HS 6	0.86	0.90	1.00	
Items	n/a	n/a	n/a	n/a
Economies				
Values	1.00			
Cases	0.81	1.00		
HS 6	0.96	0.76	1.00	
Items	0.85	0.65	0.87	1.00

Note: The table illustrates the correlation coefficients between seizure percentages across products (HS, 2-digit based) and economies calculated on the basis of *1)* values of infringing articles; *2)* cases of interceptions; *3)* number of seized items; and *4)* number of HS subheadings on the 6-digit level.

Annex 4.A2

CONSTRUCTION OF GTRIC-p

General trade-related index of counterfeiting: products (GTRIC-p)

The General Trade-Related Index of Counterfeiting for products (GTRIC-p) is constructed in three steps: (1) first, the general seizure percentages are calculated for each reporting economy; (2) from these, each product category's counterfeiting factor is established; and (3) based on these factors, the GTRIC-p is derived.

Measuring general product seizure intensities (seizure percentages)

Let $\widetilde{v}_{i,t}^{k}$ be the seizure value, or the number of seizure incidents, of product type k (as registered according to the HS on the 2-digit level) in economy i at time t from *any* origin (*i.e.* all j). Then γ_{i}^{k} is economy i's relative seizure intensity (seizure percentages) of good k over all t, where t ranges from 1999 to 2005 depending on the reporting economy.

$$\gamma_{i}^{k} = \frac{\sum_{t} \widetilde{v}_{i,t}^{k}}{\sum_{t}\sum_{k} \widetilde{v}_{i,t}^{k}} \text{, such that } \sum_{k} \gamma_{i}^{k} = 1,$$

where $k = \left\{1,...,\overline{K}\right\}$ is the range of sensitive goods (the total number of goods is given by K) and $i = \left\{1,...,\overline{n}\right\}$ is the range of reporting economies (the total number of economies is given by N). The general seizure intensity for product k, denoted Γ^{k}, is then determined by averaging over seizure intensities, γ_{i}^{k}, weighted by the reporting economies' share of total sensitive imports. Hence,

$$\Gamma^{k} = \sum_{i}^{\overline{n}} \omega_{i}\gamma_{i}^{k}$$

The weight of reporting economy i is given by

$$\omega_{i} = \frac{\widetilde{m}_{i}}{\sum_{i=1}^{\overline{n}} \widetilde{m}_{i}}, \text{ where } \widetilde{m}_{i} \text{ is } i\text{'s total registered import value of sensitive goods}$$

$(\sum_{i=1}^{\overline{n}} \omega_{i} = 1)$

The general seizure percentages for the top 15 product categories (Γ^k, $k \in$ Top 15) are listed in Chapter 4, Table 4.1.

Measuring the counterfeiting factors

The counterfeiting factors reflect the sensitivity of product infringements occurring in a particular product category relative to its share in international trade (Figure 4.2). These are based on the seizure percentages calculated for each reporting economy and constitute the foundation for the formation of the GTRIC-p. The general counterfeiting factor for a product category is simply given by the ratio of the category's general seizure percentage (described above) divided by its share of total registered imports of sensitive goods.

Define $\widetilde{M}^k = \sum_{i=1}^{N} \widetilde{m}_i^k$ as the total registered imports of sensitive good k for *all* economies, $i = \{1,...,N\}$.

Total imports of sensitive goods is then given by

$$\widetilde{M} = \sum_k \widetilde{M}^k,$$

and the world import share of good k by

$$s^k = \frac{\widetilde{M}^k}{\widetilde{M}}, \text{ such that } \sum_{k=1}^{\overline{K}} s^k = 1$$

The general counterfeiting factor of product category k, denoted CP^k, is then determined as the following (depicted in Figure 4.2).

$$CP^k = \frac{\Gamma^k}{s^k}$$

Establishing the GTRIC-p

The GTRIC-p is constructed from a transformation of the general counterfeiting factor and measures the relative propensity to which different types of product categories are subject to counterfeiting and piracy in international trade. The transformation of the counterfeiting factor is based on two main assumptions. The first assumption ($A1.p$) is that the counterfeiting factor of a particular product category is positively correlated with the *actual* intensity of international trade in counterfeit and pirated goods covered by that chapter. The counterfeiting factors depicted in Figure 4.2 must thus reflect the real intensity of *actual* counterfeit trade in the given product categories. The second assumption ($A2.p$) acknowledges that the first assumption may not be entirely correct. For instance, the fact that infringing goods in certain categories are detected more frequently than they are in others could imply that differences in counterfeiting factors across products merely reflect that some goods are easier to detect than others, or that some goods, for one reason or another, have been specially targeted for inspection. The counterfeiting factors of product categories with lower counterfeiting factors could therefore underestimate actual counterfeiting and piracy intensities in these.

In accordance with: assumption *A1.p* (positive correlation between counterfeiting factors and actual infringement activities); and assumption *A2.p* (lower counterfeiting factors may underestimate actual activities), the GTRIC-p is established by applying a positive monotonic transformation of the counterfeiting factor index, using natural logarithms, which flattens the index and gives higher relative weight to lower counterfeiting factors. Moreover, in order to address the possibility of outliers in both ends of the counterfeiting factor index (*i.e.* some categories may be measured as particularly susceptible to infringement even though they are not, whereas others may be measured as insusceptible although they are), it is assumed that GTRIC-p follows a left-truncated normal distribution, with GTRIC-p only taking values of zero or above. According to Kernel density estimation of the transformed counterfeiting factor index, this appears to be a reasonable assumption (Figure 4.A2.1)

Figure 4.A2.1. Kernel density estimation of counterfeiting factors

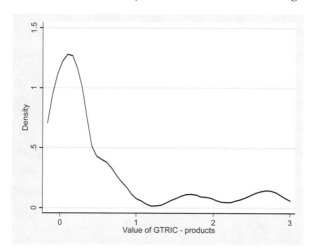

The normality assumption furthermore adds the important property that reductions in index values diminish as counterfeiting factors fall. This means that the cumulated density function for GTRIC-p follows an S-curve and implies that relative propensities for counterfeiting and piracy fall slower and slower as counterfeiting factors fall (Figure 4.A2.2).

The transformed counterfeiting factor is defined as

$$cp^k = \ln(CP^k + 1)$$

Assuming that the transformed counterfeiting factor can be described by a left-truncated normal distribution with $cp^k \geq 0$, then, following Hald (1952), the density function of GTRIC-p is given by

$$f_{LTN}(cp^k) = \begin{cases} 0 & if \ cp^k \leq 0 \\[2em] \dfrac{f(cp^k)}{\displaystyle\int_0^\infty f(cp^k)dcp^k} & if \ cp^k \geq 0 \end{cases}$$

where $f(cp^k)$ is the non-truncated normal distribution for cp^k specified as

$$f(cp^k) = \frac{1}{\sqrt{2\pi\sigma_{cp}^2}} \exp\left(-\frac{1}{2}\left(\frac{cp^k - \mu_{cp}}{\sigma_{cp}}\right)^2\right)$$

The mean and variance of the normal distribution, here denoted μ_{cp} and σ_{cp}^2, are estimated over the transformed counterfeiting factor index, cp^k, and given by $\hat{\mu}_{cp}$ and $\hat{\sigma}_{cp}^2$. This enables the calculation of the counterfeit import propensity index (GTRIC-p) across HS chapters corresponding to the cumulative distribution function of cp^k.

Sensitivity analysis of GTRIC-p

Given the uncertainty of the parameters underlying GTRIC-p, the index is subjected to an analysis of sensitivity. This is done by varying the estimated means of the counterfeiting factor, cp^k, around the standard deviation. More specifically, the upper and lower boundary of GTRIC-p is given by re-calculating the index on the basis of $\hat{\mu}_{cp} \pm 2\hat{\sigma}_{cp}$. This effectively constitutes a confidence interval for GTRIC-p of 95%, given by the shaded area in Figure 4.A2.2.

Figure 4.A2.2. Sensitivity of GTRIC-e

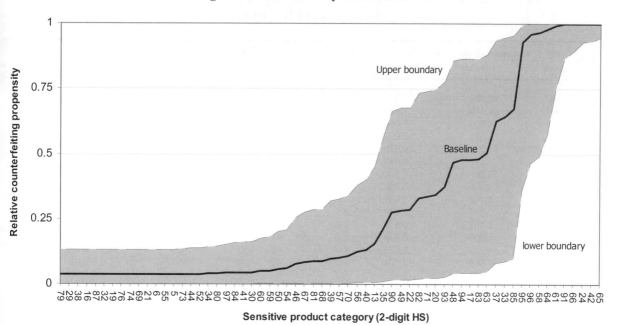

The dark line illustrates the value of GTRIC-p under baseline assumptions (mean and variance as estimated over the generalised counterfeiting factor, cp^k).

Table 4.A2.1. Relative baseline counterfeiting factors (CP^k) and GTRIC-p (products) across sensitive HS chapters

Rank	HS code	Counterfeiting factor	GTRIC-p (baseline)	Increse in sensitivity (base=rank 1)	Rank	HS code	Counterfeiting factor	GTRIC-p (baseline)	Increse in sensitivity (base=rank 1
1	65	16.183	1.000	1.0	33	68	0.124	0.087	11.3
2	42	14.949	1.000	1.1	34	81	0.124	0.086	11.3
3	24	14.606	1.000	1.1	35	67	0.119	0.083	11.3
4	66	12.440	0.999	1.3	36	46	0.109	0.076	11.3
5	91	11.326	0.999	1.4	37	54	0.085	0.060	11.4
6	61, 62	8.117	0.995	2.0	38	50	0.083	0.058	11.4
7	64	5.567	0.980	2.9	39	59	0.074	0.052	11.4
8	58	4.680	0.967	3.3	40	60	0.070	0.049	11.4
9	96	4.412	0.961	3.5	41	30	0.064	0.045	11.4
10	95	3.510	0.930	4.3	42	41	0.064	0.045	11.4
11	85	1.401	0.672	7.8	43	84	0.063	0.045	11.4
12	33	1.298	0.644	8.0	44	97	0.060	0.043	11.4
13	37	1.233	0.625	8.2	45	80	0.057	0.040	11.4
14	63	0.890	0.504	9.2	46	34	0.056	0.040	11.4
15	83	0.831	0.480	9.3	47	52	0.054	0.038	11.4
16	17	0.830	0.479	9.4	48	44	0.053	0.038	11.4
17	94	0.824	0.477	9.4	49	73	0.053	0.038	11.4
18	48	0.800	0.466	9.4	50	5	0.040	0.036	14.8
19	93	0.600	0.372	10.0	51	55	0.039	0.036	15.2
20	20	0.545	0.344	10.2	52	6	0.036	0.036	16.1
21	71	0.533	0.338	10.2	53	21	0.033	0.036	17.8
22	82	0.520	0.330	10.3	54	69	0.029	0.036	19.9
23	22	0.439	0.285	10.5	55	74	0.022	0.036	26.1
24	49	0.437	0.284	10.5	56	76	0.020	0.036	28.9
25	90	0.422	0.275	10.6	57	19	0.016	0.036	36.5
26	35	0.318	0.213	10.9	58	32	0.015	0.036	40.3
27	13	0.225	0.154	11.1	59	87	0.008	0.036	71.1
28	40	0.191	0.132	11.2	60	16	0.003	0.036	191.9
29	56	0.179	0.124	11.2	61	38	0.001	0.036	455.2
30	70	0.155	0.108	11.2	62	29	0.001	0.036	745.8
31	57	0.147	0.102	11.3	63	79	0.000	0.036	n/a
32	39	0.142	0.099	11.3					

Note: The table depicts the ranking of HS chapters in terms of their standard counterfeiting factors and GTRIC-p values. These are based on generalised seizure information and related to the total trade in each product category. The index can therefore no be interpreted as illustrating the ranking of products in proportion to total customs seizures as such. The "Increase in sensitivity" indicates the number of times that relative infringement likelihood increases, by using GTRIC-p compared to counterfeitin factors.

Annex 4.A3

CONSTRUCTION OF GTRIC-e

General trade-related index of counterfeiting: economies (GTRIC-e)

The General Trade-Related Index of Counterfeiting for economies (GTRIC-e) is constructed in three steps: *1)* first, for each reporting economy, the seizure percentages for source economies are calculated; *2)* from these, each economy's counterfeit source factor is established (based on the reporting economies' weight in terms of total imports); and *3)* based on these factors, the GTRIC-e is formed,

Measuring economy seizure intensities (seizure percentages)

Let $\tilde{v}_{ij,t}$ be economy i's registered seizures of *all* types of infringing goods (*i.e.* all k) originating from economy j at time t, in terms of either value, number of incidents, or items. Then γ_{ij} is economy i's relative seizure intensity (seizure percentage) of all infringing items that originate from economy j, over all t ranging from 1999 to 2005, depending on the data from the reporting economy.

$$\gamma_{ij} = \frac{\sum_t \tilde{v}_{ij,t}}{\sum_t \sum_j \tilde{v}_{ij,t}}, \text{ such that } \sum_j \gamma_{ij} = 1, \ \forall i, \text{ where } j = \{1,...,J\} \text{ is identified source}$$

economies.

The general seizure intensity for economy j, denoted Γ_j, is then determined by averaging over seizure intensities, γ_{ij}, weighted by the reporting economy's share of total imports from known counterfeit and pirated origins. Hence,

$$\Gamma_j = \sum_i \varpi_i \gamma_{ij}, \text{ where } i = \{1,...,\bar{n}\} \text{ is the range of reporting economies.}$$

The weight of reporting economy i is given by

$$\varpi_i = \frac{\tilde{m}_i}{\sum_i \tilde{m}_i}, \text{ where } \tilde{m}_i \text{ is } i\text{'s total registered import value from source economies}$$

($\sum_i \varpi_i = 1$)

The general seizure percentages for the top 20 source economies (Γ_j, $j \in$ Top 20) are listed in Chapter 4, Table 4.2.

Establishing the GTRIC-e

Gauging the magnitude of counterfeiting and piracy from a source-economy perspective can be done in a similar fashion as it was for sensitive goods. Hence, a general trade-related index of counterfeiting for economies (GTRIC-e) is established along similar lines and assumptions. The first assumption ($A1.e$) is that the intensity by which any counterfeit or pirated article from a particular economy is detected and seized by customs is positively correlated with the actual amount of counterfeit and pirated articles imported from that location. The second assumption ($A2.e$) acknowledges that assumption $A1.e$ may not be entirely correct. For instance, a high seizure intensity of counterfeit or pirated articles from a particular source economy could be an indication that the source economy is part of a customs profiling scheme, or that it otherwise is specially targeted for investigation by customs. The importance that source economies with low seizure intensities play with respect to actual counterfeiting and piracy activity could therefore be under-represented by the index and thereby lead to an under-estimation of the counterfeiting and piracy magnitude.

As with the trade-related index of counterfeiting for sensitive goods, GTRIC-e is established by applying a positive monotonic transformation of the counterfeiting factor index for source economies using natural logarithms. This follows from assumption $A1.e$ (positive correlation between seizure intensities and actual infringement activities), and assumption $A2.e$ (lower intensities tend to underestimate actual activities). Also, considering the possibilities of outliers in both ends of the GTRIC-e distribution, *i.e.* some economies may be wrongly measured as being particularly susceptible sources of counterfeit and pirated imports, and the other way around, GTRIC-e is approximated by a left-truncated normal distribution, as GTRIC-e does not take values below 0. According to a Kernel density estimation of the transformed counterfeiting factor index, this appears to be a reasonable assumption (Figure 4.A3.1).

Figure 4.A3.1. Kernel density estimation of GTRIC-e

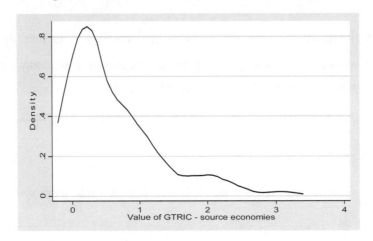

Normality also brings the property that the reduction in an economy's estimated susceptibility for being a source of infringing imports is diminishing with the level of seizure intensity. The index therefore falls slower and slower as the counterfeiting factor for source economies falls (Figure 4.A3.2)

For each reporting economy, counterfeiting factors with respect to source economies are established by dividing the calculated share of seizures from economy j with j's share of economy i's total imports.

Define $\tilde{M}_i = \sum_{j=1}^{J} \tilde{m}_{ij}$ as the total registered imports of economy i from *all* identified source economies. The share of economy i's imports coming from source economy j is then given by

$$s_{ij} = \frac{\tilde{M}_{ij}}{\tilde{M}_i}, \text{ such that } \sum_{j=1}^{J} s_j = 1$$

From this, the economy-specific counterfeiting factor is established

$$CE_{ij} = \frac{\gamma_{ij}}{s_{ij}},$$

where γ_{ij} is economy j's seizure percentage registered by economy i (for all types of infringing goods); $\tilde{s}_{ij}$ is economy j's share of economy i's total imports from all identified source economies. $i = \{1,...,N\}$ and $j = \{1,...,J\}$ indicate reporting and source economies, respectively.

The generalised counterfeiting factor across source economies on which GTRIC-e is based is then given by

$$ce_j = \sum_{i=1}^{n} \varpi_i \ln(CE_{ij} + 1)$$

Following GTRIC-p, it is assumed that GTRIC-e follows a truncated normal distribution with $ce_j \geq 0$ for all j. Following Hald (1952), the density function of the left-truncated normal distribution for ce_j is given by

$$g_{LTN}(ce_j) = \begin{cases} 0 & \text{if } ce_j \leq 0 \\ \dfrac{g(ce_j)}{\int_{0}^{\infty} g(ce_j)dce} & \text{if } ce_j \geq 0 \end{cases}$$

where $g(ce_j)$ is the non-truncated normal distribution for ce_j specified as

$$g(ce_j) = \frac{1}{\sqrt{2\pi\sigma_{ce}^2}} \exp\left(-\frac{1}{2}\left(\frac{ce_j - \mu_{ce}}{\sigma_{ce}}\right)^2\right)$$

The mean and variance of the normal distribution, here denoted μ_{ce} and σ_{ce}^2, are estimated over the transformed counterfeiting factor index, ce_j, and given by $\hat{\mu}_{ce}$ and $\hat{\sigma}_{ce}^2$. This enables the calculation of the counterfeit import propensity index (GTRIC-e) across source economies corresponding to the cumulative distribution function of ce_j.

Sensitivity analysis of GTRIC-e

GTRIC-e is, similarly as for products, subjected to an analysis of its sensitivity. This is done by varying the estimated means of the counterfeiting factor, ce_j, around the standard deviation. More specifically, the upper and lower boundary of GTRIC-e is given by re-calculating the index on the basis of $\hat{\mu}_{ce} \pm 2\hat{\sigma}_{ce}$. This effectively constitutes a confidence interval of GTRIC-e of 95% given by the shaded area in Figure 4.A3.2.

Figure 4.A3.2. Sensitivity of GTRIC-e

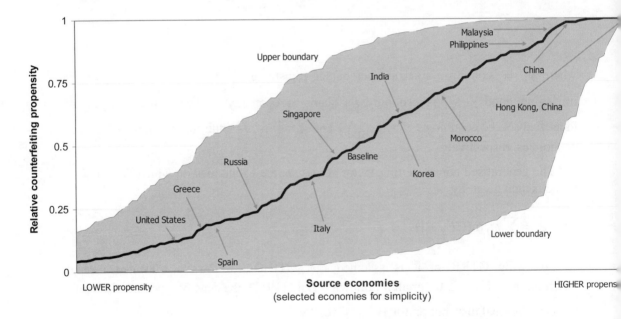

The dark line illustrates the value of GTRIC-e under baseline assumptions (mean and variance as estimated over the generalised counterfeiting factor, ce).

Table 4.A3.1. Baseline GTRIC-e (economies)

No.	Source economy	GTRIC-e	No.	Source economy	GTRIC-e	No.	Source economy	GTRIC-e
1	China, Hong Kong SAR	1.0000	48	Jordan	0.6285	95	Portugal	0.1344
2	Lao People's Dem. Rep.	1.0000	49	Cook Isds	0.6205	96	Cote d'Ivoire	0.1327
3	Afghanistan	0.9999	50	India	0.6133	97	Saudi Arabia	0.1222
4	Thailand	0.9997	51	Rep. of Korea	0.6085	98	United States	0.1204
5	United Arab Emirates	0.9993	52	Tajikistan	0.5854	99	Latvia	0.1199
6	Dem. People's Rep. of Korea	0.9984	53	Maldives	0.5746	100	United Kingdom	0.1114
7	Togo	0.9981	54	Mauritius	0.5717	101	Brazil	0.1112
8	Kyrgyzstan	0.9956	55	Luxembourg	0.5294	102	Hungary	0.1021
9	Tokelau	0.9953	56	Brunei	0.5212	103	Israel	0.1011
10	Lebanon	0.9945	57	Oman	0.5130	104	Poland	0.0952
11	Pakistan	0.9917	58	Egypt	0.5091	105	Argentina	0.0891
12	Paraguay	0.9851	59	Indonesia	0.4910	106	Denmark	0.0811
13	Cyprus*	0.9847	60	Bahrain	0.4800	107	Australia	0.0807
14	Uzbekistan	0.9830	61	Bangladesh	0.4767	108	France	0.0740
15	China	0.9748	62	Iraq	0.4685	109	Suriname	0.0700
16	Viet Nam	0.9651	63	Singapore	0.4500	110	Mexico	0.0655
17	Malaysia	0.9527	64	Senegal	0.4469	111	Belarus	0.0603
18	Albania	0.9358	65	Ghana	0.4273	112	Venezuela	0.0592
19	Rep. of Moldova	0.9057	66	Montserrat	0.3844	113	Trinidad and Tobago	0.0572
20	Philippines	0.9043	67	Kazakhstan	0.3802	114	Belgium	0.0545
21	Turkey	0.8915	68	Haiti	0.3782	115	Netherlands	0.0536
22	Yemen	0.8767	69	Italy	0.3663	116	Canada	0.0480
23	Sri Lanka	0.8724	70	Ecuador	0.3640	117	Finland	0.0449
24	Panama	0.8697	71	Bulgaria	0.3591	118	Mali	0.0439
25	Ukraine	0.8682	72	Romania	0.3447	119	Angola	0.0419
26	Georgia	0.8678	73	Bahamas	0.3421	120	Japan	0.0419
27	Other Asia, nes	0.8543	74	Honduras	0.3281	121	New Zealand	0.0419
28	Neth. Antilles	0.8519	75	Estonia	0.2964	122	Germany	0.0419
29	China, Macao SAR	0.8368	76	Madagascar	0.2809	123	Costa Rica	0.0419
30	Syria	0.8342	77	Croatia	0.2801	124	Tunisia	0.0419
31	Kenya	0.8290	78	Dominican Rep.	0.2667	125	Austria	0.0419
32	TFYR of Macedonia	0.8156	79	Cameroon	0.2596	126	Mozambique	0.0419
33	Iran	0.8022	80	Russian Federation	0.2380	127	Chile	0.0419
34	Malta	0.7962	81	Guatemala	0.2330	128	Norway	0.0419
35	Botswana	0.7706	82	Czech Rep.	0.2291	129	Bosnia Herzegovina	0.0419
36	Mongolia	0.7665	83	Colombia	0.2239	130	Uruguay	0.0419
37	Turkmenistan	0.7398	84	Algeria	0.2111	131	Slovakia	0.0419
38	Lithuania	0.7279	85	Kuwait	0.2084	132	Fiji	0.0419
39	Cambodia	0.7255	86	Switzerland	0.2073	133	Qatar	0.0419
40	Armenia	0.7190	87	Nicaragua	0.2037	134	Azerbaijan	0.0419
41	Myanmar	0.7042	88	Nigeria	0.1940	135	Nepal	0.0419
42	Morocco	0.7018	89	Spain	0.1926	136	Aruba	0.0419
43	Djibouti	0.6852	90	Serbia and Montenegro	0.1867	137	Libya	0.0419
44	Gibraltar	0.6684	91	Slovenia	0.1851	138	Papua New Guinea	0.0419
45	Bolivia	0.6555	92	Greece	0.1708	139	Areas, nes	0.0419
46	Peru	0.6440	93	South Africa	0.1623			
47	Jamaica	0.6325	94	Dem. Rep. of the Congo	0.1375			

See footnote 18 in Chapter 3.

Note: It is emphasised that GTRIC-e is based on generalised seizure information and that values are related to the total trade of each economy. The index can therefore not be interpreted as illustrating the ranking of economies in proportion to total customs seizures as such.

Annex 4.A4.

CONSTRUCTION AND APPLICATION OF GTRIC

Estimating the magnitude of counterfeiting and piracy in international trade

Let the general propensity of importing infringed items of HS category k, from any economy, be denoted P^k, and be given by GTRIC-p such that

$$P^k = F_{LTN}(cp^k)$$

where $F_{LTN}(cp^k)$ is the cumulative probability function of $f_{LTN}(cp^k)$ described in Annex 4.A2. The counterfeiting factor $cp^k \geq \varepsilon_{cp}$ where ε_{cp} denotes some small value larger than 0 to account for potential infringement activities in those product categories that were not defined as sensitive. Note that $P^k \in [\varepsilon_p;1)$, $\forall k \in \mathbf{K}$, where $\mathbf{K}$ is the set of *all* product categories and $\varepsilon_p > 0$.

Furthermore, let the general propensity of importing any type of infringing goods from economy j be denoted P_j and given by GTRIC-e, such that

$$P_j = G_{LTN}(ce_j)$$

where $G_{LTN}(ce_j)$ is the cumulative probability function of $f_{LTN}(ce_j)$ described in Annex 4.A3. The counterfeiting factor $ce_j \geq \varepsilon_{ce}$ where ε_{ce} denotes some small value larger than 0 to account for potential source economies among those that were not identified as such. Note that $P_j \in [\varepsilon_e;1)$, $\forall j \in \mathbf{J}$, where $\mathbf{J}$ is the set of all exporting economies and $\varepsilon_e > 0$.

The general propensity of importing counterfeit or pirated items of type k originating from economy j is then denoted $c(j,k)$ and approximated by

$$c(j,k) = \alpha P^k P_j$$

such that $c(j,k) \in [\alpha \varepsilon_p \varepsilon_e; \alpha)$, $\forall j,k$, with α denoting the maximum average counterfeit export rate of any type of infringing goods, k, originating from any trading partner, j, and, similarly, $\alpha \varepsilon_p \varepsilon_e$ denoting the minimum average counterfeit export rate.

Given prior values of the model's crucial parameters $(\alpha, \varepsilon_{cp}, \varepsilon_{ce})$, the value of $c(j,k)$ is calculated for 243 export partners and 96 HS chapters, as registered by the 124 reporting economies in the UNSD-OECD Comtrade database on international trade. This results in a matrix of counterfeit import propensities, denoted **C**, which is then applied on world imports, denoted by the matrix **M**. The baseline example is illustrated with a maximum counterfeit export rate of $\alpha = 0.1$ (10%). To account for counterfeit and pirated exports of products and/or from source economies that were not identified in the OECD surveys, it is assumed that $\varepsilon_{cp} = \varepsilon_{ep} = 0.05$.

The general counterfeit import propensity matrix **C** is given by

$$\mathbf{C} = \begin{pmatrix} \mathbf{C}_1 \\ \vdots \\ \mathbf{C}_i \\ \vdots \\ \mathbf{C}_n \end{pmatrix}, \text{ with dimension } nJ \times K$$

with each element, $\mathbf{C}_i$, given by economy i's counterfeit import propensity matrix

$$\mathbf{C}_i = \begin{pmatrix} c_{i1}^1 & c_{i1}^2 & & & c_{i1}^K \\ c_{i2}^1 & \ddots & & & \\ & & c_{ij}^k & & \\ & & & \ddots & \\ c_{iJ}^1 & & & & c_{iJ}^K \end{pmatrix}, \text{ with dimension } J \times K$$

Each element c_{ij}^k states the economy i's propensity of importing infringing goods of type k from trading partner k which is given by $c(j,k)$ above.

The import matrix **M** is given by

$$\mathbf{M} = \begin{pmatrix} \mathbf{M}_1 \\ \vdots \\ \mathbf{M}_i \\ \vdots \\ \mathbf{M}_n \end{pmatrix}, \text{ with dimension } nJ \times K$$

with each element defined by economy i's unique import matrix of good k from trading partner j.

$$\mathbf{M}_i = \begin{pmatrix} m_{i1}^1 & m_{i1}^2 & & & m_{i1}^K \\ m_{i2}^1 & \ddots & & & \\ & & m_{ij}^k & & \\ & & & \ddots & \\ m_{iJ}^1 & & & & m_{iJ}^K \end{pmatrix}, \text{ with dimension } J \times K$$

Hence, the element m_{ij}^k denotes i's imports of product category k from trading partner j, where $i = \{1,...,n\}$, $j = \{1,...,J\}$, and $k = \{1,...,K\}$, and $n = 113$; $J = 249$; and $K = 96$. The product-by-economy percentage of counterfeit and pirate imports, denoted Ψ, can thus be determined as the following

$$\Psi = \mathbf{C'M} \div \mathbf{M}$$

Total trade in counterfeit and pirated goods, denoted by the scalar $\mathbf{TC}$, is then given by

$$\mathbf{TC} = \mathbf{i}_1' \Psi \mathbf{i}_2$$

where $\mathbf{i}_1$ is a vector of ones with dimension nJ x 1, and $\mathbf{i}_2$ is a vector of ones with dimension K x 1. Then, by denoting total world trade by the scalar $\mathbf{TM} = \mathbf{i}_1' \mathbf{M} \mathbf{i}_2$, the ceiling of counterfeiting and piracy in world trade, s_{TC}, is determined by

$$s_{\mathbf{TC}} = \frac{\mathbf{TC}}{\mathbf{TM}}$$

The estimates resulting from the baseline assumptions described above are lastly subjected to a sensitivity analysis, as described in Annex 4.A2 and 4.A3. This analysis suggests that the ceiling of counterfeit and pirated products is likely to be between 0.2% and 2% of world trade. Holding the fix-point constant at 0.1, sensitivity analyses of other model parameters does not challenge these results.

Chapter 5

EXAMINING THE ECONOMIC EFFECTS OF COUNTERFEITING AND PIRACY

5.1. Summary

This chapter examines the effects of counterfeiting and piracy on economies. First, the general socio-economic effects are outlined, followed by the effects on rights holders, consumers and governments. Then, the effects specific to developing economies are presented.

As shown in Table 5.1, the effects of counterfeiting and piracy are wide-ranging. Counterfeiting and piracy can have broad economy-wide effects on trade, foreign invest-ment, employment, innovation, criminality and the environment. Concerning the micro-economic effects, the sales volume, prices and costs of rights holders are impacted, as are investment, royalties and brand value. For consumers, counterfeit and pirated products may offer cheap alternatives to genuine goods but are usually of inferior quality. For certain types of infringing goods, the health and safety of consumers may be put at significant risk. With respect to governments, counterfeiting and piracy have effects on tax revenues, government expenditures, and, when corruption takes place, the effectiveness of public institutions.

The potential effects of counterfeiting and piracy summarised in Table 5.1 differ in character; some occur immediately, while others are lagged and prolonged, and thus of a more indirect character. The approximate timing of the effects on key impact areas outlined in Table 5.1 is presented in Table 5.2.

Table 5.1. Summary of principal potential effects of counterfeiting and piracy

Impact area	Principal potential effects
General socio–economic effects	
Innovation and growth	– Reduction in incentives to innovate – Possible negative effects on medium and long term growth rates
Criminal activities	– Increase in flow of financial resources to criminal networks, thereby increasing their influence in economies
Environment	– Substandard infringing products can have negative environmental effects – Disposal of counterfeit and pirated products has environmental consequences
Employment	– Shift of employment from rights holders to infringing firms, where working conditions are often poorer
Foreign direct investment	– Small, negative effects on levels of foreign direct investment flows; possible effect on structure of foreign direct investment
Trade	– Negative effects on trade in products where health and safety concerns are high
Effects on right holders	
Sales volume and prices	– Reduction of rights holders' sales volumes – Downward pressures on prices
Brand value and firm reputation	– Erosion of brand and firm value
Royalties	– Diminished flow of royalties due to rights holders.
Firm-level investment	– Adverse implications for R&D and other creative activities – Reduced firm-level investment
Costs of combating counterfeiting and piracy	– Costs are incurred for: (1) investigatory work; (2) public awareness initiatives; (3) technical assistance to governments; (4) litigation to fight infringements; and (5) modifications to product packaging to deter counterfeiting and piracy
Scope of operations	– Downsizing of rights holders operations – Increased risk of going out of business
Effects on consumers	
Health and safety risk	– Substandard products carry health and safety risks ranging from mild inconveniences to life-threatening situations
Consumer utility	– Consumers who unknowingly buy counterfeit/pirated products are generally worse off – Consumers who knowingly purchase counterfeit/pirated goods are generally not in a position to properly evaluate the quality of the product; there is substantial risk that utility will fall short of expectations
Effects on government	
Tax revenues	– Lower tax and related payments (such as social charges) by rights holders – Weak collection of taxes and related charges from counterfeiters/pirates
Costs of anti-counterfeiting activities	– Costs are incurred for enforcement and public awareness initiatives, and for development and maintenance of legal frameworks
Corruption	– Bribery and extortion of government officials to facilitate counterfeiting and piracy operations weaken the effectiveness of public institutions charged with law enforcement and related government activities.

Table 5.2. Timing of the main potential effects of counterfeiting and piracy on key impact areas

	Short term	Medium and long term
General socio-economic effects		Innovation and growth
		Criminal activities
		Environment
		Employment
		Foreign direct investment
		Trade
Effects on right holders	Sales volume and prices	Sales volume and prices
	Royalties	Brand value and firm reputation
		Firm-level investment
		Costs of combating counterfeiting and piracy
		Scope of operations
Effects on consumers	Health and safety risk	Consumer utility
	Consumer utility	
Effects on governments		Tax revenues
		Costs of anti-counterfeiting activities
		Corruption

Insights into the relative importance of the effects were revealed in the surveys of governments and industries (OECD, 2005*a* and *b*). The reduction in profitability was the effect that was indicated most frequently by both governments and industry representatives, followed by health and safety concerns. Criminal activity was third in the case of government respondents, while industry highlighted reductions in consumer confidence.

5.2. General socio-economic effects

Counterfeiting and piracy can have general socio-economic effects, including those on: *1)* trade; *2)* foreign direct investment (FDI); *3)* innovation and growth; *4)* employment; *5)* the environment; and *6)* criminal activity.

Only a few studies have assessed the general effects of counterfeiting and piracy on economies. This is due in part to the lack of consistent cross-economy counterfeiting and piracy datasets. Insights may nevertheless be gained from empirical studies that examine the effects of intellectual property rights (IPR) regimes economy-wide. However, while counterfeiting and piracy and the quality of IPR regimes are related, they are not synonymous (Box 5.1); the findings from these studies therefore cannot be directly applied to counterfeiting and piracy. The studies mentioned quantify the quality of IPR protection by a series of indices (Rapp and Rozek, 1990; Ginarte and Park, 1997; Ostergard 2000); the indices are then applied in macroeconomic analyses.

Box 5.1. Weak IPR: Does it mean high levels of counterfeiting and piracy?

While a number of studies have examined the strength of IPR regimes to economic performance in various economies around the world, caution is needed in the application of their results in assessments of counterfeiting and piracy. The relationship of IPR strength to counterfeiting and piracy is complex, and indicators of IPR strength may not signal the presence of conditions conducive to counterfeiting and piracy. A country with a low score for IPR strength may not turn out to be a significant source of infringing products. Conversely, a country with a strong IPR regime could well be a major source of counterfeit and pirated items.

The variable relationship between some IPR indicators and the extent of counterfeiting and piracy in a given economy arises because of at least three factors. First, beyond a permissive IPR environment, commercial counterfeiting and piracy operations require other elements, such as capital stock, infrastructure and distribution channels. Second, even economies with relatively strong legal IPR regimes could fail to provide adequate enforcement for the prevention of counterfeiting and piracy; enforcement is not always reflected in IPR indices. Third, an index of IPR strength may capture the general quality of institutions, which can be important for certain effects but omit dimensions of particular relevance to counterfeiting and piracy.

A quantitative assessment of the correlation between various IPR indices and the trade–related indices of counterfeiting and piracy is presented in Chapter 4.

In support of the OECD project on counterfeiting and piracy, efforts were made to more explicitly explore the links between these and economic performance, through the development of an economic model that examines effects in two key areas – foreign direct investment and trade. The model used customs seizures data as a principal building block (Box 5.2).

Box 5.2. The ATRIC index

Assessing the effects of counterfeiting and piracy on trade and FDI

An aggregated trade-related index of counterfeiting and piracy (ATRIC) was constructed, based on data provided by customs officials on seizures. The index was constructed to capture the (a) intensity, (b) scope and (c) duration of counterfeit/piracy trade in a given economy. The index is used as a proxy for counterfeiting and piracy levels.

This index differs somewhat from the construction of the G-TRIC index that was presented in Chapter 4. The two most important differences between the two indices are:

The ATRIC index covers only four economies. While G-TRIC covers a large number of economies, the coverage of ATRIC is small because of the need for highly detailed data; sufficiently detailed data were only available for several economies. While this reduces the scope of ATRIC, it improves the accuracy of measurement significantly.

ATRIC examines economy/product relationships simultaneously at the outset; while G-TRIC treats economy and product relationships separately. The detailed ATRIC approach enables more specific and robust assessments of counterfeiting and piracy on trade and investment (G-TRIC, it will be recalled, is used to estimate the overall magnitude of infringement).

Further information on the index is provided in Annex 5.A1.

5.2.1. Innovation and growth

Innovation has long been recognised as a key driver of economic growth and thus welfare. It is stimulated in large part by the development and exploitation of ideas for new products and new processes that innovators protect through patents, copyrights, design rights and trademarks. That protection is the key to promoting innovation, which is often highly risky, time-consuming and expensive. The strongest form of IPR protection for innovation is patents, which provide innovators with time-limited exclusive rights over the exploitation of their innovations. The link to innovation appears weaker in the case of registered trademarks, which are used principally to differentiate products, and copyrights that apply to creative works rather than ideas. Counterfeiting and piracy, to the extent that they undermine the efforts of innovators, can therefore have an important adverse effect on the R&D intensity and on growth.

Some work has been done on a sectoral basis which links piracy to growth. Bezmen and Depken (2005), for example, examined the situation in software piracy. Covering three years -- 1995, 2000 and 2002 -- the study relates software piracy (based on BSA estimates) to economic development in 77 economies, using the United Nation's Human Development Index (HDI). A two-stage regression approach is used in which software piracy first is evaluated using various macroeconomic values, and HDI is then regressed on software piracy, Simon-Fraser's economic freedom index and GDP per capita. The results suggest that software piracy affects economic development negatively, at least in the short run.

The CEBR (2000) study referenced earlier analysed the effects of counterfeiting in selected industries of the European Union. Based on the estimates of foregone invest-ments, CEBR applied their own macro-economic model of the European economy to simulate the resulting impact on GDP. According to CEBR, the reduction in investment is estimated to have a negative effect on GDP across the EU area of EUR 8 billion.

Similar modelling techniques have been used by the Allen Consulting Group (2003) for the Australian economy, with a focus on the toy, software and computer and video games industries. According to their model, a reduction of counterfeiting by 33% over a five-year period would increase GDP by 41 million AUD per year. A study performed by IDC concluded that a drop in piracy rate in the software sector by 10% would increase world output by USD 400 billion (IDC, 2005). These estimates are based largely on approaches that assume a one-to-one relationship, or perfect substitutability, between pirated software and lost legitimate sales, which could significantly affect the final results, and partly explain the difference between the Allen and IDC results.

On the aggregate level, related work has also been carried out on the relationship of the strength of IP regimes to growth. However, since the strength of IP regimes is only an approximation of the level of counterfeiting and piracy in an economy (see Box 5.1), an application of these results to counterfeiting and piracy must be done with caution.

An example of the studies on IPR and growth is Gould and Gruben (1996), who use Heston, Summers and Aten cross-economy data to study the effects of patent protection on average yearly economic growth during 1960-1988. They find a significant positive effect of the strength of patent protection on economic growth – especially for open economies. They also find, however, that IPR may have a weaker effect in uncompetitive and closed economies.

Similarly, using average yearly growth of GDP during 1970-1985 for 112 economies, Rushing and Thompson (1996) find that stronger patent protection may contribute to economic growth, but only for economies above a certain income threshold. More recent studies find evidence that the impact of IPR on economic growth is non-linear or state-dependent. For instance, while strong patent protection may stimulate growth in economies that have reached a high level of development, this relationship does not hold for middle-income economies (Greenaway *et al.*, 2004). According to the Greenaway study, strong patent protection also appears to have a positive impact in the least developed economies -- presumably since such protection stimulates knowledge transfer through other channels. Middle-income economies have often gained imitative capabilities that can offset, at least partly, the positive impact of IPR protection.

It must be emphasised, however, that the aggregated effects on economic growth are so far generally established only for intellectual property rights, and not for counterfeiting and piracy. As already mentioned, the quality of an IPR regime is but one of the factors that determine counterfeiting and piracy activities (see Box 5.1). So far, no unified theory of economic growth takes the aspect of counterfeiting and piracy into account. Nevertheless, the relatively strong transmission between the quality of IPR protection standards and growth rates of open economies suggests that similar patterns for counterfeiting and piracy could be expected.

5.2.2. Criminal activities

As indicated in Chapter 3, counterfeiting and piracy have attracted the attention of criminal networks, as the activities are highly profitable and carry relatively low-risks. Given that counterfeiting and piracy transfer economic rents to providers of illicit goods, one can conclude that at least some of these rents eventually could be used to sustain further criminal activity.

The growth in the role of criminal networks in counterfeiting and piracy is a concern for economies as it can undermine civil society by providing those networks with the resources required to finance a range of illicit activities, in a corrupt and organised manner.

5.2.3. Environment

Counterfeiting and piracy can have negative effects on the environment. The aspects are twofold. Firstly, the seizure of counterfeit and pirated items raises environmental issues since destruction can be a costly process that creates considerable waste. In 2005, for example, the European Union seized 76 million articles.[39]

Secondly, substandard counterfeit products can have environmentally damaging consequences. A case in point is the chemicals industry, which has documented cases where the use of counterfeit fertilisers caused vast damage to the environment. Some respondents from the chemical industry (CropLife and DuPont) provided examples about the destruction of harvests in large areas in China, Russia, Ukraine and Italy due to the use of counterfeit chemicals (OECD, 2005a).

---

39.   European Union, Taxation and Customs Unit (2006).

5.2.4. Employment

At the economy-wide level, counterfeiting and piracy affect employment in a number of ways. First, as labour is one of the key input factors in production, employment shifts from rights holders to infringing parties. Internationally, the shift would result in jobs being created in economies where counterfeiting and piracy tend to be widespread, and lost in other economies. Within economies, there would be a shift in employment from recognised, traditional employers to operations that are often clandestine. As noted in the pharmaceutical sector write-up, working conditions in such environments can be appalling. It should also be noted that compounding the risk to health and safety, due to unhealthy and often dangerous working conditions, is the constant threat of detection and arrest for participating in such criminal activity. Moreover, the level of pay and benefits for workers employed in clandestine operations is likely to be far lower than in legitimate enterprises, as is job security.

A number of studies analyse the effects of counterfeiting and piracy on employment in the rights holders' economies of origin.

The CEBR study mentioned earlier analysed the impact of counterfeiting on employment in the EU.[40] Lost investment was seen as translating into a loss of 17 000 jobs in the four analysed industries.[41] In the model, the total loss of investment was treated as quarterly negative shocks to investment expenditures over the period covered. These were all assumed to be of equal size, amounting to EUR 978 million per quarter.

More detailed assessments have been prepared on a number of sectors. The Allen Consulting Group (2003) using the forecasting model presented above predicted that the 33% decline in counterfeiting and piracy would boost employment by 403 full- and part-time jobs in the sectors covered over five years. Put in relation to total employment in the industries, the effects appear to be relatively small, economy-wide.

An analysis of the effects specific to the software industry has been performed by IDC. According to their estimates, a 10 point drop in worldwide piracy, from 40% to 30%, over four years could add 1.5 million jobs (IDC, 2005). As indicated above, the IDC study assumes perfect substitutability between pirated software and lost legitimate sales, and also assumes that parties purchasing a low-priced pirated product would, in the absence of the pirated product, purchase the genuine product.[42]

Additionally, the US motion picture industry estimated that piracy resulted in a direct loss of 120 085 jobs in the US industry, with an additional 20 945 jobs lost in other affected sectors (IPI, 2006). The estimates rely on data on legitimate and infringing products obtained from surveys. Based on the estimated foregone sales, the resulting losses in employment are calculated using a set of multipliers.

In the OECD survey, evidence of the effects on employment were also provided by respondents from the music and textile industries, where cases of closures, downsizing and layoffs due to counterfeiting and piracy were reported (OECD, 2005a). In addition, related effects, on an economy-wide basis, were cited in the survey of economies. With respect to the latter, the basis of the estimates and the nature of the job losses were unclear.

---

40. For more details on the study of CEBR (2000), see Annex 5.A1.

41. Clothing and footwear, perfumes and cosmetics, toys and sports equipment, pharmaceuticals.

42. As indicated in Chapter 2, this is unlikely to be the case for most products.

It should be noted that the sectoral analyses focus on the loss of jobs that occur for affected firms and do not take into account economy-wide labour market dynamics. The loss of jobs in one sector may affect economy-wide employment (and unemployment) levels, but this depends on the extent to which workers move (or do not move) into alternative jobs.

5.2.5. Foreign direct investment

An econometric analysis of the relationship between counterfeiting and piracy and foreign direct investment (FDI) using ATRIC provides indications that there are effects. The analysis was conducted for three large economies that are major sources of FDI -- Germany, Japan and the United States -- and found that higher FDI from these economies was positively correlated with lower rates of counterfeiting and piracy (as captured by the ATRIC) in the FDI-receiving economies (see Annex 5.A4 for details). However, the ATRIC index explains a fairly small part of FDI variability, meaning that trade-related counterfeiting and piracy only serve a limited role in explaining the aggregate foregone FDI. Thus, while there are indications that reducing counterfeiting and piracy can increase inward FDI, its effect remains partial in the face of other important factors.

As with trade, considerable analysis has been carried out that examines the relationship of the strength of IPR regimes with, in this case, FDI. Again, as the indices of IPR are not an accurate proxy of counterfeiting (see Box 5.1), these studies present just a rough indication of the potential effects of counterfeiting and piracy on FDI. A survey-based study by Mansfield (1994) concludes that IPR protection is a key concern for companies when they established R&D centres, while it is of less importance in establishing sales and distribution outlets. The studies of Markusen and Maskus (2001) and Nunnenkamp and Spatz (2003), which employed gravity-like equations, suggest that the effects of IPR quality on FDI are weak but positive. Another study by Smarzynska Javorcik (2004) finds some effects of IPR regimes on the composition of FDI inflows using a sample of some transition economies. An extension of the study by Smarzynska Javorcik to counterfeiting and piracy suggests that there might be some effects of IPR violation on the structure of FDI flows.

According to an A.T. Kearny (2005) report, the effects of intellectual property protection on FDI appear to be significant in determining the R&D investment locations, which is only a part of total FDI flows. This emphasises the fact that IPR is just one component out of the set of FDI determinants and underlines the need for more detailed context-dependent analyses.

Concerning factors that are important in attracting foreign direct investment, other reasons such as the quality of the labour force and cost of investment could therefore be more important. This seems to be supported by FDI statistics. China, for example, is one of the key sources of counterfeit products but is also one of the world's largest recipients of foreign direct investment (A.T. Kearny, 2005). Thus, it is likely that other factors outweigh the negative effect of counterfeiting and piracy on foreign direct investment.

5.2.6. Trade

No studies have been done that estimate the effects of counterfeiting and piracy on trade levels (*i.e.* trade volumes), due at least in part to the lack of data. The impact analysis of counterfeiting and piracy on trade using ATRIC did not yield a definite and conclusive result about any possible correlation between counterfeiting and aggregated volumes of international trade.

However, there are indications that counterfeiting and piracy may affect the structure of trade. A simple correlation using ATRIC suggests that economies that are known to be important sources of counterfeit products have lower exports of goods, which, if their quality is substandard, could affect the health of consumers negatively (for more details see Annex 5.A2). In particular, pharmaceutical products seem to have significantly smaller shares in the total exports of economies that are important sources of counterfeit and pirated goods.

The analysis, which focuses on exports, seems to be supported on the import side as well. The relationship between the volume of imports within sectors from different economies and their degree of counterfeiting activity were examined using the gravity approach. The experience of the United States was examined, as the quantity and quality of data on counterfeiting were high. Attention focused on the situation in the pharmaceutical sector. The results suggest that counterfeiting and piracy are negatively correlated with the volume of US imports of medicines. This could reflect reluctance on the part of importers to source certain health-sensitive products from sources where the risk of substandard counterfeit products are high.

The ATRIC results are, however, highly preliminary as they rely on an extremely limited dataset. Better quality data would potentially improve the robustness of the test and the causality analysis.

Unfortunately, there are no other studies that focus on the relationship between counterfeiting and piracy and trade. However, there are some relevant empirical studies that examine the relationship between the quality of IPR regimes and trade. A selection of these studies is outlined in Table 5.3. A more detailed presentation of these studies is given in Annex 5.A3.

Table 5.3. Empirical studies on the effects of intellectual property rights on trade

Study	Principal conclusions
Maskus and Penubarti, 1995	Strong patent protection in economies has a positive impact on bilateral trade flows of manufacturing goods
Primo Braga and Fink, 1999	Stronger IPR in economies has a positive significant effect on bilateral trade flows
Smith, 1999	US exports are lower to economies that pose a strong threat-of-imitation due to weak IPR
Smith, 2001	US affiliate sales and licenses are stronger to economies with strong IPR

As indicated in Box 5.1, the approximation of the degree of counterfeiting and piracy is not the primary function of an IPR index. Therefore, one should consider the above presented studies as an indication of what the results of counterfeiting and piracy on trade might be.

5.3. Rights holders

The following section outlines the effects of counterfeiting and piracy on rights holders. Apart from formal rights holders, these effects could be further extended to the other industry players involved in the production and distribution of the legitimate goods, such as distributors and retailers.

5.3.1. Sales volume and prices

5.3.1.1. Reduction in sales

Firms affected by counterfeiting and piracy suffer a direct loss in *sales volume*.

Whereas patent infringement creates more quasi-competitive pressure for the rights holder, which translates into a smaller market share, the effects on sales of trademark- and copyright-infringing products depend in large part on the characteristics of the products/industries concerned -- in particular, on *1)* the degree of deceptiveness of the infringing product; and *2)* the quality of the counterfeit/pirated product in comparison to the genuine product.

The loss in sales volume has two components: *1)* sales lost to consumers who purchase a counterfeit/pirated product believing it is genuine (*i.e.* sales lost on the primary market); and *2)* sales lost to consumers who knowingly purchase a counterfeit/pirated product, instead of a genuine article, because of its lower price (*i.e.* sales lost on the secondary market).[43]

The impact on lost sales due to successful deception is high, since virtually every purchased counterfeit item represents a lost sale to the legitimate producer.

The impact on lost sales on the secondary market, where infringing products are knowingly and consciously bought, are harder to quantify. Some consumers of the lower-priced fakes would have purchased the higher-priced genuine product if the fake had not been available; others would not.[44]

There are also issues related to the short and longer-term effects of counterfeiting/piracy on sales. Firstly, counterfeiting and piracy can undermine the time-related marketing strategies of firms. The audio-visual industry, for example has pointed out that the intro-duction of related products (*e.g.* cinema releases, cassettes, DVDs and video online) is often timed to respond to different commercial and competitive pressures. The presence of a pirated product could have significant implications that make it difficult, if not impossible, to successfully carry out marketing plans, resulting in lost sales. Secondly, current economic theory suggests that sales of low-priced pirated products on the secondary market can, under certain circumstances, expand markets for genuine products over time (Slive and Bernhardt, 1998; Shy and Thisse, 1999). The software industry has often been used as a case in point. The retail price charged for signature software products may be at a level that discourages sales to different types of consumers. In these cases, the sale of

---

43. In terms of the formal methodology introduced in Chapter 2 (see the Annex for Chapter 2 for the formal introduction), the case when consumers are deceived translates into a reduction of total demand q^*. Those consumers that knowingly opt for the illicit substitute are represented by the volume q'.

44. This is because for some consumers, their valuation is too small compared with the price charged by the rights holder. Formally it is the case when $v(j) < p(j)$ (see Annex Chapter 2).

much lower-priced pirated copies could expand consumption of the software product and help to secure its position as a major or dominant product, which eventually could lead to higher sales of legitimate versions. The studies, which have been done on such externalities are, however, mostly theoretical and do not provide robust empirical support.

5.3.1.2. Price pressure

As counterfeiters and pirates do not incur the developmental costs related to the creation of new processes and products (*e.g.* the cost of research and development, etc.) they are able to sell products profitably, at lower prices. Thus, the presence of counterfeit products creates *price pressures* on the rights holders on primary markets.

In the case of patents, the unauthorised production of a like product puts additional merchandise on the market, which puts downward pressures on prices. In the case of trademarks and copyrights, lower prices for infringing products on the secondary market (where purchasers know the products infringe IPRs) tend to put pressure on rights holders to reduce their prices. This is notably the case in the copyright-intensive industries, where infringing products usually are largely interchangeable. In this case, a high reduction in demand for genuine products might require a significant change of pricing policy by the rights holder.[45]

5.3.1.3. Illustration

The dynamics of the primary and secondary markets and the short-run consequences of counterfeiting and piracy on rights holders are illustrated in Figure 5.1. The rights holder first establishes a price for the genuine product, expecting a certain volume to be sold. This quantity is depicted by the larger circle on the left ("primary market"), which constitutes the entirety of the market for genuine items in the absence of counterfeit and pirated products.[46]

Competition from counterfeit/pirated products is then introduced; it affects the rights holder in two ways. First, a market develops for lower-priced IP-infringing products that consumers buy, knowing the products are not genuine;[47] this market is depicted by the smaller circle on the right ("secondary market"). The overlap of the two markets, shown in the shaded area, represents the sales that counterfeiters/pirates steal from rights holders.

Additional sales are lost to counterfeiters/pirates who successfully deceive consumers into buying their products. This is illustrated by the small dark circle labelled "Deception".

---

45. Under certain conditions, the infringement of IPR gives rights holders in some sectors the opportunity to differentiate between consumers with respect to their willingness to pay for the authentic products. Particularly, when consumers with low willingness to pay decide to buy a cheaper counterfeit good, a rights holder may increase the price of the genuine product, aiming at customers with higher willingness to pay. This, in fact, may lead to an increase in the prices of genuine products (accompanied by a reduction in sales volumes).

46. Formally, the area of the circle labelled "primary market" is represented by equation A.1 in the Annex of Chapter 2.

47. The area of the circle labelled "secondary market" represents the non-deceptive demand for infringing products and is formalised by equation A.3 in the Annex of Chapter 2.

Figure 5.1. Infringement on primary and secondary market.

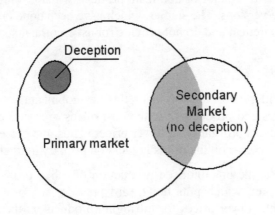

5.3.1.4. Estimating volume and price effects

Estimating the effects of counterfeiting and piracy on sales volume and prices is unfeasible at an aggregate level, but can be carried out effectively on a sectoral basis, taking the characteristics of the industry involved into account. Basic data requirements include:

- Knowledge of the demand function for the product concerned (including elasticities).

- Knowledge of the sub-market demand functions for: *1)* counterfeit and pirated products (*i.e.* the secondary market) as a whole; *2)* consumers, who would have purchased the higher-priced genuine item in the absence of the counterfeit/pirated product; and *3)* those who would not have purchased the higher-priced item in the absence of the counterfeit/pirated product.

- The price at which the rights holder is selling the product concerned.

- The prices(s) at which the counterfeit/pirated product is being sold; and

- The degree to which counterfeiters and pirates have deceived consumers into purchasing their product.

It is beyond the scope of the current project to make sectoral estimates, as sufficient data are not available. Work has been carried out by other studies, however, in a number of areas.

One of the first studies was carried out by Feinberg and Rousslang (1990), who estimated the total foregone profits due to counterfeiting for a number of sectors using simulation techniques (see below). Similar approaches were used in later studies by: the International Trademark Association (INTA, 1998); Centre for Economic and Business Research (CEBR, 2000); Business Software Alliance (BSA); International Federation of the Phonographic Industry (IFPI); Entertainment Software Association (ESA) for entertainment software; International Federation of Phonographic Industry (IFPI); Motion Picture Association (MPA); and studies by Hui and Png (2003) and the L.E.K. consulting company (2006). A summary of these studies is contained in Annex 5.A5.

All of these studies rely on market models under which consumer demand is estimated *ex-ante*. The final effect of counterfeiting is measured by comparing actual market outcome with that of the predicted market with no, or reduced, counterfeiting/ piracy. This approach requires a high degree of accuracy in quantifying the market characteristics, particularly demand elasticities, which are difficult parameters to estimate. Moreover, these parameters vary significantly across sectors and economies, which makes the aggregate result estimates particularly difficult to calculate.

5.3.2. Brand value and firm reputation

The presence of counterfeit products may damage the value of the brand and image of the producers of genuine products over time. For instance, those consumers who believed they were buying a genuine article when they in fact were buying a fake will be likely to blame the manufacturer of the genuine product if the fake did not fulfil expectations, thus creating a loss of goodwill. If consumers never discovered that they had been deceived they may be reluctant to buy another product from that manufacturer and may communicate the information to other potential buyers.

This dynamic effect of consumers' reduced trust is a well-known economic phenomenon described by Akerloff (1970). The case when consumers reduce their valuation of a given product because they expect that in some cases it may be of lower quality corresponds to the case of asymmetric information in the market. Figure 5.2 illustrates the dynamic scenario, when a large fraction of consumers expects to be deceived, even though the actual scale of deception is relatively small. Nevertheless, all consumers who expect deception reduce their willingness to buy the legitimate product, which in turn leads to further market erosion.

Figure 5.2. Dynamic effects of a deception in the primary market

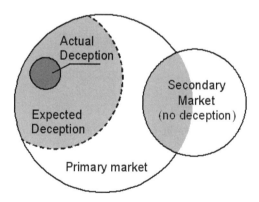

Effects of this sort were reported by several respondents to the OECD survey along the lines of "erosion of company name" or "destruction of brand reputation". Such indications came from respondents across numerous sectors, including consumer electronics, information and computers, electrical equipment, food and drink, luxury goods, sports-wear, automotive spare parts and car accessories and pharmaceuticals (OECD, 2005a).

5.3.3. Royalties

Royalties are the proceeds gained by IPR holders for permitting other parties to exercise such rights. Infringement deprives the rights holder of these proceeds. Moreover, there may be multiple parties who would be affected by lost sales of genuine products, since royalties are payable for different elements of the product, where such rights have been licensed and not purchased outright. The significance of these losses is difficult to quantify as no specific datasets about this market are readily available.

5.3.4. Investment[48]

It is often argued that strong IPR protection stimulates incentives to invest, invent and innovate.

While the predicted relationship between IPR and investment suggests that high levels of counterfeiting and piracy are therefore likely to discourage innovation and investing, only limited empirical work to support this view has been carried out. The CEBR (2000), for example, estimated that for the European Union during the period 2003-2005, the foregone investments amounted to EUR 19,6 billion in six sectors only.[49]

Given the lack of data on counterfeiting and piracy, studies have instead focused on the relationship of the items with the strength of IP regimes (rather than infringement). A potential application of these findings on counterfeiting and piracy should be made with caution, as the IPR indices are only a rough approximation of counterfeiting and piracy.

The results of studies on the relationship between IP regimes and investment suggest that strong IPR protection provides incentives to invest in the development of new products and processes. Kanwar and Evenson (2003) find that strong patent protection has a positive effect on R&D expenditures (which is used as a proxy for innovation) using panel data for 32 economies during 1981-1995. Lerner (2002) finds that the strengthening of patent protections had some positive effect on the number of filed patent applications, looking at significant changes in patent policies over 60 economies. However, when controlling for changes in the patenting environment, such as the negative effect of the Great Depression in the 1930s, the effect of increased patent protection on domestic applications was actually significantly negative. The effect on foreign patent applications, on the other hand, was strongly positive. The latter result is confirmed on U.S. firm-level data during 1982-1999 by Branstetter *et al.* (2004).

5.3.5. Costs of combating counterfeiting and piracy.

Right holders can incur significant costs related to combating counterfeiting and piracy, such as modifications to product design, special packaging, litigation, investigations and related research, assistance to governments, campaigns for increasing public awareness and "goodwill" costs associated with settling claims by customers who bought faulty counterfeit products (Table 5.4).

---

48. The term *investment* is broader than the conventional perception of investment in physical capital. It also covers research and development activities and any other form of creative activity that could result in a future stream of returns.

49. Estimates for the following sectors: clothing and footwear, perfumes and cosmetics, toys and sports equipment, pharmaceuticals.

Table 5.4. Extra costs related to combating counterfeiting and piracy

Type of costs	Characteristics
Product protection	Anti-counterfeiting modification of the product
Packaging	Special packaging, difficult to counterfeit
Litigation	Legal proceedings against counterfeiters
Investigations and research	Privately funded investigations to track down counterfeiting activities
Co-operation with governments	Resources spent to co-operate with governments in anti-counterfeiting programmes
Public awareness	Raising public awareness of counterfeiting and piracy issues
Liability	"Good will" claim settlements

Protecting products from counterfeiting and piracy can involve substantial investment in the development of technological product protection. This could include anti-counterfeiting product modifications, such as holograms or watermarks. In addition, substantial resources can be required to develop anti-counterfeiting packaging. In the liquor industry, for example, considerable sums are invested each year to combat counterfeiting via the development and use of non-refillable containers, sophisticated packaging and other devices.

IP holders also have costs related to enforcing their rights and providing compensation for the damage caused by counterfeiters and pirates. These costs are linked to: legal actions against counterfeiters; privately funded investigations working to track down counterfeiting activities; and co-operating with governments on anti-counterfeit measures, *i.e.* the training of customs authorities to assist customs officers in their enforcement activity.

Costs are also incurred in raising public awareness of counterfeiting and piracy issues. This involves educating the public and lawmakers through communication campaigns or through other national, international or sectoral action groups.

Responses to the OECD industry survey indicate that the costs of anti-counterfeiting actions can be significant. One respondent operating in the electronics sector estimates the yearly costs of such protection (holograms, etc.) to be around to EUR 20 million. In the food and drink sector, the costs of legal proceedings were stated to be on the order of USD 20 000 per case. Other respondents from the food and drink sector report yearly costs of anti-counterfeiting actions of USD 75 million (OECD, 2005*a*).

Finally, costs of invalid warranties are also related to counterfeiting and piracy. A 2005 study from the Economist Corporate Network found that two thirds of IT manufacturers cover the costs of honouring invalid warranties involving a counterfeit product (ECN 2005).

It should be strongly emphasised that all the costs presented above do not translate into higher quality for the legitimate goods. The cost of protection against counterfeiting could be spent to improve product quality or other additional productive and beneficial investments. Indeed, from the general point of view, these costs can be classified as a pure social loss, as no agent directly derives any utility from this spending at any point of time.

5.3.6. Scope of operations

Counterfeiting and piracy can also affect the scope of a firm's activities. Some survey respondents, for example, mentioned cases where reduced profitability and losses in brand value had driven companies out of the business, or reduced their scale of operations. One from the music industry reported a case of bankruptcy caused by counterfeiting and piracy; another from the same sector reported infringement-induced closures (OECD, 2005*a*).

5.4. Effects on consumers

5.4.1. Health and safety

Counterfeiters and pirates who target the primary market while seeking to maximise profits have limited, or no, interest in ensuring the quality, efficacy or safety of their products. This increases the potential for negative effects on the health and safety of consumers. Concerns about this appear frequently in the responses to the OECD surveys (OECD, 2005*a*). The industries where health and safety effects tend to occur include: automotive, electrical components, food and drink, chemicals, toiletry and household products, pharmaceuticals and tobacco products.

In the automotive sector, inferior replacement parts falsely carrying the brand name of trusted manufacturers have been problematic. Counterfeit brake pads, hydraulic hoses, engine and chassis parts, suspension and steering components and airbag mechanisms are among the items that have been counterfeited. In some instances, the deficiencies found in these products could seriously impair the safety of vehicles.[50] In the electrical components sector, counterfeit circuit breakers have been found to be calibrated wrongly or to be constructed using low-quality materials. Such deficiencies have caused fires and fatal electric shocks.

In the food and drinks sector, few people would knowingly purchase counterfeit food or drink products, due in part to the potential health risks involved. Such risks range from general discomfort, to serious illness. As discussed in the sectoral assessment, this has been the case for poorly distilled raw spirits and fake baby formula.

In the case of pharmaceuticals, trademark-infringing products are unapproved and thus potentially dangerous. Counterfeit pharmaceuticals may include correct ingredients in incorrect quantities or may be composed according to a wrong formula. Products can furthermore be made of non-active substances altogether, or even contain toxic substances. In all cases, ailments that could be remedied by genuine products may go untreated or worsen; in some cases, they may even lead to death. Significantly, counterfeit drugs have reportedly increased drug resistance among some the world's most deadly infectious diseases, including malaria, tuberculosis and HIV/AIDS. For example, in cases where fake antiretroviral drugs contain incorrect levels of active ingredients, the disease becomes more quickly resistant to first-line therapies, forcing healthcare officials to resort to second-line and potentially more toxic therapies, increasing healthcare costs and reducing access to essential medicines (see IMPACT, 2006 for further details). Patients and health providers who purchase products on the primary market are likely to be completely unaware that they have been victimised. A number of producers in this sector (*e.g.*

---

50. See Part III sectoral write–up for further details.

GlaxoSmithKline, Pfizer, VFA) reported negative effects on health and safety as one of the key negative effects of counterfeiting and piracy.

Because data are not being collected systematically, most evidence of negative health and safety effects is anecdotal in character and more work is needed to measure the effects more broadly. Healthcare providers and patients are typically unaware that a drug is counterfeit, attributing therapeutic failure to human variation. Thus, incidents of counterfeit drugs often go undetected and unreported. Moreover, few governmental data-bases concerned with public health, injuries, illnesses and consumer product safety, whether on a local or a national basis, provide for the specific collection of data on counterfeit-related incidents (Forzley, 2003). At present, precise measurement of counterfeiting related public health effects is therefore virtually impossible.

The available studies that address this issue show that counterfeit drugs are most prevalent in developing markets that fail to exercise adequate control over the drug-supply chain. The results presented by IMPACT (2006) show that developed economies with generally effective regulatory systems and market control (*e.g.* the US, EU, Australia, Canada, Japan and New Zealand) are reported to have a low percentage of counterfeit pharmaceuticals, *i.e.* less than 1% of market value. In contrast, between 10% and 30% of medicines sold in developing markets are believed to be counterfeit. Developing economies with weak drug-safety controls, including parts of Asia, Latin America and Africa, have areas where more than 30% of the medicines on sale are believed to be counterfeit. In many of the former Soviet republics, counterfeit medicines reportedly exceed 20% of market value. The proliferation of unregulated Internet sites, which can reach consumers in any market, has increased the prevalence of counterfeit drugs in both developed and developing economies. Medicines purchased from Internet sites that conceal their actual physical address are reported to be counterfeit in over 50% of cases. One needs to stress that these figures rely greatly on anecdotal evidence, and therefore they should be considered as an indication rather than an exact estimate.[51]

Another study that seeks to address the health and safety related impact of counter-feiting is Forzley (2003). The author examines material and data developed through an extensive review of available information. Covering an annual span from 1995 to 2001, these sources include, but are not limited to, anecdotal evidence, media reports, industry/association releases, as well as organisation and government reports and studies on all types of human injury associated with any type of counterfeit good. Using US and EU customs seizure data as an indicator of the most commonly counterfeited goods with potential adverse health effects, Forzley focused on pharmaceuticals, aircraft and auto parts, consumer goods and tobacco. To ensure source validation, all information was screened using six criteria including: *1)* the identification of a specific product; *2)* a specified injury or illness; *3)* a reported place of incidence occurrence; *4)* the number of persons affected; *5)* the date of the incident; and *6)* the source of a traceable report. Despite the number of years, only a few reports (21 of 120) could be validated on at least four of these criteria. A summary of these are presented in Table 5.5.

---

1. In addition, it should be noted that the pharmaceutical industry employs a broader definition of counterfeiting than that employed in this study; it includes substandard products that do not necessarily infringe IP. It is believed that statistical information on counterfeit products generally covers the broader definition.

Table 5.5. Adverse health effects from counterfeit goods

	Location	Injury	Number of incidents	Da
Pharmaceuticals				
Insulin	Volograd, Russia	Hospital admission	1000	200
Birth control pills	Brazil	Unwanted pregnancy	12	199
AIDS triple cocktail	Brazil	Panic	120	199
Androcur	Brazil	Death	10	199
Fake drugs - unspecified	China	Death	192000	200
Viagra	China	Unsatisfied customers	On-line customers	200
Seostim	US	Swelling/rash	Some patients	200
Meningitis vaccine	Niger	Death	2500	199
Medicines	Vietnam	Death (adults)	27	199
Baby powder	Vietnam	Death (chrilden)	300	199
Alcohol				
Liquor	Vietnam	Death (adults)	100	199
Vodka	Russia	Death	22	
Wine	Egypt	Death	1	191
Vodka	UK	Blindness	1	191
Beer	China	Death	Dozens	
Alcohol	China	Death	Dozens	Each ye
Food/Nutritients				
Dietary supplements	Texas, US	Adverse reaction	Complaints	20
Enfamil	US	Illness	2	20
Food sprayed with banned pesticides	China	Death	69	199
Consumer goods				
Washing powder	UK	Can cause burns	None cited	20
Cigarettes	China	Headache	Unspecified	

Source: Forzley (2003).

As for aviation, the Federal Aviation Administration (FAA) tracks data on unauthorised aircraft parts, which include counterfeit parts, but does not track associated injuries. Most of the information on these aspects of counterfeiting is therefore only obtainable by media reports and other forms of anecdotal evidence. Using the National Transportation Safety Board (NTSB) database, which contains information on annual accident reports in civilian aviation and other transportation industries in the US, Forzley found that in 1998 counterfeit parts were identified in incidents or crashes in which 110 persons were injured.

5.4.2. Consumer utility

Consumer utility is the value or satisfaction that consumers derive from products; it is based in large measure on the quality of the products and/or their performance, taking the price paid for the product into account. Consumers acquiring counterfeit or pirated products, whether knowingly or unknowingly, experience: *1)* elevated health and safety risks; and *2)* in cases when consumers have been deceived, are generally likely to experience lower consumer utility in other regards. The *consumer utility* situation is nuanced for consumers who knowingly purchase infringing products; some will gain, others will lose.

Since the quality and/or performance of counterfeit or pirated products is generally inferior to genuine products, the negative effects of counterfeiting and piracy on consumer utility tend to be particularly pronounced on the primary market. Indeed, consumer utility is decidedly lower for those individuals who pay full price, believing the product that they have purchased is genuine. A consumer who unknowingly pays full price for a low-quality, counterfeit computer component that does not operate properly, for example, gains far lower utility than someone who purchases a genuine component operating according to expectations.

The situation is more nuanced with respect to parties that knowingly purchase counterfeit or pirated products on the secondary market. Those consumers, who choose to purchase infringing products on the secondary market, deliberately make a cost-quality trade-off; thus the effects of counterfeiting and piracy on utility for this group of consumers tend to be ambiguous.

In fact, the price of fakes sold on the secondary market is expected to be lower than the price charged by rights holders on the primary market, which in turn increases the consumer utility. If the quality of such products is high, consumer utility could be higher than would be the case for higher-priced genuine articles.

However, if the quality and/or performance of the infringing products offered on the secondary market is lower, which is generally the case, consumer utility could be lower. A low-quality counterfeit watch that does not keep accurate time and that wears out quickly may bring consumers less value than an original, even though the counterfeit was purchased at a fraction of the price of the original. In this regard, it is also important to emphasise that consumers often cannot judge *ex-ante* the quality of a given product offered on the secondary market. While they know the price at which the counterfeit/pirated product is being sold, their ability to assess the quality of most counterfeit/pirated products is seriously limited. In the event they have misjudged, they have little recourse as warranties and after-sale services are not generally offered for counterfeit/pirated products.

In addition to the above-presented short-term effects, counterfeit and pirated products can have more profound longer-term implications. Less innovation by rights holders can translate into slower product quality improvements. Slower quality improvement slows in turn growth in consumer value in the longer term. In addition, consumers who are aware of the risk of unknowingly buying substandard counterfeit or pirated products may lower their expectations with respect to future purchases, thereby reducing the utility that they would derive from buying and using the products concerned.

Another effect of counterfeiting and piracy on consumers' satisfaction is the reduction of consumer confidence in given brands, or groups, of products. This particularly concerns trademarks and copyrights infringements and is related to the similar effect on rights holders (see Chapter 2, subsection 2.3.3.3 on brand value and reputation). Given that consumers are aware of potential deception in the primary market, they may adjust their expectations about future consumption. Consequently, the overall utility that consumers have from buying and using the products is therefore reduced.

Last, due to the presence of counterfeit and pirated goods, consumers may in the long term end up paying lower prices for the genuine goods sold on the primary market. This follows from the fact that rights holders may face strong quasi-competitive pressure from counterfeiters, which eventually may result in price reductions of genuine products. This is supported by the OECD industry survey, where more than one-third of the respondents mentioned price pressure as an important consequence of counterfeiting and piracy (OECD, 2005*a*).

5.5. Effects on government

The principal effects of counterfeiting and piracy on governments concern foregone tax revenues and additional costs associated with fighting counterfeiting and piracy. Furthermore, an additional indirect effect concerns the weakening of public institutions that occurs when criminal networks use corruption of public officials as a means of supporting their illegal activities.

5.5.1. Tax revenues

Lower sales volume and lower prices due to counterfeiting and piracy would lower the profits of rights holders, resulting in reduced corporate income taxes from the rights holders. The lower prices would also result in reduced sales taxes and reduced value-added taxes on sales made by rights holders. In addition, some employee taxes are foregone and customs revenue from smuggled products are lost. There are some instances where some of the tax losses would be offset by increased taxes from counterfeiters and pirates. Tax collection from these parties, however, appears to be weak.

Moreover, foreign sourcing of counterfeit and pirated products would further diminish domestic tax receipts, as any income taxes paid by infringing parties would be paid to another taxing authority. The tax revenue losses incurred by governments are particularly high in sectors such as tobacco and alcoholic beverages where excise taxes are high and smuggling to avoid those taxes is common.

Most of the empirical work that has been done estimating tax losses (Box 5.3) assumes that counterfeiters and pirates do not pay any taxes, or that if they do, they are far lower than those that would be paid by rights holders. Given the involvement of criminal networks, this is likely to be a fair presumption in many instances. It is probably not valid in the case of parties that infringe patents, however, as such parties are generally reputable concerns that are only found to have infringed an IP after a contested legal proceeding.

In making estimates, a number of factors need to be kept in mind, namely that: *1)* tax revenues are not completely foregone -- sales and related consumption taxes may be paid, depending on the terms, conditions and location of sales, and as suggested above, some producers of infringing products may pay income and others taxes, even if at lower levels; and *2)* taxes foregone in some jurisdictions may be paid, at least to some extent, elsewhere -- this is likely to be the case when the production of fake goods occurs in jurisdictions outside that of the legitimate producer.

Box 5.3. Empirical research on effects of counterfeiting and piracy on tax revenues

Assessing foregone tax revenues

Several studies have been carried out on the effects of counterfeiting and piracy on foregone tax revenues.

With a focus on the Australian toy, software, and computer and video games industries, the Allen Consulting Group (ACG, 2003) modelled the impact of a decline in counterfeiting of 33%. It was estimated that such a reduction would correspond to an annual increase in government tax revenues of AUD 34.4 million. A similar study on software piracy was conducted by IDC (2003). Using a somewhat different approach, IDC projected the effects of a 37% reduction in software piracy from 2002 to 2006 and estimated that tax revenues in this period would increase by AUD 437 million. However, these studies are very narrow and limited to only one market and one economy. Moreover, the estimated tax losses concern mostly taxes based on the corporate income and do not take into account losses from other taxes (*e.g.* sales tax or wage tax paid by workers).

Other studies rely on market models under which consumer demand is estimated ex-ante. The final effect of counterfeiting is measured by comparing actual market outcome with that of the predicted market with no or reduced counterfeiting/piracy. This approach requires a high degree of accuracy in quantifying the market characteristics, particularly demand elasticities, which are very difficult parameters to be estimated. Moreover, these parameters vary significantly across sectors and economies, which makes the aggregate results estimates particularly difficult to calculate. This approach was used by Thompson (2004), who estimated the losses for New York to be equal to USD 1.03 billion, and by the US Chamber of Commerce (2006), which estimated that the annual tax losses in Brazil due to counterfeiting in apparel and toys amount to at least BRL 12 billion.

5.5.2. Costs of anti-counterfeiting activities

In addition to lost tax revenues, governments incur certain other costs related to counterfeiting and piracy. These include costs associated with customs and related law-enforcement agencies and the resources required to process judicial proceedings. More-over, governments often commit resources to initiatives for combating counterfeiting and piracy, such as increasing public awareness of the problem. Finally, significant costs are incurred in handling seized goods.

5.5.3. Corruption

As indicated in Chapter 3, criminal networks sometimes seek to reduce disruption of their distribution channels and the risk of punishment for their unlawful activities through bribery and extortion of government officials. Such actions weaken the effectiveness of public institutions charged with law enforcement and other government activities (such as monitoring or certification), at the expense of society at large.

5.6. Developing economies

As indicated in Chapters 3 and 4, the magnitude of counterfeiting and piracy tends to be higher in developing economies, which means that the effects discussed above are likely to be more pronounced in these economies. The higher levels of counterfeiting and piracy are partly explained by the relatively weak enforcement of IP in effect in these economies (see Ostergard, 2000). With trading partners focusing increased attention on enforcement, pressures will be particularly great for the developing economies to take action to strengthen efforts, in the absence of which trade frictions could well develop.

While counterfeiting and piracy do not seem to have any effects that are specific to developing economies, there are several aspects that might be highlighted. However, these aspects relate more to the nature of IP regimes than counterfeiting and piracy in particular, as there are no studies that analyse the potential relationship between the degree of counterfeiting and piracy and development.

Some analyses on IPR and developing economies have focused on the potential drawbacks of strong regimes (*i.e.* high levels of protection, coupled with strong enforcement). These studies suggest that weak IPR regimes (or poor enforcement by a strong IPR regime) in less developed economies can help those economies close technological gaps with more advanced economies, as there may be important spill-over effects that help boost growth and improve social welfare. Proponents of this view (*e.g.* Helpman, 1993; Grossman and Lai, 2004) have often drawn attention to the value that high-quality, patent-infringing drugs - that are sold at relatively low prices -- can have for low-income economies, and the value that low-cost pirated software and books can have for individuals who would otherwise not have had access to these goods. Another often-sited consequence is the effect that production of infringing goods can have on creating employment (for an overview, see Dutfield, 2003).

However, the notion that weak IPR regimes can promote technological catch-up assumes that there are no costs associated with such transfers. There is ample evidence that this is not the case (see Coe and Helpman, 1995; Benhabib and Spiegel, 2002). The ability of economies to absorb and profit from technology transfers may, for example, require close collaboration and co-operation with foreign suppliers; hence, strong IP protection creates an additional incentive for foreign parties to share their knowledge. Moreover, as indicated earlier, weak IP regimes may have implications for the level and structure of FDI in general. Firms may be reluctant to transfer more advanced and interesting technology to economies where piracy is high, particularly if there are viable alternatives. The value of strong IPR in promoting FDI has been explored by Fink and Maskus (2004) and Park and Lippoldt (2003), who establish a positive link.

With respect to employment, as indicated earlier, the shift of workers to activities that are associated with counterfeiting and piracy comes at a cost, as working conditions may be poor; moreover, the biggest beneficiaries of the infringing operations appear to be criminal networks involved in a range of illegal activities. The cost to society of providing additional financial resources to such networks may far outweigh any apparent gains from additional employment.

Finally, IP regimes affect both domestic and foreign rights holders. Weak regimes that tolerate counterfeiting and piracy invariably undermine local innovation. In developing economies, the principal victims of weak regimes are likely to be innovative small- and medium-sized enterprises, which are a major source of new jobs in most economies.

References

A.T. Kearney (2005), *Foreign Direct Investment Confidence Index*, Global Business Policy Council, Vol. 8.

Akerloff, G. (1970), "The Market for Lemons: Quality Uncertainty and the Market Mechanism", *Quarterly Journal of Economics*, pp 488-500.

ACG (2003), "Counterfeiting of Toys, Business Software, and Computer and Video Games", Report to the Australian Toy Association, the Business Software Association of Australia and the Interactive Entertainment Association of Australia, Allen Consulting Group, Sydney.

Benhabib, J. and M. Spiegel (2002), "Human Capital and Technology Diffusion", *FRSBF Working Paper* No. 2003-02.

Bezmen, T. L. and C.A. Depken (2005), "The Impact of Software Piracy on Economic Development", Conference Paper, Academy of Economics and Finance.

Branstetter, L. G. et al. (2004), "Do Stronger Intellectual Property Rights Increase International Technology Transfer? Empirical Evidence from U.S. 50 Firm-Level Panel Data", *World Bank Policy Research Working Paper*, No. 3305.

BSA (2005), *Second Annual BSA and IDC Global Piracy Study*, Business Software Alliance.

CEBR (2000), *The Impact of Counterfeiting on Four Key Sectors in the European Union*, Centre for Economic and Business Research, London.

Coe, D., and E. Helpman (1995), "International R&D Spillovers", *European Economic Review*, 39: 859-887.

Dutfield, G. (2003), *Literature Survey on Intellectual Property Rights and Sustainable Human Development*, Department for International Development (DFID), United Kingdom.

Economist Corporate Network (2005), *China: Intellectual Property Rights. Protecting assets in the information, communications and entertainment market*, An industry report series exclusively written for KPMG in China and Hong Kong SAR, ECN.

European Union, Taxation and Customs Unit (2006), *Community-wide statistics for 2004 and major changes 2004-2005*, http://ec.europa.eu/taxation_customs/resources/documents/customs/customs_controls/ counterfeit_piracy/statistics/counterf_comm_2005_en.pdf

Feinberg, R. M. and D. J. Rousslang (1990), "The Economic Effects of Intellectual Property Rights Infringements", *The Journal of Business*, Vol. 63, No. 1, Part 1.

Fink C. and K. E. Maskus, eds. (2004), *Intellectual Property and Development: Lessons from Recent Economic Research*, Oxford University Press and World Bank, Oxford and Washington DC.

Forzley, M. (2003), *Counterfeit Goods and The Public's Health And Safety*, International Intellectual Property Institute, Washington DC.

Ginarte, J. C. and W.G. Park (1997), "Determinants of Intellectual Property Rights: a Cross-National Study", *Research Policy*, Vol. 26.

Gould, D. M. and W.C. Gruben (1996), "The Role of Intellectual Property Rights in Economic Growth," *Journal of Economic Development*, 48: 323-350.

Greenaway, D., Falvey, R. and N. Foster (2006) "Intellectual Property Rights and Economic Growth" *Journal of Economic Development*, Vol. 10, Issue 4.

Grossman, G. and E. Lai (2004), "International Protection of Intellectual Property", *American Economic Review*, Vol. 94, Issue 5.

Helpman, E. (1993), "Innovation, Imitation, and Intellectual Property Rights", *Econometrica*, 61: 1247-80.

Heston, A., R. Summers and B. Aten (2006), *Penn World Table Version 6.2*, Center for International Comparisons of Production, Income and Prices, University of Pennsylvania.

Hui, K. L. and I. Png (2003), "Piracy and the Legitimate Demand for Recorded Music", Contributions to *Economic Analysis & Policy*, Vol. 2, Issue 1.

IACC (2005), *The Negative Consequences of International Intellectual Property Theft: Economic Harm, Threats to the Public Health and Safety, and Links to Organized Crime and Terrorist Organizations*, White Paper of the International Anti-Counterfeiting Coalition, available at: http://www.iacc.org/resources/IACC_WhitePaper.pdf

IDC (2003), *Expanding Global Economies: The Benefits of Reducing Software Piracy*, IDC.

IDC (2005), Internet Commerce Market Model (ICMM) v.10.1, October, International Data Group

IFPI (2005), *The Recording Industry 2005 Commercial Piracy Report*, International Federation of Phonographic Industries.

INTA (1998), *The Economic Impact of Trademark Counterfeiting and Infringement*, International Trademark Association, New York.

IPI (2006), *The True Cost of Motion Picture Piracy to the U.S. Economy*, IPI Policy Report # 186, Institute for Policy Innovation.

Kanwar, S. and R. Evenson (2003), "Does intellectual property protection spur technological change?", Oxford Economic Papers, Oxford University Press, Vol. 55(2), pp. 235-264.

Lerner, J. (2002), "Patent Protection and Innovation over 150 Years", *NBER Working Paper*, No. 8977.

Mansfield, E. (1994), "Intellectual Property Protection, Foreign Direct Investment, and Technology Transfer", *International Finance Corporation Discussion Paper* No. 19, International Finance Corp.

Markusen, J. R. and K. Maskus (2001), "A Unified Approach to Intra-Industry Trade and Direct Foreign Investment", *NBER Working Papers* 8335, National Bureau of Economic Research.

Maskus, K. E. and M. Penubarti (1995), "How trade-related are intellectual property rights?", *Journal of International Economics*, Elsevier, Vol. 39(3-4), pp. 227-248, November.

Nunnenkamp, P. and J. Spatz (2003), "Intellectual Property Rights and Foreign Direct Investment: The Role of Industry and Host-Country Characteristics", *Kiel Working Paper*, No. 1167.

Stephens, W., A. Calder, J. Newton (2005), "Source and Health Implications of High Toxic Metal Concentrations in Illicit Tobacco Products", *Environ. Science, Technology,* 39: 479-488.

Ostergard, R. L. (2000), The Measurement of Intellectual Property Rights Protection, *Journal of International Business Studies*, Vol. 31, No. 2: 349-360.

OECD (2005*a*), Responses to OECD industry surveys, unpublished.

OECD (2005*b*), Responses to OECD economy surveys, unpublished.

OECD (2006), Responses to OECD customs survey, unpublished.

Park, W. G. and D. Lippoldt, (2003), "The Impact of Trade-Related Intellectual Property Rights on Trade and Foreign Direct Investment in Developing Countries", *OECD Papers: Special Issue on Trade Policy*, Vol. 4, No. 11, Issue 294.

Primo Braga, C. and C. Fink, (1999), "How Stronger Protection of Intellectual Property Rights Affects International Trade Flows", *World Bank Policy Research Working Paper* No. 2051.

Rapp, R. T. and Rozek, R. P. (1990), "Benefits and costs of intellectual property protection in developing countries", *Journal of World Trade*, Vol. 24, No. 5.

Rushing, F. W. & Thompson, M. A. (1996), "An Empirical Analysis of the Impact of Patent Protection on Economic Growth", *Journal of Economic Development,* Vol. 21, Issue 2.

Shy, O. and J.-F. Thisse (1999), "A Strategic Approach to Software Protection", *Journal of Economics & Management Strategy*, Blackwell Publishing, Vol. 8(2), pp. 163-190.

Slive J. and D. Bernhardt (1998), "Pirated for Profit", *Canadian Journal of Economics*, Canadian Economics Association, Vol. 31(4), pp. 886-899, November.

Smarzynska Javorcik, B. (2004), "The composition of foreign direct investment and protection of intellectual property rights: Evidence from transition economies", *European Economic Review*, Vol. 48(1), pp. 39-62, February.

Smith, P. J. (1999), "Are Weak Patent Rights a Barrier to U.S. Exports?", *Journal of International Economics*, 48.

Smith, P. J. (2001), "How do foreign patent rights affect U.S. exports, affiliate sales and licenses?", *Journal of International Economics,* 55.

Thompson, Jr., W. C. (2004), *Bootleg Billions – The Impact of the Counterfeit Goods Trade on New York City*, City of New York Office of the Comptroller, November.

US Chamber of Commerce (2006), *Global anti-Counterfeiting and Piracy Initiative.*

Annex 5.A1

AGGREGATED TRADE-RELATED INDEX OF COUNTERFEITING (ATRIC)

The Aggregated Trade-Related Index of Counterfeiting (ATRIC) is meant to assign a unique number to every economy known as being a source of counterfeit and pirated products, reflecting the intensity, scope and durability of counterfeiting activities in the economy. The main purpose this index will be used for is to assess the potential effects of counterfeiting and piracy.

ATRIC is based on four economy-specific Trade-Related Indices of Counterfeiting, referred to as TRIC. These indices were created for Japan, Germany, New Zealand and the United States. The selection of these economies assures that the main trade patterns are captured by the index, subject to the available datasets.

Each economy-specific TRIC relies on data on customs seizures and international trade statistics. Customs register, on a systematic basis, the originating economies for seizures of counterfeit and pirated goods, as well as the associated quantities, number of incidents and/or product values. These statistics offer one of the only ways to quantify the intensity to which counterfeit and pirated products originate from different economies. The indices for Germany and the United States are developed on the basis of the registered values of seized goods, whereas the indices for Japan and New Zealand are based on the number of items seized within each product category.

Moreover, since the series are often made according to customs profiling schemes, some economies that are commonly known to be sources of counterfeits can be over-represented in customs statistics. Consequently, economies with low seizure intensities could be underrepresented. To take this into account, the final dataset is presented in logs.

Construction of the ATRIC index

Step 1: Economy-specific trade-related indices of counterfeiting

Let $\widetilde{v}_{i,j,t}^{k}$ be the total value, or the total number of items, of seized counterfeit or pirated imports in sector k originating from economy j as registered by i's customs at time t.[52] Calculate the shares of counterfeit products in j's exports to i in the given category k, i.e.:

---

2. Depending on the quality of the seizures statistics, k refers to groups of sectors mostly at the 2-digit level of HS codes.

$\dfrac{\widetilde{v}^{k}_{i,j,t}}{m^{k}_{i,j,t}}$, where $m^{k}_{i,j,t}$ is the economy i's total imports of good k from j.

Remove from the sample all outliers, *i.e.* economies for which
$\widetilde{v}^{k}_{i,j,t} / m^{k}_{i,j,t} < 0.01, \forall k.$

For every industry, calculate its share of total counterfeit imports (this is meant to be a proxy for industry–specific propensity of counterfeiting). Adjust the shares presented above by industry-specific intensities[53]:

$$\frac{\widetilde{v}^{k}_{i,j,t}}{m^{k}_{i,j,t}} \frac{\sum_{j} \widetilde{v}^{k}_{i,j,t}}{\sum_{k}\sum_{j} \widetilde{v}^{k}_{i,j,t}}$$

Aggregate the industries to get a preliminary economy-specific and industry-specific index of counterfeiting (denoted by $\widetilde{\phi}^{k}_{j,t}$). In order to control for the scope of counterfeiting activity, the c.e.s.[54] methodology is being applied. It allows for balancing the scope of j's counterfeiting ("In how many sectors have counterfeit goods from i been detected?") with the magnitude ("What is the percentage of counterfeit goods in total imports from j?"). This is captured by the following formula:

$$\widetilde{\phi}_{j,t} \equiv \left[\sum_{k} \sqrt{\frac{\widetilde{v}^{k}_{i,j,t}}{m^{k}_{i,j,t}} \frac{\sum_{j} \widetilde{v}^{k}_{i,j,t}}{\sum_{k}\sum_{j} \widetilde{v}^{k}_{i,j,t}}} \right]^{2}.$$

Aggregate the economy-specific index ($\widetilde{\phi}_{j,t}$) over time to obtain the generalised index based on the information from the reporting economy i. In order to control for long-lasting, multiple detections of counterfeiting activity, apply again the c.e.s. methodology[55], *i.e.*

$$\phi_{j} \equiv \left[\sum_{t} \sqrt{\widetilde{\phi}_{j,t}} \right]^{2}$$

At this stage a preliminary, economy-specific index is obtained. By normalising the preliminary index ($\max_{j} \phi^{k}_{j} \equiv 1000$) and then taking logs, the i-specific TRIC is obtained, *i.e.*:

$$TRIC_{i,j} \equiv \log\left(\frac{\phi_{i,j}}{\max_{j} \phi_{i,j}} \cdot 1000 \right)$$

---

53.   For Japan, Germany and New Zealand, the industry-specific weights are obtained from the aggregated (world) dataset presented in Chapter 4.

54.   *Constant Elasticity of Substitution.* Given the incomplete datasets, this step has been applied only with respect to the U.S.-based index. For other indices, a simple summation over k has been applied.

55.   Given the incomplete datasets, this step has been applied only with respect to the US and German indices. For the other indices, a simple summation over t has been applied.

The values for Japan-, Germany-, New Zealand- and U.S.-based TRICs are presented in table 5.A1.1.

Table 5.A1.1. TRIC$_i$ indices

TRIC - Germany		TRIC - Japan		TRIC - New Zealand		TRIC - USA	
Uzbekistan	3.000	Korea	3.000	Pakistan	3.000	Hong Kong, China	3.000
Estonia	2.792	China	2.875	Thailand	2.597	China	2.988
Lithuania	2.676	Hong Kong, China	2.286	Hong Kong, China	2.097	South Africa	2.622
U.A.E..	2.593	Philippines	1.838	Indonesia	2.089	Malaysia	2.475
Chinese Taipei	2.364	Thailand	1.126	China	2.013	Russia	2.410
Malaysia	2.350	Malaysia	0.797	Korea	1.829	Viet Nam	2.385
Hong Kong, China	2.262	Italy	0.785	Malaysia	1.358	Korea	2.188
Singapore	2.175	Indonesia	0.474	Singapore	1.072	Pakistan	2.142
Philippines	2.122	USA	0.339			Singapore	1.917
China	1.813	Singapore	0.011			U.A.E..	1.855
Viet Nam	1.650					Panama	1.584
Ukraine	1.646					Philippines	1.520
Thailand	1.627					Netherlands	1.166
Korea	1.576					Chinese Taipei	0.982
Poland	1.464					India	0.834
Turkey	1.430					Jordan	0.764
Bulgaria	1.383					Italy	0.759
Pakistan	1.325					Thailand	0.604
Hungary	1.006					Bahamas	0.570
USA	0.563					Guatemala	0.526
Finland	0.010					Turkey	0.442
						Germany	0.365
						Mexico	0.138
						France	0.108
						Israel	0.106
						Canada	0.029
						Japan	0.007
						Saudi Arabia	0.001
						Brazil	0.001

Step 2: Calculating the Aggregated Trade-Related Index of Counterfeiting (ATRIC)

To calculate the aggregated index, create the weights for every economy i, for which the TRIC$_i$ index is available. Take economy i's share of total world imports, denoted as ω_i, as a proxy for i's importance in international trade and global economy. [56] The Aggregated TRIC then becomes:

$$A - TRIC_j \equiv \sum_i \frac{\omega_i}{\Sigma_i \omega_i} \phi_{i,j}$$

Table 5.A1.2 presents the list of significant exporters of counterfeit products with their corresponding values in the ATRIC index.

---

56.   In order to avoid double counting, set $\omega_i = 0$ if $i = j$.

Table 5.A1.2. ATRIC[57]

A - TRIC	
China	3.000
Hong Kong, China	2.957
Korea	2.580
South Africa	2.539
Malaysia	2.454
Russia	2.328
Vietnam	2.318
Uzbekistan	2.209
Pakistan	2.116
United Arab Emirates	2.087
Estonia	2.002
Singapore	1.966
Lithuania	1.887
Philippines	1.815
Chinese Taipei	1.654
Panama	1.504
Thailand	1.257
Netherlands	1.090
Ukraine	0.900
Turkey	0.821
Italy	0.791
India	0.765
Poland	0.742
Jordan	0.697
Bulgaria	0.674
Bahamas	0.511
Indonesia	0.477
Guatemala	0.470
Hungary	0.392
Germany	0.320
USA	0.235
Mexico	0.117
France	0.091
Israel	0.089
Canada	0.024
Japan	0.005
Finland	0.002
Saudi Arabia	0.001
Brazil	0.001

57. The ATRIC index presented above has been created as a tool to assess the macroeconomic effects of counterfeiting and piracy on trade and FDI. The ATRIC index is based on seizure statistics from four economies. This index does not present an economy's global ranking in the proportion of seized counterfeit or pirated goods.

Annex 5.A2

ANALYSIS OF THE RELATIONSHIP BETWEEN COUNTERFEITING, PIRACY AND TRADE

The first section of this annex presents the results for the estimation of the effects of counterfeiting and piracy on the structure of trade for a given economy. The results of a number of regressions are presented in Table 5.A2.1. The dependant variable (column "Sector") is the share of a given HS category in total exports from a given economy. The correlation coefficients between the dependent variables and the explanatory variable (the $ATRIC_j$ index) are reported in column 2. The following columns present the relevant OLS linear coefficients, standard deviations and the significance levels.

Table 5.A2.1. Dependant variables: Share of products within given categories in total exports from a given economy

Sector (HS Code)	Correlation	Coefficient	St. error	P > t
Pharmaceutical Products (30)	− 0.297	− $2.15 \cdot 10^{-5}$	− $1.14 \cdot 10^{-5}$	0.066
Products of cereals, flour etc. (19)	− 0.255	− $2.74 \cdot 10^{-6}$	− $1.70 \cdot 10^{-6}$	0.116
Misc. edible preparations (21)	− 0.250	− $2.19 \cdot 10^{-6}$	− $1.39 \cdot 10^{-6}$	0.124
Edible meat (2)	− 0.238	− $8.05 \cdot 10^{-6}$	− $5.40 \cdot 10^{-6}$	0.144
Cosmetics, perfumery, toilet prep. (33)	− 0.218	− $4.49 \cdot 10^{-6}$	− $3.31 \cdot 10^{-6}$	0.182

Observations: 39

The remaining section of this annex presents the results for the estimation of the effects of counterfeiting and piracy on the volume of United States imports of medicines. The results of the regression based on the gravity analysis are presented in Table 5.A2.2. The dependant variable is the volume of imports of pharmaceuticals (defined by the category 30 of the HS classification system) by the United States. Given the multiplicative form of the gravity equation, the controls (population size and the GDP per capita) are in logs. The columns show the relevant OLS linear coefficients, standard deviations and the significance levels.

Table 5.A2.2. Dependant variables: Imports of pharmaceuticals (HS 30) by the United States.

	Coefficient	St. error	P>t
TRIC - US	−0.807*	0.474	0.09
Population size	0.731***	0.143	0.00
GDP	2.744***	0.404	0.00
R^2	0.43		
Observations	49		

Annex 5.A3

THE RELATIONSHIP BETWEEN IPR AND TRADE: A REVIEW OF STUDIES

This annex presents the existing studies on the relationship between intellectual property rights (IPR) and trade.

The studies on the effects of IPR protection on trade were pioneered by Maskus and Penubarti (1995). Covering 28 manufacturing-type sectors in 1984, they use trade data from 22 OECD economies involving 71 destination economies. The IPR measure follows that of Rapp and Rozek (1990) and thus relates to the strength of patent protection. Maskus and Penubarti find that stronger patent protection has a positive and significant impact on bilateral imports for both small and large developing economies, with the strength of impact being more pronounced in the larger economies. From their results, however, it appears that trade is more influenced by patent protection in industries where patents are less important.

Primo Braga and Fink (1999) use a gravity model to study the effects of patent protection on bilateral trade flows. They use data for non-fuel and high-technology trade in 1989 over an 89x88 economy matrix. The gravity model follows a standard setup in which trade that flows from economy i to j depends on the GDP and population of both economies, the geographical distance between the two, a dummy to indicate whether a common border is shared, and a dummy that indicates if languages are the same. Dummy variables for preferential agreements (*e.g.* the EU, NAFTA, ASEAN) are also included.

To study how IPR affects bilateral trade flows, Primo Braga and Fink use an IPR index developed by Ginarte and Park (1997) and look specifically at how IPR affect the imports into economies. For non-energy trade flows, Primo Braga and Fink find that strong IPR has a positive significant effect on the probability that two economies will trade with one another (both imports and exports), and a positive significant effect on bilateral trade flows. For high-technology trade, however, stronger IPR is associated with a negative significant probability of trade between economies. The direct effect on high-tech imports is also negative, albeit insignificant. Since one would expect the role of IPR to be bigger on high-tech trade, the authors note that this rather surprising result could suggest that stronger market power may offset the positive market expansion caused by stronger IPR, and that stronger IPR may cause high-tech firms increasingly to serve foreign markets through FDI. Moreover, the omission of tariff and non-tariff barrier variables may have biased the results. As such, there seem to be a trade-off between the IPR related market expansion, and the monopolistic firm behaviour that strong IPR may motivate.

The approach presented by Maskus and Penubarti (1995) has been further extended by Smith (1999 and 2001) with a focus on international flows from and to the US. Smith (1999) uses the bilateral trade gravity – type equations with a control for trade distortions related to patent regimes, expressed by the Rapp and Rozek (1990) index. The main conclusion of this study is that weak-patent regimes are a significant obstacle for U.S. exports, but only when there is a threat of imitation in the partner economy. Smith (2001) presents an extended analysis of the relationship between exports and U.S affiliate sales and licenses. Consequently, the study considers not only the effect of a patent regime on the intensity of a given flow but also the decision about the type given flow (trade, affiliate sale or licensing). The degree of patent protection is expressed with the Ginarte and Park (1997) index of patent protection. Using a similar gravity–like approach leads to the conclusion that stronger patents increase US affiliate sales and licenses, especially in economies with strong imitative abilities.

Annex 5.A4

ANALYSIS OF THE RELATIONSHIP BETWEEN COUNTERFEITING, PIRACY AND FOREIGN DIRECT INVESTMENT

This annex presents detailed results for the estimation of the effects of counterfeiting and piracy on flows of foreign direct investment (FDI). To do so, a number of regressions are run, with the volume of inflowing FDI to an economy as the explanatory variable. The dependant variable (FDI_i) is the FDI inflow to a given economy i (in millions of USD) from three source economies, which are among the biggest sources of foreign direct investments: Germany, Japan and the United States. Given that the construction of the ATRIC index relies on the dataset provided by the customs of these economies, they seem to be particularly suitable for analysing the effects of counterfeiting on FDI.

The openness rank of the receiving economy and its size (in terms of population) are used as control variables. The openness measure is the ratio of GDP per capita to total trade, which proxies the degree to which a given economy is engaged in multiple processes of globalisation and its orientation towards foreign markets. This measure should be helpful in explaining incoming FDI flows. Given that openness can be expressed in current or constant prices, both measures are checked for independently. The size of the economy is meant to rule out the scale effect. Values for both rank of openness and size of the economy are taken from Heston, Summers and Aten (2006). The results of the OLS regressions are presented in Tables 5.A4.1 and 5.A4.2.

Table 5.A4.1. Dependant variable: FDI inflows from Germany, Japan and the US

	Coefficient	St. error	P>t
A-TRIC	-394.59 *	225.41	0.092
Population size	0.0041	0.0024	0.102
Openness in current prices	19.46 ***	6.923	0.009

Observations: 28

Table 5.A4.2. Dependant variable: FDI inflows from Germany, Japan and the US

	Coefficient	St. error	P>t
A-TRIC	-384.09 *	222.72	0.097
Population size	0.0041	0.0024	0.107
Openness in constant prices	18.63 ***	6.575	0.009

Observations: 28

The regression yields the following results: The linear coefficient of TRIC is negative and statistically significant at the 10% level. This means that there is a 90% probability that a higher rank for counterfeiting translates into smaller FDI flows to a given economy from Germany, Japan and the United States.

Annex 5.A5

EFFECTS OF COUNTERFEITING AND PIRACY ON PROFITABILITY: A REVIEW OF STUDIES

This annex outlines existing studies that document the effects of counterfeiting and piracy on rights holders.

Feinberg and Rousslang (1990) were among the first to produce comprehensive estimates of profit losses due to infringements of trademarks, copyrights and patents. The basis of the study was a company survey conducted in 1986 by the US International Trade Commission. Using simulation techniques, the study estimated total profits lost due to counterfeiting at USD 2.1 billion, or 1.8% of worldwide sales. There is nevertheless considerable variation across industries, with the entertainment industry experiencing the highest level of lost profits, while consumers gained USD1.9 billion. Profits for infringers were lower than the losses for legitimate producers, but varied significantly among sectors. It should be noted that these values depend crucially on how competing counterfeited products affect the prices of legitimate producers. The calculation requires good information on supply and price elasticities, which are difficult parameters to estimate. Also, the quality of counterfeit products is not taken into account, nor are the health- and safety-related costs that consumers could incur in purchasing counterfeit and pirated products. Substandard products could significantly diminish any consumer benefits. Finally, the model is a partial equilibrium model and thus gives estimates for static welfare changes only. Dynamic effects, such as the effects on investment from infringements, are therefore not considered.

A study commissioned by the International Trademark Association (INTA, 1998) estimated how counterfeiting affected revenues for trademark owners in the apparel and footwear industries. The study, which was conducted by Wharton Economic Forecasting Associates (WEFA), follows a market demand model under which consumer demand is estimated separately for both industries. As in the Feinberg and Rousslang study, it is assumed that the availability of counterfeit goods reduces the market for legitimate goods by an equal amount at all prices (*i.e.* results in a residual market), which inflicts costs on legitimate producers in terms of lost sales. The impact is thus calculated by comparing sales that would have occurred if counterfeit goods were not present, with actual sales. The actual level of counterfeiting is estimated based on the degree of trademark protection, which is assumed to be related to the industry revenues. The INTA study concludes that, across all economies, average sales losses for the 10 firms covered were 22% (+/- 4%), with a corresponding value of USD 2 billion (1995 prices). Even though the approach taken in the study makes no direct assumptions as to the level of actual counterfeiting, it relies on two other assumptions that could be critical. The first is the fact that counterfeiting affects legitimate market demand equally, regardless of the price of genuine products. The second is the assumption of a consistent relationship between the trademark protection variable and actual counterfeiting magnitude. Also of note is the fact that the coefficient on trademark protection was found to be insignificant over the period 1992-1995 when using the full model.

The Centre for Economic and Business Research (CEBR, 2000) analysed the effects of counterfeiting on revenues and profits in the four industries covering clothing and footwear, perfumes and cosmetics, toys and sports equipment, and pharmaceuticals. The general approach is similar to that of the previous two studies in the sense that impact is measured by comparing actual market estimates with those of a simulated "counterfeit-free" market. However, instead of relying entirely on product demand estimates as in INTA (1998), CEBR specifies and estimates the legitimate demand and supply for each industry.[58] Given these estimates, industry revenues in a counterfeit-free market situation are assessed assuming that the amount of counterfeit goods is transferred to the legitimate industry on a one-to-one basis. To do so, CEBR uses information on the likely level of counterfeiting in each industry obtained from the Anti-Counterfeiting Group in the UK, and from the Association des Industries de Marque (AIM) for the rest of the EU. The difference between the revenue estimates stemming from the counterfeit-free market versus those of the actual market denotes the loss of revenues due to counterfeiting. Given that genuine and counterfeit goods are not necessarily perfect substitutes, these revenue losses are likely to be exaggerated. To take this into account, CEBR adjusts the estimated losses according to the degree of substitution indicated by consumer surveys. Applying marginal profitability ratios across the aggregated revenue losses suffered by each industry in the EU, CEBR also estimated the impact of counterfeiting on industry profits (see Table 5.A5.1).

Table 5.A5.1. Annual revenue and profit losses due to counterfeiting, as estimated by CEBR (2000)

	Annual lost revenues		Annual lost profits
	Percent of total revenue	Millions of EUR	Millions of EUR
Clothing and footwear	3.2	7,581	1,266
Perfume and toiletries	7.2	3,017	555
Torys and sports goods	11.5	3,731	627
Pharmaceuticals	5.8	1,554	292
Total		**15,883**	**2,740**

Note: Lost revenues and profits in EUR millions (1998 prices).

Source: CEBR (2000).

Based on the estimates of counterfeiting and piracy magnitudes provided by BSA for business software, ESA for entertainment software, IFPI for recorded music, and MPA for motion pictures, the respective industry associations provide estimates of impact effects (see Table 5.A1.2).

. Initially, the slopes of the demand and supply curves are estimated for each industry by regressing data on actual sales volume on total disposable income and an overall retail price index for legitimate demand, and on an index of industry costs for legitimate supply. Relating demand and supply, the two regression equations jointly include the retail price index of the industry by which the slopes of the two curves are estimated. When the slope estimates are obtained, the model is calibrated, or fitted, to data on sales volumes and prices over 1995-1998, in order to estimate the curve intercepts or constants. From this, the actual market demand and supply model emerges, in which counterfeit goods are present, and industry revenues can be estimated.

Table 5.A5.2. Impact measures for business software and recorded music

Industry	Revenue losses 2004 Millions of $US						
	Global	European Union	Rest of Europe	North America	Latin America	Asia Pacific	M. East/Africa
Business software *	**32,695**	12,151	2,313	7,549	1,546	7,897	1,239
- percent of sales	35	35	61	22	66	53	58
Entertainment software (US) **	**3,000**						
- percent of sales	n/a						
Motion pictures (US) ***	**3,000**						
- percent of sales	n/a						
Recorded music **	**4,600**						
- percent of sales	14						

Note: * Retail price base, ** Pirate price base, *** Wholesale price base. All figures based on hard-copy piracy rates. Figures for entertainment software and motion pictures are 'minimum quotes' and apply to losses incurred by US companies only.

Source: Based on BSA (business software), Deloitte (entertainment software and motion pictures), and IFPI (music).

Industry losses to the business software industry are calculated by using the known size of the legitimate market and using the piracy rate to derive the retail value of the software that was illegitimately acquired. Hence, BSA assumes a one-to-one relationship, or perfect substitutability, between pirated software and lost legitimate sales. This is a questionable assumption, and the figures should be treated with care.

The ESA takes a different approach in evaluating the impact of piracy on the entertainment software industry. Instead of calculating the retail value of the pirated copies, ESA estimates expenditures on pirated products. In effect, this approach corresponds to measuring the impact on legitimate revenues based on consumers' budgets. To obtain a broader picture of the situation, however, ESA also estimates the piracy market using wholesale prices as reported by game publishers.

The IFPI follows the same general approach as ESA in its estimate of the impact of piracy on the music industry, whereas the motion picture industry (MPA) bases its estimates of losses on wholesale prices. It has not been possible to obtain impact measures for the various OECD member economies except for the business software industry. The ESA publishes impact measures in the IIPA 'special 301' submission, but these generally cover economies outside the OECD area.

Based on music piracy data from 1994-1998 obtained from IFPI, Hui and Png (2003) analyse the effect of piracy rates on music sales in 28 economies. They estimate the impact of piracy on legitimate sales to be around 6.6%, which is significantly lower than the rate estimated by the industry. The estimates, however, could be understated given that legitimate prices probably would have been higher if there had been no music piracy.

The consumer surveys-based study by LEK Consulting, Inc. (2005) estimated what revenues the movie industry would have earned without piracy. The analysis distinguishes between digital and hard goods piracy and takes into account costs of piracy to domestic and worldwide companies. The LEK study reports the losses of MPAA member companies in 2005 amounted to USD 2.4 billion due to bootlegging and USD 1.4 billion due to illegal copying.

Chapter 6

IMPROVING INFORMATION AND ANALYSIS

Available information on counterfeiting and piracy falls far short of what is needed for robust analysis and for policymaking. This chapter therefore focuses on what could be done to improve and expand information on counterfeiting and piracy. The chapter also suggests how measurement techniques could be advanced in order to produce more accurate global and sector-specific estimates about the magnitude, scope and effects of infringements on economies. Finally, the chapter concludes that these three areas should receive priority: *1)* improving information that is available from enforcement activities (*i.e.* customs and related law enforcement agencies); *2)* developing a framework for collecting information on the effects that counterfeit and pirated products are having on the health and safety of consumers; and *3)* expanding the use of surveys to collect basic information from rights holders, consumers and governments.

Far more additional analysis can, and should, be done to improve understanding of the magnitude of counterfeiting and piracy and the effects economy-wide, as well as the impact on rights holders, consumers and governments. In carrying out such assessments, the assumptions underlying approaches should be clear, as should the economic arguments; transparency is key. Outcomes should be evaluated in terms of reasonableness and, wherever possible, be subjected to sensitivity analysis to determine how variations in key assumptions affect outcomes.

6.1. Development of information

Information on the magnitude, scope, effects and factors driving counterfeiting and piracy is critical to understanding the nature of the problems being faced and how the situation is evolving. Such information is essential in designing and implementing effective policies and measures to combat the illicit operations.

As discussed below, there is considerable scope for improving the quality and abundance of information on counterfeiting and piracy. To maximise its value and usability, it is crucial that information development be: *1)* systematic; *2)* comparable; and *3)* comprehensive. Moreover, to the extent possible, it should be made accessible to interested parties.

- *Systematic.* Assessments of developments and trends in counterfeiting and piracy require that data be collected regularly, over time.

- *Comparable.* Consistent data collection is essential for ensuring data comparability across companies, sectors and economies. The ability to carry out econometric analysis in this project was seriously limited due to the inconsistency of datasets among economies.

- *Comprehensive.* Efforts to develop basic information should be comprehensive, drawing on as many different points of measurement as possible. In developing information on magnitude and scope, for example, potential sources should include data that could be obtained at four stages: production, distribution, sales and consumption (Box 6.1).

Box 6.1. Potential sources of information on the magnitude and scope of counterfeiting and piracy

Development of information on magnitude and scope would preferably rely on multiple measurement points, including:

Production: Information on production can be pieced together from various sources, including factor inputs. If the production of a counterfeit product requires a specific input that is relatively easy to track or account for, information on its usage may facilitate estimation of the production of counterfeits. An example could be the use of writable CDs in the production of pirated music CDs. Other ways of gaining insight into counterfeit production involve information on legal actions against illegitimate producers, as well as information on raids, investigative work and on-site seizures.

Distribution: Information can also be developed while goods are in transit within countries, or when crossing national borders. Trans-border shipments are particularly promising as they are subject to inspection of Customs authorities in the receiving and/or sending country. In many cases, information collected by Customs authorities constitutes the only official instance that collects information on counterfeit and pirated items on a systematic basis.

Sales: The sales of counterfeit and pirated items refer to the actual transaction between sellers and final buyers. Information may be drawn from sampling exercises, *i.e.* by sample shopping in markets suspected of supplying infringing goods, from surveying end consumers, as well as from information on seizures from market raids. Other potential sources could be the tracking of counterfeit and pirate sales through Internet sites.

Consumption: Insight into counterfeiting and piracy is also possible by focusing on actual consumption, product circulation, or the exchange of infringing goods between consumers. Consumption may also be a good point for developing better information on sub-standard fakes that have been marketed, as long as consumers have become aware that the product is counterfeit.

6.1.1. Information on product infringement

Information on product infringement is an excellent source for establishing the scope of counterfeiting and piracy. As shown in Chapters 4 and 5, infringement data can furthermore be used for providing indirect measures of the magnitude and effects of counterfeiting and piracy. Unfortunately, the datasets that are currently available are inconsistent and incomplete.

The Customs Enforcement Network (CEN), a reporting framework developed by customs agencies through the World Customs Organization (WCO), offers one of the most promising ways forward for improving information on infringement. The framework establishes the parameters for reporting on seized/intercepted products (Box 6.2).

Box 6.2. Key elements of WCO reporting framework

- Detailed description of the products involved.
- Date of seizure/interception.
- Retail value of the product.
- Quantity of the product (number of items or weight, etc.).
- Type of IPR infringement (patent, trademark, copyright, etc.).
- Origin of product.
- Routing of product (from origin to destination).
- Type of concealment (if relevant); and
- Detection method.

Drawing exclusively on information from CEN, the WCO published its first global study on counterfeiting and piracy in 2006 (WCO, 2006). In this report, the WCO notes that higher emphasis on the importance of CEN has led to a significant increase in the usage of the system; however, many countries are still inactive in reporting.

With relatively few modifications, the framework could be transformed into a template that could be used by *1)* other law enforcement agencies to record IP crime, and *2)* by industry to compile related information. The WCO's Harmonised System, for example, provides a coded nomenclature for over 5 200 items; utilising this at the detailed, six-digit level would provide much needed specificity about the products being intercepted/seized.

More recent initiatives on data development include the building of an Interpol data-base[59] that feeds on information provided by private companies. This data are to be made available to law enforcement agencies worldwide in order to assist their investigations of intellectual property crime.

6.1.2. Information on health and safety effects

There are numerous reports on the adverse effects that counterfeit products can have on public health and safety. The reports, however, have limited scope. A more systematic and extensive approach for developing data in this area is therefore needed; this was highlighted at the first OECD/WIPO experts meeting on counterfeiting and piracy.

At that meeting, a system for developing information on counterfeit medicine was presented (Liang, 2005). Under a "Patient Safety Reporting System", patients, medical practitioners and suppliers would provide inputs. Reporting would thereby not be restricted to professionals and rights holders, but would include consumers. To facilitate reporting, it was recommended that provisions be available for supplying input by email, the Internet (via web-based forms), mail or fax. While the focus of the system was directed exclusively towards pharmaceuticals, it could be adapted more widely.

---

9.   www.interpol.int/Public/FinancialCrime/IntellectualProperty/Default.asp.

Another idea advanced by Forzley (2003) would be to build a better platform for general data development by providing a means for registering infringement-inflicted harm to consumers under public health disease classifications of unintentional injury. The first step in this direction would involve the introduction of codes for harm caused by counterfeit articles in the International Classification of Diseases (ICD). This should be followed by improvement of systems used to develop and monitor statistics on health and safety, concerning transportation, food, drinks, drugs and consumer products. These systems should register the infringement-inflicted accidents, injuries and deaths.

Some progress in collecting data on effects, in a more systematic fashion, is being made, particularly in the pharmaceuticals sector. An International Medical Products Anti-Counterfeiting Taskforce (IMPACT) [60] was recently created by the World Health Organization (WHO), which among other things, has the goal of developing accessible and reliable information on the nature and extent of the problem. The taskforce has simplified the process and tools for reporting counterfeit medicine, and data collection is now facilitated by the Rapid Alert System (RAS)[61], which is a web-based reporting platform accessible to any interested party.

6.1.3. Additional information, using surveys, sampling and economic experiments

Other types of information on counterfeiting and piracy could be developed using: *1)* surveys; *2)* sampling; and *3)* economic experiments.

6.1.3.1. Surveys

Surveys are a potentially rich source for developing various types of information. They can be conducted on consumers, rights holders, intermediate suppliers, governments and organisations, and they can used for gathering information on scope, magnitude and the effects of counterfeiting and piracy. They are also good tools for developing information on consumer attitudes and industry perceptions.

The strength of surveys is their flexibility, in the sense that they can be designed to provide information on a very wide range of factors -- both quantitative and qualitative -- while allowing for numerous controls (*e.g.* gender, age and/or income). However, they are sensitive to the way questions are constructed and rely on the willingness of respondents to provide accurate responses; this could be a concern as respondents might be reluctant to report fully on unlawful behaviour. Moreover, industry might be unwilling to share information that might harm their commercial interests. Surveys must therefore be well-designed and targeted in a manner that provides information on those characteristics that are key to the analysis. A clearly defined and measurable research objective is thus critical.

To enhance their value, surveys should be standardised to the highest extent possible. The standardisation would facilitate cross-country and cross-sector analysis. Finally, repeating surveys periodically would provide opportunities for following developments over time.

---

60.   www.who.int/medicines/services/counterfeit/en/

61.   http://218.111.249.28/ras/default.asp

6.1.3.2. Consumer surveys

Consumer surveys can be used to develop information on the experience that consumers have had with counterfeit/pirated products and the effects, whether they purchased them knowingly or were deceived. Such surveys also provide a means to develop insights into: *1)* the types, frequency and quantity of counterfeit/pirated products that consumers have knowingly purchased; *2)* the factors driving the purchases; and *3)* the means through which the products were purchased. Finally, consumer surveys can also be used to develop information on consumer attitudes and perceptions.

6.1.3.3. Surveys of rights holders

Surveys of rights holders can be used to develop information on: *1)* the counterfeiting/piracy situation overall, as well as in different product markets; *2)* the effects that counterfeiting and piracy have on sales, investment, costs, brand value, etc.; *3)* the actions that industry is taking to combat the counterfeiting and piracy; and *4)* the counterfeiting/piracy situation in different economies.

6.1.3.4. Surveys of governments

Surveys of governments can similarly serve as a tool through which information on the counterfeiting/piracy situation can be developed. Conducted at regular intervals, they can provide insights into how policies and programmes are evolving, and provide a means for tracking the effectiveness of those policies and programmes in the economies concerned. Eventually, such surveys could provide inputs that can be used as a basis for strengthening international dialogue. They could also serve as a catalyst for improving domestic and international polices.

6.1.4. Sampling

Targeted or random testing of whether purchased products are infringing is in theory one of the best techniques one can apply to obtain accurate magnitude measures of counterfeiting and piracy. This technique focuses on the points of sale, and is therefore not consumption orientated; rather, it is oriented towards distribution and general product availability. As such, it is particularly useful for developing information on product areas where consumer awareness is low, or where there are no (or limited) means for validating survey results.

Like surveys, sampling techniques have limitations. In order to yield valid estimates, sampling must be undertaken for a specific product category. Furthermore, the sampling must be done from a representative set of sales/distribution points. If this cannot be obtained, the results will be biased. Prior information about the counterfeit and pirate markets is therefore beneficial. Sampling just a few products is an extensive task, and expanding the scope of the analysis makes the process time-consuming and costly.

Besides giving an indication of product infringement availability, sample results can be used for estimating total demand for the infringing goods concerned. This can be done by applying the counterfeit/pirate sampling rate to the actual sales registered, or estimated, for each relevant sales/distribution point. Examples of studies applying direct-sampling methodologies include MPA's earlier measures of movie piracy (see IACC,

2005), and studies of counterfeit drugs in Myanmar and Vietnam (WHO, 1999) and China (Clark, 2003).

6.1.5. Economic experiments

An economic experiment can be seen as a combination of a classical survey and a laboratory experiment. The experimental part arises from the fact that the "survey" includes some form of incentive schemes[62] designed to reveal the preferences and/or behavioural traits of participants. In relation to counterfeiting and piracy, such mechanisms can be useful for revealing how participants in the experiment value fake vs. genuine goods; the results can be used to help determine what consumers are willing to pay for various counterfeit and pirated items under different circumstances.

The experiments are performed in order to identify individual preferences under controlled laboratory conditions. During an experiment, participants are essentially tested to determine under what conditions they would buy a counterfeit/pirated product.

Concerning the design of economic experiments, key elements are:

- *Transparency*. Instructions and rules must be simple, easy and clear.

- *No deception*. Participants should not be deceived by the person who conducts the experiment.

- *Context-independence*. The environment in which the experiment takes place should be as neutral as possible to avoid possible framing of the participants.

The information developed through such experiments can be used to estimate or predict reactions to changes in demand for a genuine good under different rates of piracy. Knowledge of such relationships is critical when analysing the effects of counterfeiting and piracy on rights holders but difficult to develop using traditional economic and econometric tools.

6.2. Enhancing the analysis

Far more analysis can, and should, be done to improve understanding of the magnitude of counterfeiting and piracy and effects economy-wide, as well as the impact on rights holders, consumers and governments. Opportunities for doing so are particularly promising at the sectoral level. Such analysis is critical for developing effective policies and programmes for combating counterfeiting and piracy.

The approaches that are used to carry out such analysis should adhere to a number of key principles: *1)* assumptions should be spelled out; *2)* economic arguments should be clearly elaborated; *3)* to the extent possible, outcomes should be tested for reasonableness, using alternative estimation approaches; *4)* sensitivity analysis should be carried out to provide indications of potential variability of the results; and *5)* details on the approaches used should be shared with interested parties, with a view towards expanding and improving future analysis.

---

62.   These schemes, or procedures, often referred to as BDM, have been pioneered by Becker, De-Groot, and Marschak (1964) and have been further developed along with their application in modern economics. See Kagel and Roth (1995) for general reference on experimental economics.

6.2.1. Assessment of drivers

As indicated in Chapter 2, a product's characteristics play an important role in determining the extent to which it is produced and consumed in primary and/or secondary markets. Similarly, institutional factors play an important role in determining the extent to which production and consumption take place in different economies. Carrying out assessments of the factors (or drivers), even on a qualitative, non-empirical basis, can generate insights into the counterfeiting/piracy situation in different products and in different economies. In the case of product-specific assessments, results can: *1)* suggest how approaches to measuring magnitude should be structured; and *2)* indicate areas where efforts to combat counterfeiting and piracy should be focused. In the case of economy assessments, results can help to identify ways to strengthen the effectiveness of policies for combating counterfeiting and piracy.

6.2.2. Sectoral analysis – estimating magnitude and effects

As indicated earlier, opportunities for estimating the magnitude of counterfeiting and piracy are greater at the firm- and/or sectoral level than they are at the overall level; this is also the case with respect to effects. While insights can be developed through improved information, there are also possibilities for developing economic models to further enhance analysis. Such models have to be constructed taking the characteristics of the sectors concerned into account.

6.2.3. Estimating magnitude

There are two basic approaches that can be employed to estimate magnitude using models: direct and indirect.

6.2.3.1. Direct approach

A simple technique of assessing the magnitude of counterfeiting and piracy in a given sector is the direct estimation of production and/or consumption of a given infringing product.

This estimation exercise relies on information developed on product infringements, *e.g.* in the form of confiscated counterfeited products, or results from sampling techniques. In essence, this information is treated as a proxy of the infringement activity and can, given certain conditions, be extended to the entire population in order to produce an estimate of the total magnitude. An example of this type of analysis is presented in the MPA study that estimates the piracy rate in the movie industry (see IACC, 2005).

6.2.3.2. Indirect approach

The indirect approach of assessing the magnitude of counterfeiting and piracy requires the estimation of total consumption (production) of a given good, including both genuine and infringing items, and the measurement of the legitimate consumption (production). The difference between the two then provides an indication of the consumption (production) of counterfeit and pirated products. The indirect analysis has already been applied in a number of empirical studies, including the work carried out by the software industry (*e.g.* IDC-BSA, 2003).

The fundamental requirement for conducting an indirect analysis is the availability of information that would permit: *1)* estimating the total market consumption (production); and *2)* determining the legitimate consumption (production).

Actual estimation would typically rely on information specific to the industry, as well as economy-specific inputs. Two main methods of the indirect approach are presented in Annex 6.A1: the first one uses production as an entry-point (input/output estimation); and the second uses consumption (product-dependent estimation).

6.2.3.3. Estimating effects

Quantification of the effects of counterfeiting and piracy using economic models is a complex exercise. Not only does it rely heavily on accurate indications of the phenomenon's magnitude, but the effects may also take many different forms, some of which have very complex causation mechanisms. Generally, the more complex the effects are, the larger is the need for a strong data foundation in order to quantify the effects.

For rights holders, lost sales are among the principal effects and on which most research has been carried out. In order to focus analyses of the effects on sales, it is important to distinguish those sales that are lost on the primary market from those that are lost on the secondary market.

Primary market: Counterfeit and pirated goods sold on primary markets are, by definition, deceptive. Because consumers are deceived, and therefore would be as likely to obtain a genuine product rather than a fake, this implies that losses reach their potential maximum. It also means that certain measurement tools, such as consumer surveys, are not relevant for effects analysis. Counterfeiting and piracy operating in primary markets could possibly also exhibit similarities across sectors and draw legitimate rights holders together who have no connection other than facing principal threats to their primary markets. From this perspective, there can be significant benefits derived from sharing information on counterfeiting and pirate activities, even between companies that operate in different sectors.

Secondary market: The quantification of counterfeiting and piracy in secondary markets seems less challenging than for the more "clandestine" primary market. Because consumers knowingly purchase counterfeit and pirated products, demand based techniques are useful. It also becomes critical to distinguish between consumers who would have brought the genuine product but switched to low-priced fakes, and those who purchase an infringing product only because it is cheap and who would not have purchased the higher-priced genuine product otherwise.[63] Concerning the secondary market, information may be gained from a variety of sources including consumer surveys, experiments, sampling exercises, hedonic regressions, as well as product-dependent estimation.

---

63.   For example, in the absence of counterfeiting, demand for a USD 5 000 deluxe branded watch might be 100. Sales of a newly introduced copy at USD 5 might be 1 000. In this case, the sales lost because of counterfeiting would range from 0 (if no one switched from the genuine to the fake) to 100, if all consumers opted for the lower-priced infringing goods.

References

Becker, G.M., DeGroot, M.H. and J. Marschak (1964), "Measuring utility by a single-response sequential method", *Behavioral Science,* 9, pp. 226–232.

Clark, D. J. (2003), *Product Counterfeiting in China and One American Company's Response: A Case Study*, Secretary of Defense Corporate Fellows Program.

Forzley, M. (2003), *Counterfeit Goods and the Public's Health and Safety*, International Intellectual Property Institute.

International Anti-Counterfeiting Coalition Inc. (IACC) (2005), "Submission of the International Anti-Counterfeiting Coalition, Inc. to the United States Trade Representatives: Special 301 Recommendations", IACC, Washington D.C.

IDC-BSA (2003), *Expanding Global Economies: The Benefits of Reducing Software Piracy*, IDC.

Kagel, J. H., and A. E. Roth (1995), *The Handbook of Experimental Economics*, Princeton University Press, Princeton, NJ.

Liang, B. (2005), "Measuring the Impact of Counterfeit Drugs: Applying the Patient Safety Reporting System Approach", Presentation at OECD/WIPO Meeting on Measurement of Counterfeiting and Piracy, 17-18 October.

WCO (2006), *Customs and Counterfeiting 2004*, World Customs Organization, Brussels.

WHO (1999), *Counterfeit and Substandard Drugs in Myanmar and Viet Nam*, World Health Organization, Geneva.

Annex 6.A1

INDIRECT ESTIMATION OF COUNTERFEITING AND PIRACY WITHIN A GIVEN INDUSTRY

This annex presents two methods for indirectly estimating the magnitude and scope of counterfeiting and piracy in a given industry: *1)* input/output estimation; and *2)* product-dependent estimation.

Input-output estimation

The input/output estimation is a general method that could be helpful in estimating the potential supply of counterfeit production in a given industry. Broadly speaking, following this method the true output of a factory, firm or a sector is estimated and then compared to the output that is actually registered. A detected discrepancy between what is registered and what is estimated can be perceived as a proxy for counterfeit production.

Depending on the types of input that are used as instruments, one can distinguish between two general approaches: the direct and the indirect approach.

The direct input/output estimating approach relies on information on the usage of intermediate input(s) that are key for producing the product concerned. This could be, for example, a specific natural resource, a given technical component or some specialised packaging material, etc. Because production of the final product depends strictly on the quantity of the intermediate production factor, the estimates of final output should be quite robust.

The indirect input/output estimation technique is a generalisation of the direct technique. The difference is that the indirect method does not rely on one particular instrument, *i.e.* information on the usage of a key input factor, but uses a generalised set of inputs as a proxy. The generalised set of such inputs could include units of physical capital, material factor inputs, labour or energy. The economy and industry specific data on aggregated productivities, as well as economy-specific counterfeiting indices, can be applied as additional controls.

Once the output of the sector has been estimated, it is compared to the registered output of the factory. Positive discrepancies are indicatory of counterfeit and/or pirated production activities. There are few examples of actual applications of the input/output approach; however, the music industry seems to be basing some of their piracy estimates on the production of blank optical discs. It is nevertheless uncertain how this is being done; this, and other concerns, are discussed in the audio-visual sector study in this report (see Part III).

Product-dependant estimation

The product-dependent estimation is a technique that allows for estimating total demand for a given good in a given economy. Similarly to the input/output method, measures of counterfeiting and piracy are obtained by comparing the predicted demand with data on actually registered demand; the discrepancy between the two is a proxy for the counterfeit market. Also, the estimation procedure should rely on a particular set of instruments, of which the choice must be sector- and economy-specific. The analysis should furthermore be complemented with extensive use of controls. Ideally, the instruments would be goods, or phenomena that are complementary with, or necessary for, the consumption or usage of the product concerned. The following three examples illustrate potential use of this method.

The first example concerns the market for automotive spare parts. Applying econometric techniques to historical data on car sales, allows for estimating the potential demand for automotive spare parts in a given economy. The controls to be considered in the estimation of such demand are obviously subject to discussion, and should involve experts in the area; yet, one could consider including data on the quality of roads (proxied, for example, by the density of highways and/or private and public road-maintenance budgets), average number of accidents, climate, average age of car stock, etc. In addition, some macroeconomic, economy-specific indicators can be used to determine the income-driven part of demand.

A second example could be that of software piracy. In this case, historical data on sales of hardware, *i.e.* computers, can be used to proxy the total demand for software in a given economy. Controls could include individual consumer characteristics, such as educational background, income, etc. Moreover, in order to control for types of commercial use of different software packages, one could apply industry specific controls, *i.e.* industry structure, average size of companies, etc. BSA is an example of an industry association that uses such a methodology for providing figures on software piracy.

The last example considers the demand for a given pharmaceutical product. An instrument that could be successfully applied in such a case could be data on the illness, which the pharmaceutical product seeks to alleviate, or it could be statistics on prescriptions for the medicine, if such data existed. As far as controls are concerned, one would need to consider consumption of possible and potential substitutes, income, medical subsidies and insurances, etc.

Part II

COMBATING COUNTERFEITING AND PIRACY

Chapter 7

AN OVERVIEW OF GOVERNMENT AND INDUSTRY INITIATIVES

Governments and industry have been active in combating counterfeiting and piracy on a number of fronts, both independently and, equally importantly, with each other. In addition to efforts undertaken in a national context, governments have been working through multilateral institutions and on a bilateral and regional basis to address issues. Industry has also been active, nationally and internationally, both on a sectoral and cross-sectoral basis. This chapter provides an overview and assessment of the initiatives that have been taken, and Annex 7.A2 presents the situation in 15 different economies, in greater detail.

7.1. Intergovernmental initiatives

Intergovernmental initiatives have included the establishment of a comprehensive multilateral legal framework within the World Trade Organization (WTO), as well as co-operation in a number of specific fields (Table 1.1). On the enforcement front, for example, the World Intellectual Property Organization (WIPO), Interpol and the World Customs Organization have all developed specific programmes to improve enforcement of IPRs. In the area of health, the World Health Organization (WHO) is supporting specific initiatives to undermine the counterfeiting of medicines. Issues have also been addressed within the G8, and as part of a Global Congress that several multilateral institutions have organised with industry support.

7.1.1. Multilateral legal framework

As indicated above, the basic multilateral rules governing IPR are established in the WTO's TRIPS Agreement. The Agreement covers four broad issues:

- How basic principles of the trading system and other international intellectual property agreements should be applied.

- How adequate protection to intellectual property rights should be given.

- How countries should enforce those rights adequately in their own territories.

- How disputes on intellectual property between members of the WTO should be settled.

Table 7.1. Summary of intergovernmental IPR activities

Organisation	Principal activities related to counterfeiting and piracy
G8	Established experts group to examine ways to strengthen efforts to combat counterfeiting and piracy. Internet: www.fco.gov.uk/Files/kfile/PostG8_Gleneagles_CounterfeitingandPiracy.pdf en.g8russia.ru/docs/15.html
Global Congress	The Global Congresses on Combating Counterfeiting and Piracy bring together senior officials from government, international organisations and the private sector to enhance international co-ordination and co-operation and seek more effective solutions to combat counterfeiting and piracy. The Congress is organised by Interpol, WCO and WIPO, with the support of industry (GBLAAC, INTA, ICC and ISMA)*. Internet: www.ccapcongress.net
Interpol	Supports law enforcement agencies worldwide to combat IP crime through an IP Crime Programme. Established government/industry Intellectual Property Crime Action Group (IIPCAG) to advise and assist with initiatives. Internet: interpol.int/Public/FinancialCrime/IntellectualProperty/Default.asp
WCO	Provides training and technical support for governments to combat trade in counterfeit and pirated products. Works with governments and industry to address enforcement issues through information exchanges, and guidelines for effective enforcement. Established government/industry IPR Strategic Group to support initiatives. Internet: www.wcoipr.org
WHO	Engaged in building co-ordinated networks to combat counterfeit medicines around the globe. Established government/industry International Medical Products Anti-Counterfeiting Taskforce (IMPACT) to support efforts. Published guidelines for government measures to combat counterfeit medicines. Internet: www.who.int/medicines/services/counterfeit/en/index.html
WIPO	Oversees certain IP treaties and conventions containing enforcement provisions; provides technical enforcement support and training to governments. Established Advisory Committee on Enforcement (ACE) to support activities. Internet: www.wipo.int/enforcement/en
WTO	Oversees TRIPS agreement, which establishes a comprehensive multilateral legal framework governing IPR; agreement contains provisions for enforcement, consultation and dispute resolution. A TRIPS Council oversees operation of the agreement and government compliance. Internet: www.wto.org/english/tratop_e/TRIPS_e/TRIPS_e.htm

*Global Business Leaders Alliance Against Counterfeiting, International Trademark Association, International Chamber of Commerce (Business Action to Stop Counterfeiting and Piracy) and International Security Management Association.

With respect to enforcement, governments are generally obliged under the Agreement to ensure that intellectual property rights can be enforced under their laws, and that the penalties for infringement are sufficient to deter violations (WTO, 2006). Procedures must be fair and equitable, and not unnecessarily complicated or costly. They should not entail unreasonable time limits or unwarranted delays. Parties involved should be able to ask a court to review an administrative decision or to appeal a lower court's ruling.

In addition to general obligations, the Agreement includes rules for obtaining evidence, provisional measures, injunctions, damages and other penalties (Box 7.1). It indicates courts should have the right, under certain conditions, to order the disposal or destruction of pirated or counterfeit goods. It indicates that wilful trademark counterfeiting or copy-right piracy on a commercial scale should be subject to criminal prosecution and that border measures should be available to help prevent imports of counterfeit and pirated goods. Annex 1 elaborates further on the key provisions.

Box 7.1. Minimum standards set by TRIPS for IP enforcement

Civil proceedings: judicial instruments must be available to rights holders, such as injunctions, damages, evidence, right of information and provisional measures.

Criminal proceedings: members have to provide for criminal proceedings for commercial scale trademark and copyright infringement.

Border measures: measures to prevent the commercialisation of imported products that infringe trademarks and copyrights are required.

The TRIPS Agreement also contains provisions under which parties agree to consult with each other on matters relating to the agreement, including enforcement. Each member must supply information on the enforcement system (including laws and regulations, final judicial decisions and administrative rulings) in response to a written request from another member. These provisions have already been used by the United States, Switzerland and Japan in 2005 to inquire into the enforcement of IP rights in China. The Agreement also contains provisions for the adjudication of disputes.

7.1.2. Regional and bilateral agreements

In addition to the TRIPS Agreement, many regional and bilateral agreements contain provisions on IP; Annex 7.A1 provides further details on these agreements. In a substantial number of cases, the obligations contained in these agreements go beyond those contained in TRIPS, suggesting that there may be areas where the WTO disciplines could be strengthened (see below). These include expanding the scope of border measures, broadening the scope of civil and criminal remedies and expanding criminal provisions to cover a broader range of IP infringements. Further details on these, and other possible areas for strengthening the disciplines, are provided in Annex 7.1

7.2. National initiatives

Descriptions of the actions being taken to fight counterfeiting and piracy in a total of 15 OECD and non-OECD economies are contained in Annex 7.A2. The descriptions are based on information supplied by the respective economies and independent research carried out by the Secretariat[64]. A review of the situation suggests that in most of the areas examined economies have the mechanisms in place to adequately combat counterfeiting and piracy as their legal and regulatory framework are compliant with TRIPS. Civil procedures with remedies are available to rights holders, and there has been a general tendency to: *1)* increase damages available in case of IPR infringement; and *2)* to speed up the settling of cases. Many countries have also strengthened their criminal provisions by increasing prison terms and monetary fines. Enforcement, however, is still viewed by many as weak. A common criticism is that the resources devoted to IPR enforcement are insufficient and that those who engage in counterfeiting/piracy activities are not sufficiently penalised for their actions when they are caught.

---

4. It should be noted that the economy templates in Annex 7.A2 are brief overviews of the respective national IP protection regimes, but they have not been subject to review and comment by OECD members or other interested parties. These templates are not intended to be an assessment of the country's IP protection or enforcement systems or efforts to combat counterfeiting and piracy.

As resource challenges are likely to persist, governments may need to consider focusing enforcement activities on operations that will have the greatest impact. Disruption of counterfeiting/piracy activities at the points where infringement takes place is important: once items move into domestic or international trade, the chances for disrupting them are greatly reduced. As stopping infringing activities at the source is not always possible, efficient border enforcement procedures are also essential.

Raising awareness is an important aspect of combating counterfeiting and piracy and needs to be pursued vigorously. Consumers should be adequately informed about the growing threat that sub-standard counterfeit/pirated products pose to their health and safety, and consumers and counterfeiters/pirates should be aware about the legal consequences of infringing IPRs or knowingly purchasing infringing products. Raising awareness may also have beneficial effects on consumer attitudes and behaviour towards counterfeiting and piracy by making them more reluctant to purchase infringing products.

The section below presents a review of some of the measures taken by economies -- described in Annex 7.A2 -- to combat counterfeiting and piracy. The review was carried out using an analytical framework with eight key elements (see Box 7.2.), which could serve as a basis both for internal evaluation, as well as a point of departure for peer review.

7.2.1. Institutional organisation and co-ordination

A number of ministries and related government bodies are generally involved in administering and enforcing IPRs. Effective co-ordination appears to be the key to strengthening planning and enforcement. Most economies surveyed have promoted co-ordination, either by designating lead agencies, or by setting up special interagency working groups on IP protection. Japan, for example, has established a unit in the office of the Prime Minister to plan and oversee IP measures. France has created an inter-service working group that meets about three times a year to step up co-operation between administrations involved in the enforcement effort. Chinese Taipei has set up a task force for IP enforcement to review policies and improve communication. In China, a National Working Group on IP based at the Ministry of Commerce is responsible for the planning and co-ordination of IP protection. In some countries reviewed (Israel and Korea, for example), departments dealing with enforcement - mainly customs and police - have increased co-operation and intelligence-sharing through the exchange of databases.

7.2.2. Policy

A clear policy on IP enforcement that contains concrete objectives can provide the impetus needed to improve outcomes. Programmes in the countries reviewed have mainly aimed at strengthening legal and administrative structures and raising awareness. Since 2002, Japan has formulated an annual strategic programme for IP with identified priority areas. China's 2006 action plan summarises a range of initiatives in the areas of legislation, enforcement, training, education, international co-operation, awareness-raising and defines enforcement campaigns and crackdown operations.

Only some of the economies surveyed have established plans with detailed, measurable elements. In France for example, a 10-point government action plan adopted in 2004 has, amongst other things, set concrete enforcement targets for increasing seizures of counterfeit/pirated products at borders. In Brazil, work has been guided by a plan with 99 points for priority action.

7.2.3. Legal and regulatory framework

The legal and regulatory framework provides the parameters within which enforcement can be pursued. While the frameworks used by economies resemble each other in key respects, there are some differences. Under French criminal law, it is for example illegal to buy counterfeit goods, and the consumer of infringing products can be charged with a penalty. In the United Kingdom, a law allows the proceeds from IP crime to be recovered and used by enforcement agencies, thereby expanding the resources available to finance additional enforcement activities.

7.2.4. Enforcement

A good legal and regulatory framework is essential for combating counterfeiting and piracy, but it is not sufficient. Efforts devoted to combating counterfeiting and piracy on the ground are critical. Most of the economies surveyed have made enforcement a priority and have increased the resources devoted to it in recent years. In many countries, measures to address counterfeiting and piracy have been linked to efforts to fight organised crime.

Strengthening enforcement has involved organising well-publicised domestic enforcement operations aimed at disrupting counterfeiting/piracy activities. China, for example, organised a wide-ranging intensive enforcement campaign against criminal infringement of trademarks with raids of offices, warehouses and stores (*i.e.* the Mountain Eagle campaign). Brazil conducted several operations involving federal, state and municipal bodies at shopping centres and markets known for selling pirated products. The European Union launched two major joint customs multi-week operations to seize counterfeit goods in ports -- operation DAN in 2006 and operation FAKE in 2005.

Reinforced border measures are important to prevent the release of infringing goods into free circulation. A number of economies surveyed have adopted provisions allowing customs authorities, not only to check imports, but also infringing goods destined for exportation. This is for example the case in China, Korea and Chinese Taipei. Besides exports, European Union countries also control goods in transit and transhipment.

Governments have worked on strengthening the expertise of enforcement officials through the creation of specialised IP police/customs units and specialised IP courts. Korean customs, for example, have teams dealing especially with IPR enforcement. Chinese Taipei has an IP police, together with a unit specialised in identifying and dismantling optical disk operations that conduct illegal activities. Several economies, including Japan, China, the United Kingdom, Korea and Brazil have created specialised IP courts.

Many of the economies surveyed have also increased training. Chinese Taipei, for example has created a training academy for IP professionals, including judges, prosecutors, police officers or customs officials. Enforcement officials have been granted increasing powers in their enforcement activities: in a number of economies, police or customs can act upon their own initiative (*ex officio)* and are allowed to seize infringing goods without prior court order. The ease with which enforcement officials can act *ex officio* does, however, vary considerably among economies.

To increase the effectiveness of enforcement, economies like Korea and Chinese Taipei have set up reward mechanisms for informants and law enforcement personnel who have been active in seizing counterfeit products.

7.2.5. International co-operation

Counterfeiting and piracy is a global problem that needs to be addressed on a co-operative basis for best results. Most economies participate in international forums such as Interpol, WTO, WIPO and WCO. Some economies surveyed have also been active at the bilateral or regional level to exchange best practice and set common objectives in terms of IPR protection, or to provide training and engage in joint enforcement activities. France has created inter-ministerial bilateral committees with Italy and Russia to exchange best practice, set mutual annual targets and define common actions regarding IP protection. Brazil has been involved with Mercosur partners to strengthen IP protection through the adoption of a regional protection plan. In addition, it launched operation Jupiter-South America -- a cross-border police operation to target counterfeiting and piracy -- along with Paraguay and Argentina in 2004. In a joint 2004 summit, Japan, China and Korea agreed to increase dialogue and co-operation between patent offices. China, the European Union and the United States have established frameworks for regular consultation regarding IP issues.

7.2.6. Awareness

It is important for consumers, rights holders and government officials to: *1)* be aware of the counterfeiting and piracy problem; *2)* to understand what the effects are economy-wide, as well as on individual stakeholders; and *3)* to know what concerned parties can do to combat counterfeiting/piracy activities. A number of economies have developed far-reaching training and education programmes. In India, the government has set up an institute delivering training both to professionals and to the wider public. Chinese Taipei and the United Kingdom have introduced educational programmes on IP for schools.

Increasing awareness has also included the development of information through surveys. Japan, for example, has conducted detailed surveys to assess consumer awareness of counterfeiting and piracy and the adverse effects that the practices can have on rights holders. Finally, some economies have conducted media campaigns and prepared exhibitions to heighten awareness. Korea has organised an exhibition to help consumers distinguish counterfeit from genuine goods. France has launched annual wide-ranging media campaigns targeting consumers, using the press, radio and television, the Internet and information brochures. These awareness-raising efforts were operated in certain places: airports, beaches or during flights at times when consumers are most likely to buy infringing products. In some economies, governments have worked on publicising enforcement efforts. China has focused on coverage in the media. Brazil, for example, has organised the public destruction of seized goods.

7.2.7. Programme evaluation and measurement

To help monitor progress and respond to the changing nature of counterfeiting and piracy, policies and programmes need to be reviewed regularly. A number of governments have developed regular monitoring or reporting schemes and have published findings. These are important in helping to assess problem areas and evaluate progress. Economies such as Brazil, China, the United Kingdom and Korea, for example, prepare annual papers on IP protection and enforcement, while Chinese Taipei publishes quarterly reports and annual reviews.

Some economies, like Canada, have conducted special investigations -- Project Sham 2004 and Project Saffron 2000 -- to assess developments of IP crime. The United Kingdom had an independent review of its IP system conducted in 2006. The Gowers review examined the instruments of intellectual property (*i.e.* patents, copyright, designs and trademarks) to determine whether they provided incentives in an efficient manner; the final report provided recommendations on ways the system could be strengthened. In the United States, an independent review of customs enforcement was carried out by the Government Accountability Office (GAO) in 2007; a number of recommendations were made for improving border enforcement.

7.2.8. Industry and government co-operation

Industry has an important role to play in combating counterfeiting and piracy as it has the experience and knowledge to efficiently complement government action. Its involvement in the enforcement effort is essential since: *1)* rights holders have the technical expertise to distinguish counterfeits from original products; and *2)* industry may have additional information regarding the functioning of distribution channels. Industry is also an important partner in the awareness-raising task. Efforts towards stepping up co-operation are well underway in a number of the countries surveyed. In the customs area, for example, the European Union has recently set up a business-customs working group to rationalise the transmission of intelligence from rights holders to ports and airports. In the United Kingdom, an IP Intelligence system has been developed by the Intellectual Property Office, which collects intelligence gathered both by industry and enforcement agencies. In France, a national anti-counterfeiting committee (CNAC) has been set up to act as a forum for exchanges of ideas with the private sector; it has organised awareness-raising campaigns in collaboration with industry. In Switzerland, the Institute for Intellectual Property has initiated a public-private partnership with industry ("Stop Piracy") in 2005 to increase information exchange and organise awareness-building campaigns.

7.3. Industry initiatives

Industry is combating counterfeiting and piracy on many fronts. Their efforts include: *1)* collecting intelligence, conducting research and developing public awareness about C&P issues; *2)* pursuing IPR violators in courts; *3)* supporting government efforts to combat counterfeiting and piracy; and *4)* taking action to make it harder for pirates and counterfeiters to copy and market their products (*i.e.* through technology, etc.). Efforts are being pursued at the firm and sector levels, as well as across sectors. A number of cross-sector initiatives have an important international dimension (Table 7.2).

Box 7.2. Checklist for analysing policies and programmes to combat counterfeiting and piracy

1. Institutional organisation and co-ordination

Which government institutions are involved in addressing counterfeiting and piracy issues? Are their activities sufficiently co-ordinated? Could the institutional framework be further improved?

2. Policy

Has a clear policy to combat counterfeiting and piracy been developed? If so, what are the main provisions? Do policies have concrete elements against which progress can be measured?

3. Legal and regulatory framework

What are the main laws and regulations dealing with IPR and IPR infringement? Does the legal and regulatory framework meet TRIPS standards; does it go beyond? What punitive measures can be taken against counterfeiters and pirates? What is the deterrent value of these measures?

4. Enforcement

How is IPR enforcement carried out? What has been the nature and results of recent domestic enforcement initiatives/operations? Are the human and financial resources assigned to enforcement sufficient? Can enforcement agencies act *ex officio*? Could the speed and transparency of judicial and administrative actions be further improved? Are enforcement statistics compiled?

5. International co-operation

Apart from involvement in WCO, WIPO, WTO, WHO, G8 and Interpol activities, what initiatives have been taken to combat counterfeiting through international co-operation? Has there been a commitment to bilateral/regional initiatives or operations? Is information and expertise being sufficiently shared with other governments?

6. Awareness

What initiatives have been taken to promote awareness of the counterfeiting/piracy situation (public education campaigns, media campaigns, campaigns at schools and universities, surveys, training, etc.)? What have been the results?

7. Programme evaluation and measurement

What internal processes and procedures are in place for regularly reviewing policies and programmes to combat counterfeiting and piracy? Are reports/reviews prepared regularly? Could the evaluation process be improved? Is there sufficient data collection and evaluation?

8. Industry and government co-operation

What are the main initiatives where industry has co-operated with government to combat counterfeiting and piracy: in awareness-raising campaigns, in enforcement operations? Has the co-operation worked well, or can it be further improved? How can industry's role be enhanced?

Table 7.2. Examples of international/regional anti-counterfeiting associations/groups*

Organisation	Overview
AC-G (Anti-Counterfeiting Group)	Provides support and co-ordination with law-enforcement agencies and courts, and a national and international network of information, advice and contacts on anti-counterfeiting activities; maintains close links with Customs. Membership: 200 companies in 30 economies. Internet: www.a-cg.com
AIM (European Brands Association)	Liaises with European authorities and provides expert input at all levels of the legislative process; provides position papers and recommendations; works closely with customs. Membership: 1800 (through corporate members and national associations) in 21 economies. Internet: www.aim.be
BASCAP (ICC)	Unites the business community to more efficiently identify and address IP rights issues and bring these to the attention of authorities. It has created a number of practical tools to carry out its work, including those that provide for exchanging information on C & P issues in economies/sectors, brand protection techniques and intelligence reports. Membership: over 150 companies and trade associations. Internet: www.iccwbo.org/bascap
GACG (Global Anti-Counterfeiting Group)	Facilitates co-ordination among national and regional IP protection and enforcement organisations; provides education/information and promotes greater awareness of C & P issues. Promotes the formation of national anti-counterfeiting coalitions. Members: 20 organisations from Europe (including Russia and Ukraine), plus: China; Hong Kong, China; India; and United States. Internet: www.gacg.org/.
GBLAAC (Global Business Leaders Alliance Against Counterfeiting)	Promotes greater awareness of C & P issues and works with international law enforcement agencies and international government organisations; works closely with industry organisations and coalitions to improve information sharing, co-ordination and collaboration among industry groups. Will be merging with ICC/BASCAP in 2007. Membership: 13 multinational companies. Internet: www.gblaac.org/.
IACC (International Anti-Counterfeiting Coalition)	Provides anti-counterfeiting programmes and develops and conducts training for domestic and foreign law enforcement officials; works with governments worldwide and submits comments on intellectual property enforcement laws and regulations; participates in regional/international programmes aimed at improving IP enforcement standards. Membership: over 150 stakeholders [brand owners (76), law firms (39), etc.]. Internet: www.iacc.org/
INTA (International Trademark Association)	Promotes the rights of trademark owners; analyses and comments on treaties, laws, regulations, procedures and other enforcement mechanisms with respect to anti-counterfeiting. Engages and works with other anti-counterfeiting organisations and with government officials. Promotes public awareness through government roundtables, forums and publications on anti-counterfeiting. Membership: more than 5 000 trademark owners and professionals, from more than 190 countries. Internet: www.inta.org/
MARQUES (Association of European Trademark Owners)	Liaises with relevant EU and other international bodies in all matters relating to trademark protection. Provides a platform for networking and promotes the professional development of its members in the selection, management, protection and exploitation of their trademarks. Internet: www.marques.org/

This table provides an overview of cross-sectoral associations involved in anti-counterfeiting activities. Information on sectoral associations can be found at: www.wipo.int/enforcement/en/co-operation.html.

The ICC's BASCAP is one of the more recent (early 2005) and comprehensive global initiatives launched by industry. It seeks to bring firms together to pursue a more unified approach to combating counterfeiting and piracy. Its efforts include the creation of platforms for exchanging information on the counterfeiting/piracy situation in different economies and sectors, and for sharing information on effective brand-protection techniques. It also seeks to provide stakeholders with improved information on the efforts being taken to address issues, with a view towards enhancing co-ordination. At the same time, research projects are being carried out to provide more effective methods for evaluating the counterfeiting/piracy situation in different economies. On the public policy front, efforts are being made to more effectively communicate the economic and social costs of counterfeiting and piracy to governments and the general public.

Important cross-sectoral initiatives to combat counterfeiting and piracy are also being taken by a number of national organisations, in addition to which many sectoral groups have specific activities devoted to fighting counterfeiting and piracy. The US Chamber of

Commerce, for example, launched a multi-million dollar global initiative in 2004 to combat counterfeiting and piracy (www.thetruecosts.org). Objectives include strengthening IPR legal regimes, providing technical assistance to enforcement and other government bodies, and carrying out research to improve understanding of the factors driving counterfeiting and piracy and the effects on economies. The initiative has a global dimension, with specific programmes in China, India, Brazil, Russia, and Korea. Another important initiative has been launched by industry in China. The Quality Brand Protection Committee (QBPC) of the China Association of Enterprises with Foreign Investment works in co-operation with the Chinese government to promote intellectual property protection. Its work has been directed to strengthening cross-border enforcement, facilitating international co-operation, and educational and research initiatives.

7.4. Authentication technologies

As indicated earlier in this report and in the sector assessments in Part III, it has become easier for counterfeiters and pirates to deceive consumers through high-quality packaging and/or through fake products that are virtually impossible to distinguish from authentic merchandise.

In the case of trademark infringement, brand owners are constantly looking for cost-effective ways to provide retailers and end-users with a means to determine whether the products they have purchased are authentic. In addition, if a rights owner wishes to take action against anyone infringing their intellectual property they need to be able to easily prove their case. The inclusion of authentication devices on genuine products offers strong supporting evidence to the court. Such authentication devices can also facilitate the work of enforcement agencies, such as customs and trading standards, during seizure processes. Although it is relatively easy to install an effective authentication system, the drawback is that the system requires continuous monitoring and updating to ensure that the selected solution is not compromised. In addition, brand owners need to be willing to support the effective use of the system through education and training of those who need to examine it in the field.

Technologies being employed to do so take two basic forms – those that are used to authenticate products, and those that are used to track and trace the movement of products through supply chains (Table 7.3)[65].

Examples of some of the overt technologies include holograms, embedded security threats, colour change inks and paper watermarks. Hidden features that can be included in overt devices include laser images, fluorescing inks, temperature-sensitive devices and polarising elements. Covert features include security inks, micro print and a variety of molecular and nano-scale marking technologies.

---

65.   The analysis draws on information provided by Reconnaissance Internationale.

Table 7.3. Anti-counterfeiting technologies

Authentication technologies		Track and trace technologies	
Overt	Markings which are visible to an unaided human eye under standard viewing conditions.	Barcodes	Symbols printed on labels; can be combined with covert elements.
Hidden	Elements incorporated into overt features or packaging which are revealed to the human eye through the use of a handheld tool, such as a reactive pen, laser pointer, optical filter or UV light.	Radio frequency identification	Automatic identification method. Incorporated into a product for the purpose of identification using radio signals.
Covert	Not normally visible to the human eye; detection device required for viewing.		
Forensic	Require in-field assay kit or laboratory analysis, which can include analysis of the composition of the product as well as forensic analysis of the authentication marker.		

Radio frequency identification (RFID) is an emerging tracking technology. It facilitates automatic identification, relying on storing and remotely retrieving data using devices called RFID tags or transponders. In the United States, the Federal Drug Administration (FDA) has considered the use of RFID as a preferred solution to fighting counterfeiting in the pharmaceutical industry, but it has currently de-emphasised this technology due to cost, privacy and implementation issues.

The types of technology used vary according to the needs of individual industry sectors; many companies use a combination of overt and covert technologies. For example, the luxury goods industry uses, among others, RFIDs and embedded electro-magnetic identification tags in the goods themselves to track fake and stolen items. In addition to some pilot programmes using RFID, the pharmaceutical industry uses a wide range of authentication devices including holograms and colour-shifting ink labels on a large range of products. In the audio and visual sector, for example, edge to edge holograms are used on CD ROMs that feature a three-dimensional holographic image over the entire surface of the CD.

These anti-counterfeiting technologies are continuously subject to reverse engineering and brand owners are recommended to make minor changes to the designs they use at least annually to keep ahead of the counterfeiters. Suppliers of these technologies are well-aware of these threats and regularly update their offerings with new technology options.

While a range of these technologies has been introduced in the last several years, their broad use and success has been limited by a variety of factors, including costs and the ability of counterfeiters and pirates to adapt or copy the technologies.

References

Reconnaissance International Ltd. (2007), Discussions with Ian Lancaster, Managing Director (see http://reconnaissance-intl.com).

Annex 7.A1

THE INTERNATIONAL LEGAL FRAMEWORK FOR COMBATING COUNTERFEITING AND PIRACY

The scope of this annex

This annex presents an overview of the international legal instruments available to combat counterfeiting and piracy: it examines the texts adopted at the multilateral level, then those developed within regional frameworks, and finally, bilateral instruments. By building upon this review of the international discipline, the second part outlines the areas where it may be possible to strengthen the international framework against counterfeiting and piracy.

Not all IPR infringements amount to counterfeiting or piracy. For example, goods that under a licensing agreement have been manufactured or used under conditions other than those agreed upon with the rights holder are usually not considered counterfeited or pirated. Such infringements are not considered here.

In addition, although remedies may be identical for all types of infringements, some rules, such as Customs and border measures, have been specifically devised to combat commercial scale IPR infringements, in particular trademark counterfeiting and copyright piracy. Within the framework of IPR enforcement, this Annex looks particularly at these disciplines.

Specific definitions of counterfeit trademark goods and pirated copyright goods are contained in footnote 14 of the WTO Agreement on Trade-Related Aspects of Intellectual Property Rights ("TRIPS"):

> *For the purpose of this Agreement:*
>
> *(a) "counterfeit trademark goods" shall mean any goods, including packaging, bearing without authorisation a trademark which is identical to the trademark validly registered in respect of such goods, or which cannot be distinguished in its essential aspects from such a trademark, and which thereby infringes the rights of the owner of the trademark in question under the law of the country of importation.*
>
> *(b) "pirated copyright goods" shall mean any goods which are copies made without the consent of the right holder or person duly authorised by the right holder in the country of production and which are made directly or indirectly from an article where the making of that copy would have constituted an infringement of a copyright or a related right under the law of the country of importation.*

These definitions have been used in other international instruments. For example, several free trade agreements concluded by the United States contain the same wording.[66] Similar language is also used in the EC Council Regulation 1383/2003 of 22 July 2003 Concerning Customs Action Against Goods Suspected of Infringing Certain Intellectual Property Rights and the Measures to be Taken Against Goods Found to Have Infringed Such Rights (see article 2.1.a and b).

This Annex does not purport to provide an exhaustive review of every existing legal instrument relating to IPR enforcement, but rather strives to offer a general assessment of the discipline through a review of a representative selection of instruments, in particular those concluded by OECD countries and by the major world economies. It should be noted that while most of the instruments presented are legally binding, some are not.

Nor does this Annex examine whether or how the international discipline is applied or the level of compliance that OECD members and non-members have reached in the implementation of the existing multilateral, regional or bilateral rules.[67] This type of study would require a much more comprehensive set of data and would imply a detailed analysis of national legislation, jurisprudence and practice, which is outside the scope of the present work. The focus, instead, is on the assessment of the current international discipline, and how their limitations could be addressed through the strengthening of the international legal framework pertaining to IPR enforcement.

The international legal instruments for combating counterfeiting and piracy

Multilateral level

The WIPO Convention states as a primary objective the promotion of the protection of intellectual property throughout the world. This requires both the enactment of intellectual property legislation as well as the effective enforcement of rights. Treaties administered by WIPO contain some provisions on IP enforcement. The Paris Convention for the Protection of Industrial Property, the Berne Convention for the Protection of Literary and Artistic Works, the WIPO Copyright Treaty (WCT), as well as the WIPO Performances and Phonograms Treaty (WPPT) include special enforcement provisions over issues covered in the respective treaties.

However, the WIPO treaties remain relatively vague on the issue of enforcement. None of these instruments provide for a comprehensive set of rules on IP enforcement. With the TRIPS Agreement, existing rules were collated and systematised and new multi-lateral minimum standards were established. Therefore, the TRIPS Agreement constitutes by far the most comprehensive discipline for combating counterfeiting and piracy at the multilateral level. Other instruments have a more specialised nature, although some of them, such as the Interpol resolutions, may play a significant role in promoting and facilitating international co-operation in combating large-scale IPR infringements.

---

66. See, for example, the US-Australia Free Trade Agreement (footnotes 17–26 and 17–27); the US-Central America and Dominican Republic FTA (footnote 18-15); US-Chile FTA (footnote 17-31); US-Morocco FTA (footnote 15-19).

67. For an appraisal of the implementation of the TRIPS, see C. Arup, "TRIPS: Across the Global Field of Intellectual Property", *European Intellectual Property Review*, 2004, 26(1), pp. 7–16.

The WTO TRIPS

Part III of the TRIPS Agreement (Articles 41 – 61) is devoted to the enforcement of intellectual property rights. The scope of this section is not to examine in detail these provisions, for which literature is abundant,[68] but to give an overview of the commitments made by WTO Members in the enforcement of IPRs.

According to Part III of TRIPS, WTO Members are required, *inter alia*, to introduce into their legal system a set of procedures for the enforcement of intellectual property rights. These procedures and remedies constitute a minimum standard of protection[69] which is made available to IPR right holders across the whole WTO membership, developed and developing countries alike. Least-developed country WTO members are, however, not required to apply TRIPS provisions in general until 1 July 2013[70], and are exempted from protecting and enforcing patent rights and undisclosed information with respect to pharmaceutical products until 1 January 2016[71]. In addition, the TRIPS provisions permit, but do not oblige, members to apply stricter enforcement procedures and remedies, provided that the TRIPS provisions, including safeguards against abuse, are respected (Article 1.1 TRIPS). Therefore, the actual level of IPR enforcement procedures and remedies depends on the national implementation and on the individual members' interest in adopting measures which go beyond TRIPS obligations.

The TRIPS enforcement provisions can be summarised as follows:

- WTO Members must establish, under their law, enforcement procedures for effective actions against IPR infringements. These procedures must be fair and equitable, timely, accessible and in accordance with the principles of due process (Article 41 and ff.). The TRIPS Agreement also requires that such procedures shall not create barriers to legitimate trade and shall provide for safeguards against their abuse. It is also understood that there is no obligation to put in place a distinct judicial system nor to redistribute resources between IPR enforcement and law enforcement in general.

- In civil and administrative procedures, the judicial authorities must be provided with the authority to order the following minimum judicial instruments:

  i)   Injunctions to prevent the commercialisation of IPR-infringing goods (article 44).

  ii)   Seizure and destruction of the infringing goods and of the disposal of the *instrumental celeris*, *i.e.* the equipment for the production of such goods, outside the channels of commerce (article 46).

---

68.   See, for example, D. Gervais, *The TRIPS Agreement. Drafting History and Analysis (2nd edition)*, London 2003; D. Mattews, *Globalising Intellectual Property Rights. The TRIPS Agreement*, London and New York, 2002; T. Cottier, "The Agreement on Trade-Related Aspects of Intellectual Property Rights", in P. F. J. Macrory, A. E. Appleton, M. G. Plummer (eds.), *The World Trade Organization: Legal, Economic and Political Analysis*, Volume 1, New York, 2005, pp. 1102–1109. For an assessment of the first 10 years of the TRIPS, see F. M. Abbott, "Toward a New Era of Objective Assessment in the Field of TRIPS and Variable Geometry for the Preservation of Multilateralism", in *Journal of International Economic Law* 8(1), pp. 77–100.

69.   Cottier defines these TRIPS provisions as "a body of common procedural standards in international law", see p. 1103, cit n. 1.

70.   Decision of the Council for TRIPS of 29 November 2005, WTO Document IP/C/40.

71.   Decision of the Council for TRIPS of 27 June 2002, WTO Document IP/C/25.

iii) Damages adequate to compensate at least for the injury provoked in case of wilful or careless infringement (article 45).

iv) Prompt and effective provisional measures to prevent IPR infringements, in particular to prevent infringing goods from entry into the channels of commerce, and to preserve evidence in regard to the alleged infringement. Where appropriate, it must be possible to adopt provisional measures *inaduita altera parte* (article 50).

- With regard to trademark counterfeiting and copyright piracy, WTO Members have to:

  i) Adopt border measures under which authorities, upon right holders' application, can suspend the commercialisation of counterfeit trademark goods and pirated copyright goods at the point of importation (article 51). The provision for such measures is only mandatory with regard to the importation of goods. The extension of these measures to infringing goods destined to be exported is optional. Goods in transit or transhipment, as well as small quantities of goods imported for non-commercial purpose, contained in travellers' personal luggage or sent in small consignments, are also not covered by the mandatory system of border measures. Other provisions specify the conditions for a right holder's application (article 52), procedural requirements (articles 53-57) and indicate the remedies that may be applied (article 59), including the destruction of the goods. TRIPS permits, but does not oblige, members to set up procedures for taking ex officio action, *i.e.* suspension of release into circulation of goods upon the initiative of the competent authorities and without any prior request by IPR holders, provided certain safeguards are met.

  ii) Provide in their laws for the application of criminal proceedings against wilful violations on a commercial scale. Remedies available must be serious enough to constitute a deterrent and the seizure and destruction of the infringing goods and of the instruments for their production must be available (article 61).

As the above summary shows, enforcement standards found in TRIPS operate on several levels. It can be generally said that the TRIPS sets out the main fundamental principles necessary for combating IPR infringements, sometimes in very general terms and sometimes in terms of more specific measures, but overall leaving a great deal of discretion to Members. National legislation is therefore inevitably more specific. Moreover, optional measures, which the WTO members may choose to implement in their legislation, are abundant in the TRIPS enforcement section, which shows that numerous potential "TRIPS-plus" provisions, *i.e.* enhancements over the TRIPS mandatory standards, could be established. Most notably:

- The reach of the mandatory border measures is limited to only cover certain IPR infringements and to only cover imports. The TRIPS expressly suggests as an option the extension of these measures to exports, but makes no such mention in regard to other border operations, such as transhipment. Expansion of mandatory border measures has the potential of considerably reducing the trade in IPR infringing goods.

- The mandatory criminal sanctions are restricted to cases of "wilful trademark counterfeiting or copyright piracy on a commercial scale." As the TRIPS itself suggests, there is room for applying criminal sanctions to infringements of other IPRs. Moreover, the TRIPS does not contain a definition "commercial scale".

- In addition to what is required by the TRIPS, there may be scope to consider making the availability of other remedies in civil and/or criminal procedures mandatory, such as, for example, seizure of assets, other than those covered by Articles 46 and 59, foreclosure of business, or suspension of professional license.

- There are principles which are mandatory, but where the Members have several options from which to choose in their implementation. This is notably the case in criminal penalties required to be adopted by Members with respect to trademark counterfeiting and copyright infringement, where the TRIPS language "[r]emedies available shall include imprisonment and/or monetary fines" (Art. 61) would allow the Members to choose from incarceration or monetary fines, or to decide to have both. Requiring that measures include both monetary fines and imprisonment, could potentially provide for a stronger deterrent. Mandating minimum fines and sentences would also ensure a more harmonised effect of such measures and potentially strengthen their deterrence value;

- The provision for *ex officio* actions by the authorities, whether in instituting criminal proceedings or border measures is optional, although the TRIPS does offer minimum standards should Members decide to provide for such measures. Mandating the availability of such measures could strengthen the enforcement system;

- While availability of provisional measures is mandatory, the determination of their scope is largely left to each Member;

- The right of information, whereby the authorities could order the infringer identity, for example, of third persons involved in the production and distribution, is optional under TRIPS.

This annex does not go as far as examining the national laws of WTO Members, but it can be imagined that implementation of the TRIPS in national legislation could potentially take different forms[72].

TRIPS contains other provisions which may be relevant to enforcement, including article 68, which creates the Council for TRIPS to monitor the Agreement, and article 69 on international co-operation. The latter provides:

> *Members agree to co-operate with each other with a view to eliminating international trade in goods infringing intellectual property rights. For this purpose, they shall establish and notify contact points in their administrations and be ready to exchange information on trade in infringing goods. They shall, in particular, promote the exchange of information and co-operation between customs authorities with regard to trade in counterfeit trademark goods and pirated copyright goods.*

---

72. In response to a Checklist of Issues on Enforcement, prepared by the WTO Secretariat, some Members have provided concrete information on national enforcement laws and practices, see WTO Document IP/C/5 of 30 November 1995 for the checklist and WTO Documents IP/N/6/country code for responses.

For a better implementation of this article, the Council for TRIPS adopted a common procedure for the notification of contact points established under its provisions[73].

Disputes under the TRIPS can be adjudicated in accordance with the WTO dispute settlement mechanism. However, there have been only a few dispute settlement cases of relevance to enforcement so far. Three complaints have related to provisional measures as required under Article 50 TRIPS, and another one to obligations relating to criminal procedures in Article 61 TRIPS[74]. These complaints were the subject of amicable settlements. Two other cases reached the panel stage. They mainly concerned substantive rights, but also included claims relating to the availability of fair and equitable enforcement procedures, which were not upheld by the Panel[75] and the Appellate Body[76] respectively. There have been no complaints under the DSU relating to TRIPS enforcement provisions since the beginning of 2000. Hitherto, the DSU has not served to provide further guidance on the interpretation of TRIPS enforcement provisions. This does, however, not automatically imply full implementation by all WTO Members of their TRIPS obligations to combat counterfeiting and piracy.

The revision of the TRIPS rules on enforcement is not on the agenda of the Doha Development Round. However, some Members have indicated in the regular session of the TRIPS Council that they remain concerned about the increasing level of counterfeiting and piracy, notwithstanding implementation of the TRIPS Agreement. They have proposed a TRIPS Council work programme on this matter, for example to identify best practices, but without suggesting amendments to TRIPS rules. In three communications, the EC has referred to the need to assess the implementation of enforcement provisions by national authorities and to discuss solutions to the perceived deficiencies. It also raised the limited scope of border measures, which are only mandatory for the importation of counterfeit trademarks and pirated copyright goods; see WTO Documents IP/C/W/448, 468 and 471. A joint communication by the EC, the US, Switzerland and Japan has set out ideas for a TRIPS Council work programme on this matter, for example, to facilitate an exchange of information on experiences and best practices in this area and to engage in a constructive discussion of how to implement the TRIPS enforcement provisions more effectively; see WTO Document IP/C/W/485 of 2 November 2006.

A US submission has made available information on customs seizures and on modern border enforcement tools with a view to contributing to a constructive exchange of views and experiences among Members; see WTO Document IP/C/W/488 of 30 January 2007. Some other WTO members are not convinced that it would be appropriate for the TRIPS Council to take up this matter at a time when the Council had other important matters on its agenda on which work had not yet been completed. They have argued that the TRIPS Agreement leaves it to Members to determine the appropriate means of implementing enforcement measures and that there are other measures in the TRIPS Council and the WTO more generally for addressing any issues in this connection. Advocacy groups,

---

3.   See WTO Document IP/N/3/Rev.9 plus addenda for the list of contact points notified by WTO Members.

4.   WT/DS83 (*Denmark-Measures Affecting the Enforcement of IPRs*); WT/DS86 (*Sweden-Measures Affecting the Enforcement of IPRs*); WT/DS124 (*European Communities-Enforcement of IPRs for Motion Pictures and Television Programmes*); WT/DS125 (*Greece-Enforcement of IPRs for Motion Pictures and Television Programmes*); WT/DS196 (*Argentina-Certain Measures on the Protection of Patents and Test Data*).

5.   WT/DS174/R and WT/DS290/R (European Communities Protection of Trademarks and Geographical Indications for Agricultural Products and Foodstuffs).

6.   WT/DS176/AB/R of 2 January 2002 (United States-Section 211 Omnibus Appropriations Act of 1998).

governments and scholarly literature have indicated the provisions on border measures as the main area of improvement.

The World Customs Organization (WCO)

The main instrument developed within the WCO to combat counterfeiting and piracy is the Model Provisions for National Legislation to Implement Fair and Effective Border Measures Consistent with the Agreement on Trade-Related Aspects of Intellectual Property Rights. This non-binding instrument provides a model to follow when national legislations implementing border measures for the protection of IPRs are drafted or reviewed.

However, the WCO Model Provisions, which were developed first in 1995 and subsequently amended in different occasions until the last revision of 2004, go beyond the minimum standards of the TRIPS and recommend a more effective legislation to fight cross-border traffic in counterfeit and pirated goods. Their most salient and innovative elements vis-à-vis the TRIPS are that laws and regulations:

- Permit applications for enforcement actions to be submitted directly to the customs authorities that process the applications, without the need for a previous authorisation by the courts.[77]

- Permit a right holder to request customs to suspend clearance of goods infringing any type of IPRs, although with certain limitations with regard to geographical indications, and vis-à-vis any customs operation, including export or transit.

- Permit, and in certain cases require, customs powers to act *ex officio*. Under this provision, customs authorities would be obligated, on their own initiative, to suspend the clearance of goods in respect of which they have acquired *prima facie* evidence that an intellectual property right has been infringed or is about to be infringed and may also suspend the clearance of goods which they have reasonable grounds to suspect of infringing an IPR.

- Restrict the *de minimis* derogation contained in TRIPS for digital piracy to a single copy of a work for personal use. This is an increasingly important area, given that the cumulative effect of shipments of pirated goods in travellers' luggage is considered by the WCO more and more a source of commercial harm to right holders.

- Define trade in counterfeit and pirated goods as a customs offence in accordance with the national laws.

The WCO, and particularly its "Strategic Group", which works with IPR holders on combating global counterfeiting from custom's perspective, developed a Standard Application Form for IPR holders to request border measures by customs authorities.

Other guidelines that were adopted within the WCO and which are relevant to the fight against counterfeiting and piracy include the *Guidelines on Controlling Free Zones in Relation to IPRs Infringements* and the *Guidance to Industry on Information to be Provided to Customs*.

---

77.   The decisions by the customs remain subject to judicial review by administrative or civil courts.

WIPO

WIPO has announced as objectives assistance to WIPO Member States in strengthening their systems and infrastructure for effective IPR enforcement. Such measures include, *inter alia*, legal and technical assistance to Member States in relation to the development and establishment of effective IPR enforcement mechanisms and developing projects and information material for use in activities to enhance public awareness in fight against counterfeit, piracy and other IPR infringements.

Interpol

The Interpol General Assembly adopted the first resolution on intellectual property crimes in 1994 at its session in Rome (AGN/63/RES/13) and restated it in 2000 at its session in Rhodes (AGN/69/RES/6). While the impact of these documents, which have a non-binding nature, is limited, this organisation has carried out important operational activities in recent years.

Interpol has developed an IP Crime Programme and has established an Intellectual Property Crime Action Group. This group, which is composed of police and customs officials from Interpol member countries, international organisations and cross-industry representative bodies, develops initiatives and delivers solutions to stakeholders, member countries and industries affected by IP crime.

Interpol, in co-operation with the WCO, WIPO and the business community, organises a Global Congresses on Combating Counterfeiting and Piracy, the most recent of which was held in Lyon in November 2005. The Congress constitutes the largest gathering of agencies and private sector stakeholders working on counterfeiting and piracy. The Congress' final Declaration contains a set of critical elements for government and industry effective anti-counterfeiting/piracy strategies, about raising awareness, improving co-operation and co-ordination, building capacity and promoting better legislation and enforcement. In this latter field, the Congress recommended, *inter alia*, that "national governments empower competent authorities with the ability to examine export merchandise and to fully exercise that authority in taking appropriate action against counterfeit and pirated shipments."

Group of Eight

The Group of Eight (G8) has taken a number of steps to combat counterfeiting and piracy. The most significant commitments on enforcement have been taken at the Gleneagles Summit in July 2005, where the document *Reducing IPR Piracy and Counterfeiting through more Effective Enforcement* was adopted. In particular, the G8 leaders committed to:

> *promote and uphold laws, regulations and/or procedures to strengthen effective intellectual property enforcement, where appropriate, in areas such as the seizure and retention of suspected counterfeit or pirated goods, the destruction of such goods and the equipment used to produce them, and the use of clear, transparent and predictable judicial proceedings, policies and guidelines related to intellectual property enforcement.*

A similar declaration has been adopted at the St. Petersburg Summit in July 2006 (*Combating IPR Piracy and Counterfeiting*).

Within the G8, operates an IPR experts group which meets regularly to discuss co-operation on the fight against counterfeiting and piracy. In the 2006 Declaration, this group has been instructed "to study the possibilities of strengthening the international legal framework pertaining to IPR enforcement".

Regional level

European Union

The European Union's main instruments devoted to IPR enforcement are the Council Regulation 1383/2003 of 22 July 2003 Concerning Customs Action against Goods Suspected of Infringing Certain Intellectual Property Rights and the Measures to be Taken against Goods Found to Have Infringed such Rights ("Regulation") and the Directive 2004/48/EC of the European Parliament and of the Council of 29 April 2004 on the Enforcement of Intellectual Property Rights ("Directive"). A Directive on criminal enforcement is also under discussion. The EC Regulation, which is directly applicable in all Member States, is meant to improve customs actions primarily at the Community's external borders, while the EC Directive is intended to improve the protection and enforcement of intellectual property rights within the internal market. Directives, though binding as to the result to be achieved, necessitate the adoption by national authorities of measures to define the forms and methods of their implementation.

EC Regulation 1383/2003

The EC Regulation 1383/2003 defines the actions that are to be taken by the customs authorities with respect to goods which are suspected of or found to be infringing an IPR.[78] It replaces previous legislation, which was introduced already in 1986 and subsequently updated on different occasions.

The Regulation essentially addresses border measures, which under TRIPS minimum standards pertain solely to control of trademark counterfeit and copyright pirated goods. The Regulation is much broader in scope, applying in addition to goods which infringe certain other intellectual property rights, notably patents, design rights[79], designations of origin/geographical indications and plant variety rights. The measures also extend to any "mould or matrix" which is specifically designed or adapted for the manufacture of goods infringing an IPR.

Furthermore, customs controls and actions prescribed by the Regulation apply not only to goods imported for introduction into circulation in the Community territory, but also to goods which are exported or re-exported from the territory, transhipped through the territory, or which are stored in a free zone or warehouse. This goes much farther than the TRIPS, which only requires as compulsory measures for the control of imports.

The Regulation streamlines the process of application by the rights holders for customs actions with respect to infringing goods, in order to make them more predictable and easy to apply both by customs officials and rights holders. It prescribes the minimum mandatory information and supporting documents to be provided by the right holder which would enable the customs authorities to process the application, indicates the

---

78. K. Daele, "Regulation 1383/2003: A New Step in the Fight against Counterfeit and Pirated Goods at the Borders of the European Union", in *European Intellectual Property Review*, 2004, pp. 214-225.

79. Infringement of a design right is included in the definition of "pirated goods".

response times by the customs officials, and, with respect to community trademarks, provides that an application can be filed in one Member State for action in other States.[80]

The Regulation is quite detailed about the conditions and specific actions to be carried out once the application is accepted, including the notices to be provided, the duration of suspension/detention and conditions of release and the process of inspection and information exchanges with a view of determining whether the goods infringe an IPR. Finally, the Regulation lays down measures applicable to goods which are found to infringe IPRs, including for their destruction, and requiring Members to establish "effective, proportionate and dissuasive" penalties.

The Regulation also grants broader powers to customs authorities. In particular, customs authorities are expressly authorised to temporarily detain or suspend the release of suspected goods *ex officio*, when they have "sufficient grounds" for suspecting the goods of infringing an IPR. This permits the right holder, who may not be aware of the infringement, to be informed and to file an application with the customs authorities in due course. The Regulation also provides for a simplified process of destruction of the goods in question by the customs authorities, without a court order or even a formal determination of whether they infringe an IPR, on the request of the right holder and provided that the declarant/holder of the goods is duly informed and either consents or does not object within the prescribed period of time.

The Regulation contains several exclusions to its application. The first is the typical exclusion of goods which bear the trademark with the consent of the trademark holder or which have been manufactured with the consent of the holder of another IPR, but under conditions which are different from those agreed with the right holder or where the right holder has not authorised the transborder operation in question. In addition, the Regulation concentrates on infringement for commercial purposes, thus *a priori* excluding from its coverage infringing goods transported in personal baggage to the extent of the duty-free allowance granted by Community rules. However, small scale commercial trafficking is not excluded.

Directive 2004/48/EC

The purpose of the Directive 2004/48/EC is to ensure high and comparable level of protection for intellectual property in the Member States by reducing differences in the national legislation. The purpose is not to introduce a single regime, but by implementing the Directive's provisions, the national laws of the Member states are being harmonised. Nor does the Directive affect the substantive law on intellectual property or issues such as jurisdiction or recognition of decisions. The Directive thus provides for a series of legal and administrative measures, procedures and remedies to be implemented in the Member States in order to ensure the uniform enforcement of intellectual property rights[81]

---

0.   The provisions for the implementation of this Regulation are laid down in Commission Regulation (EC) No 1891/2004 of 21 October 2004, which, *inter alia*, standardises the application forms to be used by the customs authorities throughout the Member States, including the instructions for completing the forms, specifies what information and supporting documents are to be provided based on the IPR right claimed and stipulates the points from which the various prescribed time periods begin to run.

1.   The measures, procedures and remedies provided by the Directive apply widely to any infringement of intellectual property rights as provided for by Community law or by the national law of the Member concerned. The Commission has subsequently to the Directive issued a statement (2005/295/EC) of what it considers, as a minimum, to be rights covered by the scope of the Directive, listing *inter alia* copyright and related rights,

throughout the Community. The Directive concerns only the civil measures and remedies, leaving the question of criminal proceedings and sanctions outside its scope.

The Directive presents comprehensive procedures and specific conditions for obtaining information and evidence from the opposing party and preservation of evidence by provisional and precautionary measures, including interlocutory injunctions and seizures of the goods and the materials/instruments used in their production. Measures resulting from the decision on the merits of the case are also addressed in detail, including injunctions against the infringer and intermediaries as well as specific corrective measures, such as the recall of the infringing goods already on the market and the reparation of the prejudice suffered by the right holder, including the basis for the calculation of damages.

The above mentioned measures and procedures essentially correspond to the implementation of the minimum standards set by TRIPS, the specific procedures and conditions being defined in greater detail in the Directive. However, the Directive also goes farther than the TRIPS minimum requirements in several respects. Beyond the provisional measures required by TRIPS (Article 50) in order to prevent the infringement or to preserve evidence, the Directive requires that Member States provide for means to secure the recovery of damages, such as precautionary seizure of the movable and immovable property of the infringer, by blocking, including *inaudita altera parte*, the bank accounts and other assets, which can be necessary to prevent irreparable harm to be caused. The Directive also requires Members to ensure that the judicial authorities are able, at the request of the right holder, to order the infringer or others connected to the infringement to disclose information as to the origin and distribution networks of the infringing goods, this being optional under article 47 of the TRIPS. The Directive also introduces "publicity measures" intended to act as an additional deterrent and to improve public awareness, including as a minimum requiring the publication of the decision at the expense of the infringer.

A proposed Directive on criminal measures

As indicated, the Directive 2004/48/EC concerns only the civil and administrative measures and remedies which the Member States are required to make available to the rights holders, leaving the question of criminal proceedings and sanctions outside its scope. The Commission has however recently presented to the European Parliament and the Council a proposal for a Directive on Criminal Measures Aimed at Ensuring the Enforcement of Intellectual Property Rights[82], the objective of which is to align the Member States criminal law measures to more effectively combat IPR offences. The draft Directive lays down a range of penalties to be imposed for IPR infringements on both natural and legal persons intentionally committing or attempting to commit IPR infringements on a commercial scale, including those aiding or abetting and inciting such offences. In addition to setting the level of monetary fines and prison terms, the Directive provides, *inter alia*, for the temporary and permanent closure of the establishment used to commit the infringement, judicial winding up and bans on engaging in commercial activities, as well as for the confiscation of proceeds of the crime and other property belonging to the infringer. The Directive, which is still under discussion by the European institutions, also

---

trademark and trade names, designs, patents, geographical indications, utility models and *sui generis* rights of a data base maker.

82. European Commission, COM(2006) 168 Final, 26 March 2006.

provides for *ex officio* investigations and prosecutions by the authorities and requires that the rights holders be allowed to be involved in the investigation.

The North American Free Trade Agreement

The North American Free Trade Agreement (NAFTA) preceded the TRIPS and contains a very similar set of provisions regarding intellectual property. NAFTA may provide some enhancements over the TRIPS in terms of substantive intellectual property protections and procedures, but this does not appear to be the case for the enforcement provisions.

In addition to the NAFTA, the United States, Canada and Mexico initiated a Security and Prosperity Partnership (SPP) in March 2005. One of the initiatives under this framework is called "Fake Free North America", under which the three countries have agreed to develop a strategy to enhance detection and deterrence of counterfeiting and piracy, expand public awareness and outreach efforts regarding trade in pirated and counterfeit goods, and develop measurements to assess progress over time and estimate the magnitude of the problem.

The Asia-Pacific Economic Co-operation

The Asia-Pacific Economic Co-operation (APEC) Trade Ministers issued a Joint Statement on the WTO/TRIPS Agreement Implementation at the Meeting in Darwin, Australia, in June 2000, confirming their commitment to the full implementation of TRIPS and to continuing technical co-operation. Recognising the need to improve public awareness, they also undertook to increase their co-operation within the region with respect to public education programmes concerning intellectual property. APEC members reaffirmed the importance they attach to the protection of intellectual property rights and the fight against counterfeiting and piracy at subsequent meetings. In particular, the APEC Anti-Counterfeiting and Piracy Initiative and the APEC Model Guidelines to Reduce Trade in Counterfeit and Pirated Goods and to Prevent the Sale of Counterfeit Goods over the Internet was adopted at the meeting of Trade Ministers in June 2005 and welcomed at the 13th APEC Economic Leader's Meeting in Busan, Korea, in November 2005.

The Association of South East Asian Nations

The Association of South East Asian Nations (ASEAN) Framework Agreement on Intellectual Property Co-operation, concluded in Bangkok on 15 December 1995, recognises the importance of promoting and protecting intellectual property in the advancement of trade and investment. The Agreement acknowledges and reaffirms the Member States' obligations assumed under international conventions, including the TRIPS. It goes further to indicate that any arrangements implemented within the framework of the Agreement, will be in line with the standards of those treaties and the TRIPS.[83]

---

3.   It should be noted that Laos and Vietnam are ASEAN Members, but not yet members of the WTO.

This Agreement is forward looking rather than itself providing any obligations. Potential co-operative activities include cross border measures, networking of judicial authorities and intellectual property enforcement agencies, exchange of IP experts, the establishment of an ASEAN patent and trademark systems and Offices, as well as the creation of an ASEAN Intellectual Property Association and the provision of arbitration services or other alternative dispute resolution mechanisms for handling IPR disputes.

The European Free Trade Association

The Convention establishing the European Free Trade Association (EFTA), as amended in 2001, sets as one of its objectives "to provide appropriate protection of intellectual property rights, in accordance with the highest international standards" and contains a set of provisions covering substantive IP protections. On enforcement, it expressly refers to the TRIPS provisions.

Bilateral instruments

Without undertaking a complete analysis of the numerous existing bilateral agreements and other instruments, this paper presents a broad cross-section of instruments, in particular from OECD countries and the major world economies, and concentrates on their IPR enforcement provisions. While many of these instruments offer various enhancements over the existing international discipline, to the extent that these merely expand or extend substantive IPR protections and have little additional direct impact on enforcement, they will not be considered in any significant detail in this paper.

There are few existing bilateral agreements which deal specifically with intellectual property protection, and while IPRs are generally included as part of the investment assets contemplated by Bilateral Investment Treaties, the most noteworthy provisions dealing with IPR enforcement are contained in bilateral Free Trade Agreements or similar trade related instruments.

The Free Trade Agreements and Other Trade Agreements

The US Free Trade Agreements

The United States has concluded a series of Free Trade Agreements, notably with partners in the Americas and the Middle East regions,[84] in which generally the level of detail on IP issues emulates that of NAFTA. The Intellectual Property chapters of the US Free Trade Agreements[85] are quite explicit and could practically stand on their own as a comprehensive discipline in the matter[86].

---

84. Sometimes these go by a different title, *e.g.* "The Peru Trade Promotion Agreement", without differing in form or content.

85. The Agreements examined: US-Jordan (2000); US-Chile (2003); US-Australia (1994); US-Morocco (2004); US-Central America and Dominican Republic (2004); US-Oman (2006); and US-Peru (2006).

86. The Agreements also include a chapter on customs administration, which provides for co-operation and information exchange between the parties on customs matters generally and in particular cases where there is suspicion of unlawful activity.

Most of these Agreements are TRIPS Plus, *i.e.* they offer enhancements over the TRIPS discipline, in particular with respect to enforcement.[87] The main areas of strengthening of the TRIPS discipline are:

- *Civil proceedings.* The basis for the calculation of civil damages must include actual damages as well as the profits related to the infringing activity. Furthermore, the parties must provide for the possibility of statutory damages, which the right holder can choose instead of the calculated damages. Thereby, damages could be awarded even if the actual harm is not determined.

- *Criminal proceedings.* The parties are required to provide to the authorities the right to introduce criminal proceedings *ex officio*. Exportation of counterfeit and pirated goods is subject to criminal penalties to the same extent as their trafficking and distribution. In addition to infringing goods and equipment used in their manufacture, in criminal cases, the authorities may further seize and confiscate any revenues or assets traceable to the infringing activity. The available criminal penalties must include imprisonment and fines, as a minimum in case of wilful counterfeiting or piracy on a commercial scale. This notion specifically covers in some Agreements significant infringements carried out without seeking financial gain, applying therefore to significant end-user piracy. Some agreements require such penalties also in case of knowing trafficking in materials used in conjunction with the infringement, such as packaging or labels.

- *Disclosure of information.* Judicial authorities must be able to order the infringer to identify third parties involved in the infringement and disclose information about the production and distribution networks for the infringing goods and to provide the information to the rights holder, this requirement being optional under TRIPS. Furthermore, in case of refusal to provide such information, the judicial authorities can issue sanctions against the infringer and, in some cases, against their counsel and third parties.

- *Border measures.* Customs authorities must be able to initiate *ex officio* controls, and in many agreements, *ex officio* customs actions are not limited to imports. Such measures must also be available with respect to goods destined for exportation or that are in transit, when there is reason to suspect that the goods infringe an IPR. At the same time, rights holders applications for suspension of release are only required to be available for suspected imported counterfeit or pirated goods. The Agreements do not mandate access to customs procedures for rights holders for all types of transborder operations, as does, for example, the EC legislation in the matter.

Transparency and public awareness are important principles in these Agreements. They typically dedicate an entire chapter to transparency and more specifically require that the countries' laws dealing with intellectual property as well as their customs laws be published or otherwise made accessible to the public. They generally call for consultation with the other parties to the Agreements and other interested parties with respect to perspective laws in areas covered by the Agreements. The parties are also obligated to publish their decisions and rulings in IP infringement cases of general application. The Agreements go further in requiring the countries to publicise their efforts in IPR enforcement, including statistical data.

---

7. See, for example, Pedro Roffe, *Bilateral Agreements and a TRIPS-Plus World: The Chile-USA Free Trade Agreement*, 2004, available at www.qiap.ca.

The EU Agreements

The Euro-Mediterranean Agreements

A series of Association Agreements have been concluded by the European Union and its Member States with the economies of the Mediterranean region[88], known as the Euro-Mediterranean Agreements, the objectives of which are the development and enhancement of trade, economic, technical and other co-operation between the parties, with the establishment of a free-trade area as the ultimate goal.

These agreements are based on the same model. While the exact language differs[89], the Agreements commonly call for the parties to ensure protection of IPRs in accordance with the "highest international standards" and to provide effective means to enforce such rights. These stipulations in relation to IPR protection generally refer to an annex which lists the international treaties dealing with intellectual property to which the partner is required to become party, including in certain cases the TRIPS.[90] However, it is not quite evident what these "highest international standards" are. As various "TRIPS plus" provisions, notably those extending substantive protections, have emerged in European legislation and in a number of bilateral agreements containing IPR protection provisions, these "highest international standards" could eventually be interpreted as going beyond the requirements of TRIPS. In fact, some of the Agreements also contain provisions on "approximating" the parties' respective legislations, which conceivably exceeds the TRIPS minimum standards if the partner's legislation is to be aligned with that of the Community. However, it is less clear from this language whether these standards are contemplated primarily for substantive protection or to also encompass enforcement measures established by the EC.

A regular feature of these Agreements, in addition to the sections on customs co-operation, is an annexed Protocol on Administrative Assistance in Customs Matters, which evidently could also apply to assistance in combating counterfeiting and piracy, if these are considered customs offences. The assistance includes information exchange both on a regular and *ad hoc* basis, requests for surveillance and enquiries, notification and document delivery and testifying as experts or witnesses in proceedings concerning matters covered by the Protocol.

The "Cotonou Agreement"

The Partnership Agreement between the members of the Africa, Caribbean and Pacific Group of States and the European Community and its Member States, signed in Cotonou on 23 June 2002, contains certain basic provisions for the protection of intellectual property rights. The importance of adhering to TRIPS is emphasised and the parties recognise the need to "ensure an adequate and effective level of protection" of IPRs covered by TRIPS "in line with international standards". The language is not as strong as that found in the Association Agreements discussed above. The Cotonou Agreement also provides for the possibility of concluding more specific agreements

---

88. Tunisia (1995), Palestinian Authority (1997), Israel (2000), Egypt (2001), Jordan (2002), Morocco (2000), Algeria (2005), Lebanon (2006).

89. Certain Agreements call for "adequate and effective" and others for "suitable and effective" protection. Similarly, while the term "conformity" to the "highest international standards" is used, generally more nuanced terms such as "in accordance with" or "in line with" those standards are employed.

90. Algeria, Lebanon and the Palestinian Authority are not members of the WTO.

between the parties with respect to protection of trademarks and geographical indications for specific products.

EC - South Africa

The Agreement on Trade, Development and Co-operation between the European Community and its Member States and the Republic of South Africa, signed in Pretoria on 11 October 1999, provides that the parties "shall ensure adequate and effective protection of intellectual property rights in conformity with the highest international standards". The Agreement further indicates that the parties currently apply the TRIPS and "undertake to improve, where appropriate, the protection provided under" TRIPS. As do the Euro-Mediterranean Agreements, this Agreement lists a certain number of treaties in the area of intellectual property, but in this case it is a best endeavours clause rather an obligation to become a party to the treaties. The Agreement provides for possible technical assistance by the Community in preparation of laws and regulations dealing with IPR protection and enforcement and with the establishmetn of offices involved in IPR protection and enforcement, as well as personnel training in this area. The Agreement also provides for customs co-operation and includes a protocol on mutual assistance in customs matters on the same model as described above. The Agreement specifically calls for urgent consultations in case of problems in IPR protection affecting trade.

EC - Korea

The Framework Trade and Co-operation Agreement between the European Community and its Member States and Korea of 30 March 2001, provides that the parties shall conduct policy aimed at, *inter alia*, effectively protecting intellectual, industrial and commercial property. The parties confirm the importance they attach to the obligations contained in multilateral IPR conventions and to the rapid implementation of TRIPS in their legislation.

Other agreements

The Intellectual property provisions of other agreements concluded by the EC generally follow a similar approach in that they reiterate the importance of protection and enforcement of IPRs and, at least in the more recent agreements, the parties' commitment to conform to the "highest" international standards in this area[91]. The EC-Ukraine and the EC-Moldova Partnership and Co-operation Agreements (1994) call further for the partners to improve the protection of IPRs in order to provide for a "level of protection similar to that existing in the Community."

---

1. See, for example, the EC-Mexico Economic Partnership, Political Co-ordination and Co-operation Agreement (1997) and the EC-Chile Association Agreement (2002). On the other hand, the Agreement on Trade and Economic Co-operation between the EEC and the Republic of China (1985) does not mention IPR at all and the EC-India Agreement on Partnership and Development (1993) and the EC-Russian Federation Partnership and Co-operation Agreement (1994), while calling for protection and enforcemetn of IPRs, do not refer to such standards.

The Japan Economic Partnership Agreements

Japan has concluded Economic Partnership Agreements (EPAs) with Singapore (2002), Mexico (2004) and Malaysia (2005) which are, in principle, aimed at ensuring adequate and effective protection of IPR. The Singapore and Malaysia EPAs, and their implementing agreements, contain extensive IPR co-operation provisions. They establish a committee on IP to monitor and provide advice on the implementation of the IPR provisions and provide for consultation and exchange of information between competent authorities administrations about enforcement against goods suspected of infringing IPRs. The EPA with Malaysia is comprehensive, including more direct obligations on IPR protection and enforcement, such as protection of well-known trademarks, border measures, civil and criminal remedies, as well as provisions regarding transparency and promotion of public awareness concerning IPR protection.

The EFTA Agreements

On IP protection, EFTA follows a similar approach to that of its own Convention in the many agreements that it has concluded with third countries, at least the more recent ones.[92] A general statement as to the commitment to ensure "adequate, effective and non-discriminatory" protection of intellectual property rights in accordance with international standards[93] introduces more specific obligations. The parties reaffirm their obligations under the multilateral treaties to which they are all party and undertake to adhere to other treaties, in particular those to which all EFTA Members are party. Certain areas of substantive protection are specifically addressed, but as to enforcement, the parties agree to introduce "provisions under their national laws of the same level as that provided in the TRIPS Agreement, in particular Articles 41 to 61." The Agreements provide for varying degrees of co-operation in the field of intellectual property, such as assistance in the implementation of laws in the IP area and forward looking statements as to supporting initiatives to establish future international conventions.

ASEAN-China

The ASEAN-People's Republic of China Framework Agreement on Comprehensive Economic Co-operation (2002) includes as one of the areas of negotiations towards the realisation of an ASEAN-China Free Trade Area, the "facilitation and promotion of effective and adequate protection of trade-related aspects of intellectual property rights based on existing WTO, WIPO and other relevant disciplines."

Bilateral IP instruments

Of the existing stand-alone bilateral IPR instruments, several are worth mentioning with respect to enforcement of IPRs.

---

92. The Agreements examined: EFTA-Mexico (2000), EFTA-Chile (2003), EFTA-Lebanon (2004), EFTA-Tunisia (2004), EFTA-Republic of Korea (2005).

93. Unlike the EFTA Convention and many EC bilateral Agreements, "highest" international standards are not usually mentioned in EFTA Agreements.

EU – US Action Strategy for the Enforcement of Intellectual Property Rights

At the EU-USA Summit held in Vienna on 21 June 2006, an Action Strategy for the Enforcement of Intellectual Property Rights was adopted. This Strategy, without being a formal agreement, commits the two parties to taking a string of measures on enforcement in the areas of customs and border control and to engage in joint efforts vis-à-vis third countries, particularly Russia and China. It also provides for co-operation in the efforts which are being undertaken in the different multilateral fora.

US-China

The Memorandum of Understanding (MOU) on the Protection of Intellectual Property between the United States and the People's Republic of China of 1992 contains a general obligation for each of the parties to provide effective procedures and remedies, internally and at their borders, to prevent, stop and deter IPR infringements. This MOU has been followed by an Enforcement Agreement, concluded by an exchange of letters dated 26 February 1995, to which a State Council Intellectual Property Enforcement Action Plan is annexed. This Enforcement Agreement is essentially a description by China of its IPR enforcement structure, the roles of the various national IPR protection and enforcement bodies, as well as a description of China's present and future enforcement efforts. These efforts include, *inter alia,* concentrating investigations into infringements of specific products (*e.g.* audiovisual products), intensifying customs controls on imports and exports, toughening the administrative sanctions, such as the revocation of business licenses, and increasing their application, application of a new customs law which makes IPR a customs offence and provides for *ex officio* actions. It also provides for assistance by the US Customs Service, Department of Justice and Patent and Trademark Office in China's efforts to improve IPR enforcement.

US-Paraguay

The Memorandum of Understanding on Intellectual Property Rights between the United States and Paraguay dated 30 March 2004 requires Paraguay to fully comply with its TRIPS obligations and provides for specific actions to be undertaken by Paraguay in order to "achieve actual, meaningful enforcement results." Such actions include, *inter alia*, reinforcing co-ordination between the various government entities involved in enforcement of IPR violations, encouraging and enabling prosecutors to file *ex officio* criminal cases, providing for the seizure of the infringer's assets, ensuring that prison sentences are imposed, in addition to fines, with respect to offences involving commercial quantities of counterfeit and pirated goods, training of additional prosecutors and judges and improving border measures through various concrete actions, such as establishing a special IPR customs unit, training customs officials, co-operating with rights holders and increasing *ex officio* actions. Paraguay must also assume the collection and publication of information and statistics related to all of the foregoing measures.

Bilateral investment treaties

The definition of "investment" in most bilateral investment treaties (BITs) encompasses intellectual property as one of the covered assets, either by generically referring to IPRs as a whole or by listing them. The BITs extend to IPRs the classical principles of national treatment, most-favoured-nation, fair and equitable treatment. They may also provide for rules on compulsory licensing and parallel imports. However, BITs do not contain rules on IP enforcement and in this regard their most relevant aspect is their dispute settlement provisions and particularly the investor – State dispute settlement. A claim can be based on the failure of a host country to protect an intellectual property right, as any other covered asset. Such mechanisms may provide an additional venue to rights holders to ensure adequate IPR protection and enforcement.

Areas where international co-operation in the fight against counterfeiting and piracy could be further strengthened

A quite common view is that the international normative framework against counterfeiting and piracy is sufficient and that effectiveness depends exclusively on proper implementation of the existing rules. Indeed, improved implementation of the existing framework should have an effect on global piracy and counterfeiting. However, the present review highlights aspects that may contribute to tempering this widespread view. While the implementation difficulties certainly cannot be underestimated, this review shows that the international discipline is far from being adequately stringent or complete.

In recent years, the IP enforcement norms agreed at the regional and bilateral levels, developed on the basis of the TRIPS, have surpassed the TRIPS itself. These principles, some of which are still under discussion, could be scrutinised further to determine whether strengthening the multilateral discipline is warranted or desirable. Indeed, in some cases regional and bilateral rules make mandatory what in the TRIPS is just optional; in others, they provide for new solutions.

Additional measures that are being employed include:

- *Civil proceedings.* International rules could be improved in areas such as the seizure of goods and evidence, disclosure of information, and damage awards. For example, judicial authorities may be provided with a right, *inaudita altera parte*, to block the infringer's bank accounts and other assets, when necessary, to impair the infringing activity or to secure potential compensation for the rights holder. The authorities could also be granted powers to require the defendants to co-operate with the investigations carried out by the rights holders and by the authorities in order to further uncover the infringing activity; for example, requiring defendants to surrender business records to the court. With respect to damages, an element of profits related to the infringing activity could, for example, be added to the actual damage suffered. These measures are to some extent already contained in the EC Directive 2004/48 and in some US free-trade agreements (FTAs). These measures are of course binding for a limited number of parties and not necessarily for the more important players.

- *Border measures.* Experts consider border measures as one of the most effective mechanisms for stopping trade in counterfeit and pirated goods.[94] The first element in strengthening border measures could be to expand the scope of obligations to also cover exports, as well as goods in transit or transhipment. At the moment, article 51 of TRIPS provides for a mandatory system only with regard to the importation of goods, and there is no obligation to establish corresponding procedures against

---

94. See D. Gervais, "International Initiatives", in O Vrins, M Schneider (eds.), *Enforcement of Intellectual Property Rights through Border Measures, Law and Practice in the EU*, Oxford, 2006.

infringing goods destined for export. Moreover, goods in transit or transhipment are not covered by the mandatory system of border measures. Enabling customs administrations to control exports of products that infringe intellectual property rights would help to significantly reduce the trade flow at the source. Expanding the scope to include goods in transit would provide further opportunities to stem the flow of trade in infringing products. Such measures have also already been introduced in the WCO Model, US FTAs and EC instruments, such as EC Regulation 1383/2003.

- *Criminal proceedings.* In certain economies, criminal sanctions are extended to significant non-commercial piracy. In addition, *ex officio* investigations and prosecutions by authorities have been introduced, and the range of available remedies has been broadened, as in certain US FTAs and in the EC Directive currently under discussion.

- *Public information.* Public information may provide a significant element of effective deterrence, at both consumer and producer levels. Many of the regional and bilateral instruments reviewed contain some publication obligations for the parties, be they to publish the IPR protection and enforcement laws and regulations, enforcement statistics and/or the major judicial and administrative decisions against counterfeiting and piracy. The appropriateness of generalising such obligations should be evaluated.

Governments could consider the appropriateness of enhancing the existing international discipline, in particular by taking inspiration from, and building upon, the regional and bilateral rules. The EC rules and certain FTAs, particularly the most recent ones concluded by the United States, provide examples of an enforcement discipline that could be extended more widely. Other elements, especially in dispute settlement, could be taken up from investment law, and particularly from the experience of investor-State proceedings.

On the one hand, as seen above, the regional and bilateral agreements have been instrumental in ensuring a certain improvement and expansion of IPR enforcement provisions beyond the minimum standards of the TRIPS. Because, for the most part, they involve few partners, these instruments may, on an individual basis, be less challenging to put in place than a comprehensive multilateral instrument. On the other hand, as also demonstrated by this review, the dispersed bilateral/regional approach leads to diverse and uneven results.

In conclusion, continued study by national experts is needed to determine whether, and how, global IPR enforcement efforts could be enhanced by strengthening the international legal framework or the harmonisation of enforcement measures.

Annex 7.A2

ECONOMY TEMPLATES:
OVERVIEW OF ANTI-COUNTERFEITING POLICIES

BRAZIL

Institutional organisation	The National Industrial Institute (INPI), which is an autonomous federal agency under the Ministry of Development, Industry and Trade, oversees the implementation of laws and regulations pertaining to industrial property, which includes patents, trademarks, industrial design rights, geographical indications and computer programmes (WTO, 2004). (www.inpi.gov.br/)
Policy developments	In 2003, the Brazilian government stepped up its fight against counterfeiting and piracy, creating a Parliamentary Inquiry Committee on Piracy (CPI) to investigate piracy and tax evasion. A result of that investigation was the creation on 1 October 2004 of a National Council to Combat Piracy and Crimes against Intellectual property (CNCP), comprising representatives from both the public and private sectors. The Council's work is guided by a plan containing 99 guidelines for priority action. The guidelines have four principal aspects: enforcement, education, economic and institutional policies (WIPO, 2006).
Legal and regulatory framework	The 1996 Industrial Property Law provides for civil and/or criminal actions against trademark and patents infringements.
	Trademark and patent remedies for civil cases include recovery of damages, destruction of seized products, and judicial cost recovery.
	For trademark and patent law violation, imprisonment generally varies from three months to a year, but may be increased according to the infringement and the infringer (WTO, 2004).
	The 1998 Copyright Law establishes which acts are considered civil offences, while crimes are described in the Brazilian Criminal Code (WTO, 2004). Criminal penalties can vary from three months to four years imprisonment and/or a fine. In 2003, the Code was modified to increase the types of copyright infringement considered as felonies and inflict harsher penalties. For the main felonies, the minimum penalty is two years and the maximum four years: the possibility of suspension of the sentence is no longer available. In addition to imprisonment, infringing parties can be subject to a fine.
	In the case of software copyright infringements, pirated copies produced or commercialised could be subject to seizure and destruction and punishable with detention from six months to four years plus a fine [WTO, 2004].
Enforcement	The government has increased resources devoted to enforcement and efforts to publicise enforcement through the media. Together with the judicial structure, the National Council against Piracy has been working on the creation of specialised structures within the Federal and Highway Policy Forces for combating piracy. Additional resources were allocated in 2006 to enforcement bodies including the National Industrial Property Institute (INPI).
	Institutional reform has also occurred. The Brazilian Federal Court of Appeals for the Second Region, which covers the state of Rio de Janeiro and Espirito Santo, was reorganised in 2005 to include two panels specialising in IP matters. The court has Brazil's Institute of Industrial Property within its jurisdiction.
	With regard to border measures, customs authorities are able to seize trademark-infringing products on an *ex officio* basis, as well as on the request of an interested party; the principle has, however, been extended in practice to cover other types of IP infringements (Gorini and Werner, 2004). Under current practice, Customs may retain seized items for a period of 90 days, within which the rights holder must follow up. Once confirmed, illegally marked goods can be destroyed or otherwise disposed of (EC, 2006).
	The CNCP website (www.mj.gov.br/combatepirataria/) provides a direct channel of communication for enforcement and consumer protection bodies to file complaints and transmit information on piracy cases and new methods of counterfeiting. It is also possible to file complaints about corruption in actions dealing with crimes against intellectual property (WIPO, 2006).
	New additional training programmes for police officers, experts and agents of the Federal Revenue Department and the States' ministries of finance were to be introduced in 2006 with additional programmes foreseen in conjunction with the Intellectual Property Defence Association (ADEPI), a member of the CNCP (WIPO, 2006).
	Enforcement efforts have increased in recent years, as has the degree of co-operation among government agencies (WTO, 2004). Several operations involving federal, state and municipal bodies were conducted at various centres known for selling pirated products. Priority was initially given to stepping up control at strategic border points, such as Ponte da Amizade linking Brazil and Paraguay. Efforts were later made to intensify repressive measures at large markets and shopping centres in Sao Paulo, Rio de Janeiro and Brasilia. Other enforcement actions reported regularly included stepping up of raids and closures of large factories that produce counterfeit goods, and reports of arrests of criminals (WIPO, 2006). As a result, the value of merchandise destroyed by the Brazilian Revenue Service during the first six months of 2004 was almost five-fold the level of 2003. With respect to other forms of IPR infringement, there was a 16-fold increase in the value of goods destroyed during the two time periods (WTO, 2004).

Enhanced efforts continued in 2005. During the first half of the year, four major joint operations involving the Internal Revenue Service, the Federal Police Department and the Federal Highway Police Department were carried out in the TBA area (Ministry of Justice, 2005), leading to sharply higher levels of seized goods, arrests and disruption in illegal commerce.

This was also the case in 2006, with early indications that seizures reported for the period January to September 2006 had exceed those reported for the whole of 2005 (Ministry of Justice, 2006).

Programme evaluation and measurement	The Ministry of Justice published three detailed reports on efforts to combat counterfeiting and piracy during 2005-6 (www.mj.gov.br/combatepirataria/).
International co-operation	Initiatives taken at a regional level to protect intellectual property have included liaison with foreign governments to exchange information on measures directed against counterfeiting and piracy.
	Brazil has worked with its MERCOSUR partners to address counterfeiting and piracy through a 2003 amendment to its 1999 Regional Protection Plan (Carneiro and Santos, 2004). The agreement includes specific provisions for piracy and notably calls for members to: create a special department focused on the repression of piracy; improve intelligence sharing through the creation *inter alia* of a database dealing with piracy; and co-ordinate training and capacity building regarding IP enforcement.
	Operation Jupiter-South America was launched in November 2004. It was the first co-ordinated cross-industry, cross-border police operation to target counterfeiting and piracy in this way (Interpol, 2006). It involved the national police forces of Argentina, Brazil and Paraguay, the Brazilian Customs and representatives from pharmaceutical, recording, motion picture and tobacco cross-industry representative bodies. The operation centred on a number of intellectual property (IP) crime targets, all of which were significant counterfeiting plants or distribution centres. The results included a significant number of seizures and arrests.
	The Latin American Regional Forum, hosted by Brazil and Interpol, held in Rio de Janeiro in June 2005, under the auspices of the Global Congress on Combating Counterfeiting, adopted the "Rio Declaration", which recommended a series of steps to enhance the effectiveness of the fight against counterfeiting in the region, calling, *inter alia*, for better co-operation between the various stakeholders, as well as updated legislation in a number of areas (Global Congress or Combating Counterfeiting and Piracy, 2005).
	At the bilateral level, Brazil signed a Memorandum of Understanding with Paraguay in 2005 that established a bilateral group for intelligence on piracy. Brazil also signed a technical co-operation agreement on intellectual property with France in 2006 (INPI, 2007).
Awareness	One of the techniques used to increase awareness has been the publicised and open destruction of seized goods. Another is the use of the CNCP's (Ministry of Justice) website dedicated to counterfeiting and piracy related events and seizures.
	A new campaign aimed at young consumers was launched in March 2006. The campaign "Pirata: tô for a! Só uso original" (Piracy I'm out of it I only use originals) is being carried out through television, radio and advertising; in addition tee shirts, hats and stickers promoting the campaign message are being distributed. The focus was initially on fairs and popular events and will be extended to primary and secondary schools, colleges and universities. The need to focus on young consumers was supported by a recent survey that indicated that 15-24 year olds were major consumers of infringing products. Along the same lines, the Prefecture of one of the towns in the São Paulo area launched a campaign "O barato que sai caro: (cheap can be expensive), which sought to inform the public of the negative consequences of piracy.
	In 2005, several seminars, conferences and events were held by the National Council against Piracy and other enforcement agencies. An agreement signed in August 2005 between the CNCP and the Department of Consumer Protection and Defence (DPDC) provided for counterfeiting and piracy to be included in training programmes made available to state consumer-protection agencies (PROCONS). Training was also given high priority in 2006.
Industry initiatives and co-operation	The Intellectual property Rights Protection Association (ADEPI) documents co-ordination between the public and private sectors: //www.adepi.org.br/. The ADEPI provides intelligence aimed at dismantling operations and arresting distributors of infringing goods and provides training for authorities (Ministry of Justice, 2005).

References

Carneiro, Rodrigo Borges and Mauro Ivan C. R. dos Santos (2004), "Will South America Succeed in its Fight against Counterfeiting", at www.dannemann.com.br, March.

Dannemann Siemsen (undated), "Trademarks in Brazil", at www.dannemann.com.br, accessed October 2006.

European Commission (2006), "Intellectual Property: Enforcement Survey 2006", at http://ec.europa.eu/trade/issues/sectoral/intell_property/survey2006_en.htm, October.

Global Congress on Combating Counterfeiting and Crime (2005), The Rio Declaration, June, at www.ccap.net.

Gorini, Attilio José Ventura and José Henrique Vasi Werner, "Border Control of Intellectual Property Rights", at www.dannemann.com.br, 2004.

Instituto Nacional da Propriedade Industrial INPI (2006), Notícia 25/01/07, INPI do Brasil e França assinam acordo de co-operação, www.inpi.gov.br/

Interpol, 2006, Significant Cases, at www.interpol.org, downloaded August 2006.

Ministry of Justice, National Council to Combat Piracy and Crimes against Intellectual Property (2005), Brazil Against Piracy, at www.mj.gov.br/combatepirataria.

Ministry of Justice, National Council to Combat Piracy and Crimes against Intellectual Property (2006), Brazil Against Piracy, at www.mj.gov.br/combatepirataria.

WIPO (2006), Advisory Committee on Enforcement, Public Policies for Combating Piracy in Brazil, May.

WTO (2004), "Trade Policy Review Brazil", WT/TPR/S/140, at www.wto.org.

CANADA

Institutional organisation	Several Canadian government departments and agencies are involved in dealing with issues related to intellectual property rights. On the technical and administrative side, the Canadian Intellectual Property Office (CIPO) is responsible for granting and administering the greater part of intellectual property rights in Canada (CIPO, 2006 and Garland and Want, circa 2001).
	CIPO's areas of activity include patents, trademarks, copyrights, industrial design and integrated circuit topographies. Management of IPR issues related to plant breeders' rights, however, is overseen by the Canadian Food Inspection Agency (CFIA).
	Canadian Heritage and Industry Canada are the key departments dealing with IP policy and legislation, whereas Foreign Affairs and International Trade Canada are the lead departments on most international IP files.
	With respect to criminal enforcement, the Royal Canadian Mounted Police (RCMP) is involved in cases of IPR infringements involving criminal offences. So are, to a smaller extent, provincial and municipal police departments. Regarding border enforcement, the Canadian Border Services Agency (CBSA), upon a court order, can detain suspected counterfeit and pirated goods at the borders.
Policy developments	In recent years, federal enforcement policies and programmes have sought to put more emphasis on border enforcement (Government of Canada, 2006). This has entailed interception by the CBSA of suspect counterfeit goods that come to their attention while administering the Customs Act. CBSA provides information to the RCMP who may authorise the seizure of the shipment as evidence of a Criminal Code offence.
Legal and regulatory framework	In Canada, intellectual property rights (IPR) are protected primarily under the following Acts: Trade-marks Act, Copyright Act, Patent Act, Industrial Design Act, Integrated Circuit Topographies Act, and Plant Breeders' Rights Act.
	Canada's intellectual property enforcement policy has relied primarily on civil enforcement by intellectual property rights holders (Government of Canada, 2006). Rights holders themselves are largely responsible for monitoring domestic markets for counterfeit and pirated products, with federal enforcement resources reserved for forms of infringements which constitute criminal offences; these would include infringements occurring on a commercial scale, and those involving public health and safety concerns (Government of Canada, 2006).
	Most infringements are addressed by parties through civil action. The Copyright Act does, however, include provisions for criminal sanctions for serious infringements. Under the Act, criminal offences are punishable by fines up to $1 million or imprisonment for a term not exceeding five years.
	The civil enforcement is encouraged by providing rights holders with remedies, such as injunctions, seizures and damages against unauthorised and infringing uses of intellectual property. The intellectual property rights regime has been modified periodically to address a number of issues. In 1997, for example, the government introduced a statutory damages provision in the Copyright Act to provide rights holders with a greater degree of redress. This has implications for trademark infringements as well, since such infringements can, in some instances, be addressed under the Copyright Act.
	Regarding criminal provisions, there are several criteria that have to be met in order for the RCMP to proceed with a criminal investigation in the case of copyright: it must be demonstrated that the accused acted with knowledge that the subject works were infringing goods; the infringed work must be original and duly protected; genuine goods must be distinguishable from counterfeits, and licensed versions must be distinguishable from non-licensed versions; credible evidence must establish the financial impact of the infringement on the complaining party.
	While there are no provisions in the Trade-marks Act for criminal enforcement, there is a section of the Criminal Code governing forgery of trademarks and trade descriptions. The primary offence is that of making or reproducing in any matter a trademark with the intent to deceive or defraud the public or any person; the punishment involves imprisonment for a term not exceeding two years.
	As for the border enforcements, measures are taken under the Copyright Act and the Trademarks Act, which permit rights holders, on court order, to request that the CBSA intercept infringing goods at the border (Government of Canada 2006).
Enforcement developments	The RCMP has been increasing the resources devoted to fighting organised crime. Within the country, 19 investigators were dedicated to IPR enforcement issues. Also, collaboration between the CBSA and the RCMP has been increased. The RCMP provides intelligence to customs officials concerning commercial scale shipments of infringing products. Since December 2003, these two agencies have both been reporting to the Minister of Public Safety. In collaboration with the Canadian Department of Justice, and other relevant government departments and agencies, the two agencies are both currently engaged in the process of identifying Canadian intellectual property enforcement concerns (Government of Canada, 2006).

Programme evaluation and measurement	Two projects were carried out on the assessment of IP crime in Canada by the Criminal Intelligence Directorate of the Royal Canadian Mounted Police (RCMP): Project Saffron (2000) and Project Sham (a 2004 update).
International co-operation	Canada has been an active participant in various international forums dealing with counterfeiting and piracy, including the G-8, APEC, WTO and WIPO.
	Canada has also been active in promoting, through Interpol, the creation of databases that feature information and criminal intelligence useful for investigating and prosecuting copyright and trademark offences (Government of Canada, 2006). Information exchanges with other economies have also translated into common enforcement efforts and lead to some important seizures of counterfeit and pirated goods.
Awareness	In partnership with the Canadian Anti-Counterfeiting Network, in May 2006 the RCMP launched a national awareness campaign designed to educate consumers, retailers and the public in general, about the dangers and economic costs associated with counterfeit products as well as its connection to organised crime (RCMP, 2006).
Industry initiatives and co-operation	Within industry, a coalition of individuals, firms and associations have formed a Canadian Anti-Counterfeiting Network to combat counterfeiting and piracy in Canada and internationally (www.cacn.ca). The organisation has worked with government in a number of areas; activities have included the organisation of training seminars and, as mentioned above, the launching of a public awareness initiative, in partnership with the RCMP.
	Individual industry associations, particularly in the software, film, music and designer goods industries, employ their own enforcement personnel (Government of Canada, 2006). Industry investigators – often retired RCMP personnel – compile evidence and then turn it over to the RCMP to complete the investigation and pursue criminal charges.

References

Canada Border Services Agency (CBSA)(2006), response to OECD customs questionnaire.

Canadian Intellectual Property Office (CIPO) (2006), at http://strategis.ic.gc.ca/sc_mrksv/cipo/welcome/welcom-e.html.

Government of Canada (2006), response to OECD country/economy questionnaire.

International AntiCounterfeiting Coalition (IACC) (2006), "Submission of the International AntiCounterfeiting Coalition, Inc. to the United States Trade Representative: Special 301 recommendations", February, accessed April 2006, at www.iacc.org.

Royal Canadian Mounted Police (RCMP) (2000), "Assessment of commercial scale criminal copyright piracy and trademark counterfeiting in Canada", accessed in April 2006 at www.rcmp-grc.gc.ca/crimint/copyright_piracy_e.htm.

Royal Canadian Mounted Police (RCMP) (2004), "Project SHAM: A strategic intelligence assessment of intellectual property crime in Canada".

Royal Canadian Mounted Police (RCMP) (2006), Organisation website, accessed in April 2006 at www.rcmp-grc.gc.ca.

CHINA

Institutional organisation	In China, the responsibility for intellectual property (IP) is entrusted with different entities under the State Council. The State Intellectual Property Office (SIPO) is in charge of patents, the State Administration for Industry and Commerce (SAIC) is in charge of trademarks, while the National Copyright Administration of China (NCAC) is in charge of copyrights (OECD, 2005a).
	There are two levels for IP protection in China. Administrative bodies under the State Council - SIPO, SAIC and NCAC - generally examine, grant or register IPR and handle infringement cases of major importance; the local administrative authorities are responsible for the implementation of policies and for administering and enforcing IPR at the local level (WTO, 2006).
	To improve IP protection, the State Council created the National Working Group on IP protection in 2005, which comprises 17 different administrative authorities and judicial departments. The Working Group is based at the Ministry of Commerce (MOFCOM) and is administered by the State Office of Intellectual Property Rights; it is responsible for unified planning and co-ordination of national intellectual property protection and supervises important IPR cases (WTO, 2006).
Policy developments	In recent years, China has amended its IPR laws and has modified regulations on customs protection. After having focused on the improvement of the legislation, the government's focus is now shifting to enhancing law enforcement. This shift in focus is described in a White Paper on Intellectual Property Rights[95] issued by the Government in April 2005 (State Council, 2005; WTO, 2006).
	The State Office of Intellectual Property Protection issued an "Action Plan"[96] in March 2006, which sets out a number of initiatives to strengthen IP protection over the course of 2006.
	The "Action Plan" covers four major areas: trademarks, copyright, patent and import and export-related issues. It summarises a wide range of initiatives in the areas of legislation, enforcement, training, education, awareness raising, international co-operation and services to rights holders.
	The action plan also outlines enforcement campaigns with crackdown operations targeted towards trademark infringement (continuation of the "Mountain Eagle" Campaign, see below), copyright infringement (Operation "Sunshine" for audio-visual products). A special campaign is targeted towards combating infringement at trade shows (Operation "Blue Sky").
Legal and regulatory framework	In China, trademarks, copyright, patents and design are protected under three major laws and their complementary implementing regulations: the Trademark Law, which was adopted in 1982 and revised in 1993 and 2001; the Patent Law, adopted in 1984 and revised in 1992 and 2000; and the Copyright Law, adopted in 1990 and revised in 2001.
	In case of IPR infringement, civil actions accompanied by monetary fines are included in the Patent, Trademark and Copyright laws (WTO, 2006). The Patent Law allows fines up to RMB 50 000[97], or three times the illegal earnings from passing off another person's patent as one's own. The Trademark Law allows for compensation not exceeding RMB 500 000. The revised regulations of the Copyright Law authorise fines up to RMB 100 000 for copyright infringements.
	Under the Criminal Law, seven specific types of IPR infringement are regarded as a criminal act: counterfeiting registered trademarks; selling goods bearing counterfeit registered trademarks; illegally producing and selling representations of registered trademarks; forging another person's patent' copyright infringement; selling infringing reproductions; and infringing commercial secrets. For infringement of trademarks, patents and copyrights the infringer can be sentenced to up to three years of prison and/or a fine. If the infringement has particularly serious consequence - in terms of substandard quality or health and safety of the consumer - the punishment can be up to seven years imprisonment.
	The Chinese Customs Law forbids the import or export of goods infringing the IP rights protected by Chinese law. Regulations on "Customs Protection of Intellectual Property Rights" enable customs to seize imports and exports of goods infringing patents, trademarks and copyright-related rights on an *ex officio* basis (WTO, 2006). In order to enhance the efficiency of seizures by Customs, the owner of the intellectual property right may "record" or file their right in writing with the Customs (WTO, 2006). New regulations issued by the Customs administration in September 2004

---

95. See www.china.org.cn/english/MATERIAL/126297.htm.

96. See www.ipr.gov.cn/ipr/en/info/Article.jsp?a_no=3326&col_no=102&dir=200604.

97. 1 USD = 7.7 China Yuan Renmimbi (RMB) (March 2007).

	regarding administrative penalties in the Customs context provide for fines not to exceed 30% of the value of the good confiscated, or RMB 50 000, whichever is lower.
Enforcement	Since 2004, the Government has undertaken several enforcement campaigns to combat counterfeiting and piracy. Between September 2004 and August 2005, a special one-year campaign was launched to protect IPR. Relevant administrative departments investigated and dealt with major IPR infringement cases in the fields of trademarks, copyrights and patents. This campaign focused on 15 key regions, such as Beijing, Shanghai and Tianjin and major distribution channels for counterfeit and pirated goods. Pirated discs and trademark infringements were the main targets of this campaign (State Council, 2005).

In November 2004, the Ministry of Public Security launched a one-year national campaign titled "Mountain Eagle" against criminal infringement on trademarks to crack down major cases of IPR infringement (State Council, 2005). Chinese public security authorities initiated over 10 000 raids on offices, stores and warehouses. This campaign has been extended to a second phase (Nie and Wei, 2006).

China has a dual mechanism for IPR protection. Under this system, the responsibility for IPR enforcement is shared between the State Council IPR administrations and the Courts and Procuratorate bodies. The majority of IPR cases is, however, handled by the administrative authorities (80% of the cases in 2005).

<u>Administrative enforcement</u>

Administrative authorities are empowered to: question the accused infringer; examine documents; search premises; freeze assets; issue an injunction order; confiscate and destroy counterfeit goods and the facilities specifically used in the infringement; and impose a penalty[98]. If the infringements are found to be so serious as to have constituted a crime, the case would be transferred to a competent judicial authority for criminal investigation.

Regarding border enforcement, a co-operative mechanism has been set up between the General Administration for Customs of China (GACC) and other IP enforcement administrations, including SIPO, SAIC, the Ministry of Public Security and the Supreme People's Court. In addition, Customs has increased communication with enterprises to group information resources. Methods for checking and seizing infringement products have been improved.

<u>Judicial enforcement</u>

China has progressively established a system of specialised IP tribunals[99] and has developed trained judges to sit on specialised IP tribunal to hear civil cases. An IP holder may request the court to issue an injunction order or an interim injunction before formally lodging a complaint. Preservation of evidence is also available if part of the infringement is in danger of being destroyed. Under the Chinese civil law, damages are available. They are, however, compensatory, rather than punitive. Damages may be calculated based on profits gained by the infringer or losses suffered by the rights holder. Statutory damages are now also available if a plaintiff is unable to fully quantify its damage.

Regarding criminal prosecution, the public security body is responsible for carrying out criminal investigations concerning IPR infringements[100]. Minor criminal cases are heard directly by the People's Court's First Instance, whereas the procuratorial system is responsible for cases endangering public order and national interest (WTO, 2006). |
| **Programme evaluation and measurement** | SIPO/the State Council produce an annual paper on "Intellectual Property Protection" in China outlining main achievements in the area of IP protection and enforcement (see SIPO, 2006). |
| **International co-operation** | China has engaged in exchanges and co-operation with other countries in the field of IPR. China and the United States established a framework for regular consultation on IP in 2000. It relied on roundtable discussions on IPR, and since 2003, China and the US have held these discussions every year. In 2004, the Intellectual Property Protection Working Group of the Joint Commission of Commerce and Trade (JCCT) was set up (WTO, 2006). China has also established a new platform to conduct exchanges with the European Union on IPR: both parties signed an agreement in 2003 to establish a China-EU dialogue on Intellectual Property. Since 2004, China has had rounds of talks with the EU. In addition, China has established dialogues and co-operation mechanisms on IP with Japan, Korea and France (WTO, 2006). |

8. If damages are sought by the rights holder, the judicial route must be used since the administrative authority is not authorised to award damages; also the fines in the administrative system will revert to the state (China-Britain Business Council, 2004).

9. A few Basic People's Courts, which handle substantial IP litigation have set up IP tribunals. High People's Courts and Intermediate People's Courts of some cities have established IP tribunals. The Supreme People's Court set up the Intellectual Property Tribunal (now called Third Civil Chamber), whose role is to handle major IP cases and provide guidance for, and supervision of, IP cases across the country.

00. In China, an IPR dispute may be deemed criminal in certain circumstances, one of them being when the value of the goods exceeds the monetary threshold required for criminal prosecution -- there is a distinction in the threshold for individual or corporate infringement. The Supreme People's Court's interpretation on the IP sections of the Criminal Law in December 2004 lowered the minimum thresholds required for criminal prosecution for various IP violations.

	Bilateral dialogues have been established to strengthen IPR protection in China, notably through more efficient enforcement. Several US agencies, notably the Patent and Trademark Office, the Department of Justice and the Department of Commerce provided IP enforcement training. The European Patent Office has been engaged in a long-term co-operation with China since 1986 and has provided training for a large number of SIPO staff. Today, Chinese departments are in contact with corresponding departments in other countries and also with WIPO (State Council, 2005).
Awareness	Since 2004, China has been launching national public-awareness campaigns to educate the Chinese public on IPR protection. This included radio and TV programmes, newspaper inserts, awards and national local training programmes. The campaign also included the introduction of a television programme "Intellectual Fortune" broadcast in 20 provinces nationwide. Beginning 2004, the state designated a week in April every year as the week for publicising the importance of IPR protection and the government's results regarding IPR protection. This initiative aims to popularise general knowledge about IP protection and stress its vital role in promoting scientific and technological innovation.
Industry initiatives and co-operation	Industry representatives, notably the Motion Picture Association and the Business Software Alliance undertook numerous training and awareness raising programmes throughout China in 2005. Trainings have involved police, prosecutors, judges, customs officials, administrative agency enforcement personnel. The Quality Brands Protection Committee, which was established in March 2000, has launched many initiatives to broaden public awareness on the problem of counterfeiting and to strengthen the capacity of the enforcement system. Finally, Chinese companies have also formed alliances to protect their IP rights and fight counterfeiting and piracy. This is, for example, the case with the newly created copyright alliance comprising six leading Chinese companies. The alliance intends to act as a bridge between companies, government and the media and raise awareness about the damage created by piracy.

References

China-Britain Business Council (2004), "The China IPR Guidelines", www.cbbc.org/initiatives/ipr_forum/

European Chamber (2006), "European Business in China", position paper 2006/2007, www.europeanchamber.com.cn

European Commission (2006), "Intellectual Property: Enforcement Survey 2006", October, http://ec.europa.eu/trade/issues/sectoral/intell_property/survey2006_en.htm.

Nie, Jianqiang and Yanliang Wei (2006), unpublished report for the OECD Secretariat.

OECD (2005a), "Governance in China", September, www.oecd.org/document/32/0,2340,en_2649_34121_35340704_1_1_1_1,00.html

OECD (2005b), "Promoting IPR Policy and Enforcement in China", www.oecd.org/LongAbstract/0,2546,fr_2649_33703_34407674_1_1_1_1,00.html

OECD (2006), Responses to OECD customs survey, unpublished.

People's Republic of China (2006), Response to OECD customs survey, unpublished.

Quality Brand Protection Committee (2004), "Annual review of counterfeiting developments", http://www.qbpc.org.cn, January.

State Council (2005), "White Paper on IPR protection", www.china.org.cn/english/MATERIAL/126297.htm

State Intellectual Property Office (SIPO) (2006), "China's Intellectual Property Protection in 2005", www.sipo.gov.cn/sipo_English/ndbg/

WIPO, Advisory Committee on Enforcement, WIPO/ACE/2/8 of 10 June 2004.

WIPO, Advisory Committee on Enforcement, WIPO/ACE/3/16 of 15 May 2005.

WTO (2006), "Trade Policy Review China", www.wto.org.

Zhang, August (2006), "A practical review of the effect of lowered criminal threshold in China", www.iprights.com/publications/articles/index.asp, August.

Zhang, August (2005), "China: the impact of new judicial interpretations in intellectual property-related criminal cases", www.iprights.com/publications/articles/index.asp, May.

Zhou, Zhongqi (2006), "Country chapter on China", World Trademark Yearbook 2006, www.worldtrademarklawreport.com/yearbook/2006.

EUROPEAN UNION

Institutional organisation	The competence for the protection and enforcement of intellectual property rights is shared between the European Union (EU) and its 27 Member States (MS). In the legislative field, most subjects have already been harmonised by EU Regulations (which are directly applicable as law in all MS) and Directives (which define the general lines but require national implementing legislation). Intellectual property rights such as copyrights and related rights, trademarks, designs or geographical indications have most of their rules defined at EU level.
	Regarding the enforcement aspects, the EU has already regulated civil and administrative proceedings, as well as a common regime for customs IPR infringements (see below). For the remaining field, *i.e.* the harmonisation of rules regulating criminal infringements, the European Commission issued a legislative proposal in 2005 that is currently undergoing the process of approval before the European Parliament and the Council (the representatives of the MS governments).
	The external aspects of trade-related IPR, both at bilateral and at multilateral level, are exclusive competencies of the EU, which acts on behalf of its 27 MS in all acts and negotiations with the World Trade Organization and with third countries (ex: negotiation of IPR clauses in Free Trade Agreements).
	On the legislative side, many areas are already defined at EU level. However, most of the "operational" competencies, responsibilities and means to fight against piracy and counterfeiting domestically and at the external border – such as police, prosecutors, courts and customs services -- are in the hands of the individual EU member states.
	Roles are split among the EU institutions as follows:
	▪ European Commission: Has competence regarding the drafting and proposal of new laws harmonising the European IPR regime, as well as monitoring the implementation by MS of the guidelines defined at EU level. Externally, the Commission represents MS on bilateral and multilateral venues for all trade related IPR issues.
	▪ European Parliament and Council of the European Union: On IPR issues, these two institutions are responsible for the approval of legislation.
	▪ European Court of Justice and Court of First Instance: Under their general competence of examining the legality of Community measures and ensuring the uniform interpretation and application of Community law, the EU courts will issue jurisprudence relating to IPR issues on their own and in conjunction with national courts (preliminary rulings).
Policy developments	In November 2000, the European Commission issued an Action Plan on Combating Counterfeiting and Piracy in the Single Market. This Action Plan has appeared in the form of a Directive, harmonising the enforcement of intellectual property rights within the Community, covering a Regulation improving the mechanisms for customs action against counterfeit or pirated goods set by the previous Customs Regulation, and the extension of Europol's powers to cover piracy and counterfeiting.
	On the external side, the EC adopted in 2005 the Enforcement Strategy to step up the fight against counterfeiting and piracy in third countries. The Enforcement Strategy proposes the identification of priority countries where the efforts and resources of the EU should concentrate. Stress is put on technical co-operation and assistance to help third countries, but it also foresees the use of bilateral and multilateral sanction mechanisms available against countries involved in systematic violations. The European Commission also proposes a more systematic promotion of IPR mechanisms in multilateral, bi-regional and bilateral frameworks, as well as fostering awareness amongst users and consumers in third countries, and to establish partnerships with private entities, as well as with international organisations and countries sharing its concerns.
Legal and regulatory framework	The EU establishes its framework for IP protection mainly through Regulations (legislation directly applicable and with direct effect in all MS) and Directives (legislation that defines the main guidelines but that needs to be implemented by national legislation in each MS, with a degree of choice regarding the transposition.
	Directive 93/98/EEC has been replaced by Directive 2006/116/EC, which harmonises the term of protection of copyright and certain related rights. The period of protection is 70 years after the death of the author for a literary or artistic work, and 50 years after the event for the commencement of neighbouring rights.
	Concerning trademark law: in the EU, an applicant may register a trademark either within an individual EU member state (based on local trade mark regulations) or using the Community Trade Mark (CTM), which means that it is protected in all member states. Council Regulation (EC) No 40/94 of 20 December 1993 created the CTM, which is supervised by the Office for Harmonization in the Internal Market (OHIM) located in Alicante, Spain. A new Regulation adopted in 2004 made a number of changes to the Community trademark system in order to make it more effective.

The EU patent legislation is complex. The 1973 Munich Convention on the European Patent provides for patents to be obtained for a number of countries, including all EU members, through a single application to the European Patent Office (EPO, which is not an EU institution). The 1975 Luxembourg Convention was intended to give unitary effect to European patents applied for in Community territory. In 2000, a proposal for a Regulation was put forward aimed at setting up a Community patent which would coexist with national patent systems and with the Munich Convention system. This Regulation is still being finalised.

Council Regulation (EC) No 6/2002 of 12 December 2001 on Community Design creates a unified system for obtaining a Community Design valid throughout the EC.

Enforcement	The "operational" competencies, responsibilities and means to fight against piracy and counterfeiting domestically, and at the external border, are in the hands of the individual EU member states. Police forces, prosecutors, courts, customs services and other administrative forces with enforcement responsibilities are mostly a national competence of each MS. Nevertheless, some EU institutions designed for judicial and police co-operation, such as Europol and Eurojust, and some instruments (such as European Arrest Warrant, freezing property and evidence[101] and financial penalties[102] that concern the mutual recognition of criminal judiciary decisions) can be applied to cases related to the violation of IP rights.

On the legislative side, however, as mentioned above, several important areas have common rules, adopted by the EU:

Directive 2004/48/EC on the enforcement of intellectual property rights harmonises the laws of the EU member states pertaining to enforcement of intellectual property rights via civil and administrative sanctions and remedies (criminal proceedings and sanctions are beyond its scope). It covers infringements of all IP rights and is based on "best practice" found in the EU. Member States had until 29 April 2006 to transpose the Directive's provisions into their national laws.

Customs Regulation EC/1383/2003 sets out the conditions under which the customs authorities may intervene in cases where goods are suspected of infringing intellectual property rights.

A proposal for harmonising the minimum threshold for sanctions and criminal proceedings, to support the Enforcement directive, was presented by the Commission in July 2005 in the form of a Directive. This proposal is still being discussed by the European Parliament and the Council of the European Union.

Programme evaluation and measurement	The Commission's Taxation and Customs Union Directorate (TAXUD) publishes an annual compilation of statistics on customs seizures based on data from member countries. The statistics are used for evaluating enforcement efforts as well as for tracking activities in counterfeiting and piracy more generally.
International co-operation	The EU Strategy for the Enforcement of IPR in Third Countries[103] provides for technical co-operation and assistance to help third countries with IPR enforcement.

In addition, the Commission has intensified its bilateral co-operation, particularly with economies heavily affected by IPR violation practices. The main activities undertaken to implement the Enforcement Strategy:

- In October 2006, the European Commission announced a list of priority countries on which to focus activity and resources in the fight against piracy and counterfeiting. For each, an individual assessment was published[104], listing the main problems, the efforts made by the country in question and the measures to be implemented by the Commission.

- The EU established structured IPR dialogues with several priority countries. The purpose is to contribute to an enhanced protection and enforcement of IPR. EU right-holders are allowed to participate in some sessions. Assessment of progress is made at the annual high-level trade meetings.

- EU-US co-operation: At the EU-US June 2006 Summit, the parties launched an Action Strategy to combat IP infringement in third countries. It provides for closer customs co-operation, including joint border enforcement actions; joint enforcement in "third countries" with teams of EU and US diplomats sharing data and intelligence and undertaking joint surveillance activities; joint technical assistance initiatives and strongly increased collaboration with, and in support of, the private sector. A Working Group with enforcement officials from both sides was created and has been meeting twice a year, with frequent and productive contacts at the working level.

- EU-Japan co-operation: The EU-Japan Dialogue on IPR, which started in 2003, continues to hold annual meetings, where issues of mutual concern regarding IPR enforcement are discussed. Parties are currently in the process of reinforcing this co-operation.

---

01. Council Framework Decision 2003/577/JHA of 22 July 2003 on the execution in the European Union of orders freezing property or evidence.

02. Council Framework Decision 2005/214/JHA of 24 February 2005 on the application of the principle of mutual recognition to financial penalties.

03. http://ec.europa.eu/trade/issues/sectoral/intell_property/strategy_tc.htm

04. http://ec.europa.eu/trade/issues/sectoral/intell_property/ipr_epc_countries_en.htm

- IPR Experts in Delegations: IPR experts were placed in Beijing and Moscow. In Bangkok, there is a customs expert dealing also with enforcement problems in the ASEAN region. These experts work on the creation of a network with experts from the US and EU member states. They also work closely with local EU industry representatives.

- WTO: The EU has led the debate on enforcement in the WTO/TRIPs Council, by submitting a Communication in June 2005 proposing a detailed assessment of enforcement practices among the WTO membership. Since then, the US, Switzerland and Japan have joined the EU efforts.

- G8: The EU has been actively involved in the G8 IPR agenda since the 2005 Gleneagles Summit. The EU is one of the main contributors to the ambitious agenda set by the German G8 presidency for 2007, which includes customs and technical assistance best practices and increased co-ordination, technical assistance pilot projects i South America, South Africa and Indonesia, co-operation against organised crime (Lyon-Roma Group), a partnership with the private sector to promote good business practices and an outreach process to discuss innovation and IPR with emerging economies at the OECD.

- Bilateral trade agreements are increasingly becoming another important tool to promote and enforce IPR. The EU has shifted its approach towards the inclusion of detailed sections modelled on EU legislation. These provisions take into account development aspects, but also effective rules to tackle piracy and counterfeiting.

- Customs co-operation agreements: Several of these bilateral sectoral agreements cover, inter alia, customs controls of fake goods. These agreements, inter alia with India and China provide for training and exchange of best practices.

- The Commission is a major provider of trade related IPR assistance[105]. It has three regions covered by specific multi-year IPR programmes worth several million Euros each: China, ASEAN and the Balkans. In many other regions, IPR related initiatives are covered by broader trade or customs programmes. Pursuant to the Enforcement Strategy, the focus of these initiatives is increasingly on enforcement. A new multi-year programme has been launched in China (IPR II).

Public awareness	The European Commission promotes initiatives to raise public awareness of counterfeiting and piracy with a focus on third economies and European consumers:

- As mentioned above, programmes for technical co-operation and assistance for third economies are in place, and the Commission sponsors community-wide campaigns for increasing public awareness of the negative and dangerous consequences of consumer product infringements.

- The 2006 Enforcement Survey[106] was conducted and published by the European Commission. This survey gives a detailed state-of-play of the enforcement situation in 40 countries and describes the actions available against infringements, the most effective mechanisms, best practices, etc. On the other hand, there is also extensive information about the difficulties with which EU rights holders are confronted when operating in third countries. It is a useful source of information for SMEs.

- The European Commission is also reviewing the functioning of the IPR Helpdesks[107] and Innovation Relay Centres[108] to allow them to assist SMEs dealing with IPR in third countries.

- In 2005, the European Commission sponsored the drafting of a Guidebook on Enforcement of Intellectual Property Rights. The Guidebook is mainly intended to assist public authorities in developing and least-developed economies in their efforts to put in place systems and procedures for the effective enforcement of IPR.

- Seminars and Congresses: Commission officials participate frequently in the most important international IPR conferences (Global Congress on Counterfeiting, Patinnova, WIPO and WTO conferences, etc.). On these occasions, they present and promote the EU approach to IPR enforcement in third countries.

Industry initiatives and co-operation	The European Union has put in place a policy of regular consultation and involvement of rights holders in key initiatives Some examples are:

- The IPR dialogues with third countries, where on each occasion, there is a session in which the private sector participates and has an opportunity to discuss specific situations with the relevant local enforcement authorities.

- The creation of the above mentioned IPR Helpdesks and Innovation Relay Centres to assist IP right-holders.

- The association with industrial sectors and associations concerned on several IP related processes such as the transatlantic co-operation, the OECD or the G8.

---

105.   http://ec.europa.eu/trade/issues/sectoral/intell_property/pr030806_en.htm#1
106.   http://ec.europa.eu/trade/issues/sectoral/intell_property/survey2006_en.htm
107.   http://www.ipr-helpdesk.org
108.   http://irc.cordis.lu/

References

European Community legislation, http://eur-lex.europa.eu

OECD (2005), "Responses to OECD government survey", unpublished.

Office for Harmonization in the Internal Market (OHIM), http://oami.europa.eu/

FRANCE

Institutional organisation	The *Institut national de la propriété industrielle* (INPI) is involved with a range of intellectual property issues. It notably registers IP rights (patents, trademarks and design), is involved in the creation of IP law and provides advice to firms and rights holders.
	A National Anti-Counterfeiting Committee (CNAC) was set up in 1995. Its general secretariat is in the hands of the INPI. The CNAC represents rights holders and is a forum for the exchange of ideas and dialogue between government and the private sector. It co-ordinates the action undertaken by different government departments and representatives of the various sectors of activity concerned by counterfeiting. It organises efforts aimed at keeping business people informed, increasing consumer awareness and training enforcement units.
	The main players involved in measures to combat counterfeiting and piracy are the Ministry for Economic Affairs, Finance and Industry (notably the French Customs – DGDDI -- and the Directorate-General for Competition, Consumption and the Repression of Fraud -- DGCCRF); the Ministry of Defense; and the Ministry of the Interior (national gendarmerie and judicial police).
Policy developments	A 10-point government action plan[109] adopted by the Council of Ministers in 2004 has strengthened the fight against counterfeiting and piracy. Amongst others, measures have been introduced to: step up co-operation between administrations in order to increase the effectiveness of their actions (an inter-service working group has been set up); reinforce criminal action and the resources available for dismantling criminal counterfeiting networks; improve the calculation of damages for rights holders; raise public awareness; and increase international co-operation to combat counterfeiting and piracy.
Legal and regulatory framework	Intellectual property rights – copyright, neighboring rights, designs and models, patents, trademarks, topography of semiconductors, plant varieties and appellations of origin – are principally protected by the intellectual property code. Civil and criminal action may be taken against persons infringing intellectual property rights.
	By taking civil action, the injured party can ask for damages to be paid, for the counterfeiting activities to be banned and for the counterfeit goods to be confiscated.
	In the intellectual property code, the law provides victims with a procedure to facilitate furnishing proof of alleged infringement. The procedure in question, known as the "search and seizure order" (saisie-contrefaçon) permits the searching of the premises of the accused and the seizing of samples of counterfeit goods. Besides, interim measures are available to compel the infringer to stop infringing activities. The transposition of Directive 2004/48/EC will strengthen French legislation on the conservation of elements of proof, remedies, and will allow for the calculation of damages to be adapted.
	The French criminal provisions establish three different levels of sanctions. Penalties range from a: EUR 300 000 fine and three years in prison for most common offences involving copyright, trademarks, designs and models, patents, rights on a data bank; a EUR 400 000 fine and four years in prison when trademark infringement amounts to a real commercial strategy; a EUR 500 000 fine and five years in prison when the infringement is the work of an organised group[110]. Penalties also apply to the consumer of counterfeit or pirated products.
	To combat counterfeiting and piracy on the Internet, the 1 August 2006 law and the 23 December 2006 decree, introduced penal sentences in case of circumvention of the protection of digital products (protected works and software).
	Counterfeiting of trademarks is also a Customs offence in France; the Customs code provides for a prison sentence of maximum three years. It can be increased to 10 years when the offences are committed by an organised group.
Enforcement	French Customs (DGDDI) has extensive powers to conduct operations against infringements of trademarks, copyright, design and models, whether held or circulating throughout the country. Customs can act *ex officio* or on the request of rights holders; it can initiate a seizure procedure without prior authorisation if goods are presented under an infringing trademark. In line with EU regulation (EC) 1383/2003, French customs control not only imported but also exported or re-exported goods.
	The DGCCRF can act *ex officio*, or on the request of rights holders, and is responsible for addressing trademark offences on French soil. It can seize suspect goods without court order if they are a hazard to consumer health

---

109. www.premierministre.gouv.fr/chantiers/consommation_637/fiches_641/lutte_contrefacon_les_dix_50846.html

110. The aggravating circumstance of committing an act in an organized group applies with respect to trademarks, copyright, designs, models and patents.

and/or safety.

The judicial police (*gendarmerie nationale* and police) conduct investigations into counterfeiting - including those involving organised networks - under the supervision of magistrates. A special unit focuses on combating counterfeiting. Since 1999, French Customs (DGDDI) can also conduct investigations into trademark infringement.

In line with the 2004 governmental action plan, the number of controls on the French territory has increased: Customs has been set a target of 10% annual increases in seizures. Controls performed by the DGCCRF, the judicial police and the *gendarmerie* have also been stepped up. The number of firm prison sentences announced has risen.

As efforts are geared towards stopping counterfeit goods at borders, products are mainly intercepted at airports and ports. With infringing goods circulating increasingly via small consignments dispatched by post and by express freight, checks on such consignments have been stepped up. Besides, the Customs authorities have also increased their controls in markets and fairs, particularly during the summer months.

The surge in the purchases of counterfeit products via the Internet is a trend that Customs is trying to halt by intercepting goods distributed by express freight.

Programme evaluation and measurement	The CNAC records measures taken in France and abroad to combat counterfeiting and piracy and suggests ways of improving the existing system.
International co-operation	France is involved in bilateral and multilateral initiatives to increase the protection of IPRs. Inter-ministerial bilateral committees have been set up with Italy (2002) and Russia (2001) to exchange best practice, set mutual annual targets and define common actions. France has regular exchanges with Morocco and Tunisia to set up national committees to combat counterfeiting.

France has also networked intellectual property experts in the commercial and financial sections *(missions économiques)* of its embassies in over 80 countries to facilitate exchanges regarding IPR protection with other countries.

Finally, the INPI has concluded co-operation agreements with 25 countries to exchange experience on IPR related issues.

At the multilateral level, France suggested at the Essen G7 Summit (9-10 February 2007) the creation of an inter-governmental body, based on the model of the Financial Action Task Force (FATF), to develop and promote national and international policies combating counterfeiting and piracy. The objective would be to facilitate the exchange of information, the adoption of common standards and the identification of best practice.

In addition, France supports the initiatives of WIPO, the European Patent Office (EPO) and the Office for Harmonization in the Internal Market (OHIM). |
| **Awareness** | The CNAC is central to awareness-raising schemes: it has co-ordinated numerous communications campaigns with private partners.

In 2004, the CNAC organised "Danger, counterfeiting" (*Contrefaçon danger)*, a campaign designed to alert the French to the consequences of the phenomenon and increase consumer vigilance. A whole range of awareness tools was deployed using the press, radio and television, an Internet site, information brochures, and posters in town halls, shopping centres and streets in five big towns. Information sheets were published for SMEs-SMIs. A travelling stand on counterfeiting was designed for trade fairs. A travelling exhibition was put together jointly by the INPI and the CNAC. Practical guides were produced for consumers and professionals. A monthly information letter on counterfeiting and piracy (*Contrefaçon riposte*) was also released.

In April 2006, the Ministry for Economic Affairs, Finance and Industry, the INPI and the CNAC launched a wide-ranging media campaign entitled "Counterfeiting, no thank you", the aim of which was to make the public aware of its responsibilities as regards counterfeiting. The campaign used television, putting out five 15-second commercials, and also the Internet, with advertising banners and an on-line Internet site[111]. The campaign was extended through the summer months, which is when consumers are most frequently targeted. |
| **Industry initiatives and co-operation** | The *Comité Colbert*[112] and the *Union des Fabricants* have organised awareness campaigns in partnership with the public authorities. In June 2003, the *Comité Colbert* launched long-term poster campaigns in Paris airports in conjunction with Customs and under the aegis of the CNAC. In June 2004, it organised an awareness operation at Roissy-Charles de Gaulle airport, which was aimed specifically at passengers on France-Italy flights. Since 2004, the Union of Manufacturers, in partnership with the public authorities, has organised an awareness campaign on the beaches of the Côte d'Azur. |

---

111.   www.non-merci.com

112.   The Comité Colbert is an association grouping together France's leading luxury brands.

References

Comité Colbert (2006), « Le rôle du Comité Colbert dans la lutte contre la contrefaçon en France et dans le monde ».

Contrefaçon riposte n° 15, June 2006.

Contrefaçon riposte n° 13, April 2006.

Contrefaçon Riposte n° 12, March 2006.

French Customs records for 2002, 2003, 2004 and 2005.

French Government (2005), "Replies to the OECD's country/economy questionnaire", (unpublished).

Girardet, Alain (2005), « Contrefaçons – perspectives d'évolution de la sanction civile en droit interne, revue lamy droit des affaires ».

Ministry for Culture and Communication, Inspectorate-General for the Administration of Cultural Affairs (2002), « La lutte contre la contrefaçon des droits de propriété littéraire et artistique dans l'environnement numérique ».

National Assembly Delegation for the European Union (2005), « Rapport d'information sur la lutte de l'Union européenne contre la contrefaçon ».

Statement by the Minister Delegate for Industry (2005), November.

Union des Fabricants (2005), *Report on counterfeiting and organised crime*, 3rd edition.

INDIA

Institutional organisation	In India, IP laws are administered by different offices.
	The Patent Office deals with patents and design; the Trademarks Registry administers trademarks. Both the Patent Office and the Trademarks Registry have a head office as well as local branches in main towns. The Patent Office and the Trademarks Registry are under the control of the Office of the Controller General of Patents, Designs and Trademarks (Ministry of Commerce and Industry).
	The Copyright Office (Ministry of Human Resources Development) administers copyrights under the control of the Registrar of Copyrights.
	The Copyright Board, a quasi-judicial body, was constituted in 1958. The Board is entrusted with the task of adjudication of disputes pertaining to copyright and hears appeals against orders of the Registrar of Copyrights.
	The government of India has constituted a Copyright Enforcement Advisory Council (CEAC) in order to improve copyright protection. The CEAC meets about twice every year; members include representatives of copyright industry organisations and chiefs of state police forces.
Policy developments	The Indian government has taken several steps to improve IP protection. It has changed its IP legislation (see below), but also focused efforts on building infrastructure and ensuring that IP training programmes are provided. Regarding enforcement, the government has promoted the creation of specialised IP police cells at the state level.
	The government financed the modernisation of the patent information service, as well as the Trademark Registry. Intellectual Property office buildings (with Patent Offices and Trademark Registries in one location) are to be set up in Delhi, Chennai, Mumbai and Kolkata. The government has also announced the setting up of an Intellectual Property Management Institute in Delhi (Chawla, 2006).
Legal and regulatory framework	The Trade Marks Act, 1999 was modified in 2003. It provides for increased and more stringent provisions to deal with counterfeiting of trademarks. The definition of trademarks has been enlarged and now includes the shape of goods and packaging. It is also applicable to service marks, well-known trademarks and associated marks (World Trademark Law Report, 2006). Registration of trademarks, including services marks, is not mandatory under the Act, but it facilitates its validity in case of legal proceedings.
	Amendments introduced in the 1957 Copyright Act have made offences for counterfeiting and piracy more stringent. The Copyright Act provides for civil, criminal remedies and border measures to prevent importation of infringing copies.
	The Patents Amendment Act, 2005 and the Patent Rules, 2005 have incorporated changes to the patent legislation, allowing for example product patents to be introduced in the pharmaceuticals sector. The Indian Design Act, 2000 governs the copyright of an industrial design.
	Civil remedies available against infringement of trademarks, copyright, patents and design are: an injunction, damages and compensation, and confiscation of infringing articles.
	Parties can seek criminal remedies in case of trademark and copyright infringement. Punishment and fines have been enhanced. Sentences provide for imprisonment of six months to three years with, or without, a fine. Fines can range from IND 50 000, to a maximum fine of IND 200 000[113].
	In addition, the Indian Penal Code has provisions to protect consumers from being deceived by traders or manufacturers of counterfeit goods (Ranjan, Narula and Paul Taj Kunwar, 2004).
	Administrative remedies are available to copyright holders to prevent the importation of copyright-infringing goods. They can make an application to the Registrar of Copyright who is empowered to enter facilities where illegal copies are thought to exist. An order of the registrar can bring into play the provisions of the Customs Act, 1962: custom authorities will then detain and confiscate all infringing copies.
	The Indian Customs Act, 1962 has a provision to prohibit import and export of deceptive goods. Under existing provisions, once customs officials have accepted a complaint from a rights holder, they would wait for a permanent injunction from the court (Ranjan, Narula and Paul Taj Kunwar, 2004).
Enforcement	Enforcement in the Indian domestic economy is primarily the responsibility of the state governments, whereas the national customs authorities have responsibility for enforcement at the borders.
	The national government has been working on the promotion of strengthened enforcement at the state level and has

---

13. 1 USD = 44.5 Indian Rupees (IND) (March 2007).

asked each state to set up special taskforces to counter piracy. Special cells for copyright enforcement have been set up in states and union territories. Cities such as Delhi, Mumbai and Chennai have created specialised IP police cells to fight counterfeiting and piracy.

The Trade Marks Act and the Copyright Act have given police officers of a certain rank the power to search and seize counterfeit goods and all instruments involved in committing the offence, without warrant. Police can act when a complaint is made by the rights holder. Under the Trade Marks Act, a police officer must obtain the opinion of the Registrar of Trade Marks to conduct a raid (Ministry of Consumer Affairs, Food and Public Distribution, 2006; WTO, 2002).

During 2004 and 2005, police have increased *ex officio* actions. More raids have taken place in major cities, such as Delhi and Mumbai, and in some states such as Tamil Nadu, Kerala, Maharashtra and Gujarat.

Regarding judicial enforcement, Indian civil courts have handed down landmark rulings in trademark and patent cases (Anoop Narayanan, undated). Courts have been liberal in granting police assistance in carrying out search and seizure at the infringer's premises. The threshold requirement for granting an Anton Piller[114] order has been simplified. Since 2004, a damage culture has also emerged in IP litigation. Indian courts, especially the Delhi Court, have handed down a series of decisions granting compensatory, as well as punitive damages (Agrawal and Mehra, 2006), showing that there is a trend towards increasing damages being awarded.

Programme evaluation and measurement	The Office of the Controller General of Patents, Designs, Trade Marks and Geographical Indications releases an annual report that reviews the activities of the different offices.
	The CEAC periodically reviews the progress of enforcement of the Copyright Act and advises the government on measures for improving enforcement.
International co-operation	India has strengthened the dialogue with foreign partners on IPR protection in the context of a framework of understandings on trade and investment, or technical co-operation.
	The dialogue between the EU and India has been strengthened following the EU/India Summit in 2005. As part of the decision to increase bilateral trade and economic co-operation, it was decided to exchange further on IPR related issues.
	At the third ministerial-level meeting of the U.S.-India Trade Policy Forum (2006), India and the United States agreed to an action plan directed towards IPRs. The two sides committed to co-operate in the field of IPR, notably on capacity building activities, human resource development and public awareness programmes.
	Japan and India confirmed that their governments would co-operate in capacity-building activities, including the development of human resources (2006 Joint Statement: towards a Japan-India strategic and global partnership).
Awareness	The Government in association with organisations (such as WIPO or the Chambers of Commerce) or Universities, has initiated a number of seminars, workshops and roundtables throughout the country for raising awareness on current issues linked to IP and to discuss problems linked to counterfeiting and piracy in particular.
	An Intellectual Property Training Institute (IPTI) has been set up by the Office of the Controller General of Patents, Designs and Trade Marks. It organises diversified IP training programmes for various levels of user groups (government, private sector and public at large) on IP rights, including trademarks, patents, design and copyright. The training is provided by experts involved in the working of the IP system.
	Various academies and institutions in several Indian States have included IP in their regular training programmes, including: the National Policy Academy, Hyderabad; the National Academy of Customs, Excise and Narcotics, Faridabad and the National Judicial Academy, Bhopal; the Small Industries Service Institute, Delhi.
	The Government of India has taken copyright specific measures and has published a free "Handbook of Copyright Law" for raising IP awareness amongst stakeholders, enforcement agencies, scientific and academic communities and the general public.
Industry initiatives and co-operation	Industry has taken initiatives to raise awareness on counterfeiting and piracy. It has also taken concrete measures to assist public officials in the enforcement effort, conducting raids and promoting the creation of IP cells in the police of certain Indian states. Many companies have launched large-scale search and detection campaigns on their own. Some have targeted raising retail awareness on counterfeiting and piracy.
	A Brand Protection Committee (BPC) was set up under the aegis of the Federation of Indian Chambers of Commerce and Industry (FICCI) in 2000. The BPC has set in motion the creation of special IPR cells in certain states, such as Madhya Pradesh and Maharashtra. It has also initiated conducting enforcement raids in high infringing markets in Delhi, Ahmedabad, Bangalore, Mumbai and Indore.

---

114. The Anton Piller order is a court order that provides for the right to search premises and seize evidence without prior warning. It is used to prevent the destruction of incriminating evidence and is used particularly in cases of alleged trademark, copyright or patent infringements.

The FICCI has launched a National Initiative against Piracy and Counterfeiting (NIPAC) to raise awareness on counterfeiting and piracy and strengthen capacity of the enforcement system. The initiative involves mass awareness-raising campaigns, organising workshops with judges and educational institutes.

The Confederation of Indian Industry Alliance on Anti-Counterfeiting and Piracy (CAAC) held its launch programme in 2004. Its objective is to promote a stronger enforcement system by spreading awareness among enforcement agencies at central and state levels. As part of its 2004-2005 activities, the CAAC organised workshops at regional levels involving enforcement agencies of the region to facilitate the set up of an IP cell.

The Anti-Counterfeit Coalition of India (IACCI) was founded in 2006. Its efforts in fighting counterfeiting and piracy in the IT sector include high media campaigns, road shows and conferences.

The Indian Music Industry (IMI) has organised the creation of an anti-piracy cell in three regional offices Mumbai, Delhi and Kolkata. With the help of the police, IMI have raided various manufacturing units, shops in Ahmedabad, Delhi, Patna, Vishakapatnam and Chennai.

References

Agrawal, Neha and Munish Mehra (2006), "Country chapter on India", *World Trademark Yearbook 2006,* www.worldtrademarklawreport.com/yearbook/2006

Chawla, Alka (2006), unpublished report for the OECD Secretariat.

European Commission (2006), "Intellectual Property: Enforcement Survey 2006", http://ec.europa.eu/trade/issues/sectoral/intell_property/survey2006_en.htm, October.

FICCI, "National Initiative against Piracy & Counterfeiting", www.ficci.com/general/anti-piracy/anti-piracy.htm

IACCI (IT Anti-Counterfeit Coalition of India) (2004), White Paper, March.

Ministry of Consumer Affairs, Food and Public Distribution (2006), "Report of the Working Group on Counterfeit, fake, spurious and contraband products".

Narayanan, Anoop (undated), "India, a changing IP environment", www.buildingipvalue.com

Narula, Ranjan and Paul Taj Kunwar (2004), "Counterfeiting in India, where lies the solution?", www.iprights.com/publications/articles/index.asp. February.

Office of the Controller General of Patents, Designs, Trade Marks and Geographical Indications, "Annual Report for the year 2004 – 2005".

Parijat Consulting, "Intellectual property rights in India", Focus paper on IPR laws, policy issues and development debates, http://www.parijatconsultings.com

WTO (2002), "Trade Policy Review India", www.wto.org.

ISRAEL

Institutional organisation	The main institutional entity responsible for national IPR legislation is the Legislation and Legal Counsel division of the Ministry of Justice. IPR policy is co-ordinated notably by the Ministry of Industry, Trade and Labour and the Ministry of Justice. Within the Ministry, the Patent Office ensures legal protection for industrial property, and in particular, issues patents and registers designs and trademarks following an examination of their eligibility for exclusive rights. The Office also provides advice on other matters related to industrial property rights. IP enforcement bodies include the Ministry of Justice, Police, the Customs Authority, the State Prosecutors Office, and the Tax Authorities. While each of these entities has its specific function, integrating and co-ordinating those functions and institutions has been achieved through the establishment of an inter-ministerial Enforcement Forum directed by the Ministry of Justice.
Policy developments	The government has given priority to increased co-operation amongst its enforcement bodies and enhancement of its enforcement mechanisms, and to training and awareness raising programmes.
Legal and regulatory framework	A comprehensive statutory and common law system covers acquisition, maintenance, and enforcement of rights in patents, designs, registered and unregistered trademarks, trade names, appellations of origin, trade secrets, integrated circuits, plant breeders' rights, copyright and related rights. Many of the intellectual property statues in Israel find their roots in British Mandatory law. Additional and overlapping protection for IP can be obtained pursuant to other legislation, such as the Commercial Wrongs Law and the Civil Wrongs Ordinance. The Patents Law of 1967 and its amendments and the Patents Regulations govern the majority of issues relating to patents. Patents are granted for 20 years from the date of filing. Patents for medicaments in some circumstances may be eligible for a term extension of up to five additional years. Trademarks are governed by the Trademarks Ordinance of 1972. Registration of a trademark may be renewed for as long as it is in use in Israel and maintains its distinctive character. Common law rights in trademarks may be established without registration, merely on the basis of use, and will be protected pursuant to the law of passing off contained in the Commercial Wrongs Law. The major legislation relevant to copyrights and related rights includes the Copyright Act of 1911, the Copyright Ordinance 1924, the Performers and Broadcasters Rights Law and their amendments and Orders. Designs are registered and are governed by the Patents and Designs Ordinance, 1924. Statutory legislation also exists with respect to appellations of origin, geographical indications, trade secrets, topographies of integrated circuits and plant breeders' rights. The statutory and common law system provides for pre-judgment remedies, such as injunctions and ex parte [115]orders of attachment, search and seizure orders, and customs searches and seizures. Final remedies include permanent injunctions, accounting of profits, delivery up, destruction of the offending goods and monetary damages and costs. Criminal sanctions are available, *inter alia*, for counterfeiting of trademarks, copyrights and other wilful use of false trade descriptions. Copyright piracy is punishable by up to five years imprisonment and fines of up to 2 million shekels. Trademark counterfeiting is punishable by up to three years imprisonment and fines of up to 1.5 million shekels[116]. Custodial sentences to date range in duration from a few months to two years' incarceration, and the trend is towards greater judicial willingness to impose increasingly severe penalties. Over the past five years, approximately 25 offenders have served jail time in Israel for IPR criminal offences, and many others have received fines, community service and suspended sentences.
Enforcement	Civil and criminal cases are heard in the general court system, which is comprised of magistrates courts, the district courts (higher courts) and the Supreme Court. Infringement matters in all fields of intellectual property will either begin in the magistrate courts or in the district court, depending on the value of the amounts in question. Criminal infringement actions will generally be heard by the district courts. Criminal proceedings are generally initiated by the State; however, private persons may also initiate criminal proceedings in certain intellectual property cases. Increasingly, the courts have proceeded to pre-trial detention of offenders, without opportunity for release on bail, pending completion of their trials. Recidivists with prior IP convictions will frequently receive custodial sentences. In addition, piracy may lead to prosecutions for tax evasion.

---

115.   "Ex parte" means "from one side only".

116.   1 USD = 4.2 Shekels.

The commitment to enforce IPRs has been strengthened in several branches of government, in particular the police, the State Prosecutors Office and the customs and tax authorities. Additionally, legal advisers specialising in intellectual property provide regular legal support to enforcement bodies, providing them with legal opinions, co-ordinating litigation strategies, and finding solutions to problems that arise in the normal course of enforcement activities.

The Ministry of Justice, the Attorney General, the Police Units, the Tax Authority and other relevant ministries have combined efforts to combat intellectual property violations. To this end, the ministries have allocated additional funds, and have established a special Intellectual Property Unit of the Israeli Police force. The police unit is divided into several regional units, that are responsible for carrying out investigations and raids in their geographical regions, and a national unit that is responsible for co-ordinating investigations between the regional units, legal counselling and intelligence gathering on a country wide level. The Police maintain a database on intellectual property rights; and the customs, tax and police authorities have a special permit to exchange information.

The Customs Authority, in co-ordination with rights holders and prosecutors, plays a central and active role in the enforcement of intellectual property rights through its control of merchandise entering Israel. Merchandise suspected of violating trademark or copyright is detained and relevant rights holders are notified. Rights holders are given an opportunity to inspect the suspected goods prior to their release, and when a court action is commenced such goods will be detained until the end of such proceedings. Authority to prosecute offenses against specific intellectual property laws rather than general customs legislation was granted to those legal advisors in the Customs Authority who prosecute customs offences.

Programme evaluation and measurement	The members of the Inter-ministerial Enforcement Forum meet regularly to review the activities of the various enforcement agencies involved in intellectual property and to find solutions to legal and administrative problems that arise. The Forum helps to ensure that accumulated experience is constantly being reinvested into the enforcement infrastructure.
International co-operation	Customs has established training programmes with countries such as the United States.
Awareness	The Ministry of Justice takes a leading role in providing on-going continuing legal education seminars for judges, prosecutors, police, customs agents and government office legal advisers. The judiciary also engages annually in specially designed, continuing-education programmes on IPR legal issues. In 2004, the Ministry of Justice contributed expertise to the Business Ethics Center of Jerusalem for its publication of a 35-page pamphlet entitled "Educating for Intellectual Property Rights". Industry groups, too, contributed their expertise to this project.
	In addition, the Ministry of Justice IP legal advisers lecture before Bar Association groups, the Institute for Continuing Legal Education of Judges and other related professional and civic organisations. IPR awareness-raising has been an important tool in sensitising judicial and public attitudes to the gravity of IPR crimes. As a result, both the public and the courts are taking IPR crime more seriously now than they did in the past, and penalties for IPR crimes are becoming more severe.
Industry initiatives and co-operation	The Ministry of Industry, Trade and Labour is currently reviewing policy on this matter.

References

Israeli Ministry of Foreign Affairs, www.mfa.gov.il/mfa

OECD (2005), "Response to OECD economy survey", unpublished.

WIPO, Advisory Committee on Enforcement, WIPO/ACE/2/12 of 25 June 2004.

ITALY

Institutional organisation	The Ministry of Economic Development - particularly through its Patent and Trademark Office - defines industrial property policies and administrates patents, trademarks and designs rights. It oversees the drafting of IP laws and elaborates and carries out IP policy at the national level. Copyright and related rights are administrated by the Copyright Service of the Ministry for the National Heritage.
	The Patent and Trademark Office and the Custom Agency are the main actors involved in defining anti-counterfeiting and anti-piracy policies. The Ministry for Cultural Goods and Activities is also in charge of copyright piracy.
	In 2005, a special public body -- the office of the High Commissioner for the fight against counterfeiting and piracy -- was created. It serves as a clearinghouse for IPR policies: it co-ordinates policies and strategies for protecting IP rights, studies and develops proposals on legislation linked to IPR, assesses enforcement activities, is involved in awareness-raising initiatives and provides assistance to the private sector.
	Enforcement is carried out by the Customs Agency and the police forces (Guardia di Finanza, Polizia locale, Polizia di Stato, Carabinieri and Polizia Forestale).
Policy developments	Over the last four years, measures have been taken to strengthen the Italian IP system as a whole. A new Industrial Property Code was issued in 2005 (it replaces 40 previous laws).
	Specialised IP sections were established in courts in 2003, to ensure a more rapid and efficient definition of judicial proceedings on IP matters.
Legal and regulatory framework	In Italy, Intellectual Property Rights are protected by the new Industrial Property Code (D.lgs 30/05), by the Law 633/1941 concerning copyright and by EU legislation (Regulation 1383/2003 EC and Directive 2004/48/EC). A party can take both civil and criminal actions to protect its rights.
	The new Industrial Property Code has allowed for shorter timeframes for judicial decisions by replacing the ordinary judicial procedure with company law procedure. In the case of civil action, the owner of the right can ask for precautionary measures. If the violation has been ascertained, the judge can order the inhibition of manufacture, commerce and use of goods, can dispose for their destruction, and assign the goods to the rights holder. Following to the implementation of directive 2004/48/EC, the judge will also consider the negative economic consequences for the rights holder when awarding the damages (*e.g.* missed earnings, moral damages suffered from the violation). The rights holder can ask for the profits of the infringer instead of compensation for the loss of profits, or as far as the amount exceeds such compensation.
	The Italian criminal code protects IP rights under the following articles. These provisions were recently integrated into the new Industrial Property Code.
	▪ Article 473 "Counterfeiting, forgery and use of signs which distinguish creative works or industrial products". Penalties can range to up to two years imprisonment and a fine of up to EUR 2 065.
	▪ Article 474 "Introduction into the State or Commerce of products bearing fake signs". Penalties can range from two to five years imprisonment and a fine from EUR 516 to EUR 10 329.
	▪ Article 514 "Fraud against the national industry. Penalties can range from one to five years imprisonment and a fine of up to EUR 516.
	▪ Article 517 "Sale of industrial products with misleading marks". Penalties can range from an imprisonment of up to one year and fine of up to EUR 20 000.
	In addition, article 127 of the Code punishes the manufacturing, sale, display, use and introduction into the State of objects in violation of industrial property ownership with a fine of up to EUR 1 032. Both the intention to cause damage and the act of using the product are punishable by law.
	The violation of the copyright is punished with imprisonment from six months to three years and with a fine from EUR 2 582 to EUR 15 493.
	The Law Decree No. 35 of 14 March 2005 (Law No. 80/05) establishes that a consumer can be subject to a EUR 10 000 administrative fine for purchasing or accepting a product without ascertaining its legitimate origin, due to its quality, the terms of sale, or the price offered.

Enforcement	In Italy, different police forces are competent for combating counterfeiting. The Guardia di Finanza (*i.e.* financial police) is most involved and operates on the whole national territory. It is responsible for the prevention, investigation and suppression of violations of IP rights, and it also enjoys supervisory powers (*e.g.* preventive intelligence operations). It is tasked with discovering centres of production and distribution as well as commercial channels.

The Polizia locale (local police) has territorial boundaries (it can only act within a city or a province). It is in charge of patrolling city centres, seizing products, examining transit documents. It has the power to fine those who knowingly purchase counterfeit goods in markets.

Finally, the Custom Agency plays an important role in regard to the flow of goods through Italian customs. In line with Regulation no 1383/2003, the Custom Agency has the power to intervene in the case of goods suspected of violating IP rights, suspend their release, arrange for them to be blocked and to inform the rights holder. Customs action may be carried out on imports, exports and goods in transit or transhipment. Customs can act *ex officio* when there are sufficient grounds to suspect a violation, or upon request of the rights holder. As soon as the expertise on the goods has been done and evidence obtained, the Customs has to inform the Judicial Authority. Article 474 of the Penal Code can then apply.

Since 2003, specialised IP sections have been established at the Courts and Courts of Appeal of Bari, Bologna, Catania, Florence, Genoa, Milan, Naples, Palermo, Rome, Turin, Trieste and Venice. These specialised sections have jurisdiction in disputes regarding patent, utility model, trademark, new plant variety, design and copyright infringement. They are also competent for unfair competition affecting the protection of industrial and intellectual property. The actions are heard by a panel of three judges. In actions related to IPR disputes, a shortened proceeding has been introduced to speed up judicial decisions.

Programme evaluation and measurement	The High Commissioner for combating counterfeiting and piracy is notably charged with the monitoring and gathering of data on counterfeiting and piracy. He also supervises the prevention and repression activities carried out by police forces and customs. Anti-counterfeiting activities carried out in the course of the year are to be published in a report.
International co-operation	Co-operation programmes have been carried out between the Patent and Trademark Office and other agencies. A network of IP helpdesks has been set up in markets considered sensitive by Italian enterprises (China, India, Vietnam, Korea, Chinese Taipei, Turkey, Russian Federation, Brazil).

Italy has three main strands of co-operation: China, France and the United States.

- China: co-operative activities concern procedures related to granting IPR and enforcement at the administrative and judicial levels in order to build confidence and improve bilateral economic relations.

- France: a bilateral Anti-Counterfeiting Committee was established in 2002 to monitor the counterfeiting and piracy phenomenon, co-ordinate national policies and elaborate communication programmes to improve public awareness.

- USA: organisation of joint workshops (*e.g.* joint judicial workshops on IP case-law; IPR communication workshops focusing on increasing consumer awareness).

In the framework of the Ali-Invest Programme of the EU, seminars on IPR protection and enforcement (notably on patents and trademarks) have been organised in Argentina, Bolivia, Peru and Mexico.

Italy is involved in joint customs operations with other EU Member States and third countries that act as transit States. Joint Customs Operations imply more accurate controls during specified periods on target consignments considered to be risky.

The Mutual Assistance Agreement, recently signed between the Customs Agency and Chinese Customs, allows both administrations to ask for information in case of suspicious consignments.

Awareness	The High Commissioner is competent for the development of awareness campaigns. So far, several communication campaigns have been organised:

- The campaign carried out in 2006 by the Patent and Trademark Office, was aimed at promulgating messages on the damage done by counterfeiting to the economy, through a variety of communication instruments, in order to raise consciousness in consumers and lead to a change in public opinion about infringements. This campaign will be repeated in 2007.

- The Patent and Trademark Office has also organised specific training in schools targeting children from 6 to 15 years. It has prepared educational material on IPR, counterfeiting and piracy and has organised workshops for pupils and teachers.

On the Patent and Trademark Office website, a section is specifically devoted to counterfeiting (www.uibm.gov.it/contraffazione). It provides information on the phenomenon from a legal and economic point of view, on the media campaign and on the initiative in the schools. It also provides links to the websites of all the main actors involved in combating counterfeiting.

Industry initiatives and co-operation	The Confederation of Italian Business (Confindustria) has been active both at national and European level to improve regulations against counterfeiting and piracy. It also participates in the enforcement effort. In 2005, Confindustria signed a Memorandum of Understanding on the enforcement of IPR infringement with the Customs Agency and with the financial police (Guardia di Finanza).

Confindustria is currently preparing a package of measures ("Progetto competitività") aimed at supporting companies, particularly SMEs, at developing and protecting IPR. The "Progetto competitività" aims at encouraging the diffusion of a culture of IPR protection through the creation of a modern and effective system of IPR asset management, assuring rights holders a fair exploitation of their rights. Single seminars addressed to small entrepreneurs have already been organised by a number of industry associations.

The industry association Indicam has a key role in combating counterfeiting and promoting the protection of IP rights. It acts as interface between industry and the different branches of Italian Public Administration (at central and local level), the media and the general public. It delivers an annual award, the "Indicam Award" to reward outstanding anti-counterfeiting performances by local and central public agencies and the media. Its 2005/2006 activities have included

- Organising different awareness campaigns in main historic cities and touristic sites (Florence, Venice, Rome, Adriatic Riviera, etc.);

- Organising public forums on the most important current anti-counterfeiting issues (web/web auctions; international fluxes of counterfeiting; etc.);

- Running training courses for special/local police forces;

- Co-operating with the public sector (High Commissioner, Customs, Guardia di Finanza, etc.) on programmes and projects (e.g. the Italian-French anti-counterfeiting committee; the mission of the Italian government in China).

The Italian Federation of the textile and fashion industry (Smi-Ati) and the China National Textile and Apparel Council (Cntac) signed a bilateral agreement aimed at improving the protection of IPR during a mission of the Italian Government to China, in September 2006.

In 2007, Federlegno-Arredo (the Federation of Wood Furniture Cork and Furnishing Italian Industries) signed a co-operation agreement with the China National Furniture Association and a code of conduct with the China National Interior Decoration Association (in these, a section is devoted to the mutual recognition and protection of reciprocal IPR). A similar agreement has also been signed with the China Building Decoration Association.

References

The template on Italy is based on information provided by the Italian government.

JAPAN

Institutional organisation	The legal, regulatory and enforcement framework pertaining to intellectual property is overseen by different government agencies in Japan. The Agency for Cultural Affairs (MEXT) covers copyrights and related rights; the Japan Patent Office (JPO) (METI) covers trademarks, patents and design.
	An Intellectual Property Strategy Headquarters (IPSH) has been created in the Cabinet Secretariat. It involves ministers dealing with IP issues and 10 experts from industrial and academic sectors. The IPSH develops and releases a yearly Strategic programme for IP. Individual items of the programme are assigned to specific ministries, with the IPSH overseeing the implementation of policies and measures and assessing progress (IPSH, 2005).
	In addition, a Conference on Measures against Counterfeits and Pirated Copies has been established within the Cabinet Secretariat at Director-General level in July 2004 to promote concerted efforts and adjust the policies of the ministries and agencies involved in IP protection. Meetings of the Conference ensure concerted efforts in the areas: overseas markets, border protection and the elaboration of domestic regulations (IPSH, 2005).
Policy developments	In 2002, Japan formulated an Intellectual Property Policy Outline to revitalise the Japanese economy through the exploitation of IP. The Basic Law on Intellectual Property was enacted in 2003 and established the Intellectual Property Strategy Headquarters (IPSH) (see above).
	The 2006 Intellectual Property Strategic Programme developed by the IPSH stipulates that Japan would: speed up the examination of patent applications; promote harmonisation of the patent system; and work towards an international treaty of non-proliferation of counterfeit and pirated goods.
	Japan is considering prohibiting the private importation and individual possession of counterfeits (IPSH, 2006a).
Legal and regulatory framework	Civil remedies are available to the plaintiff in the case of infringement of IPR. The plaintiff may seek an injunction, with an order for destruction of infringing goods and removal of facilities used to commit the infringement. Preliminary injunctions to prevent the infringement are also available. In case of negligent or intentional infringement, compensatory damages are available. Consequential damages can be claimed if damage has been done to the reputation of the brand. There are no punitive damages available under Japanese laws (Tanaka and Kumagai, 2006).
	Criminal penalties for infringing utility model rights, design rights, and trademark rights were increased following the amendment in June 2006 to the Customs Laws and Intellectual Property Laws (the Trademark Law, the Unfair Competition Prevention Law, the Patent Law, and the Design Law) (WTO, 2007). The penalty applied for infringement of patents, trademarks or designs is either imprisonment not exceeding 10 years or fines not exceeding JPY 10 million, or both; in the case of infringement by a corporation, fines can be higher, but could not exceed JPY 300 million. Given the amendment to the Copyright Law in December 2006 - coming into force in July 2007 - the limit for penalties in case of copyright infringement will also be raised to 10 years imprisonment (IPSH, 2006b).
	Amendments have recently been made to the Customs Tariff Law to help block imports of counterfeit and pirated goods (IPSH, 2005). Customs authorities can suspend the importation of goods *ex officio*, or following a request by the rights holder. To facilitate judicial proceedings, a system was introduced whereby the rights holders are notified of the name and of the address of the importer and consignor of the goods that are deemed to have the potential to infringe intellectual property rights. In addition, customs can provide a rights holder with samples of a product that was allegedly being infringed to ease the burden of proof on the rights holder.
	To help Japan Customs better identify infringements, the Customs Tariff Law and Customs Law were amended to enable Customs to seek an opinion from other government agencies and IPR experts.
	Following an amendment of the Customs Law and the IP Laws, exportation of IP-infringing goods is regarded as an infringement (since January 2007, for goods infringing trademarks, patent rights, industrial design rights and goods violating the Unfair Competition Prevention Law). With implementation of the amended Copyright Law in July 2007, the exportation of copyright infringing goods will also be prohibited.
Enforcement	In April 2005, the Intellectual Property (IP) High Court - a special branch - was established within the Tokyo High Court to better respond to the need for technical expertise and to ensure coherent and timely IP dispute settlements (JPO, 2006). It deals with cases before the Tokyo High Court that are related to intellectual property. Both the Osaka District Court and the Tokyo District Court have specialised divisions for hearing IP cases (Tanaka and Kumagai, 2006).
	Since July 2006, Japan Customs has strengthened the enforcement on infringing goods imported in small quantities, to act against the disguising of business imports: while it is illegal to import counterfeits for business purposes in Japan, the import of counterfeits for person use is not illegal.

Programme evaluation and measurement	The IPSH releases an annual Intellectual Property Strategic Programme on a "rolling plan" basis, allowing for better monitoring of progress and a quicker response to developments in the area of IPR. In the Strategic Programme, a section on achievements assesses the progress made in intellectual property policy.
International co-operation	Japan has been actively involved in bilateral and multilateral efforts to combat counterfeiting and piracy:
	▪ In 2005, Japan promoted the necessity of establishing a new international legal framework that would combat counterfeiting and piracy more effectively at national and international levels.
	▪ At the Japan-EU summit in 2004, a "Japan-EU Joint Initiative for Enforcement of IPRs in Asia" was adopted for the purpose of tackling counterfeiting and piracy in Asia. It was agreed to further promote this initiative at the 2005 and 2006 summits.
	▪ Co-operation was also pursued with France at a Japan-France summit held in 2005. A "Declaration for New Japan-France Partnership" was adopted, which recognises the importance of promoting measures against counterfeiting in Asia (IPSH, 2005).
	▪ In 2006, at bilateral level and under the framework of the Japan-United States economic dialogue (Sub-cabinet Economic Dialogue; the Regulatory Reform and Competitive Policy Initiative[117]), Japan and the United States agreed to continue strengthening co-operation in combating counterfeiting and piracy in the Asia Pacific region and around the world.
	Japan has also been involved in regional co-operation:
	▪ At a Japan-China-Korea summit in 2004, it was agreed to reinforce co-operation among the three countries for the protection of IPR; this included enhancing co-operation between patent offices (JPO, 2005b).
	▪ The JPO and the Agency for Cultural Affairs provide support to foreign countries/regions where counterfeiting and piracy problems are serious, notably through the training of customs and police officers and court officials (JPO, 2005b).
	▪ The Japanese government has been promoting IPR protection in a number of multilateral forums, including the APEC Summit/Ministerial Meeting in 2003[118] and the Asia-Europe Meeting (ASEM) Summit in 2004.
	To facilitate information exchange, Japan Customs has strengthened co-operation with foreign customs administration through bilateral agreements/arrangements on mutual assistance (with China, South Korea, the United States and other partners). A Japan-EC mutual assistance agreement has also been reached in substance. In addition, Japan Customs exchanges information on significant seizure cases via the WCO Customs Enforcement network (OECD, 2005).
Awareness	Japan has conducted many surveys on IP in order to ensure that effective steps are taken to combat counterfeiting and piracy.
	In 2004 and 2006, the Cabinet Office organised a special opinion survey on IP to assess whether consumers are aware that they could purchase counterfeit products and to know how much they would be willing to do so (CO, 2004 and CO, 2006).
	The Japan Patent Office has been conducting annual surveys on the losses caused by counterfeiting. The surveys indicate how Japanese firms have been affected by IP infringement and they assess damages (JPO, 2004a and JPO, 2005a).
	Since 2005, the government of Japan has introduced a survey on IP infringement overseas on the request of Japanese companies (IPSH, 2006).
	The government has conducted public awareness raising campaigns using various media in 2006, such as posters, magazines, banner ads on Internet auction sites, leaflets. An "anti-counterfeiting campaign" is also conducted via TV spots. A special website has been created for the campaign.
Industry initiatives and co-operation	The industry based International Intellectual Property Protection Forum (IIPPF)[119] in Japan and the Japanese government have organised missions to China to meet with the central and local governments to promote increased efforts for combating counterfeiting; Japan notably proposed seminars on appraisals on how to distinguish counterfeits from genuine products and technical training courses for more effective enforcement (JPO, 2005b).

---

117. See www.mofa.go.jp/region/n-america/us/report0606.pdf.

118. The establishment of IPR Service Centers proposed by Japan and the Comprehensive Strategy on IPR in the APEC region were endorsed. For further information about IPR Service Centers, see www.apecipeg.org/servicecentres/default.asp.

119. The IIPPF was created in 2002 and acts as a cross-sector industry forum for companies and associations affected by the overseas infringement of IP rights. See www.iippf.jp/en/index.html.

References

CO (Cabinet Office) (2004), "Special Opinion Survey on IP", Japanese Cabinet Office, Tokyo, www8.cao.go.jp/survey/tokubetu/h16-chizai.pdf (Japanese).

CO (Cabinet Office) (2006), "Special Opinion Survey on IP", Japanese Cabinet Office, Tokyo, www8.cao.go.jp/survey/tokubetu/h18/h18-chizai.pdf (Japanese).

JPO (Japan Patent Office) (2003), "FY 2002 Survey Report on Losses Caused by Counterfeiting", JPO, Tokyo, www.jpo.go.jp/torikumi/index.htm (Japanese).

JPO (2004a), "FY 2003 Survey Report on Losses Caused by Counterfeiting", JPO, Tokyo, www.jpo.go.jp/torikumi/index.htm (Japanese).

JPO (2004b), "Survey and Analysis Report Concerning Economic Effect of Losses Caused by Counterfeit Products", JPO, Tokyo, www.jpo.go.jp/torikumi/index.htm (Japanese).

JPO (2005a), "FY 2004 Survey Report on Losses Caused by Counterfeiting", JPO, Tokyo, www.jpo.go.jp/torikumi/index.htm (Japanese).

JPO (2005b), "Annual Report 2005", JPO, Tokyo, www.jpo.go.jp/shiryou_e/index.htm.

JPO (2006), "Annual Report 2006", JPO, Tokyo, www.jpo.go.jp/shiryou_e/index.htm.

IPSH (Intellectual Property Strategy Headquarters) (2005), "Intellectual Property Strategic Program 2005", Tokyo, www.kantei.go.jp/foreign/policy/titeki/kettei/050610_e.pdf.

IPSH (Intellectual Property Strategy Headquarters) (2006a), "Intellectual Property Strategic Program 2006", Tokyo, www.kantei.go.jp/jp/singi/titeki2/keikaku2006_e.pdf

IPSH (Intellectual Property Strategy Headquarters) (2006b), "Progress of Intellectual Property Strategy Background Information of Intellectual Property Strategic Program 2006", Tokyo, www.kantei.go.jp/jp/singi/titeki2/kettei/060609keikaku.pdf (Japanese).

OECD (2005), "Government of Japan's response to the OECD Country/Economy Survey", (unpublished).

Tanaka, Kenya and Kumagai, Miwako (2006), "Country chapter on Japan", World Trademark Yearbook 2006, www.worldtrademarklawreport.com/yearbook/2006

World Trade Organization (WTO) (2005), "Trade Policy Review – Japan", Geneva, http://www.wto.org

World Trade Organization (WTO) (2007), "Trade Policy Review – Japan", Geneva, http://www.wto.org

KOREA

Institutional organisation	In May 2004, the Korean Government formed the Council for the Intellectual Property Rights Protection Policy (IPRP) under the Office for Government Policy Co-ordination. The Council comprises 10 government bodies, including the Ministry of Justice, the Ministry of Foreign Affairs and Trade, the Ministry of Commerce, Industry and Energy, the Ministry of Culture and Tourism (MCT), the Korean Customs Service (KCS), the National Police Agency (NPA), the Korean Intellectual Property Office (KIPO), the Korean Food and Drug Administration (OGPC, 2004). The IPRP plans and co-ordinates IPR matters for the different government offices. It also periodically reviews the state of IPR protection with the relevant government offices (OGPC, 2004). KIPO is the main body responsible for granting and administering the industrial property rights. The administrative branches, namely KCS, NPA, and KIPO are actively involved in the enforcement effort. MCT is responsible for copyrights. Korea has specialised IP courts.
Policy developments	Korean Government efforts have focused on improving the legal and administrative infrastructures and educating the public (OGPC, 2004). The "Customs Modernisation Plan 2010" was adopted in 2005 and provides for improved enforcement (KCS, 2006).
Legal and regulatory framework	In Korea, IPRs are protected by 11 different acts, including the Trademark Act, the Patent Act, the Copyright Act, the Unfair Competition Prevention and Trade Secret Protection Act, the Computer Program Protection Act, the Customs Act, the Industrial Design Protection Act, the Sound Records, Video Products and Game Software Act, the Seed Industry Act, the Utility Model Act, and the Semiconductor Integrated Circuit Layout Design Act (KIPO, 2005). Legal action against counterfeit and piracy is based primarily on the following laws: the Trademark Act; the Unfair Competition Prevention and Trade Secret Protection Act; the Civil Law, and the Copyright Act. Under these laws, the manufacturing, selling, importing and exporting of counterfeit and pirated goods or works is considered as an IPR infringement and an act of unfair competition (KIPO, 2005). Under the Civil Law, a trademark rightsholder can claim compensation from any person who has intentionally or negligently infringed the IP right. In addition to civil remedies, those who violate a trademark right are subject to criminal penalties with possible prison sentences of up to seven years or a fine of up to a 100 million Korean won[120]. Furthermore, if a representative of a legal entity or an agent infringes a trademark right in relation to the business of the legal entity or a person, then the legal entity or the person, in addition to the offender, is subject to a fine of up to 300 million Korean won. The Court has the authority to order the forfeiture of the assets resulting from the counterfeiting of the trademark. The penalty for infringements involving illegal duplication and distribution without the consent of the copyright holder is up to five years in prison or a fine of up to 50 million Korean won, or both. The court can confiscate the counterfeit good owned by a copyright infringer. The Unfair Competition Prevention and Trade Secret Protection Act also protects trademarks. Under this Act, those engaged in an act of unfair competition are subject to prison sentences to up to three years or a fine of up to 30 million Korean won. The Act also stipulates that KIPO and local governments can investigate acts of unfair competition and issue warnings to offenders.
Enforcement	Under the Law Enforcement Officials' Duty Act, Customs officers have the authority to investigate and arrest importers and exporters who trade in IPR-infringing goods. IPR infringement imports are suspended for clearance and seized using risk management systems, such as the Customs Data Warehouse (CDW), the Smuggling Alert system (SAS) and the Spider Web System (KCS, 2006). KCS has set up a division in charge of IPR related matters at its headquarters in November 2003, to tackle IPR infringements more effectively. Currently, Customs have 60 teams (114 officers) dealing with IPR enforcement, and two teams (10 officers) dealing more specifically with enforcement against online counterfeiting and piracy. A system called "Spider Web" is used to track down IPR infringing goods in real-time by utilising databases containing criminal records, clearance information and foreign currency transaction data. KIPO has recently established a "Counterfeiting Reporting Centre", where investigations are carried out on counterfeiting (www.kipo.go.kr/ippc). KIPO conducts joint investigation with the police, the district prosecutors office and local governments. Each year, around 250 local government official participate in this joint investigation. Also, under KIPO's guidelines and mandates, local governments can conduct initial administrative investigations. The Supreme Public Prosecutors Office also has the authority to investigate counterfeiters and distributors of counterfeit

---

120.   1 USD = 947 Korean Won (March, 2007).

goods. The Joint Investigative Center on IPR Violations in the Supreme Public Prosecutor's Office and the Regional Joint Investigation Teams in 21 major district public prosecutor's offices conduct IPR investigations.

Programme evaluation and measurement	Since 2000, the Korean government has produced an annual report on anti-counterfeiting activities, covering results of crackdowns on counterfeit goods and IPR enforcement (KIPO, 2005).
International co-operation	Korea has been involved in various international forums, including ASEM, APEC and the Global Congress. In April 2006, the international conference on IPR was held in Seoul with participants from WIPO, WCO and business.

The government has also collaborated with related international organisations, such as WTO, WCO and WIPO. The Korean Government has, for example, been involved in efforts regarding international information exchange, notably in:

- The Project Crocodile: a global information exchange system on tobacco among 16 customs administrations.

- The Customs Enforcement Network: WCO's electronic network for the exchange of investigative intelligence on drugs and fakes.

KCS signed a Memorandum of Understanding (MOU) with the European Union Chamber of Commerce (EUCCK) in Korea in October 2000 to share IPR-related information. Under the MOU, the KCS and EUCCK exchange information concerning trademarks and import goods.

MCT established a Fund-in-Trust in WIPO to promote the copyright protection environment in the Asia-Pacific region.

Awareness	The Korean government has focused its public awareness-raising efforts on the Internet:

- In 2006, KCS set up the Cyber Intellectual Property Protection Centre (IPPC, http://iprcenter.customs.go.kr/) in order to pursue public campaigns online and to provide information. Consumers can report products suspicious of IPR infringement to the IPPC centre.

- Also, KCS has opened a unique website called Cyber Exhibition of Counterfeit and Genuine Goods (http://fake-expo.customs.go.kr/) which provides the general public with information on how to distinguish counterfeit from original items.

Since 2000, the Exhibition of Counterfeits and Genuine Goods has been held annually with attendance from around 50 domestic companies and other international brands.

KIPO and KCS have introduced an "Anti-Counterfeiting Rewards System" to raise enthusiasm for combating counterfeiting and piracy. It plans to offer rewards to organisations or individuals with an excellent record in cracking down on infringing goods (KIPO, 2005).

In addition, KIPO produces and disseminates brochures, leaflets, video tapes and other informational material on counterfeiting. It also conducts campaigns on electronic signboards in major cities in order to encourage the boycott of counterfeit goods.

In 2006, MCT began to educate teenagers about copyrights by publishing a comic book and running so called "Copyright Protection Model Schools" nationwide.

Industry initiatives and co-operation	Korean industries are at the eve of forming a coalition of firms and associations to combat counterfeiting and piracy internationally.

The Korea International Trade Association (KITA), together with MOICE, has established a centre called "Anti-Counterfeiting Center for Korean Exports" (www.kita.net/stopfake).

Industries that are particularly affected by counterfeiting and piracy -- the automotive and electronics industries, for example -- are currently working on strategies and action plans to combat the phenomenon. The Korean electronics manufacturers (grouped under the Electronic Industries Association of Korea (EIAK)) are also joining forces to minimise the damages for domestic companies (www.ipac.or.kr/).

References

Korea Intellectual Property Office (KIPO) (2005), "Anti-counterfeiting Activities in Korea".

Ministry of Foreign Affairs and Trade (MOFAT) (2005), "Korea's Proposal for APEC Anti-Counterfeiting and Piracy Initiative –Model Guidelines and Related Documents".

Office of Government Policy Co-ordination (OGPC) (2004), "Master plan for IPR Protection".

Korea Customs Service (KCS) (2006), "Counterfeiting Stops Here".

The European Union Chamber of Commerce in Korea, http://ipr.eucck.org/.

World Customs Organization (WCO) (2006), "WCO News", October 2006.

U.S. Department of Commerce, "Protecting Your Intellectual Property Rights", www.buyusa.gov/korea/en/iproverview.html.

RUSSIA

Institutional organisation	In Russia several entities are responsible for IP policy formulation and implementation.
	IP legislation is formulated within the Ministry of Justice and the Ministry of Internal Affairs of the Russian Federation, in consultation with the Executive Office of the President.
	The Federal Service for Intellectual Property, Patents and Trademarks (Rospatent), under the Ministry of Education and Science, ensures legal protection for intellectual property including patents and trademarks. The main tasks of Rospatent are:
	• To control and examine applications for IP rights; and
	• To establish and register the intellectual property rights according to the legislation of the Russian Federation.
	The Department for Economic Security of the Ministry of Internal Affairs has a special division to combat intellectual property crime.
	In addition to the above listed units, in 2002 the Government Commission to Counter Intellectual Property Infringements was set up to facilitate the process of decision-making and to co-ordinate and improve legislation. In 2004, the national Duma (lower house of the Russian parliament) set up an Expert Committee on legal regulation and protection of intellectual property to channel efforts by government and industry into formulating effective measures to protect IP rights.
Policy	IPR issues are a priority for the Russian government. In recent years, the emphasis has been on the establishment of a sound system of IP protection that complies with the international standards, and on increased co-operation between the imposing and enforcing bodies.
Legal and regulatory framework	In recent decades, Russia has worked to bring its IP legislation in line with international legal standards. In the early 1990s, Russia became a signatory to most treaties including the general treaties, IP Protection treaties, Global Protection System-related treaties and Classification-related treaties.[121] It also became a member of the World Intellectual Property Organization (WIPO).
	The major change made to bring legislation in line with WTO standards was the adoption of Part IV of the Civil Code by the Duma (lower house of the Russian parliament). Part IV introduces a single law replacing most of Russia's IPR legislation. Russia has also committed to introducing legislation related to its data-protection regime, which would protect, *inter alia*, undisclosed information (such as test data) submitted to obtain marketing approval of pharmaceuticals.
	The Russian Trademark Law is found in the Law of the Russian Federation #3520-1 on Trademarks, Service Marks and Appellations of Origin of Goods. A brand or trademark is not protected in Russia unless the brand owner complies with the state registration law. This standard is in accordance with trademark law worldwide. If a brand owner applies for, and fulfils the registration requirements of the law, the owner can acquire a proprietary right to the brand. Both foreign and domestic brand owners must comply with the same law. The rights of the trademark or brand will apply at the time of completion of the registration process, and a certificate of registration will be issued. Thereupon, the rights holder will have the exclusive right of use for the trademark and the legal power to exclude others from use of the mark with respect to the goods listed in the certificate. Anyone else using the mark on the same or similar goods thereafter is an infringer, if the use occurs in the territory of the Russian Federation. The duration of the right is 10 years from the filing, but the vested right lapses if the mark is not used for three consecutive years following issuance of the certificate of ownership. In addition, the mark must be used at least once every three years thereafter. Otherwise, the brand is terminable.
	The Russian Law of Copyright and Related Rights as amended 20 July 2004 and certain international agreements, such as the Berne Convention, govern intellectual property rights for copyrightable works in the territory of the Russian Federation.
	The Patent Law of The Russian Federation is a comprehensive law. The law provides legal protection for the creations or authors of inventions, utility models and industrial designs. The document certifying or evidencing title to the creation is a patent. The patent, therefore, is the title deed to the creation. The title document, which is the patent, describes the invention, utility model or industrial design, the date of authorship to certify the priority date of the patent, and the name or identity of the author and patentee. Upon issuance of the patent, the author acquires an exclusive set of proprietary rights. The duration of these rights will be 20 years for inventions, 10 years for industrial designs and five years for utility models.

---

21. For a complete list of IP-related treaties ratified by Russian Federation, go to: www.wipo.int/treaties/en/

Enforcement	In Russia, the enforcement of IP laws is co-ordinated by the Russian Ministry of Internal Affairs. The Department for Economic Security was established in March 1999 within the Ministry for the purpose of combating intellectual property crime in Russia. Equivalent entities were created in all administrative subjects of the Russian Federation.
	Criminal procedures have been reinforced by an amendment to Article 151 of the Russian Federation Code of Criminal Procedure. Article 146 provides for investigators from the Public Prosecutors; the amendment to Article 151 provides for additional investigators from the body that has identified the offence.
	As a signatory to the European Partnership Agreement (EPA), Russia is committed to adopting a level of [IPR] protection similar to that existing in the European Community, including effective means of enforcing such rights. Some initial measures have been taken to strengthen IPR enforcement, and further efforts are being made to meet the international standards as described by the EPA (European Commission, 2006). The issue of Russian IP rights enforcement was also discussed during the bilateral negotiations between Russia and the US on WTO accession (USTR, 2006).
	Russian authorities aim to step up efforts to effectively enforce IPR. Authorities are committed to increase resources devoted to enforcement, to improve the training of enforcement officials, and to strengthen border enforcement. Russia is also committed to improving enforcement action against Russia-based websites that permit the illegal distribution of music and other copyrighted works and to strengthen the regulation of optical media plants in order to close down production of optical media containing pirated and counterfeit material.
Programme evaluation	Activities aimed at protecting the consumer market from counterfeit and pirated products are monitored by the relevant authorities and reported to the President of the Russian Federation.
International co-operation	Russia has been an active participant in various international forums dealing with counterfeiting and piracy, including the G-8 and WIPO.
Public awareness	Rospatent has established the Russian State Educational Institute for Intellectual Property (RGIIS). The Institute offers courses, seminars and workshops, as well as expert advice and information.
Industry initiatives and co-operation	In Russia, the major industry initiative that acts for the IPR protection is the Coalition for Intellectual Property Rights (CIPR). CIPR is an industry initiative that aims at rising awareness, supporting development of IPR legislation and promoting IP rights enforcement.

References

The Coalition for Intellectual Property Rights (CIPR) http://www.cipr.org/

European Commission (2006), "IPR Enforcement: Country Reviews", October 2006 http://ec.europa.eu/trade/issues/sectoral/intell_property/ipr_epc_countries_en.htm

Federal Service for Intellectual Property, Patents and Trademarks (Rospatent), www.fips.ru/

The law of Russian Federation # 3520-1 on Trademarks, Service Marks and Appellations of Origin of Goods.

Patent law of Russian Federation # 3517-1.

The law of Russian Federation # 5351-1 on Copyrights and Related Rights.

Russian State Educational Institute for Intellectual Property," www.rgiis.ru/.

Office of the United States Trade Representative (USTR) (2006), "Results of Bilateral Negotiations on Russia's Accession to the World Trade Organization (WTO), Action on Critical IPR Issues", November 19, 2006, www.ustr.gov.

SWITZERLAND

Institutional organisation	The Swiss Federal Institute of Intellectual Property (the Institute) is Switzerland's registration office for industrial property rights. It is also the governmental agency competent for all matters relating to intellectual property and it formulates IP policy. As a legal entity in its own right, the Institute is financially and operatively autonomous. When acting as the government agency competent for intellectual property policy formulation and implementation, the Institute is supervised by, and reports to, the Federal Council (Swiss government).
	Activities of the Institute include the preparation and implementation of legislative instruments in the field of IPR. It is also involved in the implementation of international treaties, the representation of Switzerland within the framework of international organisations and conventions, and participation in technical co-operation in the field of IPR.
	Other governmental agencies involved in the protection of IPR are among others: the Federal Customs Administration; the Federal Office for Police, the Federal Office of Consumer Affairs; and the State Secretariat for Economic Affairs (SECO).
	As part of the Swiss Anti-Counterfeiting and Piracy Platform (see below), a "public" contact point has been set up at the Institute to co-ordinate governmental agencies involved in combating counterfeiting and piracy.
Policy developments	The Swiss Parliament is currently debating proposals for amendments to various parts of Swiss IP legislation, in order to facilitate the fight against counterfeiting and piracy. These include:
	▪ Strengthening the penalties for infringements on a commercial scale;
	▪ Expanding border measures to allow customs authorities to seize infringing goods in transit;
	▪ Providing a simplified destruction procedure for infringing goods;
	▪ Allowing the seizure of infringing goods imported or exported for private purposes.
	Furthermore, in November 2006, the Federal Council initiated public consultation regarding a federal patent court law and a patent attorney law. These laws aim to improve the legal protection and the advisory services in patent matters to strengthen Switzerland as place of innovation.
	Together with the private sector, the Institute has initiated the Swiss Anti-Counterfeiting and Piracy Platform (STOP PIRACY), a public private partnership to fight counterfeiting and piracy.
Legal and regulatory framework	In Switzerland, IP rights are notably protected by the 1954 Federal Law on Patents for Inventions, the 1992 Federal Law on the Protection of Trademarks and Indications of Source, the 2002 Design Law and the 1992 Federal Law on Copyright and Neighbouring rights. Swiss IP laws provide both civil and criminal sanctions in case of IPR infringement.
	Civil sanctions generally include:
	▪ Action for declaratory judgment;
	▪ Action for execution, including proceedings for damages and redress and surrender of profits;
	▪ Confiscation;
	▪ Precautionary measures;
	▪ Publication of judgment.
	Criminal sanctions generally include:
	▪ Imprisonment for a term not exceeding one year or a fine of up to CHF 100 000 for infringement; or,
	▪ Imprisonment up to three years and a fine of up to CHF 100.000 for infringements on a commercial scale.
	▪ Due to the revision of the general parts of the Swiss Criminal Code, fines for criminal sanctions have been increased de facto; fines can now reach up to CHF 1 080 000 (the amount depends on the income of the sanctioned person).
	Administrative measures include border measures, such as the suspension of release of infringing goods by the customs authorities.
Enforcement	Enforcement mechanisms to combat infringements are administrative procedures undertaken by the police, judicial procedures (civil and criminal) and customs procedures; currently these are not available for patents.
	Civil and criminal enforcement procedures in Switzerland are governed mainly by procedural laws of the Cantons, by

the Federal Law on Jurisdiction and the Federal Law on the Organisation of the Judicial System, unless the federal intellectual property laws contain specific provisions for the enforcement of IPRs. Decisions concerning the civil and criminal enforcement of IPRs are made, in the first instance, by the Swiss cantonal courts. Decisions can be appealed to the Supreme Federal Court. The creation of a specialised first instance patent tribunal for civil procedures is currently under discussion in the context of the revision of the patent law.

As counterfeit and pirated goods are mainly imported into Switzerland, the number of border controls (especially at airports) has been increased. Customs can act on the request of the rights holders, but can also seize goods *ex officio* In practice, Swiss customs, however, rarely act on their own initiative. Switzerland plans to extend the provisions relating to border measures in the ongoing revision of the patent law. This would allow making customs provisions available for patents. Customs would also be able not only to check imports and exports, but also goods in transit suspected of infringing a trademark, a design or a copyright. In addition, the possibility for customs to seize small quantities of counterfeit products of a non-commercial nature infringing a trademark or a design is under discussion.

Programme evaluation and measurement	The Federal Customs Administration publishes statistics about counterfeiting and piracy every year (see www.stop-piracy.ch/en/candp/cap20.shtm).
International co-operation	As a member of EFTA, Switzerland has concluded a series of free-trade agreements with other countries. Switzerland and other EFTA Member States assist their trading partners in their national enforcement strategies through technical co-operation, by improving awareness and education and providing practical training in the field of intellectual property rights, particularly for customs and police officials.
	In addition to the free-trade agreements within the EFTA, Switzerland has concluded numerous Trade and Economic Co-operation Agreements (TECA) and Free-Trade Agreements (FTA) with third countries. Those agreements cover IP among other disciplines.
	Besides, an agreement between the Swiss government and the government of the Socialist Republic of Vietnam on the protection of intellectual property and on co-operation in the field of intellectual property was concluded in 1999. In the last three years, particular emphasis has been put on enforcement. The Institute has led three training sessions of two weeks each for representatives from the Vietnamese police, custom authorities, market police and anti-counterfeiting forces in Switzerland.
Awareness	To fight counterfeiting and piracy, the Federal Institute of Intellectual Property combined forces with the ICC Switzerland (Swiss National Committee of the International Chamber of Commerce) to create the Swiss Anti-Counterfeiting and Piracy Platform in July 2005. Activities are varied and range from building awareness among the broad public to training governmental agencies, courts and businesses.
	Awareness-raising activities have included:
	• An awareness campaign (see www.stop-piracy.ch/en/news/n10.shtm)
	• A website: www.stop-piracy.ch
	• Posters all over Switzerland
	• Flyers, t-shirts and banners on several websites (like eBay Switzerland)
	• Presence at several fairs.
	In addition, counterfeiting and piracy contact points (one for public and one for private users) have been created.
	In 2004, the Federal Institute of Intellectual Property organised a survey of Swiss companies to assess the size and impact of counterfeiting and piracy (see www.ige.ch/E/jurinfo/documents/j10711e.pdf).
Industry initiatives and co-operation	Numerous industry branches are involved in the Swiss Anti-Counterfeiting and Piracy Platform (see www.stop-piracy.ch/en/about/a30.shtm). Sectors where trademark and patented products are involved include the watch industry and the pharmaceutical, machine, food, textile and cigarette branches; those where copyrighted material is at issue include music, film and software producers.
	Through this Platform, industry exchanges information and best practice on counterfeiting and piracy issues, and it supports public awareness-raising campaigns. The platform also allows for improved co-ordination between industry and government.

References

The template on Switzerland is based on information provided by the Swiss Federal Institute of Intellectual Property.

CHINESE TAIPEI

Institutional organisation	Overall co-ordination of IPR activities in Chinese Taipei is carried out by an interagency "Co-ordination Task Force for IP Enforcement", created in 2003, which is chaired by the Prime Minister and situated at the Ministry of Economic Affairs (MOEA).
	The Task Force, comprising eight government bodies[122], meets frequently to review IP policies and strengthen inter-agency communications and co-ordination. Within the group, the Intellectual Property Office of the Ministry of Economic Affairs (TIPO) is responsible for IP registration, formulating IPR enforcement policy and promoting public awareness (TIPO, 2004 and WTO, 2006).
	The MOEA is responsible for the IPR police force. It has created the Joint Optical Disk Enforcement taskforce (JODE) to carry out raids and seizures of manufacturing devices, raw materials and products of illegal plants.
Policy developments	Chinese Taipei has modified its legislation and practice in conformity with the WTO TRIPS Agreement. This has been pursued through the "2002 IPR Action Year" and "IPR Action Plan 2003-2005". Initiatives have largely concerned fulfilling international responsibility by increasing IPR protection, strengthening government IPR enforcement mechanisms and amending related IPR laws such as trademarks, patent and copyright laws. (TIPO Annual Report, 2005).
	A new "IPR Action Plan 2006-2008" aims to strengthen Internet infringement prevention, reinforce IPR protection on campuses and provide guidance for the establishment of a copyright licensing system. In response to Internet crimes, the government introduced an Implementation Plan for Strengthening Preventive Measures Against Internet Infringements in 2005. Chinese Taipei enacted legislation in March establishing an IP Court at the end of 2007.
Legal and regulatory framework	All IP laws contain provisions on remedies in case of infringement. Rights holders may take legal actions based on civil, administrative or criminal codes.
	Under the Patent Act, the amount of reimbursement due to patent damage may be calculated on the basis of the Civil Code or on the basis of the profits earned by the infringer.
	The latest amended Patent Act, which entered into force in July 2004, allows the Judiciary to designate organisations with expertise in determining patent infringements to assist judges and prosecutors (WTO, 2006).
	In the case of civil penalties for infringement of a registered trademark, the violator shall be charged with imprisonment for no more than three years and/or a fine of no more than NT$200 000[123]. Any person, who knowingly sells, displays for sale, exports or imports the counterfeiting goods shall be charged with imprisonment of no more than one year and/or a fine of no more than NT$50 000. The latest amended Trademark Act 2003 broadened trademark protection to include goods "likely to cause confusion"; it also added protection for three-dimensional trademarks, colour trademarks and sound trademarks (WTO, 2006).
	The Copyright Act was amended in 2003, 2004 and 2006. In the 2003 amendment, public transmission and distribution rights were added and provisions for criminal sanction in the selling and production of pirated optical disks were stipulated. Regarding civil remedies, the amount of statutory compensation was increased from NT$1 million to NT$5 million for infringement ruled as serious in nature. In the case of criminal penalties, the fines can increase up to NT$8 million. The 2004 Copyright amendments provided clarification on exclusive rights and the use and protection of copyrights in the context of the current digital environment. The provisions impose heavier penalties for the manufacture, distribution and sale of pirated optical disks. In 2006, the Copyright Act was amended to comply with the Criminal Code revisions.
Enforcement	The government provides training courses to judges, prosecutors, police officers and Customs officials. In 2005, the Taiwan IP Training Academy (TIPA) was established by MOEA. It is associated with universities, training organisations and private enterprises, and it aims to train IP professionals through the sponsorship of courses and workshops. In 2005, TIPA compiled training texts and selected IP professionals to provide education to industries with respect to efficient IPR management (TIPO Annual Report, 2005)
	To increase the effectiveness of enforcement, the government provides awards to informants and law enforcement personnel upon the seizure of IPR infringing products. The government provides rewards of up to NT$10 million for a tip-off that leads to a successful crackdown on illegal optical disk plants and NT$500,000 for discovery of illegal optical disk

---

22. The Co-ordination Task Force for IP Enforcement comprises eight government bodies including Executive Yuan, Fair Trade Committee, Ministry of Justice, Government Information Office, Ministry of Finance, Ministry of Interior, Ministry of Education and Ministry of Economic Affairs, www.tipo.gov.tw/eng/prosecution/apjl.asp.

23. 1 USD = 33 NT$ (February 2007).

burners. In 2005, a total of NT$17,012,883 was granted (TIPO Annual Report, 2005). According to TIPO's preliminary statistics, awards granted in 2006 amounted to NT$ 23 million.

In the case of judicial proceedings, prosecutors may act *ex officio* in case of trademark infringement. In the case of optical disk piracy deemed to violate the Copyright Law, the prosecutor's office may initiate a public prosecution (WTO, 2006).

Customs may suspend *ex officio* the release of goods suspected of infringing IPR regulations. Cargos that are declared for import/export, delivered by parcel post, or carried by inward/outward passengers will be confiscated by Customs if infringements of patent rights, trademark rights, or copyrights are found. The offender can be fined one to three times the value of the goods.

The IPR police force continues to strengthen enforcement in traditional markets (*i.e.* night markets, side walk vendors, etc.) and the Internet. In 2005, The IPR police uncovered a significant increase of Internet infringements compared to 2004 (TIPO Annual Report, 2005).

Programme evaluation and measurement	The Government prepares quarterly and annual reports on IP protection that review developments in key policy areas and report on enforcement initiatives (www.tipo.gov.tw).
	A cross-departmental meeting, chaired by the Prime Minister, continues to be held quarterly to address key IPR issues and to review the effectiveness of the Co-ordination Task Force for IP Enforcement.
International co-operation	Apart from WTO/TRIPS, Chinese Taipei ensures co-operation on, and protection of, IPR within the framework of APEC. Chinese Taipei is not a signatory to any conventions of the World Intellectual Property Organization, but it has sought to implement cross-border IP protection requirements and obligations through bilateral arrangements and co-operation with major trading partners, such as Australia, New Zealand and the United States (WTO, 2006).
Awareness	To boost public awareness, since 2002 the government has sponsored seminars, television and cinema commercials and public displays (train stations and airports), large outdoor promotions and concerts, and a series of television and radio shows.
	To help build understanding of, and respect for, IPR from a young age, the Ministry of Education requires that all levels of schooling incorporate concepts of IPR protection into their curriculum. Furthermore, the TIPO published on-line education and entertainment programmes, distinguished by elementary, junior and high school levels, to promote and enforce IPR protection (www.tipo.gov.tw/copyright/copyright_act/copyright_act_2006.asp).
Industry initiatives and co-operation	The government and major international rights holder groups jointly host IPR awareness activities, seminars, workshops and international conferences. Industry works with the government to provide knowledge and assistance in conducting investigations into IPR infringements.

References

TIPO (The Intellectual Property Office) (2004), "Performance Report on Intellectual Property Protection in Chinese Taipei", www.tipo.gov.tw, 2004.

TIPO (The Intellectual Property Office) (2005), "Annual Report 2005", www.tipo.gov.tw.

TIPO (The Intellectual Property Office) (2006), "July-September Quarterly Report on Chinese Taipei's Intellectual Property Rights Protection", www.tipo.gov.tw/eng/

WTO (World Trade Organization) (2006), Trade Policy Review Body - Trade Policy Review - Report by the Secretariat – "Separate Customs Territory of Taiwan, Penghu, Kinmen and Matsu – Revision", www.wto.org/english/tratop_e/tpr_e/tpr_e.htm, June 2006.

UNITED KINGDOM

Institutional organisation	The UK Intellectual Property Office (IPO), under the aegis of the Department of Trade and Industry, is responsible for the national framework of intellectual property rights comprising patents, designs, trademarks and copyright. Responsibility for policy development in the IPO rests with the Intellectual Property and Innovation Directorate (IPID). www.patent.gov.uk/
Policy developments	The UK National IP Crime Strategy launched in 2004 aims to deliver better-targeted enforcement action. The National IP Crime Group (IPCG), whose members represent government, enforcement authorities and industry bodies, was set up by the IPO in 2005 to steer the work. Priority areas include improved intelligence to better target enforcement work and improvements to the enforcement framework nationally and internationally. The authorities have also made the recovery of criminal proceeds a priority. The review of the UK intellectual property system (the Gowers Review) was published on 6 December 2006. The principal recommendations of the review were aimed at: *1)* tackling IP crime and ensuring that rights are well enforced; *2)* reducing the costs and complexity of the system; and *3)* reforming the copyright law to allow individuals and institutions to use content in ways that are consistent with the digital age. The IPO has published a timetable for the implementation of the Gowers Review recommendations. www.patent.gov.uk/policy/policy-issues/policy-issues-gowers.htm
Legal and regulatory framework	The new law, Copyright and Trade Marks (Offences and Enforcement) Act 2002, amends provisions in the Copyright, Designs and Patents Act of 1988 and the Trade Marks Act of 1994. It raises the maximum penalty for the offences of sale or hire or dealing in material infringing copyright from two to ten years and an unlimited fine. The 1977 Patents Act was modified by the Patents Act 2004, which came into force on 1 October 2005. The Act makes some changes to help with patent enforcement and the resolution of disputes over patents. The Intellectual Property Regulations 2006, which came into force on 29 April 2006, implement the European Directive (2004/48/EC), which provides a harmonised approach to the enforcement of civil measures for IP rights. Although intellectual property laws apply equally in England and Wales, Scotland and Northern Ireland, there are separate legal procedures in Scotland and Northern Ireland. UK laws cover both civil and criminal actions. Action to enforce intellectual property rights is by way of civil proceedings and by criminal proceedings. There are separate court systems in the UK for England and Wales, and Scotland and Northern Ireland. Whilst there are specialised IP courts in England and Wales, there are none in Scotland and Northern Ireland. In England and Wales, the High Court (Patents Court) has exclusive jurisdiction to hear intellectual property infringement proceedings. A specialist Patents County Court is designed to provide a quick and cost-effective alternative to High Court litigation. The decision whether to commence criminal proceedings rests initially with the enforcement authority (the Crown Prosecution Service, Trading Standards), although private prosecutions are also possible. Criminal proceedings and prosecution begin in the magistrate courts.
Enforcement	Enforcement within the UK is generally carried out by local authorities. The local Trading Standards Authorities investigate and prosecute those who trade in counterfeit and pirated items. Under the Proceeds of Crime Act 2002 (POCA), they have the power to recover money which has been obtained illegally, and since 1 April 2006 they have had access to a proportion -- 50% -- of the recovered assets from POCA awards made in connection with IP crime prosecutions. Recovery of criminal proceeds is also undertaken by the Assets Recovery Agency (ARA) and the new Serious Organised Crime Agency (SOCA). The ARA, created in 2003, is a non-ministerial Department established under the Proceeds of the Crime Act 2002 and reports directly to the Home Secretary. The Agency performs Civil Recovery and Criminal Confiscation roles in England, Wales and Northern Ireland. In addition to its powers to initiate and pursue Criminal confiscation proceedings, it has unique powers to sue in the High Court to recover unlawfully acquired assets. It has undertaken a wide range of cases in both civil recovery and criminal confiscation in areas of alleged criminality, including counterfeit goods. The SOCA became operational on 1 April 2006 and was established under the Serious Organised Crime and Police Bill. Efforts devoted to organised crime include counterfeiting. There are plans to merge the Assets Recovery Agency with the Serious Organised Crime Agency, and to extend prosecutors' power to launch civil recovery action under the Proceeds of Crime Act 2002. The Serious and Organised Crime Agency has recently developed a specific programme to tackle IP crime. The IPO is a member of the Steering Board.

In Northern Ireland, the creation in 2000 of both the Organised Crime Task Force (OCTF) to develop a co-ordinated multi-agency approach for addressing the growing problem of organised crime, as well as the Police Service (PSNI), has helped law enforcement agencies in Northern Ireland to seize a vast amount of counterfeit products.

HM Revenue & Customs have extensive powers to investigate and seize goods suspected of infringing IP rights, chiefly under the EC Border Regulation (1383/2003). Customs has a dedicated IP unit based at Southend-on-Sea that notifies all regional detecting offices and frontier stations of all IPR applications in force and sets national profiles in response to intelligence.

As a result of the Gowers Review of Intellectual property from 6 April 2007, new powers under the Copyright, Designs and Patents Act, backed up with £5million in new funding, will be at the disposal of Trading Standards Officers and other UK enforcement agencies. Bringing into force Section 107a of the Copyright, Designs and Patents Act (CDPA) 1988 was a recommendation by last year's Gowers Review of Intellectual Property. It will make enforcement of copyright infringement the responsibility of Trading Standards and give enforcement officers the power to make test purchases, enter premises and inspect and seize goods and documents.

To support the national crime strategy, the IPO has developed a National Intellectual Property Intelligence System (Tellpat). The database collects the intelligence gathered by industry and enforcement agencies, to track illegal IP activities.

A new police unit created in February 2006 dedicated to combating film piracy and the organised criminal networks sustaining the manufacture and distribution of counterfeit film product was launched by the Metropolitan Police's Economic and Specialist Crime Command, in partnership with the Federation Against Copyright Theft (FACT).

Programme evaluation and measurement	In 2005, the IPO produced the first National Intellectual Property Enforcement Report, which provided an assessment of the scope and scale of IP crime during 2004 and the enforcement work carried out by government and enforcement and industry bodies involved in combating counterfeiting and piracy. A second Enforcement report issued in 2006 reports that early indications of the government's new enforcement strategy have been positive in those industry sectors where co-operation between enforcement bodies and industry bodies has been strong.
International co-operation	The IPO: ▪ Co-chairs the UN Economic and Social Advisory Group on Protection of IP rights (UNECE), which is an international partnership between government and industry; ▪ As a member of the Interpol IP Action Group has helped to develop an Investigators Guide and construct a key contacts database for enforcers; ▪ Is actively involved in the work undertaken by the G8 IPR experts; ▪ Provides training and awareness programmes around the world, including in China, Russia, Kazakhstan, Latvia and Bulgaria; ▪ Signed a Memorandum of Understanding with the US Patent and Trade Marks Office (USPTO) in 2005 to develop joint training programmes; ▪ Is a member of the Commission's Peer Review team assessing member states' and candidate countries' IP and enforcement regimes. HM Revenue and Customs: ▪ Co-operates globally with brands owners and enforcement authorities, including the Chinese Customs; ▪ Offers training to customs offices overseas.
Awareness	The IPO developed the Think kit® as an IP educational tool for schools. It is designed to generate interest and understanding of IP and creativity amongst school children. www.patent.gov.uk/education/education-school/education-thinkkit.htm
Industry initiatives and co-operation	Brand owners work closely with local trading standards officers to fight counterfeiting and piracy. An example is the Federation Against Copyright Theft (FACT, which works closely across the UK with Police services, Trading Standards, HM Revenue & Customs). www.fact-uk.org.uk/index.htm. Several raids and substantial seizures were reported in 2005 and 2006. Details are provided on its website. Other UK-based associations also work to protect intellectual property rights and increase public awareness including: The Alliance Against Intellectual Property (IP) Theft www.allianceagainstiptheft.co.uk/ The Anti-Counterfeiting Group (ACG) in the UK www.a-cg.com/ The *Piracy is a Crime* campaign www.piracyisacrime.com/

References

Asset Recovery Agency (ARA), 2006, "Proceeds of Crime Act and Trading Standards", www.assetsrecovery.gov.uk/

HM Treasury, 2006 Gowers, "Review of Intellectual Property", www.hm-treasury.gov.uk/

HM Treasury, 2006, Pre-Budget Report, "Meeting the Productivity Challenge".

UK IPO, 2006, "Annual Enforcement Reports 2005, 2006", www.patent.gov.uk/.

UK IPO, 2007, "Wicks targets bootleggers with £5M crackdown", www.patent.gov.uk/

WIPO, Advisory Committee on Enforcement, WIPO/ACE/2/11, 21 June 2004.

UNITED STATES

Institutional organisation	The US Patent and Trademark Office grants and administers patents and trademarks. The US Copyright Office is responsible for registering copyright claims.
	The National Intellectual Property Law Enforcement Coordination Council (NIPLECC)[124], established in 1999, brings together the key operational entities within the federal government that are responsible for IP enforcement, and it is responsible for co-ordinating intellectual property enforcement activities.
	The Office of the US Coordinator for International Intellectual Property Enforcement, established in 2005, promotes enforcement of intellectual property rights. Under the leadership of the White House, the Coordinator's Office leads interagency initiatives, such as the Strategy Targeting Organized Piracy (STOP!), and outreach with the private sector and international partners.
Policy developments	The STOP! initiative[125], announced in October 2004, is led by the White House and brings together the members of the NIPLECC, the Department of Agriculture, and the Food and Drug Administration.
	The STOP! initiative, through active co-operation with US Industry, focuses on 1) empowering American innovators to better protect their rights at home and abroad, 2) pursuing criminal enterprises involved in piracy and counterfeiting, 3) increasing efforts to block counterfeit and pirated goods at borders, and 4) engaging trading partners in efforts to combat global counterfeiting and piracy.
Legal and regulatory framework	Copyrights are protected by federal law under the Copyright Act of 1976, as amended. The Copyright Office is the registrar of claims to copyright, and administers the mandatory deposit provisions of the copyright law and the various compulsory licensing provisions of the law. Additionally, the Copyright Office and the Library of Congress administer the Copyright Arbitration Royalty Panels (CARPs), which meet to adjust rates and distribute royalties for statutory and compulsory licences. The United States grants automatic protection to copyrighted works, including software, from all WTO Members, Berne Convention signatories, and others (WTO, 2006).
	In the case of copyright infringement, the Copyright Act provides for both civil remedies and criminal prosecution. Civil remedies may take the form of both preliminary and permanent injunctions against copyright infringement and against violations of the author's rights of attribution and integrity in works of visual art; they may also take the form of actual damages suffered by the copyright owner and any additional profits of the infringer, or of statuary damages.[126] Criminal penalties for copyright infringement include: (for the first offence) imprisonment for not more than five years, or a fine of not more than USD 500 000 or, both, and (for the second or subsequent offences) a fine of not more than USD 1 million or imprisonment for not more than 10 years, or both.[127]
	Protection of trademarks in the United States arises from the actual use of the mark. Federal registration is not required but grants the holder additional rights, such as the legal presumption of ownership and the entitlement to use the mark in connection with the goods or services identified in the registration. Federal registration of marks, which includes trademarks, service marks, collective marks, and certification marks, is governed by the Trademark Act of 1946, as amended, and its implementing regulations (WTO, 2006).
	Unlike copyrights, trademarks can be protected from infringement indefinitely as long as they are in continuous use. Trademark law in the United States is enforced entirely through private lawsuits in either state or federal civil courts, and the trademark owner is therefore the sole party responsible for restricting infringing use of trademarks. Criminal penalties for intentional trafficking of goods with counterfeit marks, or attempts hereof, include: for the first offence, imprisonment for not more than 10 years, or a fine of not more than USD 2 million, or both; and for the second or subsequent offences imprisonment of not more than 20 years, or a fine of not more than USD 5 million.[128]

124. The Council includes: the Office of the U.S. Trade Representative; the Department of Commerce (including the US Patent and Trademark Office and the International Trade Administration); the Department of Homeland Security (which includes US Customs and Border Protection and US Immigration and Customs Enforcement); the Department of Justice and the State Department. The US Copyright Office serves in an advisory capacity.

125. STOP has five main priority areas: 1) empower American innovators to better protect their rights in the United States and abroad; 2) increase efforts to seize counterfeit goods at borders; 3) pursue criminal enterprises involved in piracy and counterfeiting; 4) work closely and creatively with industry; 5) engage trading partners to join efforts.

126. United States Code, Title 17 (Copyrights), §504

127. United States Code, Title 17 (Copyrights), §1204

128. United States Code, Title 18 (Crimes and Criminal Procedure), §2320

Patents are granted by the United States Patent and Trademark Office (USPTO), using the first-to-invent rule; the United States is the only WTO Member to use this rule (WTO, 2006).

In the case of the unauthorised use of a patent, the US Patent Law provides for civil remedies through injunction or damages. The damages awarded to the patent holder must correspond to an adequate compensation for the infringement, but in no event less than a reasonable royalty for the infringer's use of the patent, together with interests and costs fixed by the court.[129]

Enforcement

The United States Department of Justice pursues a three-front approach to ensure effective prosecution in the case of IPR infringement. The three main components are:

- The Criminal Division's Computer Crime and Intellectual Property Section (CCIPS) provides a core team of expert intellectual property prosecutors who investigate, prosecute, and co-ordinate national and international cases of intellectual property theft. These specialists furthermore help to develop and execute the Department's overall intellectual property enforcement strategy, as well as provide training and around-the- clock support to Assistant US Attorneys nationally. CCIPS has also developed a manual and training tool on prosecuting IP crimes.

- The Justice Department has designated at least one Computer Hacking and Intellectual Property (CHIP) Co-ordinator in every U.S. Attorney's Office in the country.[130] This network of Co-ordinators consists of Assistant US Attorneys with specialised training in prosecuting IP and computer crime; the individual co-ordinators serve as subject-matter experts within their districts.

- CHIP Units are strategically located in districts that experience a higher incidence of intellectual property and cyber-crime, or where such crimes have the largest economic impact. These units focus on prosecuting intellectual property offences, such as trademark violations, copyright infringement, and thefts of trade secrets. CHIP Unit attorneys are also actively involved in the regional training of other prosecutors and federal agents, and they work closely with victims of IP theft and cyber-crime on prevention efforts.[131]

Regarding border measures, the Department of Homeland Security, Customs and Border Protection (CBP) has diversified its approaches to IPR enforcement to include new techniques that complement traditional enforcement methods, such as implementing its IPR risk model, applying statistical analysis techniques and external information to the assessment of IPR risk. CBP has also included IPR audits in its national audit plan and trained a new group of employees, its regulatory auditors, on IPR to enable them to apply their auditing skills to the enforcement of intellectual property rights.

The Office of Enforcement, under the United States Patent and Trademark Office, undertakes a number of enforcement-related activities. The office:

- Consults with foreign governments and other United States Government agencies on IPR enforcement laws, including legal and judicial regimes, civil and criminal procedures, border measures, and administrative regulations.

- Gathers information on and monitors foreign national enforcement systems, and is active in co-ordinating enforcement-related activities undertaken by international, intergovernmental, regional, and non-governmental organisations.

- Advises the Office of the US Trade Representative (USTR) and the Department of Commerce (DOC) on the trade-related aspects of IPR enforcement and provides technical expertise and advice on enforcement provisions.

- Develops, co-ordinates, conducts and participates in training programmes, conferences, and seminars. The office also develops training materials to improve the level of expertise of those responsible for the enforcement of intellectual property rights.

---

9. United States Code, Title 35 (Patents), §283

) Primary responsibility for prosecution of intellectual property offences (and federal crimes generally) falls to the 94 U.S. Attorney Offices across the United States and its territories.

There are currently 25 CHIP Units consisting of approximately 80 Assistant U.S. Attorneys, in addition to the approximately 150 CHIP prosecutors in the remaining districts and Justice Department divisions.

Programme evaluation	The following activities contribute to the assessment of counterfeiting and piracy activities in the United States:
	The General Accountability Office (GAO) has produced a number of reports on issues relating to intellectual property, notably on the efficiency of the national enforcement strategy.[132] GAO also provides recommendations in order to improve programme efficiency.
	NIPLECC produces an annual report providing information on agencies' activities regarding counterfeiting and piracy.
	The Department of Justice publishes statistics on criminal cases (prosecutions, conviction, sentences) regarding IPR infringement.[133] The United States Department of Homeland Security, Customs and Border Protection publishes annual statistics on the top IPR commodities seized.[134]
Awareness	Since the STOP! initiative in 2004, the Department of Commerce has undertaken numerous activities to increase awareness. Efforts have in particular focused on assisting businesses, notably small- and medium-sized businesses (SMEs) in protecting intellectual property rights (IPR), both in the United States and abroad.
	▪ The website www.StopFakes.gov provides information on the STOP! initiative and allows businesses to file complaints about IPR-related trade problems. Such complaints are answered within 10 days by a trade specialist from the Office of Intellectual Property Rights (OIPR) of the Department of Commerce. The Department of Commerce also established the 1-866-999-HALT hotline answered by IPR experts at the Patent and Trademark Office (PTO) to help businesses secure and enforce their IPR through international treaties.
	▪ The OIPR has developed an online training programme for SMEs to learn how to evaluate, protect and enforce their IPR. The programme, which benefits from the expertise of the PTO, the Small Business Administration and the Foreign Commercial Service, is to be launched summer 2007 and will be offered free of charge to interested parties. OIPR also provides guidance to SMEs through presentations and web-based seminars.[135]
	▪ Efforts have also involved informing rights holders about the situation of IPR protection in target countries:
	▪ OIPR and PTO have together with a number of US Embassies developed country toolkits containing detailed information on protecting IPR in Brazil, China, Korea, Mexico, Malaysia, Peru, Russia, and Chinese Taipei that can be accessed on www.StopFakes.gov or on U.S. embassy web-sites. The OIPR is working with PTO, the State Department, and software developers to create a toolkit template to encourage further coverage.
	▪ The International Trade Administration (ITA) has established a programme with the American Bar Association through which SMEs can request a free, one-hour consultation with a volunteer attorney knowledgeable in industry IPR issues for a particular country to learn how to protect and enforce their IPR. Expertise is now available for Brazil, Russia, India, China, Egypt, and Thailand.
	In addition the ITA has developed a programme to promote the protection of IPR at domestic and international trade fairs. The programme involves educating trade fair attendees, exhibitors, and organisers about the value of IPR.
Industry initiatives and co-operation	The STOP! initiative has established effective communication mechanisms between business and US agencies on IP issues. This communication has notably been facilitated with the creation of the Coalition Against Counterfeiting and Piracy (CACP): a cross-industry group created by a joint initiative of the Chamber of Commerce and the National Association of Manufacturers.
	In response to encouragement from the Department of Commerce, the U.S. Chamber of Commerce and the Coalition Against Counterfeiting and Piracy (CACP) have released the "No Trade in Fakes Supply Chain Tool Kit". This document which is available online at www.thecacp.com, provides strategies that both small and large companies use to protect their supply chains from the infiltration of counterfeiters and pirates. OIPR is working with the CACP to encourage US trading partners to develop similar guidelines for foreign markets.

---

132. See http://searching.gao.gov/query.html?qt=+intellectual+property&charset=iso-8859-1&ql=&x=16&y=7

133. See www.usdoj.gov/ag/annualreports/pr2006/Appd/appd_f.pdf

134. See www.cbp.gov/linkhandler/cgov/import/commercial_enforcement/ipr/seizure/trading/fy06_ipr_stat.ctt/fy06_ipr_stat.pdf

135. In 2006, OIPR representatives travelled to 12 cities and gave 6 web-based seminars, speaking before a total of 2 audiences.

International co-operation	The US Trade Representative (USTR) and the State Department are actively promoting global enforcement of IPRs in international forums, such as G8, OECD, APEC and through partnerships with France, Japan and the EU. This includes promoting the adoption of best practices for enforcement internationally and new initiatives to improve the global intellectual property environment. Concerns related to IPR issues are moreover addressed through a trilateral Security and Prosperity Partnership (SPP) dialogue involving Canada, Mexico and the United States.

In addition, the agencies of the US government focus on enforcement by:

- Dismantling criminal enterprises that steal intellectual property — through the encouragement of foreign adoption of practices that lead to more investigation and prosecution of those who trade in fakes, and the establishment of relations and information sharing networks with Department of Justice foreign counterparts. Raising international awareness and support fighting the trade in fakes — through the encouragement of support for initiatives in key multilateral forums, including the Asia-Pacific Economic Co-operation (APEC), to improve global IPR.

- Stretching international capacity building resources — through the co-ordination of international assistance and training programmes in areas and countries where the need is greatest and increased staffing of US police in missions abroad, and an exchange programme that will bring foreign police to US soil.

- Establishing a more business-friendly environment abroad for rights holders through guidelines for government enforcement and the posting of additional US Patent and Trademark officials overseas to learn more about how foreign countries protect businesses from victimised by counterfeiting and piracy.

References

OECD (2005), "Responses to OECD customs survey", unpublished.

OECD (2006), "Responses to OECD government survey", unpublished.

United States Code, http://uscode.house.gov/

WTO (2006), "Trade Policies Review: United States of America".

Part III

INDUSTRY SECTOR OVERVIEWS

Objective

The purpose of the following industry sector overviews is to provide a snapshot of the practical, specific circumstances of various industries in their fight against counterfeiting and piracy. These sector overviews are meant to supplement the general analysis undertaken in this report; therefore, readers are advised to consider them in context, keeping in mind they were never intended to be exhaustive, stand-alone analyses of these industries.

Which industry sectors are covered?

Sixteen industry sectors were identified as being significantly exposed to counterfeiting and piracy. These sectors were not systematically derived, and do not conform to any international classification system, but they do cover a very significant (perhaps even overwhelming) proportion of all manufactured goods.

In keeping with the coverage focus of this report, only sectors that produce "physical" goods were covered; therefore neither services nor intangible products (such as the digital files exchanged over the Internet or by other electronic means) are covered, even if they fall within a broad definition of that industry sector. Music, film and software are examples of where this distinction would be important.

Selection of sectors for coverage

The 15 sectors identified, and those selected for further study, are shown in the box at the end of this overview.

The list of 15 had to be trimmed down, because it was physically impossible to cover all of the sectors with available resources. The selection of sectors for further study was based on a number of criteria:

- The first criterion was that sectors with public health and safety issues would receive priority as candidates for the sector studies.

- The second criterion was that because these sector studies were intended to reflect industry experience, industry co-operation was crucial; therefore, the choice of sectors reflects to some degree the willingness of industry to participate and to provide information and data.

- The third, and less-important criterion, was that sectors with large amounts of information available from other sources were also favoured for further study.

Information and data used in the sector reports

As snapshots of industry experience with counterfeiting and piracy, the sector overviews rely heavily on information, data and perspectives provided by the industry sectors themselves. Readers should note that neither the appropriateness of methodology used to derive data, nor the accuracy of the data provided by the industry, were verified by the OECD.

The information from industry was collected by way of a detailed questionnaire sent to top industry bodies and major companies in the respective sector, identified by the industry co-ordinating body for this project (Business and Industry Advisory Committee, BIAC). This was supplemented by direct correspondence with individual respondents from various bodies and firms. The majority of the information was provided to the OECD on a confidential basis, and this is reflected in the sector overviews themselves, in that firms or brand names are generally not named.

On some occasions, the industry information was supplemented by information and data from other sources. Where this has occurred, the source of that information is cited.

Key points to come out of the sector overviews

Common experiences

The sector reports were prepared with the deep involvement of the industries concerned, so that the material they contain was drawn from their research and on-the-ground experience. While the material and data provided by the various industry sectors was not collected or presented in identical fashion, there was sufficient commonality for the sector reports to be presented within a consistent framework, and this allowed the drawing out of a number of common experiences across the sectors investigated.

Briefly, these common experiences were:

Almost anything can be counterfeited

The sector studies highlight that counterfeiters are clever, skilled and very professsional in the way they carry out their businesses. Each industry has provided examples of items that have been successfully counterfeited, including some that require substantial investments as well as fabrication skills (the range of automotive spare parts counterfeited is an example).

Health and safety is at risk

Special emphasis was placed on sectors with health and safety issues, such as food and drink, pharmaceuticals, automotive spare parts and electrical components. The experience of these industry sectors is troublesome, as the common experience has been that counterfeiters will copy anything where there is a profit to be made, and these fakes are frequently below standard. In addition, all sectors reported that counterfeiters were becoming very adept at making fakes look like the real thing, in order to deceive consumers. Even security holograms have been reported as being counterfeited.

Sub-standard items in these sectors could cause deaths, illnesses, injuries and property damage, and this injects an even more serious public health and safety dimension that goes beyond concerns with IP rights. For example, instances of medicines, car parts and spirits have been found that are clearly fakes, even though they avoid the label of counterfeiting by not infringing trademarks, patents or registered designs.

Infiltration of legitimate supply chains

A worrisome thread that emerged from industry sectors subject to deceptive counterfeits (especially those with health/safety issues) was an increasing number of instances in which counterfeited goods were infiltrating legitimate supply chains. For example, fake auto parts were found in otherwise legitimate repair shops, counterfeited pharmaceutical products at chemists and food products on supermarket shelves.

This is a trend that moves counterfeiting away from any notions that it a relatively harmless and perhaps "victimless" activity, and entrenches it as a serious and perhaps sometimes deadly crime.

The infiltration of legitimate supply chains is not always easily achieved, and requires resources, organisation and even criminal "skills". Organised crime has these attributes (as well as access to bribes and coercion), and there are numerous comments on the involvement of organised criminal gangs in all of the sectors, but especially those that deal in potentially deceptive goods.

Distribution and logistics can be complex

It is one thing to manufacture counterfeits (which itself requires investment, skills and fabrication capacity) but quite another to transport the items to their most lucrative markets.

The logistics of moving and distributing counterfeited and pirated goods to their markets are almost always complex, and highlight the resources and skills available to those who engage in these activities.

Second, the industry sectors that we examined noted that on many occasions goods are transported on normal transport routes, in containers or (less likely) as air freight, with goods accurately described (but obviously not as fakes!) and supplied with appropriate paperwork, such as Bills of Lading. This makes it more difficult for customs authorities (and even IP owners) to identify counterfeited items.

A number of industry groups noted that the complexities of these logistics create an opportunity for organised criminal gangs to become involved in the counterfeiting and piracy chains.

However, long and complex logistic chains also create opportunities for authorities (especially customs) to interdict these counterfeited and pirated goods.

Importance vs. priority

From an industry perspective, there is frequently a difference between the importance that governments attach to counterfeiting and piracy, and the priority given to relevant authorities (such as police, customs and prosecutors) when resources are allocated, and there seems to be some logic to explain their experiences.

For example, it would be understandable that a greater proportion of resources is allocated to areas that deal with the more serious illicit activities, such as drugs, weapons and people-smuggling, or even smuggled goods that avoid excise. As a serious, but "less serious" crime, counterfeiting and piracy could find itself towards the tail end of resource-allocation priority lists.

Within the resources allocated to counterfeiting and piracy, there is also some logic for a pragmatic (if not intentional) hierarchy. For example, efforts to uncover pharmaceutical, food and drink, car parts and other items that have potential health and safety risks, may have greater access to resources than the more innocuous items, such as CDs, DVDs and t-shirts.

These priorities are matters for governments, and it is up to them to decide how to allocate their resources, but it is nevertheless worthwhile to at least note that in the experience of industry there is a clear difference between importance and priorities.

Are laws enforced effectively?

All of the industry sectors reported that in their experience even when adequate laws exist, they are not always effectively applied. From the industry perspective, this leads to difficulties in identifying and apprehending possible counterfeiters and pirates, delays in prosecutions reaching courts, and inadequate penalties applied even when convictions are obtained. In turn, this hampers efforts to deal with counterfeiters and pirates, and leads to high levels of repeat offenders.

Some industry sectors have suggested that local or regional governments, and especially those in depressed regions, see counterfeiting and piracy as tolerable (if not entirely appropriate) activities that provide employment and bring income to the area, and so they are less likely to act effectively than central governments. It is stressed that no empirical evidence was presented to support these claims, and they remain anecdotal and drawn from reported experiences of industry groups and firms that play an active role, especially in the producing locations.

Cost of remedies is increasing

A point frequently raised by industry, and recorded in the sector reports, is that the cost to industry of detecting and dealing with counterfeiters and pirates is high and growing. A scan of industry groups set up specifically to deal with counterfeiting and piracy, let alone the efforts of major corporations to protect their brands and products, is sufficient to highlight that industry considers these to be serious problems; and industry is willing to expend considerable resources to combat them.

Government revenues are at risk

In addition to losses incurred by IP owners and consumers, there are also substantial losses (largely unquantifiable) in government revenues, costs eventually borne by the public at large. Such losses are incurred whenever counterfeited and pirated goods avoid paying taxes, charges and fees that are borne by the legitimate products. These losses become particularly important when the goods concerned are subject to substantial excise taxes, for example, on tobacco and alcoholic products.

In addition to revenue losses, the avoidance of these excise taxes, by reducing the retail price of those commodities to consumers, can also negatively affect government public health programmes aimed at reducing the consumption of alcohol and tobacco (especially by minors).

Industry sectors considered for detailed study

Sectors examined in detail in the report

- Audiovisual

- Automotive

- Electrical components

- Food and drink

- Pharmaceuticals

- Tobacco products

Sectors not covered in detail

- Sportswear and other branded clothing

- Luxury goods, perfumes and fashion clothes

- Books

- Industrial and consumer motor lubricants

- Aircraft components

- Toys

- Computer software

- Personal care, toiletry and household products

- Chemicals and pesticides

Chapter 8

AUDIO AND VISUAL SECTORS

8.1. General description

In accordance with the OECD Council mandate for this study overall, the following sector analysis covers only piracy that culminates in the production of a physical product, such as a CD, a DVD or (increasingly less likely) a music or VHS cassette; that is, "hard media". Piracy of what the Council mandate considers "digital" (that is, non-physical) content, whether over the Internet or by other means, will be considered separately in Phase II of this project.

It is understood that in common industry terminology, the term "digital" is used to describe the binary (as opposed to the analogue) format of storing data, and that this format is used in the storage and transmission of all computer data, CD/DVD content as well as files and other content available on the Internet. Therefore, the use of the term "digital" could cause some confusion in instances (such as music contained on a CD) where the content is both digital and stored on hard media. To avoid any confusion, in this sector report (and by implication in Phase II of the overall Counterfeiting and Piracy study), the term "digital content" or "digital piracy" specifically refers to content that does **not involve** the use of hard media as means of passing pirated content from pirate to customer.

Nevertheless, while this sector report covers only physical piracy (see Box 8.1 for a description of the different forms of physical piracy), some references to digital piracy will be found when aspects of digital piracy are inextricably linked to piracy using hard media; for example, in instances when it has been impossible to disaggregate the different forms of piracy in otherwise useful data. Such instances are specifically identified in the study.

Two other points regarding this separation between physical and digital piracy should be kept in mind. The first is that because this overview covers only physical piracy, it will understate the full extent and effects of piracy in the music and video sectors. The second point is that the problem of distinguishing between physical and digital data and information will also exist in Phase II of this study, covering the piracy of digital content.

In addition, the OECD considered some aspects of digital piracy in reports covering broadband content (OECD, 2005, 2006*a*, *b*), and this has been drawn on in this separate analysis of piracy involving hard media.[136]

---

36. The OECD's Working Party on the Information Economy (WPIE) is undertaking analysis of the digital delivery of content. Details of this work and available studies can be found at www.oecd.org/sti/digitalcontent.

Box 8.1. Different forms of physical piracy

This phase of the Counterfeiting and Piracy study focus on "physical piracy", which is described as piracy involving the use of "hard media" and resulting in a tangible product (for example a music CD).

The most common forms of hard media used by pirates are well known to consumers; these are the CDs and DVDs that contain music and video content, as well as the older music cassettes and VHS tapes. These CDs and DVD can come in numerous formats and in different sizes; for example video CDs, or mini Discs, but they are all essentially similar, and contain music and video content that can be played in a home music system, DVD players, personal and auto CD players and so on.

These common formats are those counted by the music and film industries when they assess the extent of physical piracy and consequential losses.

However, there are other hard media formats that can also be used in the piracy of music and video content; these are computer-related storage media, such as hard drives, memory cards, flash memory drives and others.

For example, an 80Gb external hard drive can store as many as 20 000 digital song files (in formats such as MP3), which can be transferred from one person or another, and potentially used to create pirated CDs for sale to other consumers. Laptop computers, MP3 players, Personal Digital Assistants (PDAs) and even mobile telephones could be used for the same purposes.

These storage devices are something of a grey area, because while they are tangible, they do not conform to the general concept of hard media, such as CDs and DVDs, and an argument could be mounted that they are nothing more than storage devices that also permit the transfer of digital data.

Even if we were to treat them as forms of physical piracy, the transactions are generally very private and diffused, and it would be virtually impossible to identify and measure them. Therefore, this sector overview, while recognising their existence and their potential for facilitating the distribution of pirated material, does not attempt to explore them in depth, and no effort is made to identify their specific contribution to the overall piracy problem. The music and film industry have taken a similar approach, even though they are aware of these different forms of piracy (see, for example, IFPI, 2006, pp. 3-4).

Audio and video piracy has evolved substantially over the years, and changes have occurred at an increasing speed as suitable technology has become more widespread, easier to use and more affordable. In essence, the developments in audio and video piracy have evolved in parallel fashion, albeit at different speeds due to the different demands placed on technology by the duplication of audio and video content (see Annex 8.A1 for details).

As a concise summary, in both cases but at different times, this involved firstly the development of relatively expensive semi-commercial reproduction equipment that permitted moderately large scale production of pirated media, then the arrival of inexpensive computer equipment that allowed individuals to "burn" CDs and DVDs, and finally further developments in computing technology and the Internet that has allowed the transfer, copying and playing of digital audio/video files. This last stage has the potential to eventually virtually by-pass the need for the production, distribution and sale of copies on hard media; although it is unlikely that the demand for hard media products will totally disappear.

In both the music and film industries, technological advances have acted to make the production of pirated copies better, easier, cheaper, faster and importantly, local. This means that music and video pirates can produce low-cost, relatively high-quality copies on either pressed or burnt hard media that to consumers are virtually indistinguishable from legitimate products.

These pirated copies are increasingly produced locally, thus dispersing the supply chain and reducing the need for long-distance transport and complex distribution networks. Also, music and video content can now be pirated, sold and transmitted around the globe without the need to fabricate any physical goods, which is a threat not faced by other industries. Apart from software, none of the other industry sectors examined in this section face this kind of challenge to their legitimate trade, since in other sectors the necessity to produce, transport and distribute physical goods still remains.

8.2. Types of infringements

The principal form of IPR infringement being faced by the music, film and TV industries is piracy, that is, breach of copyright. When copies of original album and film covers are used on the pirated CDs or DVDs (for example, record or film company logos) then this may also involve trademark, and perhaps design, infringements of those covers and logos, if they are registered.

While there is arguably little incentive for those pirating the music to go to the extra expense of printing labels (as the item of interest is the music or the film itself, not the wrapping), when pirates do copy the packaging this can be extremely sophisticated, and music and film companies have reported that even security holograms have been copied. This can enhance the value of the pirated product, and in the case of the very best copies, these have even found their way to regular stores, to be sold alongside the legitimate versions. These high-quality pirated copies are generally produced in illicit, semi-professional mass-production workshops, rather than the small-scale piracy undertaken by individuals.

Box 8.2. What forms can video/audio piracy take?

For the purposes of this sector study, piracy is defined as copies that are made without the consent of the rights holder, and which are an infringement of copyright or related rights under the laws of the countries or territories concerned. This definition is largely consistent with (but not identical to) the definition of "copyright piracy" found in the footnote to Article 51 of the WTO's Agreement on Trade-Related Aspects of Intellectual Property Rights (TRIPS).

However, both the music and film industries have developed more detailed definitions to cover their sectors, and those definitions that define physical piracy (the focus of this study) are shown below to clarify how these terms are used in these industries. While the terms used by the music and film industries are to some degree similar, they can describe quite different things - for example the term "bootlegging" is quite different when used in a music or film sense.

To avoid confusion, when this study talks about "piracy" this should be read in the context of the TRIPS definition shown above. However, if a term is ever used in the context of a particular industry (for example when data from that industry are presented) then that term will used in a manner consistent with the definition used by the particular industry under analysis, and will be clearly identified as such.

.../...

Box 8.2. What forms can video/audio piracy take? *(continued)*

Film terminology

The film industry definitions have been drawn from the Motion Picture Association of America (MPAA, 2006), which uses the following classification of activities that involve physical piracy:

Bootlegging: Movies and other video content obtained by either purchasing or obtaining an illegally copied tape or optical disc.

Illegal copying: Making or receiving illegal copies of video content made from a legitimate cassette or optical disc.

Music terminology

The terminology for physical piracy in the music industry has been drawn from the International Federation of the Phonographic Industries (IFPI)[137]. These include:

Physical music piracy: Physical music piracy is the making or distribution of sound recordings on physical carriers without the consent of the rights owner. The term "piracy" refers to activities that are of a commercial nature, including activities that cause a commercial harm. The packaging of pirate copies may or may not be different from the original. Pirate copies are often compilations, such as the "greatest hits" of a specific artist, or a collection of a specific genre, such as dance tracks.

Counterfeit: Counterfeits are one type of physical piracy – these are made without required permission and are packaged to resemble the original as closely as possible. The original artwork is reproduced, as well as trademarks and logos in some cases, and is likely to mislead the consumer into believing that they are buying a genuine legitimate product.

Bootlegs: Bootlegs are the unauthorised recordings of live or broadcast performances. They are duplicated and sold – sometimes at a premium price – without the permission of the artist, composer or record company

Notes

i) The focus of this study is the commercial, physical piracy of music, film and video content generally conducted for profit. It is recognised that in many circumstances the use of music and video content may be legally permitted; for example, some forms of private, non-commercial copying, and these instances are not covered in this analysis.

ii) The film industry uses a definition of Internet piracy that principally covers non-physical piracy, which is outside the scope of this study (it will be taken up in Phase II). However, in the film industry, the definition of Internet piracy also covers the copying of movies illegally obtained on-line and copied onto hard media (tapes and optical discs), which does fall within the scope of this study.

Therefore, if movie data on Internet piracy is excluded, then this will tend to underestimate the size of the physical piracy problem in the film industry. Conversely, if the data are used, then the magnitude of physical piracy involving hard media in the film industry will be overstated.

Working on the presumption that movie piracy that is strictly online would constitute the overwhelming majority of Internet piracy involving films, data for internet piracy in the film industry has, whenever possible, been excluded from this analysis.

---

137. See www.ifpi.org/content/section_views/what_is_piracy.html

8.3. Modes of operation

With respect to physical piracy, present day production of pirated audio and video content involves both the traditional, centralised production of CDs and DVDs[138] in commercial quantities, and the more recent approach of limited quantity production from small-scale enterprises, using easily obtainable and inexpensive computer equipment.

8.3.1. Large-scale commercial production

Setting up a facility to replicate (or "press" from a master copy) CDs and DVDs remains a comparatively expensive undertaking, requiring substantial investment in suitable equipment, and would only be entertained by those intending to produce very large numbers of CDs and DVDs. Only well-funded and organised groups, with extensive distribution networks, would make the necessary investment for this kind of sophisticated equipment.

Apart from its cost (which would require the production and sale of large numbers of CDs and DVDs to amortise) this equipment would also need to be housed in permanent or quasi-permanent production facilities, which would greatly increase the chance of discovery.

In addition, a respondent from the movie industry claimed that the greatest occurrence of physical video piracy occurs in territories with the more "relaxed" rules of law relating to IPR, and where there is unused capacity in facilities that can produce finished DVDs (as opposed to the production of blank optical discs). The inference is that loosely regulated and controlled "commercial" manufacturing facilities are being used to produce pirated versions of popular films and TV shows; perhaps in parallel with the legitimate items. This insight was also reflected in a submission to the USTR by the International Intellectual Property Alliance (IIPA, 2006*b*).

Such sophisticated production and distribution activities would also have the capacity and resources to manage the complex piracy chain associated with an activity of this scale. For example, obtaining pre-release copies of films (in particular) can be more difficult than obtaining post-release masters (when the legitimate, commercially available CDs and DVDs can fulfil this role) and this would require leaks from the studios or from pre-release copies circulated for promotional purpose, or for someone to make a videocam copy from an early theatre showing.

The value of such pre-release copies is greatest before legitimate copies are made commercially available by the music or film studios, when copying can then be taken up by small-scale pirates. Therefore, quick production in considerable quantities is necessary, as well as a rapid and effective transport/distribution network to the eventual markets, which are generally outside the country of production.

These large-scale activities, especially those involving brand new material, would require sophisticated organisation and considerable investment, and this is likely to attract the attention of, and participation by, organised groups, including criminals, who use their organisational skills, their financial strength and other "persuasive" techniques to construct and operate a large-scale piracy chain. This is discussed in greater length later in this sectoral analysis.

---

138.   In some parts of the world, piracy is still carried out using music cassettes and VHS video tapes as the media of choice, but these are rapidly being supplanted by CDs, DVDs and the Internet.

8.3.2. Small-scale commercial production

As indicated earlier, computer technology has now reached the stage where CDs and DVDs can be copied at low cost and in relatively large numbers using easily obtainable multiple optical disc burners, operating either as stand-alone units or linked to a desktop computer. Quite clearly, this offers pirates the opportunity to enter into highly mobile, small-scale commercial production without need for the extensive investment necessary to set up the large scale production facilities referred to earlier.

By way of example, for a modest investment of around USD 700 it is possible to buy a 7-burner tower[139] that will plug in to a basic computer, and be capable of reproducing 70 or so CD-Rs an hour. Similarly, a manually operated, self-standing (*i.e.* no linkage to a computer required) unit with 10 DVD burners, costing less than USD 2 000, could produce around 90 DVDs an hour.[140]

Such units are quite small and can be easily moved around to minimise the risk of detection. Some more sophisticated models are automated and can be linked to compatible printing devices to produce pirated CDs and DVDs that would be hard to distinguish from legitimate products. This kind of production is suitable for distribution in open markets and locations where there are concentrations of tourists, thus avoiding exportation, which effectively reduces the risk of detection during transport or when moving through customs controls.

This small-scale commercial model, mentioned by most respondents to the OECD survey, is characterised by relatively small production facilities with outputs intended for local markets. Unlike other forms of counterfeiting/piracy, where skilled operators and substantial investment in production equipment is generally needed, in the audio/video sector only modest investments and few skills are required to produce copies of CDs or DVDs.

This smaller-scale production capability has meant that the piracy base has increased enormously, so that instead of a small number of pirates producing large numbers of copies for both local and export markets, there is now an increasing number of pirates who together probably produce the same quantities as the large-scale operators, but for essentially local distribution. This development has caused considerable concern amongst respondents to the OECD survey.

The production costs for these small-scale production facilities can be very low. Even purchased commercially in packs of 100 from sites such as eBay and Amazon, blank CD-Rs will cost around USD 0.20 each. Even with a jewel case and printed label, the overall cost per CD is unlikely to be more than USD 0.35-0.40 each.

For illegal DVD-Rs, the cost of production (*i.e.* the cost of the DVD-Rs and packaging) has been estimated to be USD 0.57, while their resale value is around USD 9 (MPA, 2005).

Even obtaining "masters" (from which copies can me made) is now relatively easy, as these can be found on legitimate CDs or DVDs of the content to be pirated, from "camcorder" copies of films taken in theatres or data files downloaded from the Internet. Any of these will give the pirates copies of a varying, but generally acceptable, quality.

---

139. Information from proactionmedia.com

140. Information from www.octave.com

This means that even by selling a pirated CD or DVD for the equivalent of USD 1, the pirate can net a profit of around 100%. Depending on the market, the sale price can be higher, which would then provide a margin to the pirate for transport and distribution beyond his local market.

On the audio side, in addition to changes in the mode of production, there have also been changes in the content of pirated items. Large-scale production focuses on producing a large number of the same title, such as a new album by a popular artist. The smaller-scale pirate can also do this, but in addition has the flexibility of producing compilations of different songs from the same or different artists "on demand". This additional service is facilitated by the computing power available from the same computer that will burn the pirate CD, and the availability of the Internet for customers to place such orders.

The importance of the development of small-scale enterprises is that there is now considerably less reason for pirated CDs and DVDs to be produced in one location, and then exported to markets worldwide. As well as broadening the production base, this also means that there is less need for pirated items to be exported across borders, and therefore commensurately less opportunity for interception by customs authorities. In addition, small-scale enterprises deal in much smaller quantities, which makes detection more difficult, and prosecution or civil action less attractive for enforcement authorities and owners of IP rights.

8.4. Factors that drive production and consumption of pirated items

This section examines various factors that drive the production and consumption of pirated audio-visual products. Each product sector has its own peculiar characteristics that will in part determine and shape those drivers, and the recognition and understanding of these drivers can provide insights on the propensity for that category of goods to be produced. In turn, this may provide some guidance on the likelihood that such products can be found in the market place and may support statistical data collected through customs interdictions, police raids on production and retail facilities, the results of legal action and other market-based data. Moreover, the propensities could provide important insights into how surveys and economic modelling could best be used to improve measurement.

Please refer to the summary table at the end of this chapter (Table 8.6), titled "Propensity to produce or consume pirated audio and visual goods". The drivers considered to apply to the audio-visual sector have been prepared (on the basis of available information, analysis, industry experience and qualitative judgement) on whether, and to what extent, they are favourable or unfavourable for the production and consumption of these pirated goods.

The interpretation of these propensity factors needs some caution, as not all drivers will carry the same weight in the decision-making process. As a simple example, any potential difficulties with the transport and distribution of centrally produced pirated hard media might be totally overwhelmed by the potential profits available to the pirate.

The drivers in the table suggest that for producers, the relative ease of production and distribution, the potential profits and relatively low penalties -- especially in comparison with other illicit commodities such as drugs --- are likely to encourage production. Pirates can also focus on the more popular content, and piggy-back on promotional efforts of the industry. The only downside for producers appears to be the actions of government to limit IP infringement and the active campaign being waged by the entertainment industry.

On the consumer side, the rapport between quality and price of the pirated products, the ready availability of the latest and most popular releases, and the relatively low risk of detection/prosecution, suggests that consumption would be encouraged, despite active education campaigns by music and film companies.

Overall, the drivers for the audio-visual sector would suggest that, despite these goods being subject to discretionary consumption, large-scale pirate activities can be expected, in part because of the attractiveness of the pirated items to consumers, and the relatively low financial and legal risks for both producers and consumers.

8.5. The issue of overcapacity of optical disc production[141]

In the OECD survey, respondents from both the music and film industries expressed the view that global capacity to produce optical discs (both CDs and DVDs) is a major contributor to piracy.[142] In its 2006 Piracy Report (IFPI, 2006) the International Federation of Phonographic Industries estimated that global disc capacity totalled 60 billion units, but that estimated "legitimate demand" amounted to around 20 billion units, or approximately 30%, of that production capacity.

IFPI draws its data from the US research firm Understanding & Solutions[143] (U&S), which according to IFPI uses the following definition of "legitimate demand":

> *"Legitimate demand" is measured in terms of trade deliveries in the retail distribution network rather than discs which are demanded by, e.g. a local studio/music label or software developer regardless of their final destination."*

In itself, this is a relatively narrow and technical definition of legitimate demand, but it is noted that there is no suggestion by the industry that the remaining demand (such as business and home use) would necessarily be "not legitimate".

With respect to the impact of any "overproduction" of optical discs on piracy, IFPI's own data shows that in 2005 around 1.2 billion pirated music CDs were sold (IFPI, 2006), which means that -- looking at the world average --- the actual use of optical discs for music piracy would amount to no more than 2% of claimed total optical disc production capacity, which would in turn translate to a comparatively small proportion of overcapacity (or even of actual production). While 2% might not seem a big number, the volume of pirated music discs is around a third of all music discs sold.

Overall, this 2% conversion of capacity to pirated material suggests that while overcapacity would facilitate piracy, it does not seem to be the principal driver for the production of pirated material.

---

141. Optical disc is a generic description for discs where lasers are used to read embedded data. CDs can store a maximum of 800Mb, while DVDs can store 4.7Gb. New generation Optical Discs (such as the Sony Blu-Ray, and the Toshiba HD DVD) will greatly increase capacity up to around 25-50Gb. For more information, see Optical Storage Technology Association at www.osta.org

142. For a more detailed explanation of this proposition by the industry, see (IPFI, 2003 page 44) and the Submission in (IIPA, 2006b, pages 7-11).

143. See www.uands.com for further information.

It is also noted that there is no established correlation between overcapacity in specific countries and territories (see IFPI, 2005, page 5) and piracy rates. As the prime example, for some years Chinese Taipei has been judged by the industry as having by far the highest optical disc production overcapacity (IFPI 2003, 2005, 2006), but Chinese Taipei exports around 90% of its optical disc production (Global Sources, 2005), and it is not at all clear to what extent these exports are used to pirate copyrighted material. Also, Chinese Taipei is not particularly high on the list of places with the greatest piracy losses, nor is it amongst the locations where the levels of piracy are estimated to be highest. As another example, Singapore also has substantial "overcapacity", but has very low piracy rates.

However, IFPI has also pointed out that in some specific economies (Russia was mentioned as an example) overproduction is considered by the industry to be a major contributor to piracy in those localities, often through the use of plant processing capacity (*i.e.* the pressing, not burning of optical discs – see the section on "Large scale commercial production" for more details). This point is noted.

In summary, leaving to one side the difficulties of defining and quantifying "legitimate" demand and whether it would be possible to somehow regulate the market to minimise overcapacity, there seems little doubt that the ease of availability of optical discs and computer hardware facilitates piracy in the audio/visual sector. This creates opportunities for pirates not seen in other industry sectors, which require substantial investment in skills, equipment and materials in order to produce fake copies of original items.

.6. Piracy rates and main centres of production

8.6.1. The availability of data

Generally speaking, efforts to estimate the magnitude of counterfeiting and piracy (which are covert and illegal activities) are hampered by the lack of reliable, consistent data. For their part, the music and film industries (along with software and book publishers) have been very active in collating information and data on piracy in their respective sectors, and have developed methodologies to assess the extent and sources of piracy, and the effects on their respective sectors. While measurement remains an inexact science, the responses to the OECD survey, material provided by the industry, as well as independent research by the study team, indicates that the quantity and quality of data available, even if not perfect, is generally superior to that of other industry sectors.

The key organisations in the music industry are: the International Federation of the Phonographic Industries (IFPI), which has 48 national affiliates and takes a global perspective on that industry; The Recording Industry Association of America (RIAA), which is affiliated to IFPI and represents the interests of the US music industry, has also been active in collecting and analysing information on piracy.

On the film side, the key organisations are the Motion Picture Association (MPA), and the Motion Picture Association of America (MPAA). While nominally different, these organisations are for all intents and purposes one and the same. Both share the same members (the principal US film studios), and share research data and a common website[144]. The only substantive difference between the two organisations is that while the MPAA

---

144.   Both organisations can be found at www.mpaa.org

focuses on US issues (such as piracy in the US and dealings with the US government), the MPA focuses on international piracy, liaisons with non-US governments, etc.

The consequence of this very close relationship between the MPA and the MPAA is that their data has a very strong US flavour. However, the MPA has also produced some data on losses due to piracy incurred by "local" (*i.e.* non-MPA member) producers, and this is used in this report, albeit sparingly and with some qualifications. Unfortunately, no other organisations representing film companies from regions outside the US responded to the OECD survey.

Both the RIAA and the MPAA are members of the International Intellectual Property Alliance (IIPA)[145], which in a US context is active in collating piracy data used for a variety of purposes, including providing regular reports and recommendations to the US Government's "Special 301 process"[146].

These reports, co-ordinated by the IIPA on behalf of its members, have been prepared for more than 100 countries and territories and contain estimates on the incidence of piracy, its value, the impact on the markets in those countries and territories and details of legislative protection (IIPA, 2006c).

While these IIPA reports bring together a considerable amount of information, they are structured in a way that meet the USTR requirements for the "Special 301" process, and cover only US music and film companies, which even though these constitute a very large proportion of the total market, remains a limitation. For this reason, preference is given wherever possible to IFPI and MPA data, although reference is also made to RIAA, MPAA and IIPA data when appropriate.

Additional anecdotal information was provided by the industry through the OECD survey undertaken in 2005. Many of the industry inputs were provided on a confidential basis (and are treated as such in this report) and were valuable sources of information on industry experience. Outside of the industry, detailed data on piracy is difficult to find, and independent studies tend to rely on industry data as the basis of their analyses.

Therefore, the analysis in this sector report relies quite heavily on industry information. However, the methodologies used in collection and analysis are relatively transparent, and because the data are used to provide an indication of the general magnitude of the piracy problems experienced, rather than detailed examination for subsequent action, it is suggested that the source of the data does not nullify their value.

8.6.2. Music piracy

Information for the incidence of piracy in the music sector has been largely taken from the yearly Commercial Piracy Reports issued by IFPI (IFPI, 2005 and 2006), as well as a confidential submission by that organisation to the OECD as part of the 2005 industry survey. Where relevant, this has been supplemented by data from the RIAA as supplied to the IIPA for their "Special 301" Reports (IIPA 2006b).

---

145   The IIPA members are: Association of American Publishers (AAP); Business Software Alliance (BSA); Entertainment Software Association (ESA); Independent Film & Television Alliance (IFTA); Motion Picture Association of America (MPAA); National Music Publishers' Association (NMPA); Recording Industry Association of America (RIAA).

146   "Special 301" is the part of US trade law that requires the US Trade Representative (USTR) to identify countries that deny adequate protection for intellectual property rights (IPR) or that deny fair and equitable market access for US persons who rely on IPR.

The IFPI methodology calculates the piracy rate in any given economy based on the number of pirated units sold divided by the total number of units sold (both pirate and legitimate), and is based on extrapolations from three different sources:

- Estimates received from its different national groups of sound recording producers.

- Estimates received from external consultants.

- Seizure information extrapolated from IFPI's enforcement teams and data from the national groups.

IFPI also takes into account historical estimates and academic and consumer studies when these are available, and believes that each of these sources of information brings a different perspective to the preparation of the estimates.

Some observations are necessary before attempting to draw points on the levels of domestic piracy contained in Table 8.1. The first observation is that the IFPI methodology focuses on the sale of both genuine and pirated optical discs (*i.e.* consumption, not production). Therefore, while this data are useful to establish where genuine products are under most pressure from pirated alternatives, they does not help to establish where they are produced, as pirated optical discs sold in one economy may have been imported from another economy.

The IIPA reports submitted to the USTR for the "Special 301" process on the surface offered some help here, as its methodology noted that where the RIAA (which collects the data on behalf of the IIPA) has sufficient information relating to known manufacture of pirate recordings that emanate from a third country, this loss data would be included in the loss number for the country of manufacture rather than the country of sale (for details on the IIPA/RIAA methodology see IIPA, 2005).

However, the RIAA has subsequently advised that this has been possible for only a very small number of countries, which limits the value of this otherwise potentially useful dataset to shed some light on centres of production.

The OECD's survey of customs authorities in 2006 was also examined for possible information on centres of production, but unfortunately this data was too coarse, as almost none recorded details of content, but simply that pirated optical discs had been intercepted. In any case, there was also very little information provided on the origin of the intercepted items.

However, a point that may be relevant here is the gradually changing face of music piracy as outlined in the earlier section on "Modes of Operation". That section highlighted the development of smaller-scale, commercial operations producing pirated optical discs primarily for local markets. This development would suggest that increasingly, pirated optical discs would be produced and sold locally, thus facilitating the deduction of the principal centres of production. However, there is no indication at this stage as to when that point might be reached, and all that can be recorded at present is that there is no systematically collected data that would allow a rigorous analysis of the main centres of pirated optical discs.

Table 8.1. IFPI estimates of the level of domestic music piracy, 2006

Region	Over 50%	25-50%	10-24%	Less than 10%
North America				USA, Canada
Europe	Bulgaria	Croatia	Finland	Austria
	Estonia	Cyprus[147]	Netherlands	Belgium
	Latvia	Czech Republic	Portugal	Denmark
	Lithuania	Greece	Slovenia	France
	Romania	Hungary	Spain	Germany
	Russia	Italy		Iceland
	Turkey	Poland		Ireland
	Ukraine	Slovakia		Norway
				Sweden
				Switzerland
				UK
Asia	China	Malaysia	Hong Kong, China	Japan
	India	Philippines	Korea	Singapore
	Indonesia	Chinese Taipei		
		Thailand		
Latin America	Argentina	Brazil		
	Central America			
	Chile			
	Colombia			
	Ecuador			
	Mexico			
	Paraguay			
	Peru			
	Uruguay			
	Venezuela			
Middle East	Egypt	Qatar	Bahrain	
	Jordan	Israel	UAE	
	Kuwait	Oman		
	Lebanon			
	Pakistan			
	Saudi Arabia			
	Syria			
Australasia				Australia
				New Zealand
Africa	Morocco	South Africa		
		Zimbabwe		

Source: Information provided by IFPI – 2006.

---

147.   See footnote 18 in Chapter 3.

On a purely anecdotal basis, the centres of production most frequently mentioned in the industry questionnaires were China, Russia, Pakistan, Uruguay, Nigeria, Malaysia, Indonesia and Thailand.

While the IFPI or other available data do not help to clearly identify the principal centres of production, they nevertheless indicate the extent of the problem faced by the music industry. The key point that can be drawn from Table 8.1 is the large number of economies where there is significant estimated penetration by pirated products and especially those where pirated music rates are estimated to be over 50% (29 of the 73 economies surveyed by IFPI). In such markets, the legitimate music would find it difficult to compete effectively, even if there is not a one-for-one substitution between pirated and genuine copies (the issue of substitution is taken up in more detail in the next section).

It was also evident from the detailed material provided by IFPI that piracy levels have fluctuated over the years, and that while the penetration levels have fallen slightly in some countries and territories, perhaps because of more intense and effective policing, in most places the penetration levels have remained steady, or increased.

8.6.3. Film piracy

The film industry has also systematically produced information and data related to movie piracy. In particular, the Motion Picture Association (MPA) commissioned a consultant to undertake an extensive study on its behalf (MPA, 2006). However, that study does not address piracy rates, but rather focuses on losses suffered by MPA members as well as estimating "consumer spending loss", which covers losses by governments, non-MPA production companies and others in the industry. Therefore, this study is discussed in detail in the next section on effects.

Because of the lack of data on film piracy rate in the MPA study, this section uses data produced by the IIPA in its series of country reports on piracy for submission to the USTR as part of the Special 301 process (IIPA, 2006c). The basic data for the IIPA's Special 301 reports is supplied by the Motion Picture Association of America (MPAA).

It is acknowledged that, as was the case with the music sector, the "Special 301" reports are US specific and prepared for the special needs of the USTR, and together these limitations make the data less useful to represent the experiences of the broader film industry. However, it is presented here as a general guide to piracy rates experienced by the US film industry, without extrapolating these numbers as being representative of the global film industry.

The piracy levels derived by the MPAA and passed on to the IIPA for its country reports are estimated in a variety of ways (but based on wholesale values in the country/ territory of sale to consumers) depending on the market circumstances.

As was the case with music, the video industry claims that the level of film piracy is very high, with some approaching a saturation point (over 90%).

Table 8.2. IIPA Estimates of the Level of film piracy 2004/05

Over 50%	25-50%	10-24%	Less than 10%
Bolivia	Argentina	Italy	Canada
China	Brazil	Korea	Greece
Colombia	Bulgaria		
Ecuador	Chile		
Hungary	Israel		
India	Malaysia		
Indonesia	Philippines		
Kuwait	Saudi Arabia		
Lebanon	Spain		
Mexico	Turkey		
Paraguay			
Peru			
Poland			
Russia			
Serbia & Montenegro			
Chinese Taipei			
Thailand			

Source: IIPA 2006c.

As noted earlier, the methodology used by the US film industry focuses on consumer behaviour and consumption rather than production, so the figures in Table 8.2 are not necessarily a good guide to the major centres of piracy, but rather of where pirated products are sold, and considerable trade in pirated optical discs with film content is still be taking place. This is important, as it means that there is still some incentive for the centralised, mass production of pirated items for transport to markets; even when this transport involves the crossing of borders.

However, as with music piracy, this situation is likely to change in the future, as ever-growing computing power facilitates the establishment of small-scale production facilities to meet local demand for pirated video content. This, together with faster broadband connections to facilitate the movement of large video files across the Internet, will eventually mean that at some point the bulk of pirated goods will be locally produced.

8.7. Effects of piracy on the music and film industries

8.7.1. General effects

The piracy problems faced by the music and film industries seem considerably worse than for other sectors subject to counterfeiting action, because in the age of digital recording technology, the copied video or audio product is generally authentic (the copied work is the same as the original) and the quality of the pirated copies can be very good.

This availability of good copies of the most popular versions of virtually any kind of music, TV shows and films, along with the increasingly fragmented and localised production methods now within easy reach of any would-be pirate, means that the music and film industries face challenges that are quite different, and arguably more difficult to deal with, than most other sectors. This situation is also likely to worsen, as online transfers are now also eliminating the need to transport the pirated goods long distances or across customs borders, which is when such goods are most at risk of being apprehended.

While the reported general effects of piracy are consistent with those suffered by other sectors subject to competition from counterfeited or pirated products (such as loss of market and profits, and loss of jobs), it is clear that there are also impacts that are specific to the music and film industries, although their actual extent can be hard to judge. This is principally because, in a sector as dynamic as the entertainment industry, even when changes in the market are detected it is difficult to know the degree to which these are due to piracy siphoning off potential sales from the legitimate music market, and the degree to which those changes are attributable to other reasons; for example, a decline in demand for music and films due to the growth of computer games and other entertainment alternatives (see IFPI, 2006a).

However, some specific effects were reported by respondents to the OECD survey, and while they cannot be quantified, they are useful pointers on the kinds of effects being experienced by the music and film industries.

Without exception, all respondents noted that their industries were under severe pressure and that generally markets have been slowing, or even contracting, after many years of steady and continuous growth. While respondents acknowledged the importance of other entertainment options that competed for the attention of consumers, from the industry perspective a substantial proportion of the blame for falling sales is due to the increasingly ready availability of pirated alternatives.

As a specific effect on these entertainment industries, all respondents noted declining royalties for artists and a fall-off in the number of performers that can be kept under contract, as well as a decline in interest by performers in the industries. Additionally, any reduction in activity in the entertainment industry would also result in job losses in the production, manufacturing and retailing arms.

Therefore, an industry specific effect of piracy is that it is bringing about fundamental changes to a sector that relies on having adequate revenue to develop and maintain a constant stream of creative talent to attract customers, and which in the view of the industry could be seriously compromised if intellectual property rights are not adequately protected. In some ways, this effect is similar to the pressure being placed on innovation and R&D in other industry sectors that are severely affected by counterfeiting.

The continuing erosion of the sale of legitimate music was also attributed by the industry to the competitive effect of technology on the pirates themselves, because even though the quality of pirated CDs and DVDs has improved (especially when compared with earlier music and video cassettes), the cost of production has fallen rather than risen, due to the falling cost of computers and CD/DVD reproduction equipment.

In addition, the music industry (although this may also apply to films) noted that widespread music piracy has led to special discounted pricing campaigns or programmes in certain markets. However, the legitimate industry simply cannot compete with pirate prices, as the cost structure of the businesses is completely different. Pirates do not pay tax, they do not pay anything to other rights holders, they do not invest in new talent, they do not carry the economic risk, and they do not pay for marketing or invest in creating brands.

The need for this kind of response has not been frequently faced by the owners of IPR in other sectors, who although they have to contend with cheaper look-alikes, have generally not been confronted with low-cost alternatives that can be virtually the same quality as the originals.

A respondent claimed that as the music and film industries accounted for a significant proportion of the GDP of some European economies, any shrinkage of the sector due to piracy would have national, rather than simply industry, implications, especially when reduced taxation revenues are taken into account.

In this respect, recent EU data indicates that the copyright industry (which covers music, film, software, books etc) contributed EUR 1 200 billion the EU economy, produced value added of EUR 450 billion, and employed 5.2 million persons in the year 2000. The total gross value added, which measures wealth added to the economy, represented more than 5.3% of the total value added for the (then) 15 EU Member States. In terms of employment, the industries contributed 3.1% of total EU employment (EU, 2006). This is a significant economic contribution to the EU, and would be paralleled in other economies, especially the USA, which highlights the potential broader economic losses that could flow from extensive activity by pirates.

8.7.2. Specific impacts on the music industry

While the IFPI data provides some very useful insights into the incidence of piracy in various economies, it does not provide disaggregated data on losses by IFPI members, beyond claiming that in 2005 around 1.2 billion pirated CDs were sold globally (out-numbering legitimate sales in 30 markets), that this represented about 37% of all music CDs sold, and that they were worth around USD 4.5 billion (IFPI, 2006). This dollar figure represented the value of the global pirated market at pirate prices.

IFPI does not estimate the level of substitution or displacement of genuine items by the pirated goods, so it makes no direct claims about the value of lost business due to the piracy.

However, a 2005 consumer survey carried out in the UK[148] found that 45% of respondents would definitely have purchased the original item if the counterfeited alternative had not been available. This figure would increase to 69% if those who would *probably* have bought the originals are included. This would represent a significant substitution rate (and therefore lost sales) in the UK. While broadly comparable figures could be entertained for similar developed economies, it is very likely that the substitution rate would be significantly lower in developing economies, so this figure cannot be extrapolated. Nevertheless, this survey at least shows that there appears to be a substitution effect on original products, and that this effect can be significant.

Apart for the IFPI and IIPA data, little other information on the effects on the music industry was provided in the survey, and this was based solely on the number and value of pirated items intercepted by police or customs authorities, whether by random or

---

148.   Survey *"Music Piracy in GB, March 2005"* undertaken by IPSOS, information provided by IFPI in private correspondence.

targeted searches, or by acting on tip-offs. This could provide a sense of the scale of the problem, and perhaps a hint of whether it is increasing or decreasing. However, data relating to seizures need to be treated with considerable caution, because this information is collected in a very unstructured way, and it is difficult to determine why changes have occurred. For example, a steep increase in seizures from year to year may indicate a growing production and trade, but could also indicate better (or luckier) surveillance by the owners of the IPRs, customs and police.

The scale of interceptions and confiscations reported by respondents to the OECD study was not particularly substantial, and the quantity and quality of data was uneven. For example, in 2004 a UK group reported seizures of items valued at GBP 1.4 million (basis of calculation not disclosed), while a Greek respondent reported that confiscations rose from 250 000 items in 2000 to a peak of 1.65 million in 2003.

8.7.3. Specific impact on the film industry

The MPA study "Cost of Movie Piracy" (MPA 2006) provides comprehensive information on its methodology and results. The Association claims (but the OECD has not verified) that this study is more rigorous than earlier efforts because:

- There is direct measurement of consumer purchasing/pirating behaviour.

- Estimates are based on rigorous consumer research (complemented by MPA experience).

- Data and calculations are consistent across territories.

The key elements of the MPA methodology used to estimate movie piracy rates and losses were:

- Focus groups and consumer surveys in the US and 21 other key international markets, macro-economic modelling used to extrapolate in another 42 countries.

- The directly researched countries constitute 95% of legitimate market and 80% of losses through piracy.

- Losses broken down by revenue streams (*e.g.* theatrical, home video) and source of content (*e.g.* bootlegged, copied[149].

- Adjustments for bias in survey methods and for seasonality.

- Adjustments made for "positive" effects of piracy (sampling of products by consumers).

- Results validated through several internal and external consistency tests.

- Based on this study, the losses incurred in 2005 by the MPA members (which essentially are the major US film studios) due to physical piracy were estimated to be around USD 3.8 billion.[150] Globally, these losses were broken up as shown in Table 8.3.

---

49. The MPA study also covers Internet downloading of movies, but this is not covered by this phase of the OECD study.

50. If digital and Internet piracy is included, this figure would be USD 6.1 billion.

Table 8.3. MPA member losses due to piracy, 2005

USD millions

Location	Copying losses	Bootlegging losses	Total
United States	529	335	864
21 key international markets*	593	1424	2017
Rest of world	242	648	890
Total	1364	2407	3771

Note: In this table, the terms "copying" and "bootlegging" are used in the context of the film industry as described in Box 8.2.

*The 21 key international markets are: Canada, Australia, UK, Germany, France, Sweden, Italy, Spain, Hungary, Poland, Russia, Hong Kong (China), Japan, China, Korea, Thailand, India, Mexico, Brazil, Chinese Taipei.

Source: MPA, 2006

More specifically, the top seven locations for MPA member losses, totalling around 60% of total losses, are shown in Table 8.4.

Of interest in this table is the number of OECD members in the list (perhaps indicating that even the laws of advanced economies are unable to limit access to pirated products) and the very large proportion of MPA member losses in the US and Japan attributed to copying losses rather than bootleg (implying substantial local production). Indeed, these locations are among a handful where copying losses exceed bootleg losses, and none of the others are close to these two with respect to the magnitude of the difference.

Table 8.4. Top seven locations for MPA member losses, 2005

USD millions

Location	Copying losses	Bootlegging losses	Total
United States	529	335	864
Mexico	5	430	435
United Kingdom	74	181	255
Russia	19	170	189
Japan	139	26	165
China*	2	148	150
Thailand	12	137	49

Note: The MPA noted that the calculation is based on the number of legitimate units that would have been purchased if pirated units were not available, assuming pricing and release restrictions at the time.

Source: MPA, 2006

While the figures in Tables 8.3 and 8.4 represent losses of revenue to MPA members, the industry has also suggested that a better way of representing those losses would be to look at the estimates in the MPA report *"The Cost of Movie Piracy"* (MPA, 2006) from the perspective of what the study calls "consumer spending loss", which the MPA claims represents a more complete market perspective because it also covers losses to governments, non-MPA member production, local distribution outlets etc.

The usefulness of this approach is that it provides an industry estimate not only on losses to MPA members, but also losses incurred by others in the film industry. The data has one disadvantage in that it includes both physical and digital piracy (the focus of this study is on physical piracy), but it can still be useful in providing a snapshot of the broader impacts of piracy generally. Because of the presence of digital piracy in the data, instead of monetary amounts Table 1.6 shows the percentage of consumer spending losses attributed to MPA members, as well as Local and Other products.

Table 8.5. Consumer spending losses, 2005

Location	MPA members	Local	Other
United States	94%	n/a	6%
21 key international markets	56.1%	30.4%	13.5%
Rest of world	71.5%	17.2%	11.3%
Total	64.8%	23.2%	12.0%

The list of the 21 key international markets is shown in Table 8.3.

Source: MPA, 2006.

Of interest here are the significant losses borne by local (non-MPA) producers, especially in the 21 key international markets, indicating that piracy does not just affect the US film industry (although it accounts for a substantial proportion of all film output), but also affects local interests.

8.8. Countermeasures taken

Respondents from both the music and film industries provided very similar comments to the OECD survey with respect to industry countermeasures to address the problem of piracy.

The seriousness of the piracy problem was evident in the number of respondents that highlighted the creation of special anti-piracy units, which have been given special mandates and resources to mount effective responses to the production, distribution and sale of pirated music and films.

These units are tasked to work with the appropriate authorities in many countries and territories as a co-ordinated response to piracy. From the industry's perspective this is an effective response to counter piracy.

The anti-piracy units frequently complement these prosecutions under public law with civil legal action based on the specific IP laws of the country or territory in which they operate, thus maximising the industry response to piracy through both civil and criminal actions.

The anti-piracy units also act as effective lobby groups in order to mobilise government action and to encourage governments to provide additional resources to respond to piracy threats; a task which most respondents judged to be difficult because of the lack of government priority given to piracy. This lack of priority in turn impacts on the availability of resources (for example, to public prosecution offices) to effectively undertake the necessary action against pirates.

More than one respondent noted that while governments considered piracy to be an important issue, few in practice attached commensurate priority to the problem, most likely because music and film piracy is rarely considered a serious crime and therefore less deserving of attention than other more serious illegal pursuits. The high cost to both governments and industry of counter-measures to detect and deal with pirated goods was also stressed by industry respondents.

In addition to action against pirates, respondents to the survey also highlighted the importance of educating the public on the effects of buying pirated products; in particular the effects on employees of the entertainment industries and the dangers of creative talent avoiding these industries if these are the subject of extensive piracy. These campaigns are seen as very important, and intended to achieve a long-term shift in public perceptions relating to piracy, but the short-term benefits are difficult to judge.

Some respondents, especially in the film industry, spoke about possible technical solutions to maximise copy protection, on the basis that if content was more difficult to copy, and if the originals are more easily and cheaply made available to the public, then the attractiveness of piracy would decline. From an industry perspective, the logic of this approach is hard to fault, provided that the technical solutions and any laws that support them are effective, and that consumer rights are upheld.

In addition, copy protection needs to be carefully thought through in order not to breach consumer and privacy protection laws, and no doubt these issues will be prominent as the industry moves towards the widespread adoption of High Definition TV and the move to new, high-capacity DVD formats. For a concise review of issues relating to the balance between effective IPR protection and the protection of the interests/rights of users, see OECD, 2006*a* pp 23-30.

One respondent very succinctly listed the necessary conditions for effective anti-piracy responses, and these were:

- Effective and rigorously enforced anti-piracy laws.
- Effective intelligence gathering to quickly identify sources and markets.

These conditions are straightforward and simple on the surface, but have proven very difficult to achieve in practice, and will probably become even more so, as both the music and film sectors continue to encounter the transition from piracy in hard media (CDs and DVDs) to direct transfer from one computer to another.

8.9. Organised crime

In the general sections of this report, the role of organised crime (a general term including both criminal gangs and terrorist groups) in counterfeiting and piracy has been frequently mentioned. The point of organised crime is that it is found most often where the potential for illicit profits is highest, and where there is a need for investment in production facilities, the creation and maintenance of complex transport and distribution channels, and the effective management of selling outlets.

These features are most evident in the manufacture of hard goods, which require quality blueprints, templates or masters from which to produce the fakes, the investment in machinery and the acquisition of skills, the creation of clandestine factories and the movement of (often bulky) of items to their final markets.

Music and film piracy has in the past featured all of these elements, and as a consequence has also attracted the attention of organised crime, just like every other sector where counterfeiting and piracy exists. Reports produced by both the music and film industries (MPA, 2005 and IFPI, undated) lay out clearly the attraction for organised crime of the relatively low- risk profits to be made from piracy in these sectors. Each report catalogues a number of specific instances when organised criminals and terrorist groups have been linked with music and film piracy.

However, the situation in these industry sectors seems to be changing, and as a consequence, the future role of organised crime may become more uncertain.

For a start, the attractiveness of large, centralised production facilities (which are ideal for the involvement of organised crime) is declining, as the availability of cheap and powerful computing power enables music and films to be copied and reproduced in small-scale enterprises. This reduces the ability of organised crime to control supply and distribution, and forces them to move to the control of the sale outlets, something which itself becomes more difficult as the number of potential producers/distributors increases.

The inexorable move from hard copies of music and films on CDs and DVDs to files moved directly from computer to computer through the Internet will further reduce the ability of organised crime to participate in this sector, as in most cases it is impossible to locate the distributor of the music and films, who may reside in another country or continent, and therefore out of reach of the criminals. Still, the gradual introduction of high definition and high-capacity DVDs will ensure that there will remain a valuable market for hard-media piracy.

In addition, if more effective technology becomes available to protect hard media, this may make large-scale piracy more difficult, which in turn may herald a new opportunity for organised crime to effectively re-enter the market, as they are likely to be the only groups that could extort or buy copiable versions of songs or films, and make the investments necessary for large-scale piracy in the face of new technologies. Time will tell in which direction things will move in the future.

As a final word, lest this brief analysis be interpreted as meaning that organised crime no longer has any kind of role in these sectors, a number of respondents noted the links between piracy and organised crime and terrorism, and highlighted the fact that these groups have very effectively infiltrated music and film piracy, and that as a consequence the effects of their involvement will be evident for some time to come. In particular, see the MPA and IFPI report on organised crime (MPA, 2005 and IFPI, undated).

Table 8.6. Propensity to produce or consume pirated audio-visual goods

FOR PRODUCERS	EFFECT ON PROPENSITIES TO PRODUCE
Market characteristics	
Unit profitability	**Profit margins can be generous** While the unit cost of producing pirated optical discs, especially in small-scale runs would be higher than those that are mass-produced, the cost is still well below USD1 per item, and there is sufficient profit margin (by avoiding music/film production and risk, advertising and promotion, royalty payments and taxes, *etc.*) to encourage pirates to produce items for their markets.
Market size	**Large, mass market** The entertainment market, whether for domestic or imported music and film content, is very large and widespread, and it is supported by the star status of performers and the heavy promotion of products by the industry, none of which is borne by pirates.
Genuine brand power	**Extremely strong** Artists, whether in the music or film industry, represent very strong "brands" with large, enthusiastic fan bases. Some films and songs attract a following in their own right, thus creating a strong demand on the pirate market, especially when eagerly anticipated new material becomes available.
Production, distribution and technology	
Production Investments	**Moderate investment required** Only a moderate amount of investment in computers and printers is necessary to produce potentially high-quality pirate CDs and DVDs, so that production can be undertaken in small-scale enterprises near local markets.
Technology	**Technology not a barrier** Some technology is required in order to produce the CDs and DVDs, but this is readily available, easy to use and constantly falling in price, and does not constitute a significant barrier for the production of pirated products.
Logistics	**Logistics are becoming easier** While CDs and DVDs are still being mass-produced in central locations to reduce the cost of production, even for films (which pose a greater technical challenge than music) this mode of operation is gradually moving to either small-scale enterprises, or to digital piracy, which largely remove the need to transport the products. While small runs are more expensive than mass-production, profit margins are adequate to compensate, especially as this also minimises the need for complex transport and distribution logistics, as well as the risk of detection when crossing national borders. Also, the interplay between Internet distribution of masters and the local production of hard-media pirated goods is further simplifying the logistics.
Marketing and sale	**Ready markets** Pirates can piggy-back on the extensive promotion and advertising undertaken by legitimate producers. Also, pirated music and films are in themselves innocuous items that can be sold almost anywhere, from street corners to markets, and in the case of the very best products even in legitimate stores alongside the original markets. The Internet also provides a ready way to find customers, and facilitates the placement of orders for special compilations, or particular movies.
Ability to conceal operations	**Becoming easier** As with any mass-production activities large facilities can be difficult to conceal. However, the growing move toward smaller, more mobile and more easily concealable small-scale enterprises means that this risk is diminishing.
Ability to deceive	**Deception unnecessary** The ability of pirates, through the use of easily available computer equipment to compile and produce CDs and DVDs containing audio and visual content that can be virtually indistinguishable from the original, means that there is no need for deception. What pirates offer their customers, in most cases, is essentially the equivalent of the original items, and while sound and video quality can vary, they are improving.

Institutional characteristics

Risk of discovery	**Moderate, but diminishing** As long as hard media is produced in a centralised location, with subsequent transport to markets, there is a chance that pirates will be detected, especially if they have to cross customs borders, and this remains a substantial risk. This risk declines significantly if CDs and DVDs are produced locally in small-scale enterprises, where the need to move product is minimised.
Enforcement	**High if detected** The entertainment industry is extremely active in defending its copyright material, frequently in co-operation with enforcement authorities. Pirates can expect to be aggressively pursued through a variety of public and private legal actions if detected. However, the industry perspective is that piracy holds a relatively low priority for governments in the allocation of resources.
Penalties	**Penalties appear not to deter** While the rate of success in court action (whether criminal or civil) is likely to be high, the industry experience (in line with experience in other industry sectors) is that penalties are not always applied fully, which results in high levels of repeat offenders. In particular, when penalties are purely financial (such as fines), they can be treated by pirates as simply another operating cost.

FOR CONSUMERS	**EFFECT ON PROPENSITIES TO CONSUME NON-DECEPTIVE ITEMS**

Product characteristics

Price	**Acceptable to consumers** By and large, the experience in the market is that consumers are willing to buy pirated items at the prices offered, as these are generally well below the comparable prices of the legitimate equivalents.
Quality and nature of product	**Generally acceptable** As with all counterfeited products, the quality of the products can vary. However, in the music and film sectors, technology has provided pirates with the capability of producing, as long as they have high-quality "masters", very high-quality products that can be virtually indistinguishable from the original. In other cases (such as video cam copies of theatre performances) consumers appear to be willing to trade-off quality for immediacy. In addition, the flexibility of "cherry picking" content also provides considerable incentive for consumers.
Ability to conceal status	**Not an issue in this sector** This element refers to the ability of consumers to deceive their peers into believing that they are actually in possession of an original item. In the music and video sectors, consumers generally are in possession of the equivalent of an original item, so this is not a significant issue.

Consumer characteristics

Health concerns	**None** This is not a factor in this sector.
Safety concerns	**Minimal** Apart from possible safety problems when organised crime is involved, there are no personal or public safety issues that would affect the buying decisions of consumers.
Personal values	**Not an important issue** Experience in the market, and comments made by many consumers regarding piracy, indicates this is not considered to be a serious crime; indeed many argue that piracy is not a crime at all, as nothing "physical" is stolen from the artist or music or film company. In essence, personal values do not seem to play a significant role when consumers buy pirated items.

Institutional characteristics	
Risk of discovery	**Moderate** The likelihood of detection for the consumer is likely to be moderate at best, and its impact on consumers is likely to vary according to level of local enforcement.
Risk of prosecution	**Moderate** While prosecution is aggressively carried out by the entertainment industry, including in some cases through the targeting of consumers (especially on peer-to-peer networks), the actual risk in practice of a court appearance because of the purchase of a pirated CD or DVD is probably low.
Penalties	**Generally low** While some moderately severe penalties are available to deal with offenders, in practice it would probably be unlikely for these to be applied to the casual consumer of pirated, hard-media products, especially when small quantities are involved.
Availability and ease of acquisition	**Freely available** Music and film CDs and DVDs are easily available to consumers, and can be found in most street markets around the world.

References

EU (European Union) (2006), "The Economic Impact of Copyright in the EU Single Market", http://ec.europa.eu/internal_market/copyright

Global Sources, (2005), China Sourcing Report: Optical Drives and Accessories.

IIPA (International Intellectual Property Alliance) (2005), "Special 301 Methodology", www.iipa.com/pdf/2005spec301methodology.pdf

IIPA (2006a), News Release dated 13 February 2006, "Copyright Industries Release Report on Piracy in 68 Countries/Territories and Press Their Global Trade Priorities for 2006", at: www.iipa.com/pressreleases

IIPA (2006b), "Copyright Protection and Enforcement Around the World", IIPA's 2006 Special 301 Report to the USTR, www.iipa.com/special301.html

IIPA (2006c) "Country Reports from Special 301 Recommendations submitted to the USTR", www.iipa.com/countryreports.html

IFPI (International Federation of the Phonographic Industry) (2003), Statement made by the Head of Enforcement at IFPI to the US House of Representative's Committee on International Relations Hearing on "Intellectual Property Crimes: Are Proceeds from Counterfeited Goods Funding Terrorism", in July 2003, www.Internationalrelations.house.gov

IFPI (2005), The Recording Industry 2005 Commercial Piracy Report.

IFPI (2006), The Recording Industry 2006 Commercial Piracy Report.

IFPI (2006a) Press Release "Digital formats continue to drive the global music market – World Sales 2005", issued 31 March 2006, under "News" at www.ifpi.org

IFPI (undated), "Music Piracy: Serious, Violent and Organised Crime", IFPI Secretariat, www.ifpi.org

MPA (Motion Picture Association) (2005), "Optical Disc Piracy v. Illegal Drug Trafficking".

MPA (2006), "The Cost of Movie Piracy", An Analysis Prepared by the L.E.K consultancy for the MPA, www.mpaa.org/press_releases/leksummarympa.pdf

MPAA (Motion Picture Association of America) (2006), Media Release "MPAA Releases Data from Piracy Study", 3 May 2006, www.mpaa.org/press_releases

OECD (Organisation for Economic Co-operation and Development) (2005), "Digital Broadband Content: Music", Working Party on the Information Economy, www.oecd.org/dataoecd/13/2/34995041.pdf

OECD (2006a), "Digital Content Strategies and Policies," Working Party on the Information Economy, www.oecd.org/dataoecd/54/36/36854975.pdf

OECD (2006b), "Digital Broadband Content: Development and Challenges", Chapter 5, OECD Information Technology Outlook, Working Party on the Information Economy, www.oecd.org/sti/ito

RIAA (Recording Industry Association of America) (2006a), "US Manufacturers' Unit Shipment and Value Chart", www.riaa.com/news/marketingdata/facts.asp

RIAA (2006b), "US Manufacturers' Unit Shipment and Value Chart", www.riaa.com/issues/piracy

Steven Schonherr (2002), The History of Magnetic Recording, University of San Diego, http://history.acusd.edu/gen/recording/magentic4.html.

Annex 8.A1

HISTORICAL DEVELOPMENT OF PIRACY IN AUDIO AND VISUAL SECTORS

Audio piracy

When music was sold only on vinyl records there was virtually no piracy. The technology to produce vinyl records was complicated and required substantial capital investments. Therefore, legitimate recordings, sold through authorised outlets, were virtually the only way to obtain music.

The situation changed slightly when reel-to-reel tape recorders became generally available in the 1950s, but these were basically used only by hi-fi enthusiasts, willing to go to considerable trouble to record from vinyl originals. The penetration of reel-to-reel tape recorders in the market was small, and as a consequence there was little cause for concern for music companies and artists.

The next development, and the first that caused serious concern for the music industry, was the introduction by Phillips of the Compact Cassette in 1963. The ability of the cassettes to easily record music, as well as playing pre-recorded material, meant that for the first time ordinary consumers had the means of more easily copying original music, and this opened up a new challenge for the music industry.

However, while cassette recorders were more accessible to the general public than their reel-to-reel predecessors, there were nevertheless problems with the format, which meant that piracy, even if possible on a large scale for the first time, was relatively slow to develop.

First of all, cassettes were originally designed for voice recording, and their performance for music was relatively poor. Improved music quality would have to wait for the development of supplementary technology (such as metal tapes, noise suppression mechanisms etc.). These innovations improved performance but also increased the cost of cassette machines and tapes.

Second, the principal source of original music remained vinyl records, which frequently became scratched and noisy, so that non-professional recordings were rarely of good quality.

Finally, the quality of music recorded on cassettes was generally much lower than vinyl records, even when professionally produced in a factory. This was due to the limited audio dynamics of the tape used in the cassettes and the electronics used in cassette recording and playing machines. Even more important (from a piracy perspective) was that the inherent characteristics of the tape medium meant that there was an in-built degradation of quality from one recording to the next, whereby some of the signal was lost in every generation of recordings from one cassette to another.

Nevertheless, the cassette was the first time when technology made large scale copying feasible. This was a significant milestone, for not only was home copying facilitated (especially when double cassette decks were introduced) but also this was the first time that the investment necessary to set up a pirate recording facility came within easy reach of organised pirates. High speed tape-dubbing machines became available at an affordable price and the editing and dubbing capability of the cassettes enabled compilations to be made relatively easily for the first time.

Pirated cassettes, of variable quality, initially freely available in certain "tourist" locations, were the first hint of what was to become a more serious future problem for the music industry. Also, the large scale, centralised production of pirated cassettes acted as incentives for organised crime to participate through the provision of capital to set up illicit copying facilities, to acquire "master" tapes to improve the quality (and hence the value) of the finished products and to set up transport and distribution channels.

The early 1980s saw the introduction of Compact Discs (CDs), which heralded a further revolution in the music industry. At the beginning the introduction of CDs was almost like going "back to the future", because the CDs could initially only be produced in high tech laboratories which required large capital investments. Therefore, while the quality of the original material increased considerably (the original CDs themselves could be used as the master copy) for some time the reproduction media for pirates remained the Compact Cassette.

This began to change in the early 1990s when large-scale factories in various parts of the world began mass producing pirated CDs (see later section on "Modes of Operation" for a more detailed description of commercial pressing of CDs).

This situation further changed when CDs started to be used as storage devices in personal computers. This led to the rapid development of cheap CD-R[151] burners which are now standard equipment on virtually every computer produced. This reduced the need for extensive investment in commercial scale equipment capable of pressing CDs, and allowed individuals, operating small-scale facilities, to produce potentially near perfect copies for sale to consumers. This computer driven and enabled revolution, and the major impact that it has had on the music industry, was frequently mentioned by respondents to the OECD industry survey.

Video piracy

The development of video piracy has paralleled that of the music industry, albeit initially at a slower rate due to the more rigorous technical challenges of copying the much larger quantities of data present in video content.

The copying of video content was quite difficult, and expensive, until the mid-1970s, when home video cassette recorders (VCRs) became commercially available. The VCRs allowed the recording of video content from TV broadcasts, as well as copying from one

---

51.   CD-R stands for Compact Disc-Recordable. This is the favourite means of illegally copying music. These discs are different from the multi-use CD-RW (Compact Disc Re-Writeable) which use different recording technology, and are intended for use in computer applications. Many home, motor vehicle and personal CD players will not play CD-RW discs, so these are rarely used for pirated music.

machine to another, thus giving pirates their first opportunity to sell video cassettes alongside their audio counterparts.

While pirated copies taken from high quality masters could be reasonable, in general the quality of pirated VCRs was poor, as most were taken either directly from recordings taken off TV broadcasts (often with commercials, sub-titles and language dubbing included), or from other VCR tapes, which suffered the same generational degradation of quality that afflicted their audio cassette counterparts.

Therefore, while piracy on VHS cassettes became relatively common, initially it could be argued that because of their relatively poor quality, videocassettes were probably more of a nuisance than a real threat to the movie and TV industries.

However, the introduction of DVDs[152] in the mid-1990s changed this scenario quite dramatically, as the copy protection in these could be bypassed to allow virtually perfect copies to be made in commercial quantities using sophisticated pressing equipment.

As was the case in the music sector, the rapid evolution of affordable powerful computers, and the growing availability of DVD-R burning machines, which permit home computers to copy video content just as easily as audio, meant that both sectors were now exposed to similar risks from both large and small scale pirates. Finally, the availability of sophisticated camcorders also gave pirates the opportunity of copying new movies directly from their very first screening; thus allowing pirated copies to hit the streets more quickly than ever before.

In other words, the experiences of the audio industry have been repeated in the video sector; that is, the ready availability of pristine original material, and the growing capability of pirates to copy material by either using reasonably priced commercial reproduction equipment or personal computers as a small-scale enterprise. In addition, the rapidly growing ability to move video content around the Internet has made access to content and distribution of pirated items easier, and their detection more difficult.

These developments have been unique to the music, film and software industries (although the latter has not been examined in detail in this study), and while the development of technology has not been the only reason for the growing incidence of piracy, the technological capability that is within the reach of virtually anyone with a computer has made these industry sectors more vulnerable than most to counterfeiting/piracy.

Common experiences

The effect of these parallel developments in the reproduction of audio and video content has been that, in addition to the commercial pressing of optical discs, anyone with access to a PC with a CD/DVD burner can now easily obtain high quality masters of original music and video content (either from other CD/DVDs or from digital computer files), compile them if necessary, and cheaply produce good quality copies. Piracy had now evolved into a very serious threat to these industries.

There have been further developments, and an even more serious challenge now comes from peer-to-peer file swapping using broadband Internet connections, which greatly facilitates the movement of large audio and video content (see references for Chapter 8,

---

152.   DVDs are Digital Versatile Discs, which with their much larger capacity can store both video and audio material. DVD-Rs are recordable in much the same way as their CD counterparts.

OECD, 2004 for further details). Because the Internet allows content to be moved directly from computer to computer, nothing physical ever needs to be manufactured and transported, which makes detection and countermeasures much more difficult. At the same time, the Internet has also given rise to new and very successful online business models for both music and film content, and peer-to-peer technologies are increasingly used to distribute content on commercial terms by the music and film industries (references for Chapter 8, OECD, 2006*b*).

Chapter 9

AUTOMOTIVE SECTOR

9.1. General description

The main counterfeiting activities in this sector are focused on automotive components, such as parts and accessories used in the manufacture, repair and modification of all types of motor vehicles, from motorcycles to passenger vehicles (cars, buses etc.), as well as vehicles intended for the carriage of goods.

In addition to the copying of parts and components (which would almost certainly be trademark infringements), there is also evidence that patent and design infringements, ranging from individual components to entire vehicles, are also taking place.

In common with all instances of counterfeiting, both consumers and producers of the original products are at risk from the circulation of fakes. On the monetary side, there have been estimates attributed to the US Federal Trade Commission, and not challenged by the industry, that counterfeiting costs the global automotive parts industry USD 12 billion a year – of which USD 3 billion is in the US alone (MEMA 2005). This is significant, even in an industry estimated by the Motor & Equipment Manufacturers' Association (MEMA) to have yearly global sales in excess of USD 330 billion.

However, in the automotive sector there is an additional concern beyond that of buyers simply not receiving what they intended. With motor vehicles, in addition to the economic implications of intellectual property right (IPR) infringements, the usage of counterfeit parts may also affect both the performance and the safety of the motor vehicles. When tested, counterfeited safety-related parts (for example, brake pads, suspension and steering components and air-bag assemblies) have frequently been found to be inferior, and not suited for their intended purpose; their failure could result in serious accidents involving deaths or injuries.

This adds a substantially different dimension to the consideration of the effects of counterfeiting in the automotive sector.

9.2. Types of infringements

9.2.1. Trademark infringements

The available evidence is that the copying of trademarks constitutes the greatest proportion of IPR infringements in the automotive sector. Principally, this manifests itself as the affixing of well-known trademarks to non-genuine auto parts, which are then sold as original items. Numerous instances of such trademark infringements have been catalogued covering items as diverse as disc brake pads, clutch plates, oil filters, suspension and steering components and spark plugs.

The auto parts affected may include replacement parts of relatively good quality (sometimes production "overruns" of original components) that are then illegally labelled with the original trademark to command a higher price. But they might also include complete fakes made to look like the original parts, but which may be quite inferior to the originals and perhaps even dangerous.

However, the automotive industry has also noted that in some parts of the world (especially in North America), the risk of detection of trademark infringement is increasingly driving counterfeiters to market substitute parts with no branding information, which in some cases has even led to counterfeiters creating their own brands. Strictly speaking, because no intellectual property rights were infringed, this practice would not be counted as counterfeiting, even though this results in non-original parts being sold to consumers.

9.2.2. Patent infringements

The automotive industry is characterised by technological innovations and industrial processes that are in some cases covered by patents. Since they are on the public record, these patents are therefore at constant risk of being copied or otherwise infringed; for example, through the reverse engineering of an automotive gearbox or other technical equipment. Respondents to the OECD survey noted in particular that patent breaches could also occur through production "overruns" of legitimate parts, or by the passing of specifications and production details to potential counterfeiters by contractors that are producing original components for motor vehicle manufacturers.

However, the industry also indicated that patents generally cover high order components and processes, and that these are less likely to be the target of counterfeiters, who tend to target lower order components that are less technically challenging. This would explain to a large degree the relative absence of patent infringement problems in the inputs received from the automotive sector.

9.2.3. Design infringements

Beyond the counterfeiting of motor vehicle parts (which may involve both trademark and design infringements) there are also increasing reports of design infringements involving the production of entire vehicles. In essence, this involves the copying of body shape, mechanical layouts and interior designs to create vehicles that are outwardly very similar to those that have been copied, but probably with sufficient differences to allow for the argument that they are actually derivative designs, and not copies.

The copying of the designs allows the counterfeiter to benefit from the creative innovation of others, as well as from the promotion, advertising and image-building investments made on the part of the originals.

A number of examples of such alleged design infringements are available, but just two alleged are used here for illustrative purposes.

In mid-2005, there were reports of apparent design similarities between an off-road vehicle (called the Landwind), produced in China and exported to Europe, and the GM Opel Frontera.

As of the time of writing, it was not clear whether GM would take legal action to protect its design, in part because the Frontera (and similar models in other countries) were no longer being produced, and partly because of the complications of cross alliances. Jangling Motors is a joint venture partner in the manufacture of trucks with Japan's Isuzu Motors, which is itself a GM ally, and the original Frontera design came from Isuzu Motors. There was a further twist, in that a group of Opel dealers in Germany were reported to have signed a deal with the Landwind importer to place the vehicles in their showrooms.

The Japanese manufacturer Toyota also found dual cab pick-up trucks being manufactured by a company in China that bore very close visual resemblance to its Highlux model. In addition to the possible design issue, the Chinese made vehicles were called "Tayota" (instead of Toyota), and carried a grill and bonnet emblem that bore very close resemblance to that registered and used by Toyota.

In other words, in addition to design similarities, in this instance there also appeared to be what could be described as an attempt to confuse potential buyers (especially those in less sophisticated markets) into believing that they were in fact purchasing an original Toyota vehicle, or at least a vehicle that was somehow built with the involvement of the Japanese manufacturer.

These examples of possible design infringement demonstrate both sides of the coin. On the one hand, in the above examples the similarities in the vehicle designs seem clear, and it is easy to understand the claims of the originators of the designs that their intellectual property has been interfered with. On the other hand, legally establishing that the designs are sufficiently similar to constitute an infringement of an Intellectual Property Right is quite a different challenge, and it seems that none of the manufacturers affected have been able to take positive and successful steps to deal with the apparent infringements.

In the case of the Toyota Hilux copy, it is possible that this could be prevented from being exported into other countries where design registration might offer a higher level of protection. But in the case of the "Landwind", this has already been imported into Europe, and it is not clear whether its legal status will be challenged there.

9.2.4. Summary

As a general comment on infringements, without exception the automotive industry respondents to the OECD survey indicated that the infringement of trademark was the most significant problem that they faced. Indeed, the Japanese Automotive Manufacturer's Association (JAMA)[153] noted that every one of its members had been affected by trademark infringements, while three-quarters had experienced design infringements. However, only one-third had been affected by breaches of patents. These results are broadly consistent with reports by the broader international automotive community that responded to our survey.

---

53.   Reported in confidential material made available to the OECD.

9.3. Products most affected

The most likely targets of counterfeiting in the automotive sector are products in the after-market for spare parts and accessories. The reason for this is that it is unlikely (if not impossible) that original manufacturers would source components for their new cars from anywhere other than their own factories, or from the factories of known, contracted producers of specialised parts and equipment.

Because the integrity, performance and safety of original automotive parts are so important to vehicle manufacturers (for regulatory, customer relations, image and legal/ liability reasons) it would be quite difficult for counterfeiters to infiltrate such relatively closed and tightly controlled environments. For counterfeited parts to enter the legitimate supply chain, there would almost certainly have to be inside involvement, which may be possible through either corruption in the system, or perhaps through pressure from criminals. Of course, if such infiltration did occur, then the likely rewards for the counterfeiter would be high.

However, for a number of reasons, the automotive after-market sector is a much easier, and therefore a more attractive, environment for counterfeiters to work in.

First, as already noted, the infiltration of the small number of large, influential and well resourced vehicle manufacturers, who have considerable interest in ensuring the integrity of parts used to build their vehicles, would be difficult. However, the after-market sector consists of thousands of mainly small firms involved in the repair and maintenance of motor vehicles, and an even greater number of individual car owners who purchase parts and accessories. Both of these groups are amenable to using "non-genuine" parts, if these are cheaper and thought to be reasonable substitutes.

Second, as the size of the potential market for counterfeit products broadens, the level of expertise on the provenance (and appropriateness and safety) of the parts diminishes, because in the vehicle after-market many such parts are purchased on the basis of an acceptable visual similarity between the copies and the originals, rather than on comparisons of their technical performance. Because of this, there is growing concern about the greater sophistication being shown by counterfeiters, who use readily available technology to make the fake products look and feel identical to the originals, even though their actual performance may be well below that of the original items.

Third, as the potential market broadens, price and not provenance become the principal yardstick for buying decisions. Therefore, car service and repair yards may substitute non-genuine parts to increase their profits, as well as reducing the cost to their customers of the work undertaken. Private car owners, with even less expertise regarding the suitability of replacement parts, are also more likely to treat cheap car parts as "bargains".

There are no readily available extensive data to provide specific guidance on which motor vehicle parts are most frequently counterfeited, but industry experience is that parts most likely to be affected are those on vehicles that have been on the market for at least three or four years (in order to maximise the size of the available market), and they affect those parts that are the fastest moving, the easiest to copy and provide the best profit margins for the counterfeiters.

Examples of such parts would be spark plugs, shock absorbers and filters of various types (filters were identified by a major truck manufacturer as easily the most counter-feited part in its range). Brake components (including pads and linings), suspension and steering components, body panels, bearings, windscreens, tyres, all types of lights and engine parts (including engine mounts) have also been frequently mentioned in survey responses as targets for counterfeiting. Some parts may also affect the quality of emissions released into the environment.

In some cases, the items that bore the fake trademark were not part of the affected manufacturer's production line, and while these examples could be viewed as simple misuse of trademarks and brand names rather than the counterfeiting of specific parts or components, there could still be damage to the affected manufacturer.

The observation from a major truck manufacturer was that although the scope of products being infringed has remained relatively constant over the past few years, the number of infringements detected has increased.

The following table (Table 9.1), provided by a major European motor vehicle manufacturer, provides some additional guidance on the range of products affected and their relativities, as measured by the value of components seized by the company concerned in 2005, during co-ordinated action with law enforcement authorities.

Table 9.1. Volume of auto parts seized in 2005

EUR millions

Auto part	Value	Percentage of total
Brake discs	2.7	18.0%
Control arms	2.6	17.3%
Brake pads	2.5	16.7%
Engine mountings	2.4	16.0%
Steering components	0.8	5.3%
Oil and oil filters	0.5	3.3%
Oil pumps	0.5	3.3%
Water pumps	0.5	3.3%
Accessories	0.4	2.7%
Belt tensioners	0.3	2.0%
Miscellaneous	1.8	12.0%

Similar data provided by a North American manufacturer contained the following break-down of affected components:

- 30% filtering products
- 25% accessories
- 20% brakes and spark plugs
- 25% other components.

The most troublesome aspect of this information is the fact that some of the most widely represented items (*e.g.* brake and steering components) are all capable of seriously affecting the safety of the motor vehicle, and their failure could result in serious accidents, which in addition to causing serious injuries or deaths could also be attributed to the manufacturers of the motor vehicle, even though they could in fact be blameless.

9.4. Magnitude, scope and trend of infringements

Because counterfeiting is an illicit activity, information on the extent and level of incidence in particular markets is unavoidably unreliable, and data are generally derived (as they are for other illicit activities) from shipments intercepted and the discovery of counterfeited items available in the market place.

One of the problems with this derived information is that apart from incomplete, it is also difficult to establish whether changes in interception rates are attributable to changes in the manufacture, trade and sale of counterfeits, or changes in the success rate of detections, or both. Acknowledging these limitations, the following indicators came to light during the OECD survey of counterfeiting in the automotive sector.

A manufacturer provided an indication of the incidence of trademark infringements in the Middle East, which, in brief, showed that the number of cases exposed rose from around 50 in 2000 to over 200 in 2003, and that the number of counterfeited items involved also rose from almost 400 000 to over 1.3 million over the same period.

Another manufacturer estimated that with up to 30% of all spare parts sold in some Middle Eastern and Asian markets being fakes, these were the regions with the greatest penetration by counterfeits. The corresponding number for the EU market was around 5%[154]. This concentration of counterfeiting activity (if not actual manufacture) in the Middle East was also reflected by other firms in the automotive sector.

A similar figure on market penetration was identified by the Automotive Component Manufacturers Association of India, which found in a 2003 study that in the local after-market there was a 37% chance of a counterfeited part being used[155].

Of interest is that a group of motor-vehicle manufacturers have established the "Automotive Brand Protection Coalition",[156] located in Dubai, to educate the public and lobby governments to strengthen their protection of IP rights.

Whether intended or not, the location is significant, as the UAE has been frequently mentioned as a favourite gateway used by counterfeiters, and statistics produced by the Coalition tend to support this status.

In July 2005, the Coalition reported a seizure of a quarter million fake car parts. This was described in the report as representing just the "tip of the iceberg". The Coalition also listed a report in the "Gulf News" that USD 1 million dollars worth of Chinese-made fake sparkplugs, labelled with the names of various motor vehicle manufacturers, had been seized at Jebel Ali Port in 2005.[157] The Coalition's website contains numerous other similar reports of discoveries and seizures.

---

154. The substantially lower penetration in the EU was attributed by the industry to the EU's direct distribution systems, which prevent the direct selling by third parties to distributors and re-sellers of automotive parts.

155. See www.acmainfo.com

156. The Coalition's members are: BMW, GM, Honda, Mercedes Benz, Nissan and Toyota.

157. Report in the Arab News, drawn from the Coalition's website at www.nofakeparts.com.

As a guide to the size of the potential automotive counterfeit market, a major manufacturer also reported that counterfeit production volume for both domestic and export markets in North Asia may reach EUR 100 million a year, based on the local retail value of genuine parts.

The same manufacturer also reported that it had itself seized counterfeited parts and accessories in China with a retail value of some EUR 6 million, and that it deals with around 600-700 cases of IPR infringements each year.

In addition, an Intellectual Property Working Group, established by the representatives of most of the major global motor manufacturers endorsed an estimate by the US Federal Trade Commission that losses by the US auto industry approach USD 3 billion in the US, and USD 12 billion globally. The WG also reported that annual losses incurred by the Japanese machinery industry (including motor vehicle manufacturers) in Asia approach USD 7.5 billion[158].

.5. Factors that drive counterfeiting production and consumption

This section examines various factors that drive the production and consumption of counterfeited automotive parts and accessories. The recognition and understanding of these drivers can provide insights on the likely propensity for that category of goods to be produced. In turn, this may provide some guidance on the likelihood that such products can be found in the marketplace and may support statistical data collected through customs interdictions, police raids on production and retail facilities, the results of legal action and other market based data. Moreover, the propensities could provide important insights into how surveys and economic modelling could best be used to improve measurement.

Please refer to the summary table at the end of this chapter (Table 9.5), "Propensity to produce or consume counterfeited automotive goods". The drivers considered to apply in the automotive sector have been judged on whether, and to what extent, they are favourable or unfavourable for the production and consumption of these counterfeited goods.

The interpretation of the propensity factors in Table 9.5 needs some caution, since regardless of the strength of their effect on propensity, not all drivers will carry the same weight in the decision-making process. For example, the difficulties with transport and distribution of counterfeited auto parts may not be sufficient to overcome the prospective profit margins available to the counterfeiters. For another example, unlike drug-dealing, the penalties for producing/distributing counterfeits tend to be comparatively minor, and this would tend to increase the propensity for organised crime to redirect its organisational skills towards counterfeiting rather than other forms of crime (an observation made by a number of respondents to the survey).

The drivers that operate in the automotive sector lead to the broad conclusion that there would be considerable propensity for the manufacture and consumption of counterfeited auto parts and components. Principally, this is because there is likely to be a strong profit motive for manufacturers, together with potentially very large global market opportunities for the goods. In addition, because the counterfeited items would generally be considered as relatively innocuous from a manufacturer, distributor and customer point of view, there are fewer prospects of detection and prosecution, and in any case, penalties are likely to be lower than for some other kinds of illicit activity.

---

58.   Information provided to the OECD by the automotive industry IP Working Group.

The only issues that could raise some concerns for counterfeiters is that auto parts require a certain degree of investment in fabrication equipment and technology, but for the right people (*e.g.* those with surplus manufacturing capacity) this is unlikely to be a serious problem. The other negative factor is the complexity of transporting and distributing the counterfeited goods to their markets (which implies the possibility of detection at customs borders), but again, this is unlikely to deter counterfeiters backed by substantial resources and organisational skills, such as those available to organised crime.

Overall, the drivers for the automotive sector would suggest that this would be a sector subject to substantial counterfeit activity, with manufacturing likely to be located in areas/countries with excess manufacturing capacity and lax IP rights protection. On the consumer side, the market is likely to be worldwide, given the penetration and growing homogeneity of motor vehicles, and the problems with detecting the consumers of such items, especially since many are designed to deceive the final customer (acting against consumers effectively protecting themselves by avoiding fake items).

9.6. Centres of counterfeit production

With respect to trademark infringement, China has been repeatedly identified as the principal source of counterfeit activity in the automotive sector, involving both trademark and design infringements. For example, a major Japanese manufacturer indicated that in its experience almost 90% of the cases affecting its products involved China. Other locations identified as being very significant were Chinese Taipei, Thailand, Turkey, Russia, the Middle East and Latin America.

Table 9.2 provides a summary of the frequency with which localities were mentioned in the OECD survey in conjunction with counterfeiting activity.

Table 9.2. Number of times localities mentioned as centres of counterfeiting

Frequency	Locality
Frequently mentioned	China, Latin America, Middle East, Russia, Chinese Taipei, Thailand, Turkey
Moderately frequently mentioned	Eastern Europe, India, Iran, Philippines, Saudi Arabia, UAE, Vietnam
Sometimes mentioned	Argentina, Brazil, Indonesia, Italy, Malaysia, Pakistan, Poland, South Korea, Ukraine

Source: OECD Survey of the Automotive Industry, 2005.

Another motor vehicle manufacturer found that the vast majority of counterfeit auto parts are manufactured in China, with specific regions focusing on counterfeiting specific products. For example, a city in southeastern China is claimed to be saturated with factories producing counterfeit spark plugs.

More specifically, a major North American manufacturer reported a case study involving a major trade (valued at over USD 150 million) in fake spark plugs manufactured in Yancheng, China, and distributed to the US, Canada, Europe and the Middle East.

While some counterfeit auto parts are used domestically in China, the majority are exported worldwide, including to the Middle East, North Africa, Eastern Europe, Mexico and North and South America.

With respect to design infringement, the situation is less clear, even though there have been numerous accusations over the years of such breaches around the world. Part of the problem with this type of infringement is that although there may be recognisable similarities between the design of motor vehicles (as well as other goods), this of itself does not prove the existence of an infringement of the design; therefore, complex (and expensive) legal actions may be necessary to establish that an infringement has occurred. Advice from the automotive industry is that such actions are few and far between, especially in developing and emerging markets.

The inclusion in this report of some examples of claimed design infringement originating in China, should not be taken as evidence that China is the only, or even the principal, place where such infringements may be taking place; rather, it is a reflection of the existence of claims in the public arena by major car manufacturers when this report was being drafted.

.7. Modes of operation and movement of counterfeited goods

Many of the counterfeited goods in the automotive sector are produced for export to other markets. This is particularly the case for copied items intended for luxury cars, as these items would carry a price premium if they can be sold as originals to unsuspecting buyers.

Generally, car parts are voluminous and heavy, and therefore do not lend themselves to casual, small-time smuggling into export markets. Therefore, these items tend to be consigned as relatively large shipments in containers, through normal transport routes, as if they were legitimate consignments.

During a series of investigations in China, a respondent found that counterfeit producing factories, which vary in size and output, respond to orders for counterfeit goods placed by export companies, usually located in a large Chinese port city. The export companies themselves tend to be hired by offshore business entities to fulfil counterfeit orders. According to the respondent, these entities are often located in Hong Kong (China) and Chinese Taipei.

The counterfeit parts would be shipped from these factories to the exporter via truck, who would then arrange for their export via shipping container. The goods are then shipped worldwide, either directly to their final destinations or to an intermediate way-point or gateway, to minimise the chances of detection at the final destination.

While motor vehicle parts are sometimes smuggled, the industry experience has been that counterfeiters tend to rely for protection on the low rate of container inspection, the generally innocuous nature of the items being transported, and the relatively low priority given to counterfeited goods by customs border controls, which are more likely to target drugs, explosives and weapons.

Generally, the contents of such containers would be accurately labelled (*i.e.* air filters would be described as air filters) and would be accompanied by correct Bills of Lading and other documentation. It would be left to customs officers to somehow detect that the items were counterfeited, which in many cases would be difficult given the sophistication of the accompanying packaging and labels. Generally, it would be very difficult for a customs officer to know whether a part was genuine or fake from a simple visual inspection, and technical testing by the manufacturer of the original parts may be necessary in order to identify fake parts. One respondent noted that even holograms, which constitute one of its major security devices, are being perfectly imitated, which increases the complexity of identifying the counterfeited items.

In addition, sophisticated counterfeiters take additional precautions to minimise the chance of detection. For example, many counterfeits are shipped without specific packaging or trademarks, and these would be described simply as "generic" goods (say filters, or brake pads). At this stage, there would be no obvious trademark infringement, and it would be difficult for such goods to be intercepted and held by customs or other authorities. The appropriate markings and packaging would be added prior to entering the market in the country or region of final destination.

Another characteristic of the trade in counterfeited automotive components is that the counterfeiters frequently ship their goods through intermediate ports, or "gateways" that are likely to attract less attention by customs officers at final destination. In particular, free-trade zones that exist around the world were identified as such "gateways" by survey respondents in the automotive sector. As a general rule, as long as goods do no enter the territory of the country in which the free-trade zone is located, and unless there is clear evidence of criminal/terrorist involvement in the goods, then custom inspections would not be carried out in the free-trade zones.[159] These free-trade zones are sometimes also used to value-add to the goods (perhaps by packaging or re-labelling them), or to trans-ship them, so that their actual origin can be disguised.

One respondent to the OECD questionnaire noted that Hong Kong (China), Turkey and the United Arab Emirates were the most often used gateways to transport counterfeits of their company's parts and accessories.

Another respondent noted that the majority of counterfeited auto parts are first sent to key transit points before being exported to their final destinations. In that respondent's experience, the main counterfeit product distribution point in the Middle East is Dubai, which is used as the gateway for Saudi Arabia, Egypt and Lebanon, as well as being a major point for redistribution to European destinations.

Again, in that respondent's experience, the key distribution area for North African countries (including Morocco, Algeria and Tunisia) is Malta, while Colombia is the key transit area for the distribution of counterfeit products into Latin/Central/South America. A respondent has claimed that counterfeit goods intended for the United States appear to go through Canada. Finally, Bulgaria has been identified by that respondent as a possible transit point for the distribution of counterfeit products to other Eastern European countries.

Table 9.3. Number of times localities mentioned as transit points for counterfeited goods

Frequency	Localities
Frequently mentioned	UAE/Dubai, Hong Kong (China)
Moderately frequently mentioned	Lebanon, Singapore, Turkey, Eastern Europe
Sometimes mentioned	Bulgaria, Canada, Colombia ,Egypt, Jordan, Malta, Saudi Arabia, Chinese Taipei

Source: OECD Survey of the Automotive Industry, 2005.

---

159. The World Customs Organization (ACO) is considering proposals for better controlling goods entering and leaving free-trade zones, perhaps through measures that apply to goods in transit in other ports.

All this suggests that there are highly developed networks in place for sourcing, transporting and distributing counterfeit automotive parts and components. This is quite consistent with the nature of such components, which require relatively sophisticated equipment and manufacturing skills to fabricate them. Only a limited number of localities can produce these counterfeited products, while markets span the globe, thus requiring quite substantial and complex transport and distribution arrangements to move the goods to their respective markets.

As additional evidence of the breadth and depth of distribution of counterfeited automotive parts, a raid undertaken by authorities on behalf of a major European manufacturer on a large counterfeit manufacturing plant in Chin, yielded a mass of shipping documents related to the transportation of the fake parts being produced. The table below shows the number and location of individual organisations and individuals that the factory was dealing with in various parts of the world[160].

Table 9.4. Number of individual entities shown as recipients of fake auto parts

Country/region	Number
China	315
Middle East	115
SE Asia	97
East Asia	23
Western Europe	21
Central Europe	5
Africa	3

With respect to design infringements, there seem to be no issues related to the transportation of goods, as most of the copies are sold in home markets, while those that are exported (even to the country of origin of the original item) are done so quite openly. The launch of the "Landwind" off-road vehicle at the 2005 Frankfurt Motor Show, and its open sale in Belgium, Germany and the Netherlands is the most obvious and recent example.

9.8. Effects of counterfeiting in the automotive sector

9.8.1. General effects

Within the automotive sector, the producers of original items, customers and the economies of the countries concerned experience impacts that are similar to those of other counterfeited products. That is, the producers of the originals suffer loss of markets and profits, the reputation and value of their brands and trademarks is diminished, they suffer a loss of market exclusivity, and considerable efforts must be expended in the hunt for counterfeits and counterfeiters. Their employees suffer through job losses when the demand for the original products diminishes.

---

160. Information provided confidentially to the OECD.

Also, because auto parts are generally purchased only when needed (for repair or maintenance) and are therefore not discretionary, it can be assumed that the purchase of a counterfeit part will imply the loss of a sale by the producer of a genuine or legitimate substitute part. Industry experience is that such losses can be substantial, and the estimate made by a major North American manufacturer of global losses approaching USD 1 billion per year is believable.

Consumers that are deceived by the counterfeits suffer from not receiving what they believed they paid for, and may receive products that are inferior to the originals, and which will almost certainly not be covered by warranties or guarantees. The counterfeits may also not be suited for the purpose for which they were intended, which adds to the loss of utility by consumers.

Countries in which the sale of counterfeit goods is prevalent may suffer the loss of tax and other revenue, and this may be reflected in loss of government services and generally poorer economic conditions.

Countries where counterfeits are produced may experience higher employment but of a transient kind, and may find that the lack of adequate enforcement of Intellectual Property rights may be reflected directly in falling direct foreign investment. Also, some companies may choose not to do business in these countries because of their inability to deal with the complexities and costs of defending their IP rights, and as a result may direct their investment or business elsewhere.

9.8.2. Automotive sector-specific effects

The distribution and sale of genuine parts for the automotive after sale market is complex and extremely well organised. While many "genuine" parts are interchangeable (in other words, one specialised manufacturer may supply different vehicle manufacturers with the same parts), many are specific to particular makes or models and may not be suitable for other vehicles.

This complexity requires a highly organised distribution system, principally through the network of dealers that specialise in specific brands and/or models. In addition, wholesale and retail automotive distribution points may also carry genuine spare parts. The entire network relies to some degree on investments made by the manufacturers on design, technical innovation, reliability, quality control, advertising and marketing. Original parts are tested and certified by the appropriate authorities and are generally accompanied by service backup and warranties. All of these costs are built into the price of the parts.

Counterfeited parts presented as originals (not replacement parts sold under their own brand names as suitable replacements for the originals) bypass most of these organisational, quality and regulatory complexities and financial commitments, and their only cost is to make the parts look like the originals, but not necessarily perform like them. Therefore, freed from unnecessary R&D, development and testing, marketing costs and backup service and warranties, the parts can be placed in the market at prices that are below those of the genuine articles. Even allowing for a price discount built into the counterfeited part to make it attractive to consumers, parts can still be priced close to the originals; the low cost of production of the counterfeited items guarantees high profits for the counterfeiters.

When counterfeited parts are offered for sale at prices that are slightly lower that the originals, the industry reports that there is a natural tendency for the price of original parts to be lowered in an effort to compete. However, this is of course a battle than cannot be won on price alone (because of the factors mentioned above), and generally achieves nothing more that further distorting the market of the original parts.

Of particular concern to the automotive manufacturers is that if the counterfeited parts are purchased in the belief that they are original, then not only will the reputation of the original manufacturer be harmed if these parts fail, but there will also be pressure from customers for warranties and service commitments to be honoured. Legal and liability obligations may also affect the original manufacturers in some cases.

The automotive sector noted that one of the responses available to them, when challenged by unchecked competition from counterfeited parts, would be for them to move to locations with lower costs of production, which may be in, or near, centres where counterfeiting is prevalent. By reducing their own costs of production, auto manufacturers hope to partially counter the advantages held by the counterfeiters by reducing the potential margins of profit available to them.

However, this strategy has two downsides. First, locating manufacturing plants near the centres of counterfeiting activity exposes those manufacturers to the possibility of even more counterfeiting, perhaps through production overruns by unreliable suppliers and contractors entering the "grey market". Also, the strategy would result in additional, large-scale loss of manufacturing employment in exiting production locations, particularly Europe, North America and Japan, which may be of concern to some manufacturers.

9.8.3. Special safety-related effects

Beyond the effects noted above, the automotive sector has identified some specific, and very important, motor vehicle performance and safety effects resulting from the use of counterfeited parts.

Air/oil filters, spark plugs and clutch plates are among parts that could affect the performance of motor vehicles to which they are fitted. For example, poor-quality spark plugs will last for a shorter time and may seriously affect engine performance, as well as perhaps increasing fuel consumption and the emission of air pollutants.

While these unwanted by-products of using fake car parts are obviously of concern to the manufacturers of original items, they are less serious than the use of fake brake pads, hydraulic hoses, engine and chassis parts, suspension and steering components and air bag mechanisms, which could seriously impair the safety of vehicles. The concern of the industry is that the inferior performance, or even outright failure, of these parts could lead to crashes or could fail to protect vehicle occupants and pedestrians, which in turn may lead to injury and loss of life.

The manufacturers of original parts are seriously concerned that counterfeited parts could go unrecognised, and that if these were linked to serious accidents then the manufactures of the original parts could be held responsible for those accidents, with potential legal and liability implications, as well as the loss of company reputations for quality and safety.

A particularly graphic example of the safety implications of counterfeiting was given by the automotive industry's IP Working Group[161] with respect to counterfeited bonnets for a popular European car. First, while the original bonnet was made of aluminium, the counterfeit was made of steel, which was therefore much heavier and much more rigid, and consequently more dangerous to pedestrians, than the original. Also, the counterfeited item lacked the specially engineered "fuse zone" (also known as crumple zones) which would provide protection to the occupants of the car in a serious collision, by absorbing much of the energy generated in the crash.

Other material provided by the IP Working Group highlighted tests by a motor manufacturer that found, and documented, instances of brake pads that cracked and separated from their metal backing, and in some cases caught fire under heavy use. Similarly, oil filter seals failed, and spark plug electrodes melted due to the use of poor quality materials in the counterfeited parts. All of these failures could contribute to accidents, possibly causing injury and deaths.

9.9. Countermeasures taken

The automotive sector's principal response has been to initially create an awareness of the problems associated with counterfeiting both within their own organisations (including distributors) and the general public, and wherever possible to train customs officers to recognise counterfeited parts.

The use of product verification technology (both overt and covert) has also been recognised by the industry as being helpful in combating counterfeiting in legitimate supply lines, but cost is a consideration, as is the difficulty of alerting all "legitimate" customers on how to recognise and assess the markings in order to identify possible fakes.

External investigators are widely used to detect infringements, which are then referred to the appropriate authorities in order to prevent further instances. Co-operation with customs and other law enforcement authorities, as well as actively pursuing private legal action against counterfeiters, are seen as key strategies by the automotive sector.

In addition, the automotive industry believes that widespread publicity of successful raids and court cases will heighten public awareness, and may reduce both the incidence of counterfeiting and demand for such items. Therefore, public awareness campaigns are considered to be important tools, especially because of the serious potential safety risks associated with the use of some replacement parts.

However, such actions can be time consuming and expensive; for example, a North American respondent reported that an action involving products valued at around USD 200 000, required three lengthy court cases before it was satisfactorily resolved.

Respondents claim that their individual success rate in combating (trademark) infringements is generally high. However, caution was also expressed, as in some jurisdictions (Turkey and Italy were specifically mentioned amongst others) problems were being encountered because the legal measures to enforce trademarks were limited or inadequate, and actions taken in such jurisdictions can be lengthy and expensive.

---

161. Drawn from material provided in confidence by the IP WG to the OECD.

There were also claims that ambiguities and inconsistencies in judgments involving trademark infringements were also hampering efforts to deal with those infringements. For example, confidential material provided by a Japanese motor manufacturer indicates that it has faced a number of instances of counterfeiting claims in China on which it has taken legal action to redress those infringements. The company has reported that judgments relating to the misuse of its logo were inconsistent, with some claims being upheld, while others, which it believed were equally similar to the original, were rejected.

In addition, the relatively light penalties that exist in many countries for trademark infringement (it is understood that in China this can be less than USD 1 000) are not adequate deterrents, and consequently there are many repeat offences. For example, in China, the same manufacturer indicated that in its experience the repeat offence rate is approximately 90%, which appears to support the view frequently put out by the industry that the penalties are inadequate to overcome the profitability of the counterfeiting action. Other manufactures of original parts reported similar experiences, and this type of comment was also frequently made in other sectors investigated during the course of this study.

One respondent to the OECD survey noted what when customs authorities in Lebanon started to take a hard line against counterfeited automotive components, their sales of genuine parts increased by 10%, only to slip back again when the attention of customs authorities was re-directed elsewhere. A similar experience was reported by a North American respondent who noted that strong action against the sale of counterfeited car parts in Turkey resulted in the sale of genuine parts significantly increasing -- in some cases doubling or trebling.

While there is no specific empirical evidence to link these events, there is a strong intuitive sense that there is some causal relationship between them.

An effect also noted in the automotive sector is that counterfeiters are now defending their actions much more aggressively, especially in jurisdictions where laws to protect IP are poor, ineffective or loosely enforced. This is greatly increasing the cost of IP protection for companies affected, as well as further reducing the protection available to them.

For example, the industry noted that actions taken to defend patent infringements are particularly expensive, and that in the United States the average patent litigation case costs around USD 1 million. However, such high-cost routes may be the only remedies available if counterfeiters breach patents but avoid using trademarks, which would give IP owners a less expensive enforcement route.

In the field of design infringements, despite several well-publicised instances of claims by motor vehicle manufacturers of such infringements, this seems to have had little effect on the production and sale of the "copied" items. Unlike trademarks and patents, design infringements are much more difficult to establish. So far, instances of claimed design infringements involve major corporations (mostly Chinese) that openly market their vehicles in both domestic and export markets.

This may be an area where additional government and private action may be needed to clearly establish where design infringements have taken place, and put some opportunities for remedial action in place. Otherwise, there is a risk that Intellectual Property rights involving designs will become ineffective, since each potential transgression that goes unchecked provides a precedent that will make others bolder, and the enforcement task more difficult.

9.10. The role of organised crime

Respondents to the OECD survey noted that the production, distribution and sale of counterfeited auto parts is potentially very lucrative, with some suggesting that it could almost rival the drug trade for profitability. Also, the breach of trademarks was generally considered by the public, police and legislators alike as being far less serious than dealing in drugs, and as a consequence comparatively fewer customs, law enforcement and prosecution resources are allocated to counterfeited goods. In addition, even when prosecutions and legal challenges for counterfeiting are successful, the penalties are considerably lower than other illicit activities.

These characteristics make the counterfeit trade quite appealing to organised crime, and many of the respondents noted increasing criminal activity in the sector. Virtually all of them noted that the incidence of intimidation, threats and physically violent acts perpetrated on investigators was increasing.

One major European manufacturer observed from its experience in the market that when organised criminal groups were involved in the manufacture and distribution of counterfeited auto parts these could represent up to 30% of the market for fast-moving items.

There was also concern shown that the involvement of organised crime in the manufacturing and distribution chain could also lead to bribery and corruption of public officials and key personnel in the distribution network. The Motor Equipment Manufacturers Association (MEMA) suggested that the infiltration of counterfeit parts into taxi, bus and limousine fleets could be attributed to this.

Table 9.5. Propensity to produce or consume counterfeited automotive goods

FOR PRODUCERS	EFFECTS ON PROPENSITIES TO PRODUCE
Market characteristics	
Unit profitability	There are balancing considerations here. On the one hand, even if counterfeiters avoid R&D, promotional and warranty costs, they still need to fabricate parts and mark and package them to look like the originals. On the other hand, because consumers can be relatively easily deceived, the prices of the fakes can be set closer to the original than might otherwise be the case. On balance, the judgment is that the available profits would make this activity quite desirable for certain people and enterprises.
Market size	This is potentially very large, as it can cover the majority of the auto after-sales market. This market exists for a large variety of motor vehicles in virtually every country in the world. The widely differing sophistication of the market also allows counterfeiters plenty of scope to differentiate their products, and the growing globalisation of marques greatly increases the size of potential markets.
Genuine brand power	The major automotive brands have traditionally been sold in various guises around the world. Brand names and trademarks have become well known and they are heavily advertised and promoted internationally. This aids counterfeiters as they have plenty of brands to choose from, and can re-route their counterfeited components to different destinations to exploit advantageous conditions.
Production, distribution and technology	
Production investments	Auto parts need to be fabricated to at least closely resemble (and in many cases to some degree operate in the same ways as) the original parts. This requires technical skill, and fabrication capability and capacity. Generally the design and fabrication of auto parts is relatively complex and requires considerable investment, so this sector is unsuitable for small scale production as production.
	However, production runs tend to be large, which tends to reduce unit costs. In addition, secret (and probably illegal) production overruns by suppliers of legitimate original components may further reduce the production costs.

Technology	Some technology is required in order to fabricate parts, especially those that are intended to deceive. Again, this technology is unlikely to be available to small or casual counterfeiters, and as a consequence will be limited to large-scale manufacturing concerns.
Logistics	These can be complex. Automotive components tend to be bulky and produced in large centralised facilities. This means that they have to be transported to markets and then somehow infiltrated into the legitimate supply chain (especially for deceptive parts). In many cases, as well as long transport routes the parts will cross national borders, where they may be subject to customs inspection and possible detection. The upside for counterfeiters is that auto parts are inherently innocuous, and until labelled and packaged are probably also legitimate.
Marketing and sale	Like most other counterfeits, automotive components can (and are) sold in open markets. However, as they are mostly specialised components, the majority tends to be sold to auto-repair establishments and retailers of after-market components. The infiltration into the legitimate (and grey market) supply chain of these establishments can be difficult.
Ability to conceal operations	The production of most automotive components will require substantial manufacturing capability, involving machinery and skilled operators. Such facilities would be relatively immobile, and are generally part of the facilities used to produce other (frequently legitimate) manufactured and fabricated items. It would generally be difficult to conceal the operations, but because on many occasions components are labelled and packaged elsewhere (when they physically become counterfeits), then such concealment may not often be necessary.
Ability to deceive	In addition to realistic packaging and markings, the likelihood of consumers being deceived into believing that auto parts are genuine is high, as end users (the motorists) do not possess the technical knowledge to detect fakes, especially if they appear to operate correctly, which is possible, even though they are inferior in quality to the original.
Institutional characteristics	
Risk detection	Auto parts are generally innocuous, and therefore less likely to attract attention in their own right (and rarely need to be hidden or smuggled). However, they do have to be transported long distances, which will increase their chance of detection, especially at customs controls near their final destination.
Role of the Internet	Apart from improving communication and perhaps assisting counterfeiters to find some customers, the Internet is unlikely to be either a facilitating or an obstructing influence.
Enforcement	Most counterfeit auto parts are undetected until they hit the market, and the experience in the auto industry is that prosecution (or civil action) against producers is relatively rare. This appears to be especially so in countries of production where ineffective laws, local sympathy and lack of official resources reduce further the effectiveness of prosecution.
Penalties	The reported experience of the automotive industry is that even when prosecution is successful, the penalties (available and applied) appear to be inadequate to act as genuine deterrents.
FOR CONSUMERS	**EFFECT ON PROPENSITIES TO CONSUME NON-DECEPTIVE ITEMS**
Product characteristics	
Price	For deceptive goods, a price lower than for the original product would help convince the buyer that he has found a bargain. For non-deceptive items, the price would have to be substantially lower than the original to convince the consumer that, possible safety risks notwithstanding, the counterfeited items would be acceptable substitutes.
Quality and nature of products	The outward appearance of most counterfeits is close to the originals, and some are so close that even manufacturers of the original need to test them to establish that they are fakes. For the consumer, who generally does not have the technical skill to make such an assessment, if the components look the same few would be able to make a judgment on their quality.
Ability to conceal status	The status of possessing something that looks like a brand original would only sometimes be a factor in the acquisition of the component.
Consumer characteristics	
Health concerns	Negligible perceived risks.
Safety concerns	If products deceptive, negligible perceived risks, even if actual risks may be high. For non-deceptive components consumers may be prepared to take risks if they believe they are saving money.
Personal values	Probably not a factor, especially when consumers see counterfeits as alternatives to necessary, but expensive components.

Institutional characteristics	
Risk of discovery	Likelihood of detection by authorities is likely to be low, as components are frequently sold in automotive repair and retail establishments. On many occasions components may be fitted without the owner's knowledge.
Prosecution	Likelihood of prosecution is low, and those consumers who were deceived into buying the fakes would tend to be considered as victims rather than offenders.
Penalties	Even if detected and prosecuted, penalties imposed on final consumers are likely to be low.
Availability and ease of acquisition	Except for components sold in open markets, the specialised nature of many of the components means that in general they would be sold through automotive repair establishments and retail outlets, which could limit their availability if a consumer was specifically searching for them.

References

MEMA (Motor & Equipment Manufacturers Association) (2005), "Stop Counterfeiting of Automotive and Truck Parts".

Chapter 10

ELECTRICAL COMPONENTS SECTOR

0.1. General description

For the purposes of this report, the electrical components industry is defined to include components used in the **generation**, **transmission**, **distribution**, or **consumption** of electric power. These fall under five sub sectors:

- Power distribution and transformers;

- Switchgears;

- Motors and generators;

- Industrial controls;

- Steam, gas, and hydraulic turbines and turbine generator sets.[162]

Some examples of these components would be relays, contacts, timers, circuit breakers, fuses and wiring accessories. Excluded are consumer electric and electronic devices, such as shavers, radios and components solely produced to be embedded into consumer goods, such as plasma screens, TV and radio antennas or CD and DVD drives. Batteries are also briefly covered in this report.

The electrical components sector is somewhat different from other sectors covered in this study because the items are generally not consumer goods, but items sold to other manufacturers and assemblers. In turn, these items are then integrated into goods for final sale. These could encompass items ranging from generators for power plants to fuses and wiring systems for homes, appliances, etc.

Counterfeit electrical components are generally meant to deceive purchasers into believing they are buying an original item. However, cases in which commercial entities, as well as consumers, have knowingly bought fake goods were mentioned by respondents, and there is evidence that in some markets counterfeit goods are readily recognisable. Given the potential safety risks associated with the failure of sub-standard electrical components, this would seem to be quite irrational behaviour by the users, and must raise concerns about the apparent success of counterfeiters in convincing buyers that fake products are acceptable substitutes for the original items.

---

162.   *Source*: Standard Industrial Classification (SIC).

10.2. Types of infringements

Trademark infringements are the most widespread type of IPR violations faced by the producers of electrical components. In most cases, the counterfeiter independently manufactures low-quality "look-alikes" and then marks them as high-quality brands. These products often do not conform to certification standards, and it is a common technique to buy cheap substitute "generic" items to then re-label and pass off as high-quality (and therefore high-priced) originals.

Patent infringements occur, but do not seem to be as common as trademark violations. It is not certain whether this is because there is a low-level of infringement or due to the fact that patent infringements are harder to detect. Also, patent infringements are costly to pursue, especially in countries in which IP rights are not yet sufficiently protected, and this may not only discourage some manufacturers from patenting their technologies, but may also discourage them from pursuing the less serious breaches.

Some respondents to the OECD survey noted that a large number of counterfeit products are not being marked with brand logos to avoid direct infringement of intellectual property rights. Instead, the counterfeiters imitate the technology and the look of the products, which are sold at close to full price with the inference that they are originals. While this practice may be of concern to companies, strictly speaking it does not represent a trademark violation, although the products may infringe patents or designs if these are registered.

10.3. Products most affected

The electrical components industry indicates that counterfeiters have focused on low cost, non-complex items, such as circuit breakers, fuses, switchgears, distribution boards and wiring accessories that can be easily mass produced with relatively little input (no advanced machinery, no specialised labour force, etc.). This provides them with the opportunity to receive a high return on investment since the mark-ups on branded products include significant costs associated with marketing, certification and research and development.

Also, industry responses and customs data indicate that while the counterfeiting of large pieces of equipment is not unheard of, counterfeiters tend to focus on relatively small items that can be easily transported in large quantities by truck or in containers.

Another type of counterfeiting action involves the production of electrical products that look similar to several well-known brands, and which can be labelled with different company logos without modification of the item. This increases the complexity of the supply chain for the individual brands, and makes it harder for investigators to trace back the fake items. This ploy also reduces the risk of confiscations in those countries where seizure orders have to be issued for each brand separately. Since investigators operating in these countries often only carry documentation for one brand, the remainder is frequently left untouched.

In common with other industry sectors, the electrical components industry claims that many products bearing unauthorised trademarks are not in the portfolio of the trademark holder. One respondent reported several incidents in which labelled goods unconnected with his business were intercepted. In other instances, devices in which the design belonged to one company had been copied and labelled with a trademark from a different company.

Box 10.1. Batteries: one of the world's most consumed items

Dry cell batteries (excluding wet-cell batteries used for automotive, marine and aviation purposes) are widely used as energy sources for mobile phones, laptops and other electronic and mechanical devices, including some items used for medical purposes.

It appears that there are significant problems with potentially dangerous, sub-standard counterfeit products, especially for the popular AAA and D-sized alkaline batteries. The National Electrical Manufacturers Association (2004) reports that a retail market sampling conducted by the battery industry in 2004 suggested annual estimated sales losses (domestic value) due to counterfeiting of USD 12 million in the US, USD 4 million in South America and USD 7 million in Europe.

US customs data show seizures of fake batteries with a domestic value of USD 2.3 million in fiscal year 2004, representing 2% of overall seizures made in that time period (US Customs and Border Protection and US Immigration and Customs Enforcement, 2006). One respondent to the OECD questionnaire noted that 34 million batteries carrying its brand name had been seized in 2004, of which over 3 million came from the US, over 15.5 million from China the remainder from the rest of the world.

The statistics for 2005 suggest an upward trend in US seizures, since over 7.3 million batteries of this particular brand were seized in the first half of 2005, while numbers for the rest of the world had declined.

The principal safety risk associated with poor-quality batteries revolves around the adequacy of venting. Quality batteries of almost any type contain a vent designed to release internal pressure within the battery in case of a malfunction or misuse. Fake batteries often do not contain this vent. If pressure is generated inside a vent-less battery, it cannot escape, resulting in an explosion. Also, poorly constructed fake batteries are prone to leakage of electrolyte, which can occur at any time during the life of the battery.

Battery electrolytes are potentially harmful to body tissues as well as damaging to many commonly used materials and circuitry in electronic devices, and reputable battery makers take great care to design products where leakage is essentially prevented. In addition, counterfeit batteries have been found to violate environmental regulations as some contain mercury, which appears to have been intentionally added in violation of US and EU laws and regulations.

Finally counterfeit batteries are sometimes slightly larger or smaller than their genuine counterparts, which makes them impossible to fit properly into devices. This has been reported especially for mobile phone and laptop batteries.

Trademark violations are the most common type of counterfeiting in the battery business, especially concerning batteries as consumer goods.

Reference:

NEMA (National Electrical Manufacturers Association) (2004), "Dry Battery Counterfeit White Paper", www.nema.org/gov/anti-counterfeiting

In addition to the products themselves, the electrical components industry expressed concern about the possession and unauthorised usage of printing plates, printed labels and packaging (including holograms and certification marks) for sale to factories producing the fake goods. Although the monetary value of such labels or printing plates is relatively low, their real value is in the fact that a (so-far legal) "look-alike" good becomes a counterfeit when the brand logo is added without the permission of the stakeholder.

In some jurisdictions (*e.g.* North America) the mere possession of labels and tools bearing counterfeit and infringing marks is not against the law. However, trafficking in, or engaging in commerce in labels, packages, containers and the like, bearing counterfeit or infringing marks is an infringement. And possession of such labels and tools can be evidence of trafficking or engaging in counterfeit commerce. In most jurisdictions, if trafficking is uncovered, labels and tools can be seized.

10.4. Modes of operation

Reports on industry investigations, according to respondents to the OECD study, indicate that much of the counterfeiting of electrical components is carried out by registered companies. These firms operate like normal companies, with relatively modern infra-structures and equipment, which in addition to producing counterfeited items often also produce goods under their own brand name, support their own web pages, exhibit "their" products in fairs and conventions (*e.g.* the Canton Fair in China) and even possess a marketing division. It has been reported that some of these companies are authorised manufacturers of genuine products and utilise surplus capacity to manufacture counter-feited products, sometimes of an inferior quality, but nevertheless equal in outward appearance to the genuine product. To an outside observer, they seem to be legal contractors of the brands they imitate.

In addition, goods are also fabricated in "underground" factories, where the production and storage of the counterfeited goods take place in crude facilities that can be relatively easily relocated to avoid detection. In the view of the industry, in recent years there has been a steady drift from large factories to smaller, unlicensed units, so that orders can be split into smaller consignments to reduce the risk of an entire order being seized.

As to distribution, in addition to straight transport using normal transport routes (with owners expecting little risk of inspection because of the generally harmless nature of the products) respondents also noted the legal export of component subsets (to be embedded into the final product) to destination or transit countries, where they would then be assembled into the final product, labelled and then further distributed for sale. China has been especially mentioned as a major exporter of subsets, particularly to Africa.

Because the subsets in themselves are legal, customs authorities can rarely take action against them, unless there is clear proof that they will be transformed into counterfeited goods. The view of respondents was that this is a way for counterfeiters to secure their supply channels, but it does also mean that final preparation of the fake items would have to be carried out in the destination country, which may provide authorities with some opportunities to apprehend them.

Because electrical components are generally sold to intermediate manufacturers or institutional end users (rather that to private individuals as is the case with more consumer-oriented products), counterfeiters generally need to devise ways of breaking into the legitimate supply chain within their sales markets, and this is done in a variety of ways.

One respondent noted that the most common way to sell the items is to mix genuine and counterfeited goods in a significant but limited proportion in wholesale and retail stores, since this lowers the risk of the fake goods being detected. For the counterfeiters, this maximises their profit margin since the fake goods are being sold at full price, next to genuine goods.

In other cases, the counterfeiters try to market their fake products through traditional wholesale channels that supply major commercial users (*i.e.* manufacturers, construction firms, etc.), although breaking into the relatively tightly controlled formal supply network might not always be easy.

The Internet also provides counterfeiters with the possibility of selling their goods in a cheap and relatively safe way. One respondent notes three types of disposal channels for counterfeited electrical components:

- Web pages operated by exporters in source countries displaying counterfeited goods as genuine items and selling them to retailers in target markets.

- Web pages operated by importers in target markets selling counterfeited products to consumers in these markets over the Internet.

- Bidding sites in which anonymity allows counterfeiters to sell their products with relatively low risk.

The advantages of using the Internet, even though yields to the counterfeiter might be lower, are obvious. There is no paperwork proving the origin of the goods, except the address on the Internet page. For properly documented small consignments, the chances of inspection by customs are small, and direct shipment to the buyers provides an easy way of transportation. The transactions are carried out across jurisdictions, which complicates legal and remedial action even if the counterfeits are detected.

0.5. Factors that drive production and consumption of counterfeited electrical components

This section examines various factors that drive the production and consumption of counterfeited electrical components. Each product sector has its own peculiar characteristics that will in part determine and shape those drivers, and the recognition and understanding of these drivers can provide insights on the propensity for that category of goods to be produced. In turn this may provide some guidance on the likelihood that such products can be found in the market place and may support statistical data collected through customs interdictions, police raids on production and retail facilities, the results of legal action and other market based data. Moreover, the propensities could provide important insights into how surveys and economic modelling could best be used to improve measurement.

Please refer to the summary table at the end of this chapter (Table 10.1), "Propensity to produce or consume counterfeited electrical components". The drivers that are considered to apply to the electrical components sector have been compiled on whether, and to what extent, they are favourable or unfavourable for the production and consumption of these counterfeited goods.

The characteristics of the electrical equipment industry suggest that even though there are some problems for the counterfeiters, this would still be a relatively attractive market for them. On the producer side, counterfeiting seems to be attractive as the market is large and profit margins are also relatively high. On the other hand, the risk of detection and difficulties in penetrating established distribution chains are limiting factors. On the purchaser side, the market for "non-deceptive" counterfeits is seen as low, given the high safety risks and the risk of purchasing low-quality items, although it reportedly still occurs. The majority of purchases of fake items would be a result of the buyer being deceived as to the true nature of the goods.

10.6. Magnitude and scope of infringements, and trends

Information provided by the industry suggests that counterfeiting is a substantial problem in the electrical components sector. The respondents to the OECD survey have suggested a steady growth in both the quantity and geographical scope of counterfeiting. A critical area over the past three to five years has been Africa, where the industry believes an estimated 25% to 75% of the mass-produced electrical components market has been captured by counterfeited goods.

Zones with existing problems, where counterfeited goods are capturing increasing market shares are Asia (especially China, where 10% to 40% of the market is believed to be composed of counterfeits), the Middle East (20% to 40% counterfeit) and Eastern Europe (10% to 40% counterfeit). The UK, India, Ireland, Italy, Spain and Portugal have also been mentioned as being subject to a significant and increasing presence of trademark or patent violations. Australia, France, Germany, the Netherlands and the Nordic countries are reported as not being substantially affected by counterfeiting.

Particularly noteworthy is the increasing tendency towards counterfeiting in South America, where links with organised crime have been mentioned, along with linkages between counterfeiting groups and the drug trade. One respondent noted that in many cases there has been a marked shift from the very risky trade involving drugs to the trading of counterfeited goods, including electrical components, which presents significantly lower risk to organised criminals. This perception is consistent with similar reports from other industry sectors.

As far as source countries are concerned, China is reported to be the leading supplier of counterfeited goods in the electrical components sector. Although counterfeiting is taking place in the entire country, Guangzhou and Wenzhou have been mentioned as principal production areas. Guangzhou is the largest and fastest-growing industrial and foreign trade centre in southern China, and every spring and autumn hosts the China Export Commodities Fair (also known as the Canton Fair), which is the largest exhibition of this kind in the world. The electrical components industry regularly examines this Fair for exhibitors that show counterfeited items, and they report numerous violations of IP rights on every occasion.

Respondents also noted that products manufactured in China are typically either shipped or transported by air directly to "importers" in different countries, which then sell the products through local distributors. The second channel includes the usage of a transit point. This gives the counterfeiters the possibility of concealing distribution channels by simply changing delivery companies or splitting the load into smaller parts, to be then shipped to different countries using different delivery services and modes of transportation. Such transit points are the Middle East (Kuwait and Saudi Arabia have been mentioned most frequently) and a few African (Kenya, Tanzania, Uganda) and European (Italy, UK, Ireland, Malta, Poland) countries.

0.7. Effects of counterfeiting in the electrical components sector

Since electrical components are not generally consumer goods, the immediate effects of counterfeit products are likely to fall on the manufacturer of the genuine product and the firms that buy components and integrate them into products for sale. Subsequently, consumers are likely to be affected if goods containing the counterfeit components fail (for example an electrical switch used in house construction that starts a fire).

For producers of the original items, the effects are two-fold: sales losses and pressure on prices. As to sales losses, if the counterfeited electronic components are meant to deceive the purchaser (which is most often the case), it can be assumed that every counterfeited item bought is a lost sale for the producer of the original item, since the purchaser has bought an item assuming it to be genuine. However, as has already been mentioned, in some countries purchasers seem to knowingly buy counterfeited items. In this case, it is uncertain whether the purchasers would have bought the genuine item if the counterfeit product had not been available, or whether they would have opted for a different product. Nevertheless, to different extents both cases represent lost sales. Lost sales worldwide are estimated by the European Electrical Installation industry to have ranged between EUR 2 and 4 billion in 2005 (based on retail value).

With respect to the pressure on prices, the calculation of the final price of a product includes a substantial portion for design, quality management, ensuring that the product conforms to certification standards as well as investment in research and development and marketing. Counterfeiters do not have such commitments, and they often use low-quality materials, as well as very cheap labour parts, for the fabrication of the products. Also, the avoidance of taxes can increase the profit margin. Therefore, the imitation of a well-known, genuine quality product can be sold much more cheaply (30% to 50% was mentioned by one of the respondents) while still yielding the counterfeiter a good profit margin.

For the intermediate and final consumers, financial losses are incurred when the fake component causes a defect of the product in which it is embedded. This will then lead to costs for the consumer as well as the producer of the device if it is under guarantee. In addition, intermediate consumers can experience damage to their brand names, and this was one of the most often mentioned negative effects. Of particular concern for the manufacturers of end-products for retail sale is that consumers would not (indeed could not) be aware that a faulty component had been unknowingly used by the manufacturer, who believed it to be an original component; inevitably it is the manufacturer's brand-name reputation that pays the price.

Safety is also a potential major issue associated with the widespread use of counter-feited electrical components. Many fake electrical items are of low-quality and may not perform satisfactorily, and in some cases they could malfunction in ways that could cause injury or death. A circuit breaker, for example, is intended to stop the flow of electric current in a suddenly overloaded or otherwise abnormally stressed electric circuit, and its performance is dependent on the calibration made during the manufacturing process and the material quality of its components. Counterfeited circuit breakers have been found to be incorrectly calibrated, and/or constructed using low-quality materials, which could result in a malfunction. Incidents involving below-quality components, especially those used in the belief that they were original items, could result in heightened risk of electrocution or fires.

10.8. Countermeasures taken

10.8.1. Industry co-operation

In the electrical components sector, actions have mostly been taken by industry associations, such as: the French Association of Electrical Installation Manufacturers (DOMERGIE); the National Electrical Manufacturers Association (NEMA); and the British Electrotechnical and Allied Manufacturers Association (BEAMA). An extensive internal reporting policy (including an intranet database) among the members of the associations and within the associations themselves has been established to monitor developments in counterfeiting. One of the aims of this initiative is to also address the problem of counterfeiting being perceived as a crime that cannot be combated efficiently, and therefore the investments made to support anti-counterfeiting efforts and actions are wasted.

The associations also function as lobbying entities to influence and advise govern-ments and to establish and strengthen contacts with other bodies, such as customs and certification authorities, anti-piracy organisations, trade fair organisers and wholesaler associations.

10.8.2. Training and public awareness

Increased educational efforts have also been mentioned as a major issue. These include courses for customs officials to improve their ability to identify fake electrical components, public campaigns against counterfeiting, and advertising actions during trade fairs to warn exhibitors showing counterfeited goods. Respondents have noted positive effects resulting from these actions, especially those involving custom officials.

One respondent noted a positive outcome from using the media as a means of increasing public awareness and educating people about the negative effects of counter-feiting. It seems that counterfeiting is no longer an ignored topic, and is widely addressed by public comment as well as detailed, analytical case studies. However, according to the industry, here, too, it appears that media interest in the electrical components sector is being eclipsed by the more high-profile sectors, such as pharmaceuticals, car and aircraft parts and tobacco products.

10.8.3. Technology

Another measure taken against counterfeiting is the adoption of technical methods for product identification, as well as special packaging. An example of a current system is that employed by the members of the French DOMERGIE group. NOTACOPY, an authentication system based on the secret and unique numbering of each legally produced item, enables the purchaser of a good to immediately verify whether or not the item is registered as a genuine product. The verification is free of charge and accessible through the Internet. The purchaser of the item also has the opportunity to enter his/her address and the address of the retailer. The information collected through this system allows producing companies to identify the region where fake goods have been detected, and can indicate the level of counterfeiting in different regions throughout the world (SARL Notacopy.com).

10.8.4. Facility relocation

A more strategic approach mentioned by the industry is the relocation of production facilities close to recognised counterfeit hotspots. The argument for this is that not only are the costs of production reduced, since manufacturing of fakes usually takes place in low-cost countries, but that the presence of stakeholders in these regions may also disrupt counterfeiting activities, due to the increased risk of the counterfeiter being detected.

However, this strategy may also cause an opposite effect. Some contracted suppliers to well-known members of the electrical components industry have been reportedly selling production over-runs in the "grey market", and possibly violating patent and/or trademark rights by selling original items marked with their own brand. One respondent mentioned that some of the formerly contracted companies have now become official producers themselves, producing the same items they used to produce for genuine manufacturers, yet marked with their own brands. These companies even invest in R&D and intellectual rights protection to secure their own goods from being counterfeited.

10.8.5. Marketing strategies

Another method used by genuine manufacturers to make the counterfeiting of their products more difficult, is to frequently change their product designs. However, the effects of such changes are time-limited, because as soon as the newly introduced design becomes known, counterfeiting will reappear. In addition, this strategy has no effect for the low-end market segment where basic functionalities and low pricing are the critical factors.

10.8.6. Enforcement actions

Eventually, field actions organised by associations as well as single industry members are the tools principally used against counterfeiters. For this industry sector, the advantages are: *1)* relatively low costs (about USD 210 000 for a six-month operation has been reported); *2)* relatively efficient, discrete treatment of the counterfeiting problem; and *3)* no long-term commitment to actions in specific regions, since investigation teams are mobile.

Also, the lack of effective IP rights protection in some producing economies, and the large number of repeat offenders, have led brand owners to the conclusion that the best way to combat counterfeiters is to continually raid and seize as many products as possible, which would hurt the infringers financially. These actions are undertaken on a case-by-case basis, in co-operation with government enforcement agencies, to encourage the use of criminal proceedings, instead of the generally less-effective civil action.

An example of successful anti-counterfeiting initiatives indicating the dimension of counterfeiting and piracy in this industry is the recently launched coalition of several electric manufacturer associations, including the French DOMERGIE and the British BEAMA. A number of anti-counterfeiting operations in China, Africa and the Middle East have been carried out within the framework of this initiative. The number of items confiscated by private investigators in co-operation with law enforcement agencies exceeded 10 million products between 2001 and 2005 (over 150 factories raided), including one four-month operation in China, in which 220 000 switchgears, 125 000 power sockets, 1 900 circuit breakers and 260 000 wiring accessories were seized.

10.8.7. Co-operation with governments

As far as governments are concerned, the opinions of respondents to the OECD survey differ as to the level of help they can expect from government authorities in actions against counterfeiting in the electrical components sector. One concern expressed by industry was the perceived lack of co-operation between governments and enforcement agencies to address the problems associated with trans-border counterfeiting activities.

The EC was given special mention for its support of anti-counterfeiting programmes, but the sense in this industry sector remains that other products, like pharmaceuticals, are more likely to receive priority. The United States was also reported as having been helpful in targeting electrical products for surveillance and prosecution, and was also considered by the industry respondents as also having taken some useful initiatives against counterfeiting in general.

Respondents also noted greater awareness and engagement by China and the Middle East countries in enforcing anti-counterfeiting measures, but as yet the level of IP protection is still considered by the industry to be insufficient in those locations. The experience in South and Central America has also been that government agencies have proven to be helpful when cases are brought to them. On the other hand, various African countries were named as being very hard places in which to enforce IP rights, due partly to insufficient IP laws and a lack of awareness by local governments.

As a general observation, respondents in this industry sector have noted that developing countries are likely to take action and provide assistance, if the stakeholder delivers information and proof on counterfeiting activities. However, the lack of public awareness, poorly educated customs and enforcement officials, as well as the perceived low risk of counterfeiting when compared to other illegal activities, all hinder the successful combating of counterfeiting in this sector.

Also, one respondent noted that the time and expense of criminal enforcement can serve as a deterrent to some governments and their agencies.

Table 10.1. Propensity to produce or consume counterfeited electrical components

FOR PRODUCERS	EFFECT ON PROPENSITY TO PRODUCE
Market characteristics	
Unit profitability	The industry claims that fake goods are being sold about 30% to 50% cheaper than their genuine counterparts, if counterfeiters do not intend to deceive the purchaser. This implies that the profit margin is high, giving counterfeiters considerable latitude in pricing their products. Where the products are deceptive, then profit margins can be even higher.
	Even when the costs for packaging and labelling are comparable to genuine products, the differences in production costs are due to the low-quality of the technical parts used, as well as the lack of R&D, certification and marketing.
Market size	Electrical components are widely used, since they are components in the manufacture of consumer electronics and other, specialised electronic devices, as well as in the construction industry. However, they are not generally considered as consumer goods.
Genuine brand power	While there are some very well-known brand names in electrical components, these are not consumer items, and brands have less attraction here than in other sectors. The exception might be when a brand name is also known to meet necessary specifications and standards, which would increase the market value of the counterfeits.
Production, distribution and technology	
Production investment	Electrical components do not require a high investment, as counterfeiters concentrate on producing simple devices, where the most important factor is the appearance and labelling. Production most often takes place in underground factories and does not require expensive machinery or skilled labour.
Technology	Generally no sophisticated technology is required for the production of most counterfeited electrical components. Some technology may be required for production of some of the more sophisticated components.
Logistics	The established transport and distribution channels can be risky (from a detection perspective) whenever they cross national borders, and because the items are shipped in large numbers they can also be bulky. However, the traditional channels remain the preferred choice for most counterfeiters, who rely on the relatively innocuous nature of the products to escape close examination.
Marketing and sale	As items that are basically used as components in end products, these items need to be infiltrated into established distribution chains, which could be difficult.
Ability to conceal operations	Some fabrication and production facilities needed, which could be difficult to conceal. However, machinery could be used for other purposes to disguise counterfeiting activities.
Ability to deceive	As it is impossible to detect low-quality items in electrical equipment without technical examination, the appearance of the item, the label and certification mark, as well as the packaging, are the principal factors of deception. As stated by respondents, the production of these items does not pose any problems to counterfeiters. The only variable to then indicate a good as being counterfeited is the price, which can also be controlled.
Institutional characteristics	
Risk of discovery	The risk of detection is considered by the industry to be relatively high, principally because of their efforts in combating counterfeiting. The industry noted improvements in reduced counterfeiting of some brands in some countries.
	However, some respondents considered government anti-counterfeiting measures to be insufficient (or in some cases non-existent), especially in developing countries. This facilitated the work of counterfeiters.
Enforcement	It appears that the risk of prosecution (as opposed to the imposition of fines and the seizure of goods) is very low, especially in developing countries. Therefore, this is not a major barrier for counterfeiters.
Penalties	Legal action under criminal law in China, the USA and the EU could (in theory) result in substantial penalties due to safety risks associated with potentially defective fakes. However, in practice counterfeiters seem to face only minor penalties if sentenced.
	Even the seizure of plant and equipment and stock would result in high, yet not crucial costs for the counterfeiter.

FOR CONSUMERS	EFFECT ON PROPENSITIES TO CONSUME NON-DECEPTIVE ITEMS
Price	This point contains two aspects. On the one hand, purchasers are deceived by almost perfect imitations, and would buy the items believing them to be the original items. In these instances, none of the other drivers would have any relevance.
	On the other hand, some characteristics of the electrical components (such as where they are sold, or unexpectedly low prices) may suggest that the good is counterfeited.
	In these instances, the purchasers would have made some judgments about the utility of the items, including the importance of the price, and the possible belief that they would be "good enough" for their purposes.
Quality and nature of products	Items are used in construction and as components in the manufacture of other goods. Industry experience is that generally they appear visually similar to the originals but are fabricated from lower-quality materials.
Ability to conceal status	The image of goods being counterfeit would not influence the decision to purchase the item.
Consumer characteristics	
Health concerns	Health risks are not factors in this sector.
Safety concerns	Safety risks associated with fake items should be a very strong negative factor, but the lack of understanding of those risks, or the belief that the items would perform acceptably, or the attractiveness of the prices, or a combination of all of these, may diminish the weight that buyers give to this important element.
Personal values	The potential safety implications of using counterfeited components should be a factor for consumers, but no indication of whether this is the case in practice.
Institutional characteristics	
Risk of discovery	The likelihood of detection is low since governments and the electrical components industry concentrate on suppliers rather than purchasers.
Risk of prosecution	The likelihood of being prosecuted is very low, since the generally deceptive appearance would probably act to turn the purchaser into a victim.
Penalties	The penalties on purchasers, even if prosecuted or facing private legal action, are likely to be low.
Availability and ease of acquisition	As many components are specialised, and intended to be used in the construction industry, or in the manufacture of end-products (such as generators), they are generally distributed through normal supply chains, which could be difficult for counterfeiters. This may act to limit the extent of their availability to consumers.

References

BEAMA (British Electrotechnical and Allied Manufacturers' Association), "Counterfeit campaign success", www.beama.org.uk/Newsletter/issue3/articles/beamainstallation.htm#3

French Association of Electrical Installation Manufacturers (DOMERGIE), "Panorama 2002 – 2006", www.domergie.fr/content/Default.asp?pageID=6

SARL Notacopy.com, "Notacopy concept", www.notacopy.com/E/procede2.php

US Department of Commerce, McGraw-Hill, Standard & Poors, International Trade Administration (1998), US. Industry & Trade Outlook '98 (1998), McGraw-Hill Companies, New York.

Chapter 11

FOOD AND DRINK SECTORS

11.1. General description

The following analysis focuses on IPR (Intellectual Property Rights) infringements affecting alimentary products (food and drink). It should be noted that the broader interpretation of "counterfeiting" that appears to be commonly used within these sectors includes "fake" products that are misrepresented (*e.g.* a bottle containing some kind of alcohol, such as vodka, that is sold without infringing a trademark). However, while important from a public policy perspective, such products are beyond the scope of this project, which limits itself to instances of counterfeiting that infringe intellectual property (IP) rights.

Also, Geographic Indicators, including controlled-denomination designations (such as the *Denominazione di Origine Controllata* -- DOC in Italy, and the *Appellation d'Origine Contrôlée* -- AOC in France) are not covered in this analysis, as these will be examined separately in a subsequent phase of this study.

It is also noted that the food and drink sector is somewhat sensitive, because of the possibility of contamination and/or the use of poor-quality ingredients in products intended for human consumption. Apart from the major concern about possible health problems associated with such products, there is also understandable concern by the producers of the genuine items that their brand names could be tainted if associated with public health problems, even if these were not of their making.

Because of the possibility of potential consumer backlash, food and drink producers are understandably very cautious about widespread public discussions of counterfeiting that could involve their own brands. Because of this potential problem, the discussion in this sectoral analysis avoids the naming of specific firms or brand names.

11.2. Types of infringements

The majority of IPR infringements in the food/drink industry involve the misappropriation of trademarks or registered designs, especially for types of foodstuffs or drinks where the original product can be easily replaced by a substitute, and where it is difficult to establish by physical observation that it is not the original. Kiwi fruits and baby formulae are examples of foods, and tea and Scotch whisky are examples of drinks, found to have been substituted in this way.

According to the industry, the incidence of infringement is considerably lower when physical counterfeiting is necessary to misrepresent the product (as opposed to simply copying the packaging, labelling, trademark and the general appearance of items being substituted), as this requires a considerably more sophisticated enterprise to successfully carry out the substitution and convince retailers and the buying public that they are original items. For example, the counterfeiting of frozen or canned food is much more difficult as this would require specialised equipment to produce the substitute items, as well as to store and transport them, and this severely reduces the potential incentive for counterfeiting.

Because of the importance of the appearance of the counterfeited item (in order to deceive the buyer into thinking that it is the original item), as well as trademark infringements, it can also be expected that there will be infringement of designs that have been registered to protect the special appearance and/or the packaging of particular products.

Finally, it is conceptually likely that some processes and formulas for the preparation of food and drink items may be covered by patents, and these patents may be breached when items are counterfeited. However, this is not a problem specifically mentioned by any of the respondents to the OECD survey. In fact, a number of them noted their unwillingness to seek patents for their processes and recipes, as these would then place them in the public domain. Rather, they expressed a preference to treat these as "trade secrets", protected through close monitoring of those processes and recipes, and the extensive use of confidentiality and non-disclosure agreements.

11.3. Products most likely to be affected

In the experience of the industry, products most subject to counterfeit action are those that are the simplest to replace with passable substitutes, and whose substitutes would not be readily detected by the consumer (and sometimes the wholesalers and retailers). Tea, rice and vodka were examples of such items provided by respondents to the OECD survey.

In these instances, the food or drink item could be easily substituted with cheaper (and probably inferior) products, with maximum effort going into reproducing the packaging so that it is practically indistinguishable from the real thing. Virtually all respondents noted the increasing sophistication of counterfeiters in reproducing packaging that is virtually indistinguishable from the original, including the copying of anti-counterfeit security devices, such as holograms and tax labels.

In this respect, the experience of the food and drink sector mirrors that of other sectors, in that the proliferation and falling cost of equipment, especially computers and associated peripherals, has made the task of the counterfeiters considerably easier.

Several respondents noted that counterfeiting and infringement of trademarks in food are relatively low compared to other products, due to generally low profit margins and the significant logistical challenges associated with the production, handling, transport and distribution of food products. These characteristics would be further magnified for perishable products, which require even more sophisticated handling and distribution chains capable of handling these products efficiently.

The apparent perception in the industry of relatively low propensity to counterfeit in this sector was to some extent supported by the survey of customs authorities undertaken by the OECD in parallel with the industry and government surveys on counterfeiting and piracy. In the responses by those customs authorities, food and drink products were rarely separately identified, and when they were, the quantities/values involved were comparatively small. One inference that could be drawn from this (but with some caution as there are confusing signals) is that food and drink products are something of a difficult target for counterfeiters, and that their efforts are more likely to be directed towards other easier, and perhaps more profitable, targets.

However, while this may be true for food that requires elaborate processing or transformation, there are many food and drink products that could be copied (or at least substituted) with little organisational effort and small investments on the part of the counterfeiters. An example of this could be the substitution of cheap bulk tea for prime quality leaf tea, or the substitution of baby formula with a powder that is made to look like the original but with few active ingredients. In these cases, the quality of the packaging would be sufficient to attract a buyer, and in many cases those buyers might not even realise that they have purchased a counterfeit in place of the original item (but might be discouraged from buying that brand again).

Alcohol products are prime targets for counterfeiters in the drinks sector, because of their brand value (and the price premium that they attract) and the high tax and excise component of the final price, both of which add to the prices that can be charged by counterfeiters. Alcohol was one of the more frequently mentioned food/drink products in the survey of customs authorities, and respondents to the OECD industry survey noted that the most common infringement was the refilling of original bottles with inferior substitutes. Categories of alcohol commonly used in mixed drinks are also particularly attractive, as the mixer can mask the distinctive taste of the underlying alcoholic base.

While many of these substitutions use original bottles and are carried out as small-scale cottage industries, according to the industry there is increasing evidence of large-scale operations that include the use of semi-automated bottling lines as well as sophisticated printing machines. The investment in such operations could also include bottle moulds, production of packaging and the production of raw spirit. Respondents to the survey also indicated that the production of fake products at this scale -- sometimes international in nature -- would almost certainly involve organised crime.

1.4. Production and distribution

By and large, food and drink products are bulky, often perishable and difficult to transport. Therefore, counterfeits are more likely to be produced for local consumption rather than counterfeiters going to the trouble and expense of transporting them to export markets.

The local production of counterfeit items was emphasised in a number of responses to the OECD survey, with the most specific comment coming from a major international producer of spirits, which noted that the distribution and sale of counterfeit brands were largely localised operations, with counterfeiters selling directly to liquor outlets, bars etc., and with little international distribution.

One of the principal characteristics of local production, distribution and consumption is that it avoids crossing national borders, where counterfeiters could expect greater vigilance from customs authorities, especially when products such as spirits, with high excise potential, are involved. This in turn not only reduces the risk of discovery, but also when discovery does occur the quantities are far smaller than when container loads of counterfeited goods are moved around the world. This generates less pressure for prosecution, and penalties may be smaller.

The other effect of relatively small local production is that this will be carried out in many more locations than when counterfeiting is undertaken in large production runs to feed international markets. For example, an international producer of spirits listed some 30 economies (both developed and developing) where legal seizures were made over the past few years, and noted that it needed to maintain a sophisticated global counterfeit recognition programme in over 150 countries and territories in order to deal with counterfeit products.

On the other hand, the European Brands Association (AIM) reported that figures from Customs seizures of food and drink products showed substantial increases over recent years (about 250% increase in the number of articles seized between 2003 and 2005), indicating that trans-border distribution of these products still exists, and should not be ignored (AIM, 2005; EC Taxud, 2003 to 2005).

As with virtually every other sector, China was frequently mentioned by respondents as the source of manufacturing, distribution and sale of counterfeit food and drink products, but in this instance, it is not the sole or dominant producer, further highlighting the largely domestic focus of this group of products.

11.5. Factors that drive counterfeiting production and consumption

This section examines various factors that drive the production and consumption of counterfeited food and drink products. Each product sector has its own peculiar characteristics that will in part determine and shape those drivers, and the recognition and understanding of these drivers can provide insights into the propensity for that category of goods to be produced. In turn, this may provide some guidance on the likelihood that such products can be found in the market place and may support statistical data collected through customs interdictions, police raids on production and retail facilities, the results of legal action and other market-based data. Moreover, the propensities could provide important insights into how surveys and economic modelling could best be used to improve measurement.

Please refer to the summary table at the end of this chapter (Table 11.1), titled "Propensity to produce or consume counterfeited food and drink goods". The drivers that are considered to apply in the food and drink sectors have been judged (on the basis of available information, analysis, industry experience and qualitative judgement) on whether, and to what extent, they are favourable or unfavourable for the production and consumption of counterfeited goods.

The interpretation of these propensity factors needs some caution, as not all drivers will carry the same weight in the decision-making process. As a simple example, the difficulties with the transport and distribution of counterfeited food and drink products, as well as the potentially low profit margins could be overwhelmed by the sheer size and diversity of the potential market, and the ease with which consumers can be deceived when faced by recognisable brands and familiar packaging.

Based on the appraisal of drivers in Table 11.1, it is suggested that the relative ease of deception, as well as the size of the market for well-known brand products, provide strong incentives for the counterfeiting of those goods. However, the generally low profit margins, the challenges associated with transporting and distributing products and the potentially serious consequences of prosecution are also limiting factors.

On the consumer side, the relative ease with which misleading packaging can be produced means that few will detect counterfeits before purchase or consumption, and therefore the drivers that could deter consumers (especially health concerns) would rarely apply. In instances when counterfeits are detected, consumers (especially those with less disposable income) might be tempted to take a risk on the possible health problems associated with counterfeited products, if these are priced well below the genuine items.

Overall, the drivers for the food and drink sector would suggest that this would be a sector subject to some counterfeit activities, with manufacturing likely to be located locally because of the difficulties in transporting many of the products. To some degree, this would tend to support the view in the industry (as evident in responses to the OECD questionnaire) that the food and beverage area is one of the more difficult sectors for counterfeiters to operate in.

1.6. Magnitude and scope

Unfortunately, the survey has shed very little light on the actual magnitude and scope of counterfeiting in the food and drink sector. Part of the reason for this is that there seems to be genuine and widespread misunderstanding in this sector of what is actually covered by counterfeiting.

Many respondents seem to hold the view that apart from actual cases of fake products sold as being original, anything that might be construed as hinting that the product was of a generic origin could be considered as a sign that it was being counterfeited. Therefore, a respondent claimed that the use of names that evoked images of a particular country, or the use of a flag or other distinguishing symbol, was sufficient to justify the conclusion that this was counterfeiting. One group even coined a name for this: "*Italian Sounding*" to cover instances in which words were used to evoke a similarity to things Italian, even though the words themselves were often not actually Italian. A similar case could no doubt be made for words that sound French, Spanish or any other language.

It is highlighted that, in the context of this study, counterfeiting means the deliberate misleading of customers through the infringement of IP rights, such as trademarks, registered designs and patents.

Such a broad view of what constitutes counterfeiting rapidly escalates the claimed losses suffered by the producers of the original items. For example, the Federazione Italiana dell'Industria Alimentare (FEDERALIMNETARE) estimated in a 2003 study that while in 2002 legitimate exports of Italian food products in 2002 totalled EUR 13.9 billion, there were also EUR 2.6 billion in sales of "illegal" imitations (FEDERALIMENTARE 2003).

While large, this number was dwarfed by the report's estimated sales in the same year of "Italian Sounding" (and therefore not necessarily illegal) products, which totalled a massive EUR 52.6 billion. Clearly, such numbers need to be handled with care in order to avoid grossly overstating the losses incurred by industry; but at the same time, the "Italian Sounding" figures can give some indication of the problems being faced by legitimate producers in dealing with imitations of all kinds.

With respect to the drinks industry, the European Brands Association (AIM) reported that during 2004 the spirit industry's global anti-counterfeiting actions resulted in the seizure of over 1 million counterfeit items, and the closure of 148 counterfeit manufacturing sites. The industry's evaluation of these manufacturing sites was that over a 12-month period their cumulative production capability was 155 000 cases with a potential full revenue value of around EUR 19 million.

A startling report published in the Food & Drink Europe website[163], claimed that some 40% all alcoholic beverages, and 36% of all foodstuffs on sale in Russia during the first half of 2003 were counterfeited, and that this was part of a worsening problem that was costing Moscow over USD 1 billion per year.

The report quoted the latest figures from the State Trade Inspectorate of the Ministry of Economy, which was itself based on some 3 000 inspections carried out during that period, of which 48% were found to be in violation of the law. More than 2 000 trading outlets were shut down, and counterfeited goods to the value of USD 1 million were confiscated.

A 2005 report quoted in the related Food Production Daily.com[164] quoted the Russian Agency for Health and Consumer Rights as saying that fake food products in Russia comprise up to 94% of the market in some sectors. In 2004, the agency seized products worth almost EUR 10 million, and issued numerous orders to destroy counterfeit goods after inspection of the food by industry associations and producers.

The European Commission reported that while the number of cases registered has remained relatively constant in recent years (and represents a very small proportion of total cases), 5.2 million items of counterfeited foodstuff, drinks and alcohol were seized in 2005, a 118% increase over 2003 (EC Taxud, 2005). The EC report also noted that most fakes seized were normal household items (which would include most food, drinks and alcohol) rather than luxury goods, and that the high quality of fakes often makes identification impossible without technical expertise.

Some care needs to be taken with these reports, especially since (as alluded to earlier in this section), it is not clear that all of these reported instances would actually involve infringement of intellectual property rights. However, they do provide a snapshot of the extent of problems being detected (if not necessarily accurately measured) in some major markets; at the very least, such reports indicate that substantial intrusions of one kind or another are occurring in the food and drink industry.

---

163.   www.foodanddrinkeurope.com/news 31 October 2003.

164.   www.foodproductiondaily.com/news 13 May 2005.

1.7. Dominant effects of counterfeiting in this sector

11.7.1. Effects on producers

The food and beverage industry has provided relatively little information of the effects of counterfeiting on firms. In terms of economic impact, one respondent in the liquor industry reported that it had assessed its global exposure to counterfeit risk at a minimum of USD 54 million in lost sales. In addition, in order to counter the threat from counterfeiting, the company invested considerable sums each year to ensure that it afforded workable anti-counterfeiting protection to its brands. The nimbleness of counterfeiters in responding to changes in packaging and other security measures meant that these had to be constantly updated. These measures include non-refillable elements, sophisticated packaging and overt and covert devices and images to authenticate the original products.

The annual cost to the company of this rolling programme of anti-counterfeiting measures is not less than USD 75 million. Together these sums indicate the degree of financial exposure, both in lost sales and precautionary measures, faced by firms in this sector with a large number of trademarks to protect. In addition, it highlights the extent to which producers are cognizant of the effects of counterfeiting on brand valuation.

11.7.2. Health considerations

Because food and drink products are intended for human consumption, the sector is vulnerable to the possible health effects of sub-standard counterfeited products reaching an unsuspecting market. The industry points out that these health problems could extend from headaches to people dying from the consumption of such products.

Examples involving baby formula (which led to the death of a number of babies) have been reported in China and other locations, as have incidents involving internationally branded spirits (mostly vodka because of its relatively neutral taste), which had been substituted by poorly distilled, and therefore potentially dangerous, raw spirits.

Generally, few consumers would knowingly purchase food or drink products that they knew to be fakes or substitutes unless they somehow also had prior knowledge of the suitability of those counterfeited products. In the case of food and drink, the possibility of serious health consequences would probably be too great for most consumers to take the risk. Therefore, counterfeiters do everything possible to make their counterfeited items appear as close to the original as possible, a task that is becoming increasingly easier.

As well as deceiving consumers through its appearance, there is also a risk that the more attention (and cost) that goes into the packaging, the less will be devoted to the product inside, thus increasing the possibility that the fake goods could carry health risks. However, as a counterpoint it is unlikely that counterfeiters would purposely produce harmful products, which would hinder their sales and reduce the potential returns of their investments.

Of course, even harmless fake products could negatively affect the producers of the genuine items. This is especially the case when the buyers are unaware that they have purchased a fake, and therefore believe that they had consumed the genuine item. Food and drink producers claim they are particularly prone to such reactions from customers, especially if there is ever any suspicion (even if unjustified) that there may be health problems associated with the substitutes.

Such secondary effects could devastate a market, as it may require extensive recalls of products, and it could take the producer of the genuine items years to rebuild consumer confidence. These concerns were mentioned a number of times by respondents to the OECD survey. In this respect, food and drink producers share some characteristics with other sectors where health and safety are involved (such as pharmaceuticals and auto parts), and this results in problems that are quite different from those experienced by sectors with less-sensitive goods, where health and safety are not considerations.

Therefore, food and drink producers face two potential downsides from counter-feiting: *1)* the usual negative effects on sales, revenues, brand value and customer loyalty; and *2)* potential regulatory and legal issues, if consumers become ill or die as a result of consuming counterfeited products, even if the producers of the original items are totally blameless.

11.7.3. Other effects

A further specific point worth mentioning here is that with spirits (as is the case with cigarettes) there is the likely loss of government revenue from excise duties and other taxes to consider; this is a direct effect that is less evident for other goods subject only to general taxation.

11.8. Actions taken

A unique characteristic of the food and drink sector is that the production of many of the goods is based on old, traditional and frequently secret processes and recipes. Such specially produced goods would normally be protected by patents, but several respondents noted that they had little trust in the national and international legal systems at their disposal for defending those recipes and processes should they become publicly known; those respondents therefore simply preferred to keep those processes and recipes secret. Some of those survey respondents described elaborate security measures to ensure that their secrets remain protected. Perhaps significantly, none of the survey respondents reported either patent infringements or breaches of confidentiality arrangements.

The majority of problems reported related to substitutes and look-alikes (essentially trademark rather than patent infringements). Responses to such infringements were largely restricted to civil action on the part of the IP owners, such as "cease and desist" letters requesting retailers to cease infringing those trademarks or registered designs. Raids, undertaken with the assistance of local authorities were also mentioned, although this greatly increased the cost of any protective action.

As an example of this, one respondent noted that in China it is possible to initiate action at the "administrative" level (*i.e.* local and city level administration) to conduct raids and have infringing material destroyed at quite short notice -- for a cost of around USD 2 000 to USD 5 000 per action. Taking a major perpetrator to court is also an option, but litigation costs are estimated to start at around USD 20 000 for even a simple case.

While virtually all respondents advised that they carry out their own trademark watching service by using staff reports and observing market activities, some went much further, by hiring investigators and local agents. These permit deeper penetration and enable greater control to be exercised at the local level, as well as facilitating the establishment of direct contacts and networks with local police and enforcement authorities. This kind of action is relatively effective, but it is also expensive for the companies concerned.

The most extensive co-ordinated action has been taken by the international spirits producers, which some 20 years ago formed and funded an industry association (the International Federation of Spirits Producers [IFSP])[165]. The IFSP includes eight major companies, with regional and local representation by a number of others, and its aims are to:

- Combat the counterfeiting of alcoholic beverage products;

- Support legal actions taken by law enforcement agencies or other authorised bodies against those concerned in the production, sale or distribution of counterfeit spirits; and

- Liaise with all appropriate authorities and provide information, analytical techniques training and assistance relating to counterfeit spirits.

In response to the OECD survey, the industry noted that the IFSP provides a single industry contact point for law enforcement agencies, thus enabling the industry to avoid duplication of investigative effort, and allowing producers to speak with one voice in public and private forums. The IFSP also targets those markets where there is pronounced production of counterfeits, or where counterfeit producers find safe havens for exporting their products. However, the industry also reports that despite these extensive and quite costly efforts (the cost of the IFSP is around USD 3 million per year), there is no demonstrable reduction in the levels of counterfeiting.

Other actions taken by firms in this sector involve technological deterrents to counterfeiting, such as holograms, microdots, modifications to printed data codes, use-by dates, batch numbers, markers and so on. However, respondents also noted that counterfeiters were becoming more nimble in responding to these technical solutions, emphasising that counterfeiters were being aided and abetted in this by ever improving (and cheaper) manufacturing, computing and printing technology.

An observation made by most respondents to the survey, and one which has been reflected in all other sectors covered by the OECD survey, is that government resources (police, investigators, prosecutors, court facilities, etc.) allocated to deal with counterfeiting are generally inadequate, and reflect the relatively low priority (if not necessarily low importance) attributed to counterfeiting when compared to other breaches of the law, such as drugs or the smuggling of weapons and people. The industry noted that this has been especially troublesome in cases when well-defined underlying laws apply, yet effective implementation has been difficult to achieve.

In other words, the experience in this sector reinforces the more generally held view that while counterfeiting is considered by governments and authorities as an important economic problem, it is generally thought of as a relatively "soft crime" (and in many instances not a crime at all), and that this results in counterfeiting being given relatively low priority compared to other illicit activities when scarce resources are allocated.

Associated with the above, is another point made by many respondents (in all sectors surveyed): from their perspective, prosecution and other legal action against counterfeiting is difficult and expensive to carry out, and penalties and punishments are rarely

---

165. See www.ifspglobal.com

sufficient to deter counterfeiters. This reflects a general view (that appears in virtually all industry responses to the OECD survey) that until the seriousness of the problems associated with counterfeiting are recognised, efforts to combat this growing phenomenon will always be inadequate ultimately.

With respect to the food and drink sector, the following issues were frequently mentioned as being evidence that counterfeiting is not a "soft crime" and that it has real victims:

- Many food and drink products could be sub-standard, contaminated or otherwise dangerous, and can therefore cause serious health problems, and even death, if consumed.

- There is evidence of the involvement of organised crime in the sector, especially in the spirits sub-sector, which requires substantial investment by the counterfeiters to realise substantial profits.

- Some respondents noted that their staffers were being threatened and attacked by interests wishing to protect their counterfeiting activities.

- With some products (in particular spirits), counterfeiting reduces government revenue from excise and other taxes.

- Counterfeit activity undermines the rule of law by creating affiliated, upstream and downstream industries.

Finally, there were some statements made in support of well co-ordinated government action to combat counterfeiting, with the European Union Customs Regulations facilitating the identification of suspect goods so that they can be acted upon. In addition, the EC Directive on the enforcement of IP rights[166], which will provide a more co-ordinated approach to the handling of IP infringements, was specifically mentioned in this context. Such action was considered by respondents as indicating the kind of support that is given by some governments and administrations to protect IP rights, and which in turn strengthens private actions taken by the owners of those rights.

However, as a counterbalance to this, the point is also frequently made that in the end the combat of counterfeiting does not appear to have sufficient official government support and resources, and that from the industry's perspective, the combined efforts are a long way short of adequately addressing the problems raised by counterfeiting. In some cases, respondents noted that local laws were either inadequate, or were ineffectively implemented, and this constrained and frustrated the efforts of both customs and regulatory personnel, as well as the IP owners themselves, from effectively dealing with counterfeiting.

11.9. Possible specific actions to address problems in this sector

In their responses to the OECD questionnaire, respondents offered a number of suggestions to enhance the ability of governments and the industry to combat counterfeiting and piracy:

---

166.   Directive 2004/48/EC.

- Enhance and harmonise the registration and control of trademarks, and actions to combat counterfeiting and piracy.

- Introduce strong criminal sanctions to punish offenders and to act as deterrents, rather than relying heavily on civil actions.

- Governments and international organisations need to bring together all law enforcement agencies and genuine industries to share intelligence and improve the effectiveness of enforcement operations.

- Training of law enforcement officers and the judiciary is vital.

- Explore the possibility of modifying Article 51 of the TRIPS Agreement to extend its scope to export, transit and trans-shipment controls in all jurisdictions.

- Enhanced consumer education and public awareness campaigns to address the dilemma that most consumers see nothing wrong in purchasing counterfeited products (presumably this refers to products that are clearly fakes and sold as such, and not to instances where consumers are deceived into buying a product believing it to be the real thing).

1.10. Summary

Perhaps surprisingly, there seems to be a view within the food and drink sectors (although the actual extent of this is not clear) that the level of sophistication required to produce certain products, the difficulties associated with the handling and transport of food and drink products (especially those that are perishable), and the low profit margins involved, would discourage many would be counterfeiters, and that therefore the levels of counterfeiting experienced in the sector are comparatively low.

On the other hand, some respondents identified serious instances of counterfeiting and trademark misappropriation, and commented on the growing sophistication of counterfeiters in replicating the original look and feel of the packaging.

One respondent even went so far as to say that as technologies rapidly develop, the counterfeit operations are becoming much more advanced, and that the better counterfeits not only look good but the quality of the products themselves are passable, and the counterfeiters are almost creating their own businesses of acceptable fakes, to which consumers will return for those products.

It is suggested that this growing sophistication, and the ever-present threat of serious health risks from consumers unknowingly consuming fake food and drink products, should remove any complacency that may exist is this sector, since producers may face serious market, financial and legal repercussions if their products, rightly or wrongly, are linked by customers to possibly harmful fakes and substitutes.

Despite some government acknowledgement of the problems caused by counterfeiting, the general level of commitment by them, especially in the allocation of resources to combat counterfeiting, are still considered by this industry as being inadequate.

Table 11.1. Propensity to produce or consume counterfeited food and drink goods

FOR PRODUCERS	EFFECT ON PROPENSITIES TO PRODUCE
Unit profitability	**Generally low profit margins** The industry view is that even if counterfeiters avoid R&D and promotional costs, they still need considerable manufacturing, transport and distribution effort (especially for bulky or perishable items), and that the low margins available would discourage many would-be counterfeiters
Market size	**Large, mass market** This is potentially very large, as food and drink products are universal, so the whole world is a potential market.
Genuine brand power	**High** Many brands in the food/drink sector have global reach, and some are as well known as the best brands in other sectors. Many will also have built up a reputation for safety, quality and consistency, and branded products are supported by advertising and promotions.
Production, distribution and technology	
Production investment	**Moderate investment required** A moderate amount of investment is necessary to produce food and drink items, but most can be just a matter of substitution (*e.g.* a low-quality tea for the higher- quality, higher-value original), and technology can easily produce identical packaging. This is therefore unlikely to be a substantial barrier to potential counterfeiters. Production costs of high-quality packaging and the production of some counterfeit items could be close to the cost of the originals; while on the other hand, when lower-cost, lower-quality substitutes are used, the production costs could be considerably lower. On balance, this could be considered to be a relatively low negative factor.
Technology	**Technology not a barrier** Some technology is required in order to manufacture some of the food and drink products, but this would not be a substantial barrier, especially in instances where the counterfeiting action would be a substitution with lower-value items.
Logistics	**Logistics are problematic** The industry view is that the handling, transport and distribution of food/drink are substantially more complex and expensive than other products, especially for perishable products. Therefore, counterfeiters need to be specialised and/or well organised to handle many products in this sector, which would tend to reduce the attractiveness to counterfeiters.
Marketing and sale	**Could be difficult** Generally, food and drink products that are intended to deceive consumers must be distributed and sold through recognised supply chains and recognised retail outlets. This could be difficult in many cases, and would limit the attraction of these types of products to counterfeiters. On the other hand, this may encourage the participation of organised crime, which would be well-placed to deal with these complexities.
Ability to conceal operations	Depends on items. Some will require considerable assembly of ingredients, as well as production and packaging equipment. This could be difficult to conceal effectively. On the other hand, simple substitutions could be carried out in small, mobile production units.
Ability to deceive consumers	**Easy to deceive consumers** Many food and drink products are purchased on the basis of their brand name and physical appearance. Low-cost technology enables counterfeiters to produce realistic packaging and markings that will generally deceive consumers. Consuming the product may/or may not reveal the product as counterfeit, especially if the consumer has no prior knowledge of the original product to provide a comparison.

Institutional characteristics	
Risk of detection	**Low, but closely watched**
	The quantity of food and drink products that are produced, transported and consumed every day, all over the world makes detection of counterfeited items much more difficult. On the other hand, because of the potential health risks (not necessarily involving only counterfeited items), there is considerable supervision and testing to ensure products meet health standards, and this increases the likelihood of detection. Overall, this is a driver that could both encourage and discourage counterfeiters.
Enforcement	**If detected, risk of prosecution probably high**
	Because of the potential health risks associated with inferior products, the probability of prosecution could be very high, and would be a factor to be accounted for by counterfeiters.
Penalties	**Penalties likely to be high**
	Because food and drink is concerned, their counterfeiting or substitution could attract substantial penalties, especially if legal action is taken under criminal, rather than civil law.
FOR CONSUMERS	**EFFECT ON PROPENSITIES TO CONSUME NON-DECEPTIVE ITEMS**
Product characteristics	
Price	**Cost savings relatively low**
	For most foods (excluding up-scale, premium brands), the cost of counterfeit products is likely to be lower than that of genuine items, but not by large amounts, especially where considerable effort goes into deceiving the consumer. However, lower prices may encourage consumers to treat counterfeits as acceptable substitutes, despite possible health risks.
Quality and nature of product	**Outwardly close in appearance to originals**
	Reportedly, appearance of counterfeited products is very close to originals. Consumers may not be able to differentiate any differences in taste.
Ability to conceal status	**Image not a factor**
	Apart from some limited products, such as sports drinks, some spirits and some luxury goods (*e.g.* caviar), image is unlikely to be major factor in encouraging the consumption of counterfeited food and drink products.
Consumer characteristics	
Health concerns	**Could be high and dangerous**
	This should be a very important driver, given the potential after-effects of poor or contaminated ingredients in food and drink. However, the success of counterfeiters largely hinges on consumers being deceived into believing they have purchased genuine items. On balance, it is suggested that health concerns would be overwhelming, especially if consumers are put on their guard about the potential dangers, and this should act as a brake to the purchase (witting or unwitting) of counterfeited products.
Safety risks	**Not a significant factor**
	No apparent safety issues.
Personal values	**Not a factor**
	Unlikely to be a major factor in this sector.
Risk of detection	**Low**
	Likelihood of detection for the consumer is likely to be low, as consumers would most likely be treated as victims, and detection efforts would be most rewarding when directed towards manufacturers, distributors and sellers.
Risk of prosecution	**Low**
	Likelihood of prosecution is low, especially as the deception of consumers would tend to make them the victims, rather than the offenders, if counterfeited products are consumed.
Penalties	**Low**
	Even if detected and prosecuted, penalties imposed on final consumers likely to be low.
Availability and ease of acquisition	**Not necessarily easy, or at least obvious**
	As food/drink items are generally distributed through normal supply chains, consumers may not always find (or realise) they have counterfeited items.

References

Association des Industries de Marque (AIM), 2005 – "Briefing Paper – Faking it: Why Counterfeiting Matters", www.aim.be/docs

FEDERALIMENTARE, 2003 - "Cibo Italiano, tra Imitazione e Contraffazione"(Italian Food, between Imitation and Counterfeiting), December 2003.

European Commission (EC), Taxud (2005), "Statistics Recorded at the External Borders of the EU", 2005.

EC Taxud (2004), "Statistics Recorded at the External Borders of the EU", 2004.

EC Taxud (2003), "Statistics Recorded at the External Borders of the EU", 2003.

Chapter 12

PHARMACEUTICALS

2.1. General description

The purpose of this chapter[167] is to provide an overview of counterfeiting activities in the pharmaceuticals sector, assess the magnitude and trends of these activities, examine the effects on patients/consumers, companies and governments, as well as analyse the measures for combating counterfeiting and piracy activities.

The counterfeiting and piracy of pharmaceutical products involves the deliberate deception of patients, healthcare providers and suppliers of genuine products, such that they unknowingly acquire products of unverified quality, safety and efficacy. Thus, counterfeit pharmaceuticals very often infringe intellectual property rights, violate health and safety legislation and regulation, and create the potential for serious public health consequences.

Pharmaceuticals are understandably amongst the most heavily regulated products due to their direct impact on human health. Consequently, the counterfeiting and piracy of pharmaceutical products is, in most jurisdictions, subject to a myriad of laws and regulations, including those applicable to the regulation of pharmaceutical products, to intellectual property rights, in the criminal and penal field, to customs and border control, etc.[168] In addition to the applicable national legislation, from an international intellectual property perspective, the Agreement on Trade-related Aspects of Intellectual Property Rights (TRIPS Agreement) is also applicable. While this chapter will examine the issue of counterfeit and pirated pharmaceuticals primarily from an intellectual property perspective, it is important to highlight that the most harmful consequences of counterfeit pharmaceuticals are their nefarious implications for and impact on human health.[169]

---

167. This chapter was completed in mid-2007 and uses data and information mostly from 2004, 2005 and 2006. A more in-depth report covering exclusively the counterfeiting of pharmaceuticals will be published by the OECD in 2008 and will cover the latest data and information for 2007-08.

168. In fact, the same event may be viewed and counted from different perspectives. For example, the production of a counterfeit drug may constitute an intellectual property rights infringement, a regulatory violation and a criminal activity, and it may be pursued under any of these headings.

169. According to the World Health Organization (WHO), a counterfeit medicine is "a medicine, which is deliberately and fraudulently mislabelled with respect to identity and/or source. Counterfeiting can apply to both branded and generic products". IMPACT, "Counterfeit Medicines: An Update on Estimates", issued 15 November 2006.

Table 12.1. Global pharmaceutical sales by geographic region (in USD), and by % of global sales

Pharmaceutical global sales Total world market Audited and unaudited data	2001 USD billion	%	2002 USD billion	%	2003 USD billion	%	2004[1] USD billion	%	2005[2] USD billion	%	2006[3] USD billion	%
North America	181.8	47.0	203.6	47.8	229.5	46.6	248	45.1	265.7	47.0	289.9	47.7
European Union	88.0	22.7	90.6	21.2	115.4	23.4	144	26.2	169.5	30.0	181.8	29.9
Japan	47.6	12.3	46.9	11.0	52.4	10.6	58	10.5	60.3	10.7	56.7	9.3
Rest of Europe[4]	-	-	11.3	2.7	14.3	2.9	9	1.6	NA	NA	NA	NA
Asia, Africa & Australia	27.9	7.2	31.6	7.4	37.3	7.6	40	7.3	46.4	8.2	52.0	8.6
Latin America	18.9	4.9	16.5	3.9	17.4	3.5	19	3.5	24.0	4.2	27.5	4.5
Unaudited Countries	22.8	5.9	25.4	6.0	26.7	5.4	32	5.8	NA	NA	NA	NA
Total	**387**	**100%**	**426**	**100%**	**493**	**100%**	**550**	**100%**	**565.9**	**100%**	**607.9**	**100%**

Notes:

1. Global pharmaceutical sales in 2004 are derived from IMS audits, which covers 95% of the market, the remaining 5% are estimates from IMS World Review. The 2004 numbers are missing data from Belarus, Bulgaria, Dominican Republic, Estonia, Lithuania, Russia and Ukraine as data was not available at time of analysis. Constant USD.

2. Excludes "unaudited data": information current as of 27 February 2006. NA = Not Available

3. Excludes "unaudited data": information current to 20 March 2007.

4. European countries not part of the European Union.

Source: IMS Health, 2007

The basic components of pharmaceutical products - active pharmaceutical ingredients (APIs) and excipients – have been the subject of counterfeiting activities. The finished pharmaceutical products – tablets, capsules, syrups, and injectibles – are commonly counterfeited. The packaging of pharmaceuticals has also been counterfeited and pirated.

Within the scope of this report, the term "pharmaceutical"[170] will be employed to include medicines requiring a prescription, medicines not requiring a prescription (*i.e.* over-the-counter products), vaccines, and herbal medicines/remedies where regulated. As well, the term "pharmaceutical(s)" will reference not only chemically-based products but also biologics. However, for the purpose of this chapter, this term will not cover medical devices or traditional medicines (*i.e.* homeopathic remedies), although it should be noted that counterfeiting and piracy has also expanded to these areas.[171]

Precise data on the size of the global pharmaceutical market are difficult to obtain, thus only a general picture is presented.[172] The audited and unaudited data for global pharmaceutical sales provides a general overview (IMS Health, 2007). The data demonstrate that the size of the global market, measured by sales, has increased annually and across all regions, having risen from USD 387 billion in 2001 to approximately USD 643 billion in 2006 (IMS Health, 2007). Specifically from 2005 to 2006, IMS reports that the global pharmaceutical market grew by 7%, to USD 643 billion.[173]

In 2005, the top 50 pharmaceutical companies accounted for USD 419.05 billion in global sales and spent USD 75.25 billion in research and development (R&D) (PharmaExec, 2006). The top 10 of the top 50 companies accounted for USD 249 billion in global sales and spent almost USD 45 billion on R&D. Amongst the top 50, the headquarters, on a per country basis, are predominantly situated in the United States (*i.e.* 20) and Japan (*i.e.* 12). In 2005, the top 10 selling products brought in sales of USD 56.9 billion, with Lipitor, the best selling pharmaceutical, bringing in USD 12.90 billion. In 2005, 13 products broke into the ranks of the blockbusters, bringing the number of products with total sales of more than USD 1 billion annually, up to 94 (Gray 2006). The top 10 therapeutic classes brought in sales of over USD 184 billion in 2005.

---

70.   Within this paper, the terms "pharmaceutical product(s)", "pharmaceutical(s)", "medicine(s)", "drug(s)" will be used interchangeably.

71.   As counterfeit medical devices and traditional medicines also raise health and safety concerns, they ought to be the subject of separate and detailed studies, and are beyond the scope of this report. The topics of parallel trade or re-importation are also beyond the scope of this chapter.

72.   A more precise picture is not feasible due to a number of factors including the number and breadth of entities involved in this sector, including small, medium and large manufacturers (both brands and generics), whole-salers, distributors, retailers, pharmacies, and more recently, biopharmaceutical companies; the differences in statistical standards and definitions; the unavailability of data from privately-held entities; and the cycle of expansion and contraction of the sector. When these factors are multiplied across many jurisdictions, the information and data are difficult to collate and are disparate at best. The data and estimates provided are from various resources, including from public and private resources, media and filings with securities commissions.

73.   The discrepancy between USD 643 billion used in the text and USD 607.9 billion reported in Table 12.1 is due to *1)* USD 643 billion includes unaudited data and *2)* variation in availability of information.

Figure 12.1. Top 100 R&D spending

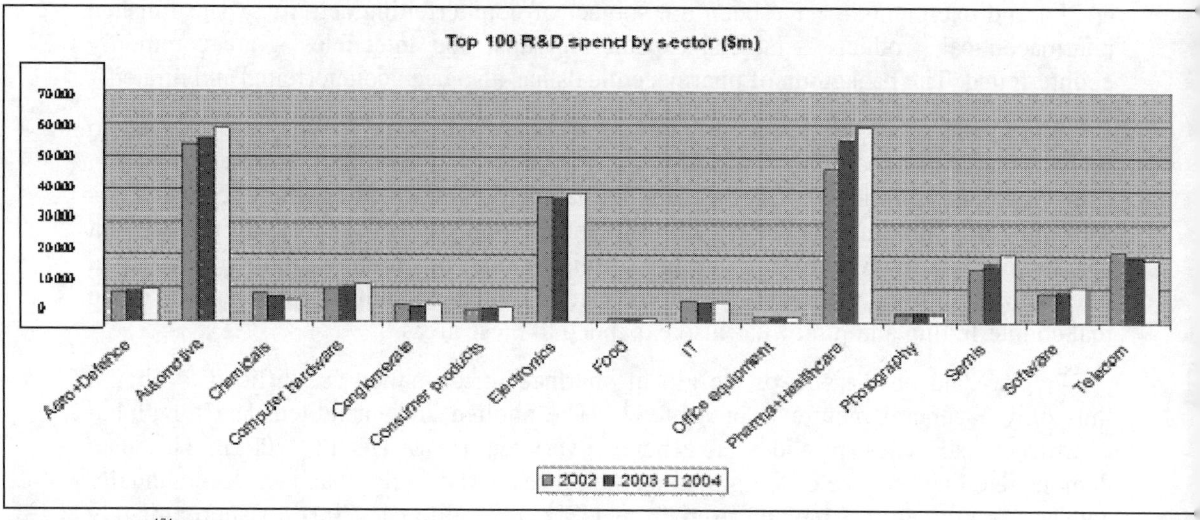

Source: Cientifica[174], 2005.

The R&D of new pharmaceutical products is a lengthy (estimates vary, with average considered as 10 to 15 years), costly and complex process (OECD, 2006). One contributing element is the investment required for obtaining regulatory approval. For example, in the United States, only .01% to .02% of the compounds tested (*i.e.* 1 out of 5 000 to 10 000) receives regulatory approval (PhRMA, 2007). As Figure 12.1 illustrates, the pharmaceutical sector is one of the most research intensive (Cientifica, 2005). Based on a survey of 100 global corporations in a variety of fields, in 2004 the top two spenders in R&D by sector were pharmaceuticals and healthcare, at USD 59.33 billion[175], and automotive, with USD 58.83 billion. As seen above, in 2005, the top 50 companies spent USD 75.25 billion on R&D. R&D intensity charted by sector reveals software as the leader for 2004 at 18.2%, followed by pharmaceuticals at 12.5% (Cientifica, 2005). As such, this sector uses intellectual property, especially patents, trade secrets/know-how, trademarks, and copyright and design rights, to protect its investment in R&D.

12.2. Types of infringements

While the counterfeiting of pharmaceuticals violates health and safety legislation and regulation, it also involves the infringement of intellectual property rights through the intentional and deceptive falsification of one or more different aspects, including the bulk ingredients, the finished pharmaceutical product and the packaging. Counterfeit pharmaceuticals also compromise legitimate production/manufacturing activities, shipment and distribution/supply chains.

---

174. Cientifica carried out a global analysis of 100 corporate spenders on research and development over the last three years. Data was obtained from annual reports and encompasses corporations from Merck KGAA (USD 732 million spent in 2004), to Microsoft (USD 7 779 million spent in 2004).

175. The discrepancy between the figures presented by Cientifica and those above (based on the Pharmaexec.com study) are due to differences in the companies surveyed and the period covered by the surveys.

Numerous acts constitute patent rights[176] violation, including unauthorised production, use (including theft), offering for sale, sale or importing of the patented active ingredient, irrespective of the quantity of the active ingredient that is actually employed within the counterfeit pharmaceutical product. Moreover, patent rights are also infringed when a patented process or method is employed by the counterfeiters, as unauthorised users, to produce the active ingredient(s), excipient(s) or finished product(s).

The "name" or logo employed for sale of a product, the colour and shape of the tablets and pills, the packaging of the product, and any distinguishing feature may be the subject of a trademark. Under the new *Treaty on the Law of Trademarks*[177], which is awaiting ratification, rights holders will also be able to protect new types of marks, such as hologram(s), motion, colours, and marks consisting of non-visible signs, such as sound or taste. Counterfeiters pirate the logos, packaging, label, including holograms, shape, size and colour of the product in order to deliberately deceive the consumer into believing that they are acquiring the genuine product. In certain cases, the trademark for a given pharmaceutical product may become quite a valuable asset. For example, many (whether they use the product or not) are familiar with the trademark "Viagra", its distinctive blue colour and the lozenge shape of the tablet. Highly valuable trademarks may create additional incentive for counterfeiters. By using the rights holder's trademark, the counterfeiter is able to usurp the goodwill and product integrity associated with the valuable trademark, without the necessary investment or safeguards.

Copyrights are applicable to the packaging, the labelling, as well as the product information, instructions and inserts of pharmaceutical products. As such, when counterfeiters make or use unauthorised copies of such proprietary information, they engage in copyright infringing activities. Furthermore, use of packaging or labelling, which is inaccurate or misleading, will often also violate health and safety regulations.

Proprietors may also register the colour of the tablets or pills, as well as their unique shape, pursuant to industrial designs. Design rights are also applicable to the shape of vials or receptacles for the pharmaceuticals products. In jurisdictions where a product and its features may be protected by multiple intellectual property rights, IP holders may pursue counterfeiting and piracy activities on a multitude of bases.

2.3. Products most affected

12.3.1. Bulk ingredients

The most important component of a pharmaceutical product is the Active Pharmaceutical Ingredient(s) (API). APIs are produced or purchased in bulk by manufacturers for use in the manufacturing of finished pharmaceuticals. The difficulties in detecting counterfeited bulk API lies in part in the difficulties that some authorities face due to lack

---

76. Pursuant to Article 28(1) of the TRIPS Agreement, "a patent shall confer on its owner the following exclusive rights: *(a)* where the subject matter of a patent is a product, to prevent third parties not having the owner's consent from the acts of: making, using, offering for sale, selling, or importing for these purposes that product; *(b)* where the subject matter of a patent is a process, to prevent third parties not having the owner's consent from the act of using the process, and from the acts of: using, offering for sale, selling, or importing for these purposes at least the product obtained directly by that process.

77. *Treaty on the Law of Trademarks*, ('Singapore Treaty'), adopted 27 March 2006, www.wipo.int/wipo_magazine/en/2006/03/article_0002.html.
While this treaty was adopted it was not in effect on 1 August 2007.

of capacity and technology. For example, one company reports an increase in the existence of counterfeit APIs and increased difficulties in distinguishing between the genuine and the counterfeit (OECD Survey, 2005). As many bulk ingredients are imported from foreign jurisdictions, there is considerable difficulty for the regulatory authority of one country to control and detect counterfeit APIs entering its borders. For example, one company detected in 33 countries counterfeit APIs sourced in India (OECD Survey, 2005). For example, in a 2000 testimony, the US FDA indicated that it was unable to detect or control all imported counterfeit bulk drugs from entering the United States, since there were, in 2000, over 1 200 foreign bulk drug producers (GlobalOptions, 2003). Pharmaceutical products also contain inactive, but important ingredients, known as excipients, which play an important role in the therapeutic performance and shelf life of both solid and liquid dosage forms.[178]

The intellectual property rights most often implicated in counterfeit bulk ingredients are patent and trademark rights. When the genuine API is protected by trademarks, counterfeiting activities constitute infringement of those rights. Bulk ingredients may be pirated through mislabelling or misbranding. To the extent that an API is protected by patents, the unauthorised use, production or adulteration of the API constitutes patent infringement. Counterfeit APIs may infringe not only product patents but also process and method claims, if the counterfeit is produced through processes and methods that are the subject of patent protection. However, since the detection of process and method infringement is more difficult than product patent violation, these types of violation are invoked less often. While the counterfeiting of excipients is less significant, the violation of intellectual property rights for excipients follows the pattern for APIs.

In addition to intellectual property issues, the counterfeiting of bulk ingredients raises health and safety concerns. Bulk ingredients are often manufactured in unapproved factories and under conditions not consistent with applicable health and safety regulations. For example, the counterfeiter may choose to mislabel an impure or inactive chemical as an API; to substitute the correct API with a lower or higher potency/dosage; to substitute the intended, often more-costly API with a cheaper one; or to re-label an expired API with a new and false expiration date (GlobalOptions, 2003).

12.3.2. Finished pharmaceutical products

Different data sources illustrate that finished pharmaceutical products covering a spectrum of therapeutic classes are being counterfeited. Examination of data for the European Union and North America shows that counterfeiters have targeted a wide range of modern drugs, including steroids, cancer (*e.g.* anti-tumour and anemia), erectile dysfunction, cardiology (cholesterol-lowering and hypertension), and hormones. By contrast, the most commonly counterfeited drugs in developing countries are the basic medicines against infection (antibiotics, anti-malarials, anti-retrovirals and anti-tuberculosis), analgesics, anti-inflammatory and anti-histamines and vitamins.[179] Figure 12.2 provides a limited global perspective on the frequency by which each therapeutic category is linked to counterfeiting, diversion and theft incidents.

---

178. According to the International Pharmaceutical Excipients Council (IPEC Americas, FAQs), excipients can be classified into the following functions: binders, disintegrants, fillers (diluents), lubricants, glidents (flow enhancers), compression aids, colours, sweeteners, preservatives, suspensing/dispensing agents, film formers/ coatings, flavours and printing inks.

179. The data analysed represent a snapshot in time based on only 31 countries, including both developed and developing nations.

Figure 12.2. Incidents by therapeutic category

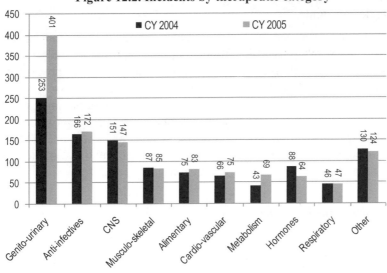

Note: "Other" includes: blood agents, cytostatics, dermatologicals, hospital solutions, parasitological & sensory organs.
Source: PSI Situation Report, 2005.[180]

The types of intellectual property rights most implicated in counterfeit finished pharmaceutical products include patents, trademarks and industrial design. The infringement of patent rights occurs when there is the unauthorised production, use, sale, importation of a patented active ingredient or excipient, or use of a process or method. An example is when the counterfeit pharmaceutical contains some active ingredient but the manufacturer is not an authorised licensee, such as the production of counterfeit "Levitra" in China (OECD Survey, 2005). The infringement of trademarks occurs when, for example, the counterfeiter is passing off the counterfeit as the genuine pharmaceutical product. Given that "passing off"[181] lies at the very heart of counterfeiting activities, trademarks, by their very nature, are the most easily and most frequently infringed IPRs. In other words, trademark infringement will arise even when there is no patent infringement; for example, a trademark violation may occur -- even when there is no use of a patented active ingredient, process or method -- as long as the counterfeit product uses an identical or confusingly similar trademark and is made to look and pass-off as the genuine product. For example, every counterfeit "Viagra", "Cialis", "Levitra", etc., tablet placed on the market in Europe violates the respective trademark. Industrial design rights are infringed any time the counterfeiter has copied the design of the genuine pharmaceutical, which has been registered in the applicable jurisdiction. Recently, more and more companies have begun to register the shape and design of particular pharmaceutical products. For example, for "Cialis", the shape of the tablet, the stamped lettering on each different dosage tablet (*i.e.* C10, C20), and the "C", have all individually been registered

---

80.   The number of reported cases of counterfeit pharmaceuticals cited is very small compared with the true number of counterfeit drugs produced in this timeframe; and it is not possible to indicate with exactness to what extent the cases are representative of the drug categories involved, or the type of counterfeiting committed.

81.   Article 16 of the TRIPS Agreement states that: "The owner of a registered trademark shall have the exclusive right to prevent all third parties not having the owner's consent from using in the course of trade identical or similar signs for goods and services which are identical or similar to those in respect of which the trademark is registered where such use would result in a likelihood of confusion. In the case of the use of an identical sign for identical goods or services, a likelihood of confusion shall be presumed."

in Europe under the Community Design.[182] Thus, every counterfeit "Cialis" tablet is violating these design rights.

A recent and worrisome occurrence, which may foreshadow the emergence of a new trend, is illustrated by the case of "Rimonabant"[183], a drug to treat obesity. It was advertised for sale over the Internet in March 2006, prior to its having received marketing authorisation by the European Commission (EU, 2006). In this case, the violation of intellectual property rights occurred prior to the rights holders having even placed the genuine product on the market, prior to their having begun to recoup on their investment, and even prior to the product having been declared safe for patient use. This example of the launch of a counterfeit prior to the actual marketing authorisation for the genuine product clearly represents a violation of health and safety regulations.

12.3.3. Packaging and labelling

Counterfeit packaging and labels raise violations of copyright, trademark and design rights. Counterfeiters achieve their deceptive goal of passing off their products as the genuine item because they are able to copy the packaging and labelling of genuine products, re-date expired genuine products, or package counterfeit products in genuine packaging obtained through unauthorised means. One study examined 286 incidents and found that 67% had both counterfeit pharmaceutical and packaging, 28% had only counterfeit pharmaceutical and 5% had only counterfeit packaging (PSI, 2005). Counterfeiters employ state-of-the-art technologies to produce counterfeit labels that, on their face, are indistinguishable from the genuine original labels and apply them to the counterfeit bulk ingredients or finished pharmaceuticals. They have the ability to make and stamp tablets with company logos and even to package them in blister packs.

For example, in one seizure presses and punches that were used by counterfeiters to emboss the terms "Pfizer", "VGR 100" and "VGR 50" were seized (Pfizer, 2005). Investigations have highlighted that counterfeiters are able to reproduce tube vials and holograms, violating design rights. For example, very sophisticated holograms to protect genuine artesunate, an anti-malarial, have been copied by counterfeiters in Southeast Asia (Newton, 2006). They are often able to replicate them sufficiently well to deceive the average patient and possibly even the unaware medical professional. The presence of sophisticated holograms on the counterfeit product, even when the genuine packaging does not contain holograms, has been reported to increase consumer's acceptance of the counterfeit as genuine (Collier, 2005).

Another counterfeiting practice is to prolong the original and approved shelf life by replacing the date label, or repackaging the drugs with altered-date labelling. In this case, the pharmaceuticals have been obtained at low cost due to their being very close to, or having passed their approved expiration date. Such a drug is still a counterfeit, despite being produced by an authorised manufacturer through an approved process with the approved quantities of active ingredients under appropriate quality conditions. This situation raises a multitude of intellectual property, as well as health and safety violations.

---

182.   For trademark information, see *e.g.* the Community Trademark database:
        http://oami.europa.eu/CTMOnline/RequestManager/en_DetailCTM_NoReg.
        For design information, see *e.g.* the Community Design database:
        http://oami.europa.eu/RCDOnline/RequestManager.

183.   Developed by Sanofi Aventis. EU Commission, "Commission warns about fake drugs on the Internet", press release, Brussels, IP/06/375, 27 March 2006.

Figure 12.3. Examples of counterfeit pharmaceuticals packing and labelling[184]

![Novalgina Dipirona packaging examples]

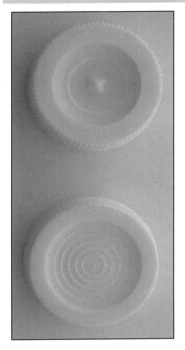
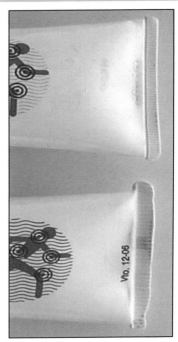

op = original; Bottom = fake)

ource: Instituto Nacional de Medicamentos – ANMAT, 2006.

---

84.   Colour pictures which better illustrate the differences between the original and the counterfeit packaging are available at www.oecd.org/sti/counterfeiting.

12.4. Magnitude, scope and trends

Counterfeiting of pharmaceuticals is an opportunistic activity which violates intellectual property, health and safety and criminal laws, amongst others, places patients' health at risk and whose detection and prevention is difficult. Assessing the prevalence of counterfeiting activities, both on a global and regional scale, is a difficult objective given the paucity of reliable data. The underlying reasons for such paucity include use of divergent definitions and terminology across jurisdictions, uneven or no data collection either within or across jurisdictions, differences in measurement techniques, variety of legislative and regulatory mechanisms pursuant to which investigations and prosecutions are carried out, a multitude of enforcement agencies involved in anti-counterfeiting activities, and the clandestine nature of such activities. Nevertheless, the available data suggest a rise in pharmaceutical counterfeiting, both in terms of volume and diversity of products affected. The analysis below aims to provide an overview, rather than a precise evaluation, and is based on OECD survey work and additional research.

Today, few jurisdictions, whether developed or developing, are immune from counterfeit pharmaceuticals and the infringement of intellectual property rights, as such activities have been reported on all continents (OECD Survey, 2005)[185]. A figure providing a global magnitude is not representative, since reports by region indicate a wide level of divergence. For example, the magnitude of counterfeit pharmaceuticals has been reported as low (*i.e.* less than 1%) for jurisdictions such as Australia, Canada, the EU, Japan, New Zealand and the U.S., versus 10% to 30% for some developing countries.[186] Jurisdictions are often the victims of multiple acts including production, sale, importation and export of counterfeit pharmaceuticals. For example, one entity reported that counterfeits of its pharmaceutical products sourced in China were detected in 42 countries (OECD Survey, 2005). Similarly, counterfeit active pharmaceutical ingredients have been reported as exported from India to 33 jurisdictions (OECD Survey, 2005). Data systematically collected by one entity provides some insight into the scope and magnitude of counterfeiting activities in different jurisdictions[187] (PSI, 2005, 2006).

---

185. With the exception, at the current time, of the two Poles.

186. WHO (2006*a*). "Counterfeit Medicines", Fact Sheet No. 275, revised November 2006.

187. It should be noted that the number of reported incidents and seizures in a specific jurisdiction is not necessarily indicative of the full scope of the counterfeiting and piracy problem in that jurisdiction, or the relative magnitude of pharmaceutical counterfeiting in one country vis-à-vis other countries worldwide. Reported incidents likely represent a small percentage of pharmaceutical counterfeiting activities in a particular country. Conversely, the fact that a jurisdiction has a relatively large number of reported seizures may speak more to its enforcement efforts than to the prevalence of counterfeiting.

Table 12.2 reveals that in 2005, the jurisdictions with the most reported incidents[188] were: 1st China, 2nd Russia and 3rd the United States. However, when measured by the number of seizures, the results were: 1st Russia, 2nd China and 3rd South Korea. In 2005, based on the European Commission's TAXUD statistics, 75% of the cases of counterfeit medicines originated from India, 7% from Egypt, and 6% from China (TAXUD, 2005). It should be noted that the incidents reported in the Table represent a small percentage of pharmaceutical counterfeiting activities in any given jurisdiction. One aspect that the Table does highlight is the dearth of data available for some jurisdictions, such as the African continent, and some other developing jurisdictions.

Table 12.2. Top 10 jurisdictions by incidents and by seizure

Rank by reported incidents	Total incidents	Rank by seizures	Number of seizures
1.China	158	1. Russia	93
2. Russia	102	2. China	87
3. United States	100	3. Korea	66
4. Colombia	71	4. Peru	54
5. Korea	67	5. Colombia	50
6. Peru	61	6. United States	42
7. Brazil	51	7. United Kingdom	39
8. India	46	8. Ukraine	28
9. United Kingdom	46	9. Germany	25
10. Ukraine	30	10. Israel	25

Source: PSI, 2006.

A worrisome trend is that counterfeits are increasingly being detected as having entered the supply chain of some of the most regulated jurisdictions. For example, in 2005, "Lipitor" tablets awaiting distribution through the UK's National Health System were determined to be counterfeit (OECD Survey, 2005). Similarly, in 2003, 18 million tablets of "Lipitor" had to be recalled in the United States due to the co-mingling of counterfeit tablets with genuine tablets by counterfeiters (OECD Survey, 2005). Counterfeit products, whether or not distributed through the legitimate supply chain, violate protected IP rights.

---

188.   The PSI (Pharmaceutical Security Institute) defines an incident as a discrete event triggered by the discovery of counterfeit, illegally diverted or stolen pharmaceuticals. PSI considers an incident to be a unique occurrence for which it must have adequate factual information, such as a particular date, time, place and type of pharmaceutical product involved. Incidents vary by magnitude, scale and timeframe. Magnitude refers to the quantity of counterfeit medicines found. An incident may involve small quantities of a single product or conversely, hundreds of thousands of counterfeit pharmaceuticals representing multiple products. Scale refers to the size of the organisation involved. Lastly, incidents can vary by timeframe. Incidents may occur over an extended period of time. An incident may be reported by anyone -- including drug inspectors, customs officials, police officers or the general public. The discovery of illegally diverted or counterfeit pharmaceuticals may be the result of government or industry market surveillance. Pharmaceutical Security Institute (PSI) (2006), "Annual Situation Report", 2005.

An examination of the data also points to an increase in the number of incidents/ activities reported and prosecuted in the last few years. For example, one source reports an increase in number of incidents of approximately 27% between 2004 and 2005 (PSI, 2006). Another illustration is the recent occurrences in the UK of three types of counterfeits reaching patients through the legitimate supply chain: counterfeit "Viagra", "Cialis" and "Reductil", in 2003 and 2004. According to MHRA, these were the first cases of counterfeit drugs to penetrate the regulated UK supply chain since 1994 (MHRA, 2005). However, such increases cannot be attributed solely to an increase in counterfeiting activities, but are also a result of better surveillance, improved detection and increased prosecution. For example, in the US there was an increase of approximately 93% in the number of cases opened between 2003 and 2004, which was attributed in part to increased awareness and vigilance at all levels of the distribution chain, increased co-ordination between state and federal law-enforcement agencies and better communication with drug manufacturers (US FDA, 2005). Similarly, the US Customs and Border Protection reported a 144% increase of IPR-seized counterfeit pharmaceuticals from mid-2005 to mid-2006, as determined by value (US CBP, 2006a).

The cases mentioned above also highlight another trend, namely diversification of the types of products targeted. Examination of data for the European Union and North America reveals that counterfeiters have targeted a wide range of modern drugs, including in the areas of cancer (anti-tumor and anemia), erectile dysfunction, cardiology (cholesterol-lowering and hypertension), hormones and steroids. Counterfeiters are tempted by these high-value pharmaceuticals, especially since often they are the best-selling drugs in the world. In light of their high-value nature, these pharmaceuticals are protected by a plethora of intellectual property rights, which are registered and protected in these jurisdictions, and are violated by the counterfeits.

In developing countries, the most-often protected and violated intellectual property rights are trademarks, copyrights and less often design rights. In developing countries, the data reveal that the most commonly counterfeited drugs include the basic medicines against infection, i.e. antibiotics, anti-malarials, anti-retrovirals and anti-tuberculosis. For example, holograms applied to protect anti-malarials are being counterfeited, violating design rights (Newton, 2006). It has been reported that trademark infringement actions are amongst the most effective means to pursue legal action against counterfeiters. Thus, measures are taken to ensure that high-risk trademarks are recorded in as many jurisdictions around the world, where recordation is possible (OECD Survey, 2005). However, the challenge, in addition to registration, is enforcement of rights. For example, in some jurisdictions, private civil actions for trademark infringement can be expensive and time-consuming, while criminal and administrative enforcement of trademark laws may be weak. Another challenge arises when counterfeit pharmaceuticals are so prevalent that the limited resources are unable to control the problem, wherein many rights holders leave the jurisdiction, as occurred in Nigeria. Prior to 2001, when counterfeit pharmaceuticals were estimated to comprise as much as 80% of the Nigerian market, pharmaceutical companies abandoned rights (NAFDAC, 2006).

Regulation, investigation and enforcement activities in the pharmaceutical sector are governed by a multitude of legislation and regulations covering diverse fields, including regulatory approval and safety (*e.g.* drug administration, quality control, pharmaceutical distribution, importation, manufacturing, marketing, patient information, licensing practices), criminal and penal activities (*e.g.* contraband activities, racketeering, endangering life), intellectual property (trademark, patent, copyright, industrial design), customs and border activities, consumer protection, *etc.* Counterfeiting activities often will simultaneously violate a number of statutes in diverse areas. Whether an action is brought pursuant to a particular charge will depend on a number of factors including which charge will have the highest success rate and result in the most severe penalties. Criminal laws often not only provide the breadth of investigative powers and seizure authority necessary to penetrate and dismantle counterfeiting operations, but also ensure that more severe penalties can be imposed on counterfeiters. Thus, although many counterfeiting activities violate intellectual property legislation, often the prosecution will be brought under criminal law, due to the more severe penalties that can be imposed on the counterfeiters. For example, in a high-profile counterfeiting case involving a global best-selling pharmaceutical, the counterfeiter was sentenced to 13 and one-half years of imprisonment without parole and to the restitution of millions to the government (US DOJ, 2006*c*), because the action was brought under criminal law rather than IP law.

In trans-border counterfeiting, the initial determination with respect to intellectual property violations most often lies with the customs authorities[189]. Given the enormous quantities of products in all sectors that pass through borders on a daily basis and often the limited time periods in which customs authorities must deal with any given shipment, any assessment of potential violation of intellectual property rights must be made quickly. In light of this, the simplest determination of an intellectual property right violation will be a trademark, as this often only requires a visual inspection. Conversely, a determination that patent rights have been violated, in the case of pharmaceuticals, involves the more complex process of chemical analysis, which may take several days or longer. Arriving at an assessment of whether a product is infringing a process patent is even more complicated as this will require an investigation of the process used in the jurisdiction of origin for the manufacturing of the allegedly infringing good. Obviously, this results in patent infringement being alleged in border seizures only infrequently. In addition, there may be other complicating factors for determining possible patent infringement. For example, in some countries, such as the United States, patents cannot be recorded with the customs authorities. Rather, in the United States, the rights holder must obtain an order from the International Trade Commission requiring customs to exclude any product that purports to infringe a patent.

The use of trademark violations as the basis for retaining suspect products at borders is reflected in the data emerging from the European Community's Taxation and Custom Union ("TAXUD") statistics. These statistics reveal that the overwhelming percentage of intellectual property rights invoked in border seizures is trademarks (Table 12.3).

---

189. The term "custom authorities" is employed in a generic sense and may include customs, border patrols, etc., authorities. The powers granted to customs authorities vary considerably across the world, from search, seizure and destruction to simple detention for limited time periods.

Table 12.3. Breakdown by type of intellectual property right covered under regulation (EC)3295/94, as % of cases

	Trademarks	Copyright and related rights	Designs and models	Patents and supplementary protection certificates	Data not communicated
2001	83%	9%	5%	3%	-
2002	80%	18%	0.50%	1.5%	-
2003	83%	13.5%	1.50%	2%	-
2004	74%	14%	2%	5%	5%
2005	79%	5%	7%	1%	8%

Source: TAXUD, 2001-2005.

Table 12.4. Extrapolation of number of registered cases by trademark and product type (pharmaceutical)

2000-2004[1]

	2000	2001	2002	2003	2004
Austria	0	0	0	0	0
Belgium[2]	0.96	0	1	12.6	2.04
Denmark	0	0	0	1	0
Finland	0	0	0	0	0
France[3]	0	0	0	0	9.24
Germany[4]	226.24	0	50.4	6.08	35.28
Greece	0	0	0	0	0
Ireland[5]	0	0	0	0	0
Italy[6]	0	0	0	0	0
Luxembourg	0	0	0	0	0
Netherlands[7]	0	0	0	0	4.69
Portugal	0	0	0	0	0
Spain[8]	0	0	0	0	0
Sweden[9]	0	0	0	0	82.56
United Kingdom	0	2.16	2.97	89.7	69.72
Total	**227.2**	**2.16**	**54.37**	**109.38**	**203.53**

Notes:

1. It should be noted that the newly admitted member states of the European Union have not been included, since the comparative data from 2000 were not available. The new member states are Estonia, Hungary, Latvia, Lithuania, Malta, Poland, Slovakia and Slovenia.

2. For Belgium in 2004, the unidentified percentage was 64%.

3. For France in 2004, the unidentified percentage was 41%; for 2002, it was 52%; and for 2001, 42%.

4. For Germany in 2004, the unidentified percentage was 60%; for 2003, it was 54%; for 2002, 41%; and for 2001, 46%.

5. For Ireland in 2004, the unidentified percentage was 40%.

6. For Italy in 2004, the unidentified percentage was 54%.

7. For the Netherlands in 2004, the unidentified percentage was 43%; for 2001, it was 47%; and for 2000, 52%.

8. For Spain in 2004, the unidentified percentage was 62%; for 2003, it was 42%; for 2002, 61%; and for 2001, 49%.

9. For Sweden in 2004, the unidentified percentage was 45%; for 2003, it was 42%.

Source: OECD extrapolation from TAXUD data.

This perspective of IPR violation is also borne out in the field of pharmaceuticals. The challenge to using TAXUD data is that until 2005 there was no separate category for pharmaceuticals, as there is for "clothing accessories" or "computer equipment". Rather, pharmaceuticals were part of the catch-all category "Other Goods". Table 12.4 and Figure 12.4 have been developed by extracting from the category "Other Goods" the figures that pertain to pharmaceuticals. Table 12.4 presents an approximation of the number of cases registered as trademark violations with TAXUD for the field of pharmaceuticals.[190] In 2005, TAXUD decided, for the first time, to collect statistics for seizures of pharmaceuticals as a separate category. In 2005, there were 148 cases pertaining to medicines registered with TAXUD. The breakdown of the number of medicine cases registered expressed as a percentage by origin/provenance reveals that in 2005, 75% of the cases involved provenance from India, 7% from Egypt, 6% from China, 4% from Thailand, and 1% from Argentina. The 148 cases pertaining to medicines that were registered with TAXUD constitute 1% of all the cases registered for all product types. While this data should not be interpreted as indicating that there are few counterfeit pharmaceuticals being imported into the EU, it does highlight that few cases of intellectual property rights violation are registered with the border enforcement authorities, and may highlight issues in regards to border enforcement.

Figure 12.4. Number of registered cases by trademark, 2000-04

Number of registered cases by trademark and product type: Other Goods - Pharmaceuticals

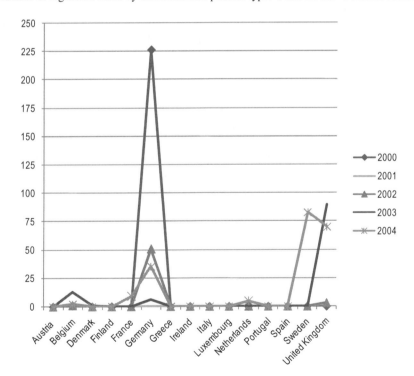

urce: OECD extrapolation from TAXUD data, (2000-04).

)0.   These figures are an extrapolation from the percentage of cases identified as pertaining to a particular trademark and the total number of cases per member country in the "Other Goods" category. In certain circumstances, these numbers may be skewed as the unidentified percentage of cases in the "Other Goods" category was significant (defined as over 40%).

Another reason that trademark violations are more often invoked than patent violations is that often trademarks outlast the applicable patents. An analysis of 37 counterfeit pharmaceutical incidents reported in the United States illustrates this point. The reported incidents involved 30 drugs, of which only 20 still had valid patents.[191] However, all 30 pharmaceuticals had registered trademarks that were infringed by the counterfeit products.[192]

While a global figure on the economic value of trade in counterfeit pharmaceuticals is not feasible, an examination of the potential profit from the counterfeiting of certain patented and trademark-protected pharmaceuticals provides some insight into the economic motivation underlying this activity. In the United States, some biologics have been counterfeited because they are of high value. This is the case for "Epogen Injection" and "Procrit Injection" (both epoetin alfa). Vials of "Epogen" and "Procrit" containing 2 000 U/ml of epoetin alfa were acquired by counterfeiters in the USA, re-labelled as 40 000 U/ml and re-introduced into the supply chain (Amgen, 2002; Ortho Biotech, 2002*a*, 2002*b*, 2002*c*). The theoretical profit from this crime may be calculated as follows. At the time, the cost of a vial of the 2 000 U/ml was USD 22 while the cost of a vial of the 40 000 U/ml was USD 445. The number of vials involved in this counterfeiting operation is believed to have been 110 000. Consequently, an outlay of USD 2.42 million to purchase the 2 000 U/ml vials would result in a sale price of USD 48.95 million at full price (Jaret, 2004). The actual profit obtained would have been less than USD 46.53 million since the 40 000 U/ml were sold at a discounted price in order to provide the incentive for buyers in the secondary market to purchase them and allow these buyers a mark-up leading to a profit for themselves. Even so, the potential profit is still significant as the counterfeiters simply had to remove the original labels by soaking the vials, print new labels and apply them.

12.5. Modes of operation

12.5.1. Manufacturing and production

Within many jurisdictions, the manufacturing and production of pharmaceutical products is a heavily regulated process. Conversely, the illicit nature of counterfeit pharmaceuticals signifies that they are not subject to any regulatory process. Counterfeit pharmaceuticals, whether API or finished product, may be manufactured and produced in the most dismal and unsanitary conditions (see Figure 12.5). They are not produced according to Good Manufacturing Practices (GMP) or approved procedures and most often use unskilled workers. Counterfeit pharmaceuticals enter the legitimate supply chain through a slew of activities including grey markets, imports, "overruns" sold at a discount, diversion and theft (Beckett, 2005).

---

191.   As indicated in the Orange Book database.

192.   As indicated in the Trademark database.

Figure 12.5. Examples of conditions of counterfeit pharmaceuticals manufacturing and production

Source: Instituto Nacional de Medicamentos – ANMAT, 2006.

Figure 12.6. Examples of equipment/technology employed

Source: Name withheld.

Source: Instituto Nacional de Medicamentos – ANMAT 2006.

Counterfeiters are able to mass produce tablets and blister packs in significant quantities through the acquisition and use of equipment for pressing tablets, often rudimentary and not prohibitively expensive, and through the use of abundant cheap labour.

While the pictures above represent the production of counterfeit pharmaceuticals in developing countries, as the following pictures illustrate, the conditions are not greatly improved when production occurs in developed countries. Below are pictures of labs producing counterfeit pharmaceutical products in the United Kingdom that were discovered through investigation and subsequently dismantled (MHRA, 2005). Such counterfeiting activities obviously operate outside the strict regulatory framework governing pharmaceuticals (including their manufacture, labelling, safety and efficacy as well as distribution).

Figure 12.7. Counterfeit operation in the UK

Source: MHRA, 2005.

12.5.2. Distribution/supply chain

The business of counterfeit pharmaceuticals is fluid and fast moving. While there are numerous approaches, in general, brokers or "middlemen" attempt to connect buyers and sellers through a series of "comfort transactions", in which both parties attempt to develop a level of mutual trust. A generalised view of the legitimate and illegitimate distribution channels is presented in the following graphics. The illustrations show how counterfeit products may enter the legitimate distribution channels from sources in the illegitimate channel. Note that diversion and tampering can occur at any point, but the main entry points appear to be at distribution and at retail levels.

Figure 12.8. Possible flows of counterfeits to the legitimate distribution channel

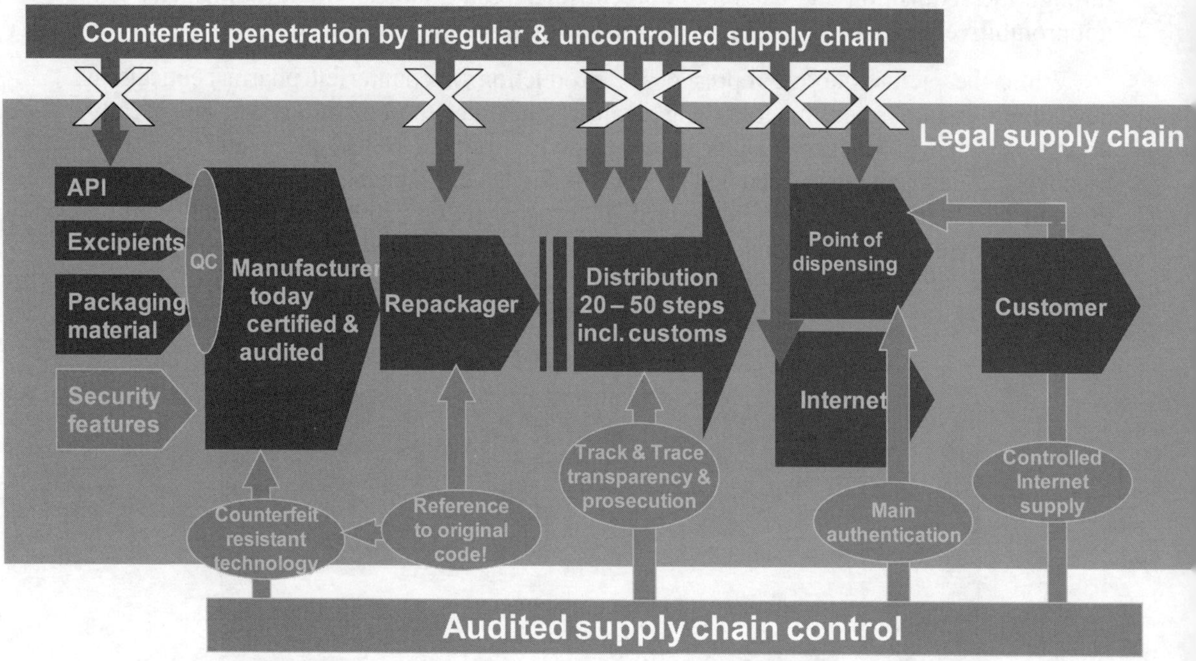

Source: EFPIA 2005.

The distribution of pharmaceutical products throughout the world is complex and varies significantly from jurisdiction to jurisdiction. Many pharmaceutical counterfeiters operate on a multi-jurisdictional basis. For example, investigations have revealed that producers of active pharmaceutical ingredients in China and India distribute in Korea, Chinese Taipei, or surrounding countries for finishing and packaging (Confidential). Counterfeit products are distributed through multiple distribution channels – mainly paths of least resistance, limited law enforcement, and free trade zones. Many producers flourish in developing countries and their products are not necessarily intended for local consumption. Often the products are produced for retail pharmacies and distributors and Internet-based customers throughout the world. For example, investigations have revealed that locations in the Middle East have been identified as distribution points for counterfeit products sourced from Asia and destined for Europe (Confidential). Investigations also revealed that a free trade zone within Central America had been identified as serving as a distribution point for products destined for North America. Figure 12.9 provides examples of flows of counterfeit products. It should be noted that this provides a snapshot fixed in time, as the movement of counterfeit pharmaceuticals is constantly changing and adapts to modifications in legislation, regulation, and policies; enforcement activities; disruption; demand; new illicit gateways; etc. (Confidential).

Figure 12.9. Example of some flows of manufacture and distribution of counterfeit products

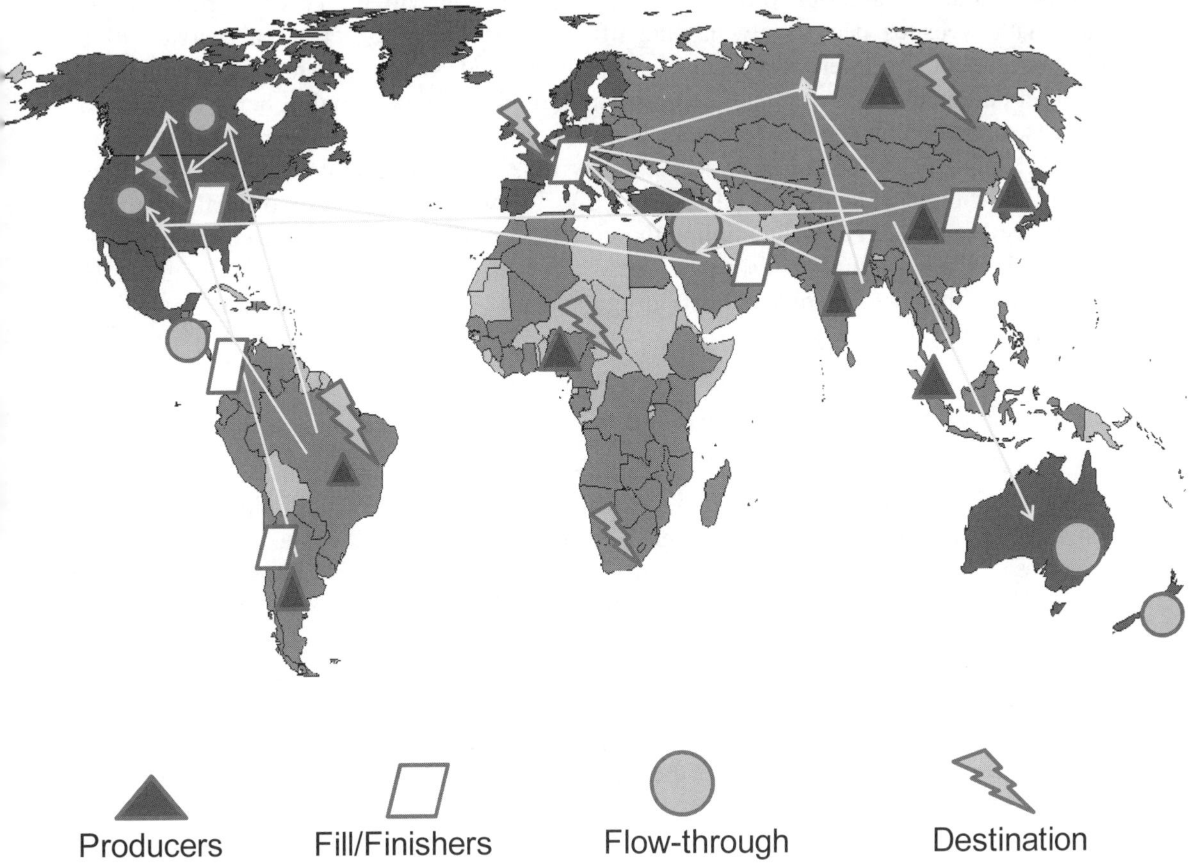

Producers   Fill/Finishers   Flow-through   Destination

Source: Name withheld.

12.5.3. Internet

The popularity of the Internet, coupled with efficient search engines, has beneficially enabled patients and consumers to seek information on health topics. Conversely, the Internet has also led to the availability of medicines from websites, and encouraged the phenomenon of consumers to self-medicate, including without the guidance of physicians or pharmacists. The willingness of patients to buy medicines through the Internet has been quickly recognised by criminals as a profitable way to supply counterfeit medicines to unsuspecting customers. Of the three types of Internet pharmacies (*i.e.* prescription, resident medical professional and non-prescription) the last category will be examined so as to highlight the concerns that arise with many Internet pharmacies. Non-prescription Internet pharmacies dispense pharmaceutical products without any prescription and without any medical professional consultation (GlobalOptions, 2003). While it would be extremely difficult to ascertain with any degree of certitude the exact number of Internet pharmacies existing, it appears that the majority of online pharmacies fall within this last category. This type of online pharmacy raises the most concern with respect to counterfeit drugs. Generally, there is no professional diagnosis, prescription or monitoring, nor is there any control of safety, efficacy or quality of the products dispensed since this type of Internet pharmacy is not subject to any legislation or regulation.

While some of these Internet pharmacies may be dispensing authentic pharmaceutical products, this type of online pharmacy may also be established by unscrupulous counterfeiters who sell counterfeit products to the unsuspecting patient. This is especially the case with websites deceptively passing off counterfeits as a 'generised' version of a pharmaceutical. As Internet websites are easily created, counterfeiters may establish an Internet pharmacy, exploit it and then dismantle it when the potential of being discovered increases. Thus, this type of Internet pharmacy presents a readily available distribution channel and may be located anywhere in the world, irrespective of its advertised location, and often without a fixed location. In April 2005, in the "Bansal" case, officials from the United States through co-ordination with numerous countries, arrested the key individuals involved in an international Internet network that illegally sold "vast quantities of controlled substance pharmaceuticals drugs and non-controlled prescription drugs" via the Internet (DOJ, 2005c).

12.5.4. Corruption, organised crime and terrorist activities

The criminals responsible for the manufacture and distribution of counterfeit drugs range from individuals, including medical professionals such as pharmacists and physicians, to criminal groups, organised crime syndicates, rogue pharmaceutical companies, corrupt local and national officials and terrorist organisations (DEA, 2006). For example, within the Russian Federation, criminal organisations have been indentified as manufacturing and distributing counterfeit pharmaceuticals in some cases in collusion with local officials (Confidential). A survey of pharmaceutical manufacturers conducted by AIPM-CIPR in 2002, cited corruption of government authorities, political influence and lack of political will as three of the top five obstacles to anti-counterfeiting efforts. While actions have been taken, the situation has not been completely redressed (Confidential).

While the primary objective of counterfeiting activities is financial gain, in some cases, secondary objectives can include funding of political aims, such as terrorist activities. For example, the link between terrorist activities and counterfeiting was again brought to light recently in March 2006 in an indictment issued by the United States government against 19 individuals on charges of operating a global racketeering conspiracy. Profits made from illegal enterprise, including through the counterfeiting of pharmaceuticals, were reported to have been provided to an organisation listed by the US government as a foreign terrorist organisation (US Newswire, 2006).

12.6. Effects of counterfeiting and piracy of pharmaceuticals

12.6.1. Patients/consumers

The most significant implications of counterfeit pharmaceuticals for patients are the health hazards from direct use and the loss of confidence in the health system, especially in regard to counterfeit pharmaceutical products resulting from brand theft and patent violations (OECD Survey, 2005). Pharmaceutical counterfeiting has been described as the "perfect crime" since if the patient's condition improves, there is no investigation, and if the patient's condition deteriorates, it will be attributed principally to the medical condition or disease. The loss of faith in genuine pharmaceuticals will occur in areas where drug quality is perceived as being poor and results in a loss of confidence in the health-care system and the drug regulatory authorities (Newton, 2006). This will be the case especially if drug regulatory authorities are viewed as not taking adequate action.

In developing countries, the failure of counterfeit drugs to produce the desired therapeutic effect can undermine the confidence of the public in the effectiveness of western-style medicines and can result in patients turning to traditional local herbal remedies and faith healers. Not only does the patient not get well, but in the case of the use of antibiotics, the use of sub-therapeutic doses may contribute to the development of resistant strains of bacteria (Newton, 2006). There is concern that drug-resistance may increase as a result of counterfeit pharmaceuticals. In addition, the failure of pharmaceutical products due to their counterfeit nature may result in a loss of confidence in healthcare professionals (OECD Survey, 2005). On the economic side, the purchase of counterfeit medicines not only wastes the financial resources of the patient, but when the patient does not get better, may also necessitate treatment for adverse reactions (OECD Survey, 2005).

From a clinical perspective, the negative consequences of taking counterfeit drugs are many and range from inconvenience to death. In the case of therapies for non-life-threatening conditions, the effect on health may be modest and perhaps limited to the absence of a clinical effect. Numerous cases of counterfeited "lifestyle" drugs used to treat erectile dysfunction, for example, have been reported with no API, resulting when taken, in unsatisfied customers. Unfortunately, in most cases the effect on patients is not systematically recorded. Records of the actual clinical effects of counterfeit drugs are most often kept only in cases involving successful prosecutions or multiple deaths, and thus present an incomplete picture. For example, it was reported that over 2 500 deaths occurred in Niger in the period 1995 to 1996 in a meningitis outbreak when over 50 000 people were inoculated with counterfeit meningitis vaccine that contained only water (WHO, 2006a). Deaths from counterfeit medicine can also occur due to the presence of toxic ingredients. There have been a number of tragic occurrences involving the ingestion of diethylene glycol, an anti-freeze agent, either as a contaminant in glycerin or as a deliberate replacement for propylene glycol. The literature points to over 350 reported deaths attributed to diethylene glycol during the 1990's in four jurisdictions (Bangladesh, Haiti, India and Nigeria). More recently, in October 2006, in Panama, at least 30 deaths were attributed to the use of four medicines contaminated with diethylene glycol (DRN, 2006).

Serious side effects can also occur when a drug has been substituted for the active ingredient stated on the label. In 2002, bottles of the antiretroviral drug "Ziagen" were relabelled as the antiretroviral drug "Combivir" in the USA (GlaxoSmithKline, 2002). While both drugs treat the same disease, approximately 5% of the patients who take "Ziagen" develop a potentially life-threatening hypersensitivity adverse reaction. If a hypersensitivity reaction occurs, patients are counselled never to take "Ziagen" again, since another dose can rapidly produce more severe symptoms that may include life-threatening hypotension and death. Since neither the prescribing physician nor the patient would know that "Ziagen" was present in the counterfeit "Combivir", the full implication of a mild hypersensitivity reaction could be missed, and the dosing could continue with severe medical consequences.

The emergence of avian influenza and the concern of its spread to humans demonstrate one of the difficulties in fighting counterfeit drugs and the possible implications for human health. There have been several cases of counterfeit "Tamiflu" in the USA, a drug which would be used in the event of a pandemic outbreak of influenza. The US Customs and Border Protection seized 51 shipments of counterfeit "Tamiflu" in south San Francisco in late 2005 and 250 parcels in New York in January 2006 (US Customs 2005, 2006). These incidents also illustrate the opportunistic nature of this criminal activity.

The acquisition of pharmaceuticals over the Internet may appear attractive to patients. From the advertisement on the website, patients may assume that they are purchasing the authentic product rather than one from an unknown jurisdiction with either no active ingredient, inappropriate levels, wrong active ingredients, toxic active ingredients, expired producfs with a false new expiration date, unapproved pharmaceutical products, products that have been improperly stored or transported, products that were not manufactured according to GMP, products without or with inappropriate packaging or labelling in terms of providing the patient with advice on drug usage, counter-indications, safety concerns, and potential side effects, etc. All of these factors increase the health risk for the patient. Investigations have shown that it is possible to order and receive very dangerous medicines without a prescription.[193] Studies have shown that patients purchasing pharmaceuticals over the Internet are more likely to be the subject of deceptive practices. For example, an August 2005 study showed that 85% of Internet drugs purported to come from one jurisdiction actually came from 27 other countries, including India, Costa Rica and Vanuatu (FDA, 2005).[194]

12.6.2. Private sector

For the private sector, ensuring continued confidence of patients in their products, and in the healthcare system in general imposes the primary burden. For pharmaceutical manufacturers, this involves activities to secure the supply chain, investigate and detect counterfeiting activities, and prosecute counterfeiters. In many cases, the manufacturer has put in place a product security or anti-counterfeiting strategy, which involves the allocation of resources (OECD Survey, 2005). Pharmaceutical manufacturers put in place anti-counterfeiting technologies to safeguard their products, which may involve considerable investment. For example, the cost of anti-counterfeiting measures for one product in one jurisdiction has been estimated at 10%-20% of total sales per annum (OECD Survey, 2005). Moreover, pharmaceutical manufacturers must continuously update the technologies employed in order to outwit counterfeiters, who are able to copy or crack these technologies.

As reliance on technology alone is not sufficient, many large pharmaceutical manufacturers also have staff that, in collaboration with governmental authorities and police forces, carry out investigation and detection of counterfeiting activities. The operation of such investigative activities is an additional cost. While frequently the information about counterfeiting activities is shared with authorities for the prosecution of counterfeiters,

---

193. Schedule II and III Controlled Substances, such as the prescription painkillers "OxyContin" (oxycodone), "Percocet" (oxycodone + acetaminophen) and hydrocodone were ordered and received over the Internet without a prescription (U.S. General Accounting Office, 2004*a*, *b*).

194. See FDA News (2005), "FDA Operation Reveals Many Drugs Promoted as "Canadian" Products Really Originate from Other Countries", P05-102, 16 December 2005, www.fda.gov/bbs/topics/NEWS/2005/NEW01277.html

there are also instances in which the counterfeiter is pursued by the intellectual property rights holder. Intellectual property litigation is often a costly endeavour. Alternatively, some actions are best or only accessible to the rights holder. For example, the use of the Uniform Domain Name Dispute Resolution Policy (UDRP) is open to the rights holder against the alleged third-party registrant. A number of pharmaceutical manufacturers have employed this mechanism to close down unauthorised websites. However, where the domain name does not contain the rights holder's trademark, an UDRP action is not available.

From an intellectual property rights perspective, the potential damage to the value of the IP right, whether trademark, copyright or patent, is a direct consequence. The potential for brand dilution is especially high for famous or well known brands (Shaw, 2005). Companies are trying to ensure the protection of their valuable trademarks and IPRs around the world (OECD Survey, 2005). However, to date, there are no available statistics that counterfeiting activities are directly impacting the value of individual IPRs in the pharmaceutical sector. A corollary is the potential effect on sales of the genuine products, whether prescription or non-prescription. To some extent, sales will be impacted by the non-purchase of the genuine product as patients purchase the counterfeited product. For example, in El Salvador, the INQUIFAR (El Salvador's Association of Pharmaceutical Companies) estimates industry losses of around USD 40 million per year due to counterfeits (Encarna, 2005). Sales may also be affected by a loss of confidence if the quality, safety and efficacy of a product should it be the subject of widespread counterfeiting, and especially if it may be substituted by another product. Furthermore, sales may also be lost due to recalls of counterfeit products (Shaw, 2005).

Another corollary is the potential liability of manufacturers and others in the supply chain. The *Fagan* v. *AmerisourceBergen Corp.* case, one of the few cases brought by a victim of a counterfeit pharmaceutical product, illustrates this point (Beckett, 2005).[195] The suit was brought against the manufacturer, the wholesaler and the retailers. In a preliminary judgement, the wholesale distributor and retailer failed to have a claim against them struck out, as it was held that they were in the best position to control movement of drugs and failed to exercise the highest practicable degree of prudence and vigilance. The claim against the manufacturer failed, as it was held that the manufacturer had no duty to anticipate and prevent criminal conduct by third parties, or to design a product in such a way as to anticipate and frustrate criminal tampering. Such negligence claims against the manufacturer were reinstated on appeal, and the case was settled soon thereafter.

The counterfeiting of pharmaceuticals has spurred on the development of the anti-counterfeiting technologies industry. Previously costly technologies, such as RFID (Radio Frequency Identification Tagging), are being refined for use with pharmaceutical products. Some analysts have estimated that if RFID adoption expands to pharmaceuticals, the industry could expand considerably in the next decade (Business Insights, 2005*b*). Moreover, preventing counterfeiting activities may spur the development of new technologies.

---

95. *Fagan* v. *AmerisourceBergen Corp.*, 356 F. Supp.2d 198, 209 (E.D.N.Y. 2004).
   Fagan v. *AmerisourceBergen Corp. and others*, discussed in N. Beckett, "Just Say No", *Fighting IP Theft*, May 2005.

12.6.3. Governments

For governments, the impact of counterfeit and pirated pharmaceutical products is an extension of the impact on patients and businesses. Where a public health authority uses government and taxpayers funds to purchase pharmaceuticals that turn out to be counterfeit, this results in a waste of financial resources, an increase in healthcare costs and the potential lack of available genuine pharmaceutical product. For example, this used to be the situation in Nigeria, where limited availability led to the purchasing of counterfeit pharmaceuticals (NAFDAC, 2006). Patients not benefiting from the therapeutic value of the genuine pharmaceutical or having adverse reactions to the counterfeit pharmaceutical may require hospitalisation, or longer hospitalisation, both resulting in increased costs for healthcare systems. In the *Fagan* case mentioned above, the patient who brought the suit required considerable additional medical attention as a result of the use of counterfeit pharmaceuticals. In addition, patients not benefiting from the therapeutic value of the genuine pharmaceutical may take longer to return to being productive members of society, which in turn has implications for themselves, their families and their employer.

Governments must also expend limited resources for law enforcement activities in order to investigate and halt counterfeiting activities. For example, the Zhejiang province, China, established a nationwide reporting and complaint hotline and a reporting centre for intellectual property violations (Li, 2006). As well, increasing reports of investigations being carried out by authorities reflect the re-orientation of resources to fight counterfeiting activities. As pharmaceuticals are more complex and sophisticated products, combating counterfeiting in this sector requires specially trained personnel, such as pharmacists, or individuals with medical/scientific training, etc. Combating counterfeiting also requires additional customs and border actions, which increase costs for the public purse. As counterfeiting activities increase, this implies even greater resources will need to be deployed. While counterfeiters take from the public purse directly when their products are purchased with public funds, they also most likely rob governments of tax receipts.

12.7. Measures to combat counterfeiting

Counterfeiting of pharmaceuticals is a global problem that has implications for patients and consumers, governments, companies and international organisations. In order to properly address this problem, the collaboration and involvement of all these parties is required. Moreover, it is a multi-factorial and multi-dimensional problem that requires simultaneously co-ordinated actions from all these parties. Some of the categories in which action needs to be taken in order to redress the problem of counterfeit and pirated pharmaceuticals include: the use of technology; the use of legislative and regulatory mechanisms; the strengthening of enforcement mechanisms, including through the availability of appropriate resources and international collaboration; education of, and communication with, the public; and through more stringent practices/control within the supply/distribution chain. Each of these actions may involve one or more actors working in the manufacture, distribution, sale and regulation of pharmaceutical products.

12.7.1. Technology

One component for combating counterfeiting is the use of technological applications.[196] However, reliance only on technological solutions will not redress the problem of counterfeit pharmaceuticals. Moreover, the use of more than one technological solution is often required. Experience has demonstrated that even when more than one technological solution has been employed, counterfeiters are able to produce counterfeited and pirated products. The feasibility of use of a particular technology across different jurisdictions will vary in light of existing conditions and resources. Moreover, the availability of particular technological solutions will be heavily influenced by the level of economic development in a particular jurisdiction. For example, the application of RFID technologies in developing countries in Africa or Southeast Asia, where significant counterfeiting activity is occurring, may not be feasible for cost and technological reasons (Brand News, 2006). In these jurisdictions, governments, international organisations and industry are considering which type of technology would be most effective.

Currently, a multitude of technologies are applied to pharmaceutical products in order to thwart counterfeiting activities. A survey of 179 industry executives found that currently the most commonly employed security measures are, in descending order, bar codes, blister packaging and colour printing (Business Insights, 2005). While unit-of-use, such as blister packs and tamper-proof packaging, are the commonly used preventative technologies to deter counterfeiting, these are being reproduced by counterfeiters in jurisdictions where labour is abundant and inexpensive.

Overt technologies (*i.e.* visible to the eye), covert technologies (*i.e.* not visible and requiring equipment for authentication) and forensic technologies are increasingly being employed as anti-counterfeiting measures. Nevertheless, highly complex holograms have been copied by counterfeiters with such detail that it was impossible to detect the counterfeit with the naked eye (Newton, 2006). So as counterfeiters become adept at reproducing technologies, manufacturers need to continuously modify and increase investment in the technologies they employ. For example, an international pharmaceutical manufacturer is carrying out trials of employing forensic technologies (*i.e.* DNA security labels) in Latin America (Brand News, 2006). If the trials are successful, the company intends to use the item-level DNA labels to replace the currently employed holograms as its anti-counterfeiting measure. Two components, one in the label and the other in the reader, produce a colour change if a product is genuine. However, the upgrading and continuous modification of technologies also raises its own challenges, including, for example, increased costs, and ensuring that the supply/ distribution chain is aware of the nature and timing of the changes.

Many consider track-and-trace technologies as forming an important component for combating counterfeiting. While there are a number of track-and-trace technologies, each with different characteristics and advantages, only two examples are discussed herein: 2-D Bar Codes and Radio Frequency Identification tagging (RFID). The adoption of any given technology is a complex question involving issues, amongst others, of cost, compatibility, feasibility and reliability, and there are divergent views on which technologies should be adopted and the timing for their adoption.[197]

---

96.   The in-depth technical examination of each of the technologies referenced is beyond the scope of this chapter.

97.   It is beyond the scope of this report to recommend the use or adoption of any given technology.

2-D (*i.e.* data-matrix) barcodes are a more sophisticated version of the black-and-white barcode, in that they may permit storage of increased information along the height and length of the symbol and can be used in very small applications. Employed in the distribution of pharmaceuticals, the use of 2-D barcodes would permit the storage of significantly more information, such as lot number, expiration date, reimbursement information and other data. It is being advocated as an anti-counterfeiting measure for use within the European Union, in light of the complex supply chain (EFPIA, 2006). It is advocated that the use of a unique, randomised (*i.e.* not sequential) serialised number for each secondary packaging unit distributed and sold across Europe will enable identification and verification across the entire supply chain, thereby improving transparency, patient safety and combating counterfeiting (EFPIA, 2006). In a repackaging scenario where the product and barcode would be separated, the 2-D barcode would no longer fulfil its purpose. The use of 2-D barcodes is viewed as complementing the eventual use of RFID tags (EFPIA, 2006).

Although the use of RFID (Radio Frequency Identification Tagging) technology continues to be viewed as expensive, it is beginning to be explored within the pharmaceutical sector (Brand News, 2006). Given the relative newness of using RFID technology for pharmaceuticals, in 2004, a pilot programme called the "Jump-Start Initiative" was carried out in the United States by a network of 14 companies – pharmaceutical manufacturers, wholesalers and retailers in collaboration with the US FDA; bottles and cases of selected drugs were tagged and then traced throughout their supply chain journey. The trials permitted product pedigree information to be accessed in real-time via a web portal. Through recall or diversion simulations, unknown or missing products (as well as those whose expiration date was soon to be reached) were singled out and dealt with, and recalls were facilitated, as the location of the product was known. The pilot project was deemed a success. The US FDA continues to advocate a phased-in approach to the adoption of RFID technology by the pharmaceutical sector starting with products most vulnerable to counterfeiting and diversion. The US FDA also recognises that there remain numerous outstanding issues with RFID which will need to be addressed (US FDA, 2006c).

Some pharmaceutical manufacturers are considering, or have begun to incorporate, the use of RFID into the packaging of their products (Business Insights). For example, by December 2005, Pfizer ensured that every package, case and pallet of "Viagra" (sildenafil citrate) shipped in the United States contained RFID tags (Pfizer, 2006). To date, Pfizer's application is not yet capable of "tracking and tracing" pharmaceutical products through the entire distribution system, because complete track-and-trace requires that all actors within the supply chain invest in the compatible technology and agree to capture and share information about product movement (Pfizer, 2006).

Figure 12.10. Sample of the Viagra label highlighting the security features

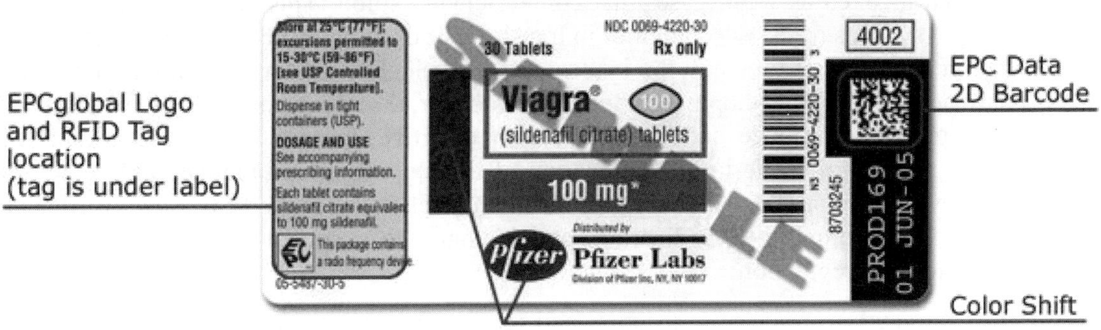

Source: Pfizer, 2006.

RFID technology for use on pharmaceuticals is still under development as there remain a number of outstanding issues (Confidential). There are issues pertaining to costs as the unit price for a RFID tag is considered still relatively high, and tracing equipment for downstream segments is also capital intensive. The cost issue continues to be a barrier for complete rollout for all pharmaceutical products, even within developed countries. This is an even greater concern for pharmaceutical products supplied to developing countries, where marginal differences in prices are significant. Concerns pertaining to equipment persist. For example, tags and readers continue to fail. Concerns also pertain to data standards. The establishment of standards could also play an important role in lowering costs. However, depending on the nature of the standard, it could also increase costs and complexity. Concerns also exist about the effect of RFID on the product quality/integrity. While these concerns may not arise for most products, they centre on the interaction between the RFID tag and different types of pharmaceutical products or their packaging, such as biologics, liquids and foils. Issues pertaining to the maturity of the technology in terms of its readability and reliability persist. Challenges pertaining to the access, ownership and sharing of information throughout the supply chain continue. The rate and speed of adoption of a RFID system across the supply chain is another issue. Privacy concerns have been expressed as certain versions of the tags have the ability to collect patient information, and it is unclear where and how such data would be captured and maintained. Finally, as noted above for the 2-D barcodes, in a repackaging scenario where the product and tag would be separated, the tag would no longer fulfil its purpose.

12.7.2. Legislative and regulatory mechanisms

The combating of counterfeiting relies on a combination of a multitude of legislation and regulations covering a broad spectrum of areas, including: intellectual property (trademark, patent, copyright, industrial design rights); regulatory approval (*e.g.* drug administration, quality control, pharmaceutical distribution, importation, manufacturing, marketing, patient information, licensing practices); enforcement; custom and borders; consumer protection; and criminal and penal activities (*e.g.* contraband activities, racketeering, endangering life). While pharmaceutical counterfeiting is first and foremost a public safety concern that involves countries' health and safety legislation, intellectual property and criminal law are also important.

The lack of adequate legislation, regulation and especially enforcement and penalties, are often invoked as weaknesses that counterfeiters exploit. This is especially noted for the legal systems of many economies in transition or developing economies. For example, Nigeria is working to remedy the inadequacy of its legislation for combating counterfeit pharmaceuticals by developing guidelines. Moreover, the myriad of applicable legislation and regulations produce another obstacle to effective and efficient prosecution. The challenges also often lie in the application of the legislation and regulations. This brief overview will highlight the challenges from an intellectual property perspective. It is a difficult and complex determination, and beyond the scope of this report, to assess legislation and regulation.

A survey covering the legislation and regulations of a number of countries reveals that many jurisdictions, including ones often viewed as major sources of counterfeit pharmaceuticals, have in place a system of legislation and regulation that provides recourse against counterfeiting activities (PhRMA, 2006). For example, Brazil, China, India and Russia, all have enacted trademark laws that provide for both civil and criminal remedies. In these cases, both fines and terms of imprisonment are options available to the deciding authorities. Often, there are even graduated levels of fines and terms of imprisonment. Similarly, legislation covering the active pharmaceutical ingredient, the finished product and the packaging are in place. However, very few jurisdictions have enacted laws that specifically address pharmaceutical counterfeiting, *per se*, or the full range of upstream and downstream activities that contribute to the manufacture and supply of counterfeit medicines.

While the remedies may be available, one challenge is the non-application or the inefficiency of these remedies and measures (PhRMA, 2006). For example, in China there is a reluctance to invoke criminal remedies against trademark counterfeiters, which is exacerbated by high quantitative and monetary thresholds that in many cases preclude criminal enforcement against commercial counterfeiters (PhRMA, 2006). While provisional measures are available on an *ex-parte* basis pursuant to the PRC trademark law, and while courts are required to decide an application within a 48-hour period, often the timeframe varies between two weeks and one month before a decision is rendered. In Russia, civil actions are virtually not employed due to the difficulty of obtaining provisional measures, which courts are reluctant to grant. Parties must rely on the use of the criminal or administrative actions available for trademark infringement. In Brazil, law enforcement authorities lack *ex officio* powers to investigate trademark counterfeiting offences (PhRMA, 2006).

Another problem is judicial and administrative systems and their agents that are overwhelmed (PhRMA, 2006). In India, for example, due to the sheer volume of litigation, judicial delays are common. In India, as a result of the complex structure of the local police and metropolitan magistrates, inadequacy of police resources and inexperience of prosecutors, particularly in the specialised field of pharmaceuticals, there is a low conviction rate (*i.e.* about 2%). However, in some metropolitan cities, IPR Cells that have jurisdiction to investigate and prosecute trademark counterfeiters across the entire city are being established.

There are numerous legislative and regulatory lacunae. For example, the Russian trademark law does not expressly provide for injunctive relief or provisional measures. While these are available pursuant to the Russian Civil Code, they are practised in a limited manner. Similarly, in India and in Brazil, administrative remedies are not available for trademark infringements, except with respect to border enforcement. In Brazil, civil actions are more favoured against trademark counterfeiters, given that rights holders must bear the significant burden of prosecuting criminal actions. Good manu-facturing practices (GMP) and good distribution practices (GDP), for example, are not in place in many jurisdictions. Legislation regulating Internet pharmacies is lacking in most jurisdictions. For example, Brazil, India, Russia and many OECD countries do not have legislation or regulation targeting the sale and distribution of pharmaceuticals through the Internet.

However, within some jurisdictions, measures specific to counterfeiting of pharma-ceuticals are being undertaken. For example, the European Commission has developed a draft Directive that would provide for criminal measures for the violation of IPRs. The International Pharmaceutical Federation has developed Good Pharmacy Practice (GPP) guidelines with a view to providing assistance to pharmacists and others in developing countries (FIP, 1998).

12.7.3. Education and communication with the public/patients

Education and communication with patients and the public with respect to counterfeit pharmaceuticals raise a number of challenges. Public education and communication about counterfeit and pirated drugs must involve all stakeholders. The information must be accurate, delivered in a manner that is accessible to the average non-expert individual and provided by a trusted entity. In case of an incident, the information must be timely, but neither cause fear nor prompt patients to discontinue using their prescription pharma-ceuticals. In terms of general education of the public about the dangers of purchasing and using unapproved pharmaceuticals or obtained from unapproved sources, the information must be communicated in a balanced manner, by trusted professionals, so as to not cause alarm and distrust in the health system. In order to be the most effective, this type of communication will also need to take into account cultural differences.

At the international level, the International Council of Nurses has published informa-tion and an action toolkit entitled "Counterfeits Kill" (ICN). This publication has the dual purpose of educating nurses and national associations of nurses, as well as the general public, about the nature of counterfeit pharmaceuticals, and providing them with the tools required for better detection of counterfeits. For example, it contains a "Tool for the Visual Inspection of Medicines". This document has been used by nurses to carry out education campaigns, in collaboration with industry and public health authorities.

At the government level, numerous public education and information campaigns have been undertaken both in developing and developed jurisdictions. In order to be most effective, such initiatives need to be tailored to the circumstances existing within a given jurisdiction, to the needs of the population and to the culture of that jurisdiction. For example, Nigeria's national medicines regulatory agency has undertaken a "Public Enlightenment Campaign" that involves dialogue, education and persuasion of the public in order to achieve behavioural change, so that the use of counterfeit pharmaceuticals from open-air markets is halted (NAFDAC, 2006).[198] Many pharmaceutical regulatory

---

98.   Discussions with authorities.

agencies provide information for both patients/the public and for pharmacists. A number of governments, including the German Ministry of Health, the UK Medicines and Healthcare Products Regulatory Agency (MHRA) and the US Food and Drug Administration, provide information on their respective websites for the public about counterfeit pharmaceuticals, as well as information about the purchase of pharmaceuticals over the Internet. Recently, MHRA and the Royal Pharmaceutical Society of Great Britain issued "Guidance for Pharmacists" and a "Guidance for Patients", in order to assist both of these groups in detecting and reporting incidents of counterfeit and pirated pharmaceuticals (MHRA, 2006*a, b*).

12.7.4. Enforcement

There are a number of challenges faced by authorities in enforcement activities against counterfeit pharmaceuticals. As examined above, the multitude of complex legislation that is applicable and administered by different entities within any government is an enormous challenge when aiming to combat counterfeiting activities. Thus, the first challenge for most governments, whether developed or developing, is to ensure proper co-ordination and communication between the various entities involved in enforcement activities. Another significant challenge is that not all jurisdictions have put in place agencies for monitoring, tracking and combating counterfeiting activities in a co-ordinated manner, both nationally and internationally. For example, the Argentinean "Division Fraude Marcario" (*i.e.* Fraudulent Marks Division) was created at the beginning of 2006. The Italian government is intending to establish a Task Force in order to monitor and evaluate the phenomenon of counterfeited pharmaceuticals, to co-ordinate activities of diverse entities and to establish countermeasures.[199]

International efforts at co-ordination include work by the World Custom Organization, Interpol, the establishment of the Pharmaceutical Security Institute and the World Health Organization's IMPACT. The limited or lack of resources, whether human or financial, for enforcement activities is another key obstacle to redressing the problem. Of 841 arrests reported in 2005, 230 were made at points of distribution[200] and 214 at the point of sale (PSI, 2006). Such data provide some guidance to enforcement authorities for allocating their limited resources in the most effective manner. Enforcement also involves the collaboration between private sector investigations and law enforcement authorities.

Policing of Internet pharmacies is a complicated activity, and generally involves co-operation of national and international law enforcement agencies and the private sector. For example, the US FDA has undertaken measures to identify and shut down fraudulent and illegal Internet pharmacies. Its approach is to carry out criminal investigations, that can involve arrests, and to issue warning letters to both domestic and foreign pharmacies. In 2005, the US Drug Enforcement Agency concluded an investigation that dismantled a large online counterfeit prescription drug ring. This operation shut down 200 illegal Internet pharmacies. Similarly, states and state medical boards are also aiming to shut down illicit Internet pharmacies. For example, in 2002, New York prosecutors charged individuals and companies for making and selling counterfeit "Viagra". The investigation uncovered a distribution ring that stretched from fake pill mills in China and India to Internet sellers in Nevada and Colorado (GlobalOptions, 2003). Pharmacy boards as well

---

199. Discussions with authorities.

200. Distributors report that wholesalers and individuals were arrested at warehouses where counterfeit goods were being stored.

as medical professional associations have also begun to take disciplinary actions against Internet pharmacies. In Canada, where the dispensing of pharmaceutical products is regulated by provincial Colleges of Pharmacists, the policy of the Ontario College prohibits Canadian Internet pharmacists from entering into agreements for the purpose of co-signing or re-writing prescriptions for out-of-country residents. In 2002, the Ontario College of Pharmacists filed charges against an Internet pharmacy for unlawfully operating an unlicensed pharmacy (GlobalOptions, 2003).

In order to address the issue of counterfeit sales of medicines over the Internet, some countries have established, or are considering establishing, mechanisms for ensuring safe and efficacious Internet pharmacies. The National Association of Boards of Pharmacy (NABP), which represents the state boards of pharmacy within the USA, eight Canadian Provinces, two Australian States, New Zealand and South Africa, developed the Verified Internet Pharmacy Practice Sites (VIPPS) programme in 1999. This voluntary programme certifies pharmacies that comply with the licensing and inspection criteria of their state and each state to which they dispense drugs, according to the NABP criteria. The VIPPS programme provides a way for patients to verify the authenticity of Internet sites selling drugs but has a limited number of registered sites (12 sites in May 2006), which may not be known to the public. In 2006, the Royal Pharmaceutical Society of Great Britain prepared a Guideline that gave comprehensive advice to pharmacists who provide Internet pharmacy services.

The private sector also carries out investigations and undertakes legal actions against fraudulent and illicit Internet websites. Often an entity will register numerous domain names bearing similar or misleading information to attract patients. Companies use the Uniform Domain-Name[201] Dispute Resolution Policy (UDRP) process of the ICANN [202] in order to deal with unauthorised websites that use trademark protected terms, such as "Viagra" (OECD Survey, 2005). This administrative process provides efficient, relatively inexpensive, as compared to litigation costs, and fast resolution to the abusive use of a domain name. Nevertheless, its effectiveness is limited since it applies only to top-level domain names incorporating trademarks and does not prevent the registration of additional domain names. e-Bay, the Internet trader, has in place a programme called VeRO ("Verified Rights Owner"), through which it implements its "notice and take down" policy (e-Bay, 2006). In addition, e-Bay permits pharmaceutical sales by e-pharmacies only if these are licensed.

---

201. The Domain Name System (DNS) helps users find their way around the Internet. Every computer on the Internet has a unique address called its "IP address" (Internet Protocol address). Because IP addresses (which are strings of numbers) are hard to remember, the DNS allows a familiar string of letters (the "domain name") to be used instead. Rather than typing "192.0.34.163," one types "www.icann.org".

202. www.icann.org/new.html. WIPO Arbitration and Mediation Centre – Domain names Disputes: http://arbiter.wipo.int/domains/guide/index.html.

12.7.5. Securing the distribution/supply chain

12.7.5.1. Government action

Certain governments are undertaking a number of proactive measures to better secure the distribution/supply chain for pharmaceuticals. Each government is employing a combination of legislative, regulatory and technological approaches. For example, in Europe there are the *Guidelines on Good Distribution Practice Medicinal Products for Human Use* and in the United States, both at the national and at the state level, there is legislation pertaining to the supply chain (*i.e.* the pedigree requirements). In Europe, a number of countries, such as Italy, Belgium and Spain, have put in place, or are putting in place, systems for better tracking products with the objective of securing the supply chain. Although each system is different, the idea is that pharmaceuticals may be tracked from manufacturing through distribution to dispensing. A positive aspect of these systems is that they permit comprehensive tracking of pharmaceuticals throughout the supply chain in the given jurisdiction. However, some have expressed concerns that if each jurisdiction within Europe were to adopt a unique system, this could result in a fragmented market and could involve increased costs for manufacturers (EFPIA, 2006). Concern has been expressed that some of these systems may affect patient privacy.

Figure 12.11. Bollino System

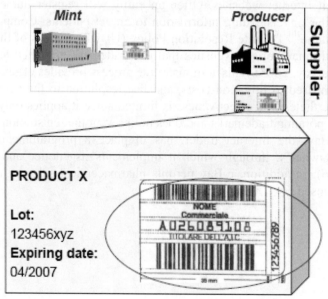

Source: Bergamaschi, 2006.

To illustrate the functioning of these types of systems, the Italian approach will be briefly outlined. In order to combat fraud and counterfeiting, Italy will implement tracking, through the "bollino" ID system, which will collect and store information in a central database. This approach is possible since within Italy, pharmaceuticals are almost all pre-packaged. The national mint (INZP) produces the unique "bollino" labels that are sent to the pharmaceutical producer/supplier. Each pharmaceutical will be affixed a "bollino" displaying: *a)* the AIC code of the drug; *b)* the product's denomination; *c)* the AIC owner; and *d)* the progressive identification of the single package – unique identifier. The "bollino" will enable the tracking of each package from the manufacturer down to the point of dispensing.

12.7.5.2. Private sector action

In light of the complexity of the distribution and supply chain in many jurisdictions and the potential this has for the entry of counterfeit pharmaceuticals, some manufacturers have adopted new approaches to the distribution of their products. For example, in the UK, Pfizer announced that it will no longer distribute through its major wholesalers (Hawkes, 2006). Instead, it decided that it will distribute its products to pharmacies and dispensing doctors with the aid of a single delivery company, UniChem. This will guarantee at least one source of authenticate products to pharmacies and hospitals. It has been indicated that this measure will have no effect on prices (Hawkes, 2006). Similarly, Johnson & Johnson decided that it will sell only to distributors who agree to its contractual terms, which stipulate that they cannot purchase from other distributors and re-distributors. Eli Lilly and Company is taking similar actions to enhance its supply chain through wholesale contracts, monitoring and auditing of the supply chain (Shaw, 2005).

2.8. Conclusion

The counterfeiting of pharmaceuticals is a global concern that has serious implications for patients and consumers, governments, companies and international organisations. Although the establishment of precise figures is extremely difficult, this activity appears to be on the rise. While it is first and foremost a global public health problem, counterfeiting of pharmaceuticals also has significant implications for intellectual property rights. As a global concern, it needs to be addressed on a global scale. Properly addressing this problem requires the collaboration and involvement of all parties. Moreover, it is a multifactorial and multi-dimensional problem that requires simultaneous and co-ordinated actions from all parties.

Some of the categories in which action needs to be taken in order to redress the problem of counterfeit and pirated pharmaceuticals include: the use of legislative and regulatory mechanisms; the use of technology; the strengthening of enforcement mechanisms, including through the availability of appropriate resources and international collaboration; education of, and communication with, the public; and through more stringent practices/control of the supply/distribution chain. Each of these actions may involve one or more actors working in the manufacture, distribution, sale and regulation of pharmaceutical products.

Table 12.5. Propensity drivers to production and consumption of counterfeit pharmaceuticals

PRODUCTION	CHARACTERISTICS
Market characteristics	
Unit profitability	**Profit margins can be very large**
	While the unit cost, and therefore profitability, varies depending on the amount of genuine active ingredient used, on the sophistication of the packaging and labelling, and on the number of products sold, there is still a significant profit margin to incite counterfeiters, even in developing countries where the price of pharmaceuticals is much lower.
Market size	**Larger market in jurisdictions with weak regulations and enforcement**
	There is a much larger market for counterfeits in jurisdictions where regulation and enforcement is weakest, such as many developing countries. There is a much smaller market for counterfeits in jurisdictions with strong regulation, which make penetration more difficult, as is the case for most developed countries. However, no country is immune to counterfeit pharmaceuticals, irrespective of its level of development.
Genuine brand power	**Strong in developed countries; less strong in developing ones**
	In developed countries, the brand of the pharmaceutical will be very strong, especially for blockbuster and prescription "lifestyle" drugs. However, in developing countries, since the most commonly used pharmaceuticals are essential medicines, the brand tends to be less important.
Production, distribution and technology	
Production investments	**Investment required varies with sophistication**
	The level of investment will vary according to how sophisticated the counterfeit is. Investments are required for numerous elements including for purchasing bulk ingredients, to produce the counterfeit, the packaging, the labelling and for access to the distribution system. This is even more significant if there is a trans-border element. However, the investment required to produce a crude counterfeit and distribute it locally can be quite modest.
Technology	**Technology not excessive barrier**
	Technology required to produce counterfeit products, packaging and labels is for the most part rather easily accessible. Copying more advanced technologies is a challenge/obstacle, but for a relatively short period of time.
Logistics	**Logistics are a complicating factor, especially in heavily regulated jurisdictions; Internet facilitates the penetration of counterfeits even in heavily regulated jurisdictions.**
	It is much more difficult to bring a product to a physical market that is heavily regulated, as is the case with developed countries. The penetration of counterfeits in jurisdictions with weak regulation and enforcement is much easier. The Internet facilitates the penetration of counterfeits into markets, whether developed or developing.

Marketing and sales of products	**Quite difficult to penetrate the supply chain in developed jurisdiction; easier to penetrate supply chain in developing countries. Internet provides parallel supply chain, greatly facilitating penetration.**
	It is quite difficult to penetrate the legitimate distribution channels in heavily regulated jurisdictions, such as those of developed countries. Easier to penetrate distribution channels in jurisdictions with weak regulations, such as in developing countries. The Internet creates the opportunity for separate distribution channels not requiring the penetration of a regulated supply chain.
Ability to conceal operation	**Moderately more difficult in developed jurisdiction, easier in developing jurisdictions.**
	The ability to conceal a counterfeit pharmaceutical operation is easier in jurisdictions with weaker regulatory systems, where resources and monitoring activities are lowest. The ability to conceal is more difficult within jurisdictions with strong regulatory frameworks and the resources to investigate.
Ability to deceive	**Deception very necessary**
	The key element for a successful counterfeit pharmaceutical is that it is accepted by the consumer as genuine. Thus, the counterfeit must be sophisticated enough to pass off for the genuine product, packaging and label. The more sophisticated the genuine product, its packaging and labelling, the more costly it may be for the counterfeiter to reproduce.
Institutional characteristics	
Risk of discovery	**Higher risk of discovery in heavily regulated jurisdictions; moderate rate of detection in jurisdictions with weak regulation.**
	In heavily regulated jurisdictions, the risk of detection is higher, especially when there are important resources allocated to the detection of counterfeiting activities. However, in many jurisdictions where the regulatory framework is weaker, and where there are no, or limited, resources for investigating counterfeiting activities, the risks are much lower. The risks are also lower for activities carried out over the Internet.
Legal and regulatory framework	**Extremely complicated framework**
	The legal and regulatory framework for pharmaceuticals is extremely complicated, involving a multitude of diverse fields, including: regulatory approval (*e.g.* drug administration, quality control, pharmaceutical distribution, importation, manufacturing, marketing, patient information, licensing practices); criminal and penal activities (*e.g.* contraband activities, racketeering, endangering life); intellectual property (trademark, patent, copyright, industrial design); customs and border activities; consumer protection, etc. Some jurisdictions have a weak legal and regulatory framework. Often, even when legislation exists, prosecution is difficult for a multitude of reasons.
Enforcement	**High if detected in developed jurisdictions; weaker in developing jurisdictions.**
	Enforcement action will be taken against detected counterfeit activities in developed jurisdictions. Enforcement has been considered to be much weaker in developing jurisdictions.
Penalties	**Penalties deter where imposed**
	The application of penalties to detected counterfeiting acts as a deterrent. However, the challenge is to ensure that appropriate penalties are provided for in the legal and regulatory framework, and that they are applied to the counterfeiters.

CONSUMPTION	CHARACTERISTICS
Product	
Price	**Developed jurisdiction, no price difference; developing jurisdictions and Internet, significantly lower price.**
	Physical distribution network:
	In developed countries, the objective is that the counterfeit pharmaceutical enters the legitimate supply chain, so the end price to the consumer at the pharmacy will be the same. However, the counterfeiter profits by having cheap production costs, and so the profits realised are significant. In developing countries, the lower price of counterfeits, coupled with the lack of knowledge of the difference between the counterfeited and genuine products, increases the propensity to purchase.
	Internet:
	The lower prices advertised on Internet sites increases the propensity to purchase, especially since these products are seen as genuine.
Quality and nature of product	**Critical element – expectation of same therapeutic effect**
	Whether in developed or developing jurisdictions or purchased over the Internet, the expectation is that the medicine will have the therapeutic effects that it is intended to have.
Ability to conceal status	**Not an issue for physical distribution; easy to conceal for Internet purchases.**
	For the physical distribution, there is no issue. For Internet purchases, once products are in hand, the ability to conceal is relatively easy, especially since the product is consumed.
CONSUMER	
Health & safety concerns	**Extremely high**
	The health and safety concerns of consumers in regard to the consumption of counterfeit pharmaceuticals are extremely high. The challenge is that many consumers are not informed of what constitutes a counterfeit and the associated health hazards and are thus unable to detect counterfeits.
Personal income	**Higher prices and/or lower incomes create higher incentives for consumers to seek counterfeits**
	In jurisdictions where medicines are available at accessible prices to the population, there is less incentive for consumers to seek alternative sources of medicines and therefore expose themselves to counterfeit medicines. In jurisdictions where incomes are low and/or the price of medicines is high, there is higher incentive for consumers to seek alternative supplies of pharmaceuticals, thereby increasing their risk of purchasing counterfeit medicines.
Personal values	
Institutional	
Risk of discovery	**Very moderate for Internet purchases**
	A consumer seeks to know of counterfeits in the legitimate supply chain so as to avoid them. The likelihood of detection for the consumer who purchases over the Internet is very small. If the Internet purchase crosses borders, the risk of detection is somewhat higher.
Risk of prosecution	**Very low**
	Low risk of prosecution of consumers.
Penalties	**Varies, but low risk**
	Depending on the legislation, the applicable penalties may be the same as for the counterfeiter. However, there is low risk of prosecution.

Availability and ease of acquisition	**In developed jurisdictions, physical acquisition is quite difficult; physical acquisition in a developing jurisdiction and on the Internet is much easier.**
	Acquisition of counterfeits is quite difficult in heavily regulated jurisdictions. In jurisdictions with weak regulatory frameworks and over the Internet, acquisition is easier.
Socio-economic factors	**Education and awareness play an important role**
	The less educated and the less informed are at greater risk of purchasing and using counterfeits. Irrespective of the level of development, education and awareness play an important role in deterring the purchase and use of counterfeits.

References

Amgen Press Release (2002), "Important Drug Warning: Counterfeiting of Epogen", 8 May 2002.

Beckett, N. (2005), "Just Say No", Fighting IP Theft, May 2005, pp.12-16.

Bergamaschi (2006), "Il sistema dello bollino", February 2006.

Brand News (2006), "Pharmaceutical Company Trials DNA Labels" Vol. 3, 26 January 2006.

Business Insights (2005*a*), "Pharmaceutical Anti-Counterfeiting Strategies", Business Insights Ltd.

Business Insight (2005*b*), "The RFID Market Outlook: New applications, best practices and future profit opportunities", July 2005.

Cientifica (2005), "Global R&D Spend, 2002-2004", Survey, October 2005.

Collier, P. (2005), "Hologramme sur faux medicaments", Contrefaçon Riposte, mars 2005.

Dominican Republican News (DRN) (2006). "Panama Registers 30 Deaths due to Contaminated Medicine", Wednesday, 25 October 2006.

EFPIA (2006), "Identification and Coding of Pharmaceutical Products in Europe", EMEA Briefing Paper, 27 September 2006.

Encarna Nunez Diaz (2005), "Counterfeit Drug Trace Causes USD 40 million Loss to Pharma Industry in El Salvador", *World Markets Analysis*, Nov. 24, 2005.

EU Commission (2006), "Commission warns about fake drugs on the Internet", Press release, Brussels, IP/06/375, 27 March 2006.

GlaxoSmithKline Press Release (2002). "GlaxoSmithKline Alerts Patients, Pharmacists and Physicians to Watch for Third-Party Tampering that Incorrectly Label Ziagen as Combivir", 10 May 2002.

GlobalOptions Inc. (2003), *An Analysis of Terrorist Threats to the American Medicine Supply*, Signature Book Printing Inc., Gaithersburg, Maryland.

Gray, N. (2006), "Changing Landscapes: A Special Report of the World's Top 50 Pharma Companies", *PharmaExec.com*, May 2006.

Hawkes, N. (2006), "Drug Giant will sell direct to beat the Counterfeiters", Timesonline, 5 October 2006.

IMS Health (2006), "Global Pharmaceutical Sales – 2005", IMS Health, 2006.

Jaret, P. (2004), "Fake Drugs: Real Threat", *Los Angeles Times*, 9 February 2004.

Li, L. (2006), "Unified IPR Violation Hotline" *China Daily*, 29 August 2006.

Medicines and Healthcare Products Regulatory Agency [MHRA] (2005*a*). Press Release, "Reading Estate Agent Punished for Illegal Sale of Counterfeit", 28 June 2005.

Medicines and Healthcare Products Regulatory Agency [MHRA] (2005*b*), "Drug Alert Ref. MDR 23-07/051", 28 July 2005.

Medicines and Healthcare Products Regulatory Agency (MHRA) and the Royal Pharmaceutical Society of Great Britain (RPSGB) (2006*a*), "Guidance for Pharmacists", May 2006.

Medicines and Healthcare Products Regulatory Agency (MHRA) and the Royal Pharmaceutical Society of Great Britain (RPSGB) (2006*b*), "Guidance for Patients", May 2006.

National Agency for Food and Drug Administration and Control (NAFDAC) (2006), "Strategies Employed In Combating Drug Counterfeiting In Nigeria", 2006.

NewKerala (2006), "Half of Medicines Sold in Pak Are Fake", posted 9 March 2006.

OECD (2006), "Innovation in Pharmaceutical Biotechnology", 2006.

OECD (2005), "Counterfeiting and Piracy: Industry Survey", July 2005.

Ortho Biotech (2002*a*), "Important Drug Warning: Counterfeiting of Procrit", June 6, 2002.

Ortho Biotech (2002*b*), "Important Drug Warning: Counterfeiting of Procrit (Epoetin Alfa)", Additional counterfeit lot, 7 June 2002.

Ortho Biotech (2002*c*), "Important Drug Warning: Additional Counterfeit Product Labelled as Procrit (Epoetin Alfa)", bearing lot number P004582, 11 October 2002.

Pfizer (2005), "Counterfeit Medicines – A Clear and Present Danger", 2005.

Pfizer (2006), "Pfizer Introduces Radio Frequency Identification Technology to Combat Counterfeiting, Protect Patient Health", Press Release, 6 January 2006.

Pharmaceutical Security Institute (PSI) (2006), "Annual Situation Report", 2005.

Pharmaceutical Security Institute (PSI) (2005), "Annual Situation Report", 2004.

PharmaExec.com (2006), "World's Top 50 Pharmaceutical Companies", 7th Annual Report, May 2006.

PhRMA (2006), "Survey of Pharmaceutical Counterfeiting Laws and Remedies", September 2006.

Shaw, C. (2005), "Combating Pharmaceutical Counterfeiting", Lilly, November 2005.

TAXUD (2005), "Statistics Recorded at the External Borders of the EU", 2005.

TAXUD (2004), "Statistics Recorded at the External Borders of the EU", 2004.

TAXUD (2003), "Statistics Recorded at the External Borders of the EU", 2003.

TAXUD (2002), "Statistics Recorded at the External Borders of the EU", 2002.

TAXUD (2001), "Statistics Recorded at the External Borders of the EU", 2001.

TAXUD (2000), "Statistics Recorded at the External Borders of the EU", 2000.

U.S. Customs and Border Protection (2005), News Release, "San Francisco Customs and Border Protection Officers Seize Counterfeit Tamiflu", December 19, 2005.

U.S. Customs and Border Protection (2006a), "Intellectual Property Rights – Top Commodities Seized – Mid Year FY 2006", July 2006.

U.S. Customs and Border Protection (2006b), News Release, "CBP Seizes More Suspect Tamiflu at Mail Facilities",13 January 2006.

U.S. Department of Justice (2005a), Press Release, "Internet Pharmacy Operator Receives 51 Month Prison Sentence", 21 January 2005.

U.S. Department of Justice (2005b), Todd P. Graves, Office of the United States Attorney, Western District of Missouri, "Pharmaceutical Distributors Indicted for USD 42 million Lipitor Smuggling", *Counterfeiting*, 31 August 2005.

U.S. Department of Justice (2005c), United States Attorney, Eastern District of Pennsylvania, "International Internet Drug Trafficking Network Shut Down", 20 April 2005.

U.S. Department of Justice, (2006a), R. Alexander Acosta, United States Attorney for the Southern District of Florida, Press Release, "Defendants Sentenced on Fake Botox Case", 26 January 2006.

U.S. Department of Justice (2006b), "Hi-Tech Pharmaceuticals & 11 Individuals Indicted for 'Generic' Pill Fraud Scheme", 20 September 2006.

U.S. Department of Justice (2006c), "Florida Man Sentenced in Fake Lipitor Conspiracy", News Release, 23 October 2006.

U.S. Food and Drug Administration (2005), "Combating Counterfeit Drugs: A Report of the Food and Drug Administration Annual Update", 18 May 2005.

U.S. Food and Drug Administration (2006a), "Fraudulent, Unapproved Influenza-Related Products", *FDA Consumer Magazine*, March-April, 2006.

U.S. Food and Drug Administration (2006b), "Combating Counterfeit Drugs: A Report of the Food and Drug Administration Annual Update", May 2006.

U.S. Food and Drug Administration (2006c), "FDA Counterfeit Drug Task Force Report: 2006 Update", June 2006.

U.S. Newswire (2006), "DOJ: Nineteen Charged with Racketeering to Support Terrorist Organization", 29 March 2006.

World Health Organization/UNICEF (2005), "World Malaria Report 2005".

World Health Organization (2006a). Counterfeit Medicines. Fact Sheet No. 275. Revised November 2006.

Chapter 13

TOBACCO SECTOR

3.1. General description

This sector overview covers the international tobacco industry, focusing on cigarettes, as these constitute by far the greatest proportion of tobacco products, as well as yielding the greatest volume of information.

The tobacco industry is almost unique, in that taxes constitute the major component of the final retail price, which makes tobacco, and especially cigarettes, lucrative for smugglers.

The same profit potential for smugglers of counterfeited tobacco products, of course, also exists for the smugglers of genuine tobacco goods, and they share many characteristics, such as transport and distribution channels and the involvement of organised crime. As a consequence, it is frequently impossible to differentiate between them, as data sources may mix them up; for example, customs authorities would probably not normally differentiate between smuggled genuine and smuggled counterfeit cigarettes. While every effort has been made to differentiate between these two quite different illicit activities, this has not always been possible, and as a consequence some information may not be totally reliable.

From comments made by industry respondents to the OECD survey indicating that consumers are reluctant to knowingly buy counterfeited cigarettes, it has also been assumed that the entire range of counterfeit tobacco products are intended to deceive the consumer.

3.2. Types of infringement

Abuse of trademarks (brand names) is by far the most common form of intellectual property infringement in the tobacco sector. There may also possibly be instances of patent or design infringement, but these are rare. Copyright infringements do not apply to this sector.

3.3. Products most affected

The products most affected by counterfeiting are cigarettes. They combine certain characteristics that make them very convenient for counterfeiters, such as being consumed in very large quantities, small in size, do not require any special transportation or storage, and they are capable of being easily produced on a large scale with a relatively small investment. Together, these characteristics make them hard to track, which is likely to give the counterfeiter a perception of low risk. Other tobacco products (such as cigars, roll-your-own tobacco and snuff) may also be counterfeited, but these would be a very small segment compared to cigarettes (about 5% according to one industry respondent).

The market for cigarettes is very large, with the World Health Organization estimating that some 5.5 trillion are consumed every year (World Health Organization, 2002).

13.4. The importance of excise and other taxes

Tobacco products share with alcohol the distinction of being unique consumer products because their retail price includes very high excise and other taxes. These taxes can vary widely. An industry study estimated that taxes represent around 50% to 60% of the retail price of cigarettes, but in some cases taxes can constitute up to 70% to 80% of prices (VicHealth and World Bank, 2001).

This means that compared to most other products, production costs and brand values play a relatively minor role in the retail price of a pack of cigarettes, and this creates a situation in which counterfeiters can generate very high profit margins by not only producing cheap fakes, but also by avoiding all of the tax burden.

For example, in the United States, a typical carton of cigarettes retails for around USD 35; in addition to a federal tax of USD 3.60 per carton, States impose per-carton taxes that range from USD 0.70 in South Carolina to USD 24.60 in Rhode Island[201] (Federation of Tax Administrators, 2006; GAO, 2004). The final pricing highlights the potential profit for smugglers, especially as a carton of counterfeit cigarettes would cost around USD 3.00 to produce.

Based on these numbers, each container that is seized in the United States (ca. 8.5 mill sticks) has a street value of USD 1 million to 1.5 million, yet the cost to the manufacturer of producing the counterfeit product in the container is about USD 120 000 to 130 000, plus around 25% to 30% for shipping costs (when China is the source market, for example). It is reported that every day, eight to ten containers of counterfeit cigarettes produced in China are unloaded from ships at the port of Los Angeles and enter the United States undetected under false import documentation (Chow, 2003).

For another example, in the UK, 86% of the retail price of cigarettes is taxes (National Center for Chronic Disease Prevention and Health Promotion, 2006), and with similar production costs as in the US example above, when China is the source country.

In the EU in general, the overall tax incidence on cigarettes, including VAT, is typically a little lower than in the UK, between 70% and 80% (International Tax & Investment Center, 2003).

13.5. Modes of operation

In the vast majority of countries and territories, cigarette manufacturers do not sell cigarettes directly to the public. Instead, they sell cigarettes in bulk quantities to distributors, wholesalers, or in some cases government monopolies, which then pass them down the distribution chain to consumers. Typically, the number of cigarettes sold is reduced at each step of the chain, as the initial bulk shipment of cigarettes is divided and subdivided until it reaches the retailer, who then sells cigarettes in either cartons or packs

---

201.   The median for all states is USD 8.00.

to the individual consumer (Phillip Morris International, 2004). This complex network may lead to a lack of transparency and creates loopholes for counterfeiters to infiltrate the supply chain with their fake products.

According to survey respondents, a typical transaction involving production in China for export to other markets, would have the products being manufactured to order, with orders placed by traders based overseas who control the distribution and sale of the product in the target market, and who would finance the deals and reap the majority of the profits.

In the case of counterfeits produced outside China (*e.g.* Paraguay, Middle East) it is often the owners of the factories who control the business and who take the greatest share of the profits.

With regard to the supply of inputs, in the case of China it is usually brokers who provide the non-tobacco materials, with tobacco apparently sourced from local tobacco farmers who produce more than their state-allocated quotas. Factories outside China often produce both legal and counterfeits together (sometimes described as production overruns). These factories source their materials directly from the same entities that supply legitimate manufacturers, and the factories' input requirements for their legitimate volumes provide "cover" for the counterfeit volumes.

Transport of counterfeits is usually by container, using the same distribution systems as legitimate products, with the products either falsely declared, or shipping documents changed prior to arrival at their final destination to facilitate smuggling. One respondent claimed that shipments are often falsely declared or trans-shipped through free-trade zones to complicate document trails. Large-scale counterfeiters, who transport counterfeit cigarettes via sea or land, are now increasingly using transit or trans-shipment points in geographically diverse ports or free-trade zones, as a means of disguising the nature of the product and complicating the tracking and detection of the shipments.

As the product approaches its target market, the load is then de-stuffed from the container and broken up into smaller units for onward transportation by a variety of trans-ports. This also reduces the risk and impact of any losses incurred at the points of entry.

As some respondents noted, these smuggling operations also utilise sophisticated disguising techniques, such as innocuous top loadings and fake documentation, to hide the true nature of their cargoes.

One respondent also suggested that all these actions are intended to divert the attention of customs authorities, who may have doubts about their jurisdictional rights over transhipments, and so may not feel compelled to investigate cargoes destined for destinations outside their own borders.

As a general observation, the transport and distribution networks for major smuggling operations are highly organised, secure and difficult to detect, often because of the participation of organised crime in the movement and sale (but rarely in the production) of the counterfeit products, which provides the sophisticated financial and logistical support that make the networks difficult and dangerous to infiltrate.

These organised criminal groups, which often already have established trading networks for other commodities, such as drugs, are now turning to counterfeit cigarettes due to the relatively lower risks and penalties, and the convenient use of their pre-existing smuggling and distribution networks (Chow, 2003). In addition, unlike narcotics and other illicit substances that must constantly be hidden before sale to the consumer, counterfeit cigarettes, once smuggled into the target market, can be moved relatively openly, thus reducing the cost of warehousing and distribution.

One respondent stated that criminal organisations with entities active in the United States, China, and Hong Kong, China are known to be very active in smuggling counterfeit cigarettes. Reportedly, the primary target markets of the criminal organisations seem to be high tax and volume markets within the EU -- with the United Kingdom market appearing to be the most attractive.

Also, industry noted the substantial use being made of courier and airmail parcel post services to smuggle counterfeit tobacco products into foreign markets. The high retail value of the product (because of high taxation) makes the smuggling of even relatively small volumes of product sufficiently profitable for individuals to accept the risks.

In some localities, particularly in areas near borders where taxes on one side of the border differ from those on the other side, there can be an incentive for individuals to carry small quantities of cigarettes across the border to sell them. While this small-scale smuggling (of both genuine and counterfeit tobacco products) is seen by the industry as being of lesser concern than large-scale, organised smuggling, it can nevertheless constitute considerable volumes due to the high number of participants.

In addition, some respondents noted that the Internet has clearly become a popular mechanism for consumers purchasing tobacco products, as this is a convenient, and increasingly significant, way of circumventing taxes. Moreover, the sale of counterfeit tobacco products over the Internet provides counterfeiters with a vehicle for expanding sales to minors. Many of the industry respondents explicitly noted that they have not authorised anyone to sell tobacco products on the Internet on their behalf, and are not selling themselves.

13.6. Factors that drive the production and consumption of counterfeit tobacco products

Each product sector has its own peculiar characteristics that will in part determine and shape those factors that drive production and consumption, and the recognition and understanding of these drivers can provide insights on the propensity for that category of goods to be produced. In turn, this may provide some guidance on the likelihood that such products can be found in the market place and may support statistical data collected through customs interdictions, police raids on production and retail facilities, the results of legal action and other market-based data. Moreover, the factors could provide important insights into how surveys and economic modelling could best be used to improve measurement.

Please refer to the summary table at the end of this chapter, Table 13.1, titled "Propensity to produce or consume counterfeited tobacco products". The drivers that are considered to apply in the tobacco sector have been judged on whether, and to what extent, they are favourable or unfavourable for the production and consumption of these counterfeited goods.

The analysis of factors that drive the production of counterfeit tobacco products indicates that counterfeiting in this sector is a high-risk enterprise, especially if the goods are smuggled, but that the rewards, in the form of potentially very high profits, appear to be more than sufficient to encourage extensive counterfeiting activity.

The greatest profits are available to counterfeiters if they successfully smuggle their products into a market, as this allows them to avoid the very high taxes that normally apply to tobacco products, and which can constitute up to 70% to 80% of the final retail price of tobacco products.

From the consumer's perspective, the principal issue is that the majority of tobacco products are manufactured to deceive the purchaser, and most buyers would thus not be aware that they have purchased a counterfeit product. The ability of counterfeiters to produce tobacco products that superficially are virtually indistinguishable from the original, and the complexity in definitively establishing the phoniness of a product (probably requiring a chemical analysis), makes this one of the more difficult products to be identified as counterfeit by consumers.

For consumers who willingly purchase counterfeit cigarettes, there is little risk (apart from the obvious potential health risks) from their purchasing decision, as they are unlikely to be apprehended and prosecuted for the purchase of small quantities of these products.

The significant and increasing role of the Internet, for both producers and consumers, should be noted.

3.7. Magnitude, scope and trend of infringements

Although the smuggling of genuine cigarettes is not the subject of this analysis, it is worth exploring the relationship between these and counterfeit cigarettes, and how the smuggling of genuine cigarettes and counterfeited cigarettes has developed proportionately in recent years, indicating the two are quite clearly linked.

During the late 1990s, manufacturers of genuine products, working with governments, increased controls over distributors and retailers, thereby making less genuine product available for smuggling. The smugglers responded by increasing production and trafficking of counterfeit products, as these would not be captured by the more stringent regulations affecting the genuine items. Reportedly, the ease with which counterfeiters have access to state-of-the-art cigarette manufacturing and printing facilities to faithfully reproduce packaging materials has facilitated the growth in the counterfeit products.

The industry believes that the shift in emphasis from the smuggling of genuine to counterfeit products is already significant and will increase, so that as one form of trade replaces the other the overall threat to the tobacco industry will not be greatly altered.

The perceived shift in illicit cigarette trading, from originals to counterfeits, is supported by Customs statistics and other studies. In 2000/01, illicit tobacco was estimated to account for 25% of all cigarette sales in the United Kingdom, with counterfeits accounting for 5% (UK House of Commons, 2002). In 2002, Customs & Excise in the UK seized 2.6 billion cigarette sticks, of which 2.2 billion were smuggled genuine products and only 390 million counterfeits (15%). However, in 2004, of 1.8 billion sticks seized by UK Customs & Excise, 828 million were genuine items, while 972 million were counterfeits (54%) (The Organised Crime Task Force, 2006).

A more recent study in the UK (HM Treasury, 2006) indicated that of all cigarettes seized by Customs & Excise, the proportion that was counterfeit had risen from 15% in 2001/02 to 48% in 2005/05.

A similar shift occurred in the United States. By 2003, seizures of counterfeit products substantially exceeded those of genuine cigarettes, estimated to be USD 45.8 million vs. USD 5.1 million, respectively (United States General Accounting Office, 2004).

US Customs seized cigarettes worth USD 9.6 million (domestic value) in FY[202] 2005 (USD 24.2 million in FY 2004), which is about 10% of overall seizures (17% in FY 2004) (US Customs and Border Protection and US Immigration and Customs Enforcement, Department of Homeland Security, 2006). Interestingly, cigarette seizures were zero in 1998 and USD 0.3 million in 1999 (United States General Accounting Office, 2004), which further supports the notion of a rapid increase in counterfeiting in the late 1990s.

In the EU, customs statistics show that around 8.3 billion cigarettes were seized in 2004, a rise of 25% compared to 2003 (European Union, Taxation and Customs Unit, 2005). Statistics for 2005 are not available, nor are breakdowns between original and counterfeit products.

13.8. Centres of counterfeit production and distribution

With respect to the origin of counterfeited cigarettes, EU Customs' data reveals that in 2004 around 47% of all items seized came from China, 7% from the UAE and 6.5% from Gambia (European Union, Taxation and Customs Unit, 2005). Statistics for FY 2003 are not available, neither are statistics for FY 2005.

As reported by US Customs, the main source country for imported fake cigarettes also is China, with USD 9.5 million in domestic value in FY 2005 (USD 22.1 million in FY 2004, USD 33.2 million in FY 2003), which is about 99% of the overall amount of items seized (91% in FY 2004, 80% in FY 2003) in terms of value (US Customs and Border Protection and US Immigration and Customs Enforcement, Department of Homeland Security, 2006).

Industry experience, as reported by respondents to the OECD survey, tends to support the quantitative data from EU Customs, suggesting that more than 50% of the overall counterfeit cigarette production takes place in China, where industry estimates that around 100 billion counterfeit cigarettes are produced each year, with considerable domestic consumption.

The map in Figure 13.1 shows some known transportation patterns of counterfeited tobacco products originating in China.

While China has been identified as the largest producer of counterfeit cigarettes, it is not alone, and other economies were identified by industry respondents as being involved in counterfeiting activities. For example, in the Asia region in 2005, Customs agents in South Korea and Chinese Taipei seized shipments of imported counterfeit cigarettes valued in the millions of dollars. Criminal syndicates in North Korea are also believed to be producing cigarettes; Thailand, Vietnam, Malaysia, Paraguay and the Middle East were also mentioned by survey respondents.

---

202.   FY: fiscal year; in the US, the fiscal year 2005 starts 1 October 2004 and ends 30 September 2005.

Figure 13.1. Transportation patterns

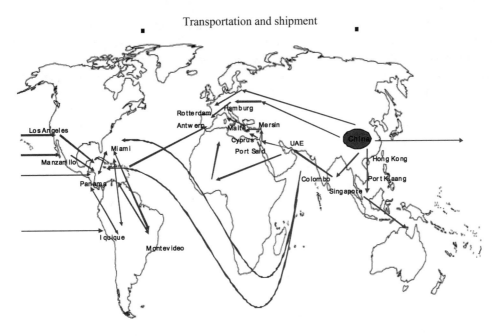

Note: See footnote for Table 8.2 in Chapter 8.

Some respondents also noted that there has been an increasing shift away from the unauthorised use of surplus tobacco-manufacturing capacity by contracted manufacturers for ultimate sale in the grey markets of Central and Eastern Europe (Russia, Albania, Latvia, Ukraine were named). Instead, there has been increasing exportation of both skilled personnel and machinery to major EU markets in order to set up illegal manufacturing facilities inside those markets. Thus, the number of illegal factories within the EU producing counterfeit cigarettes has been increasing (Germany, Poland, Netherlands, the Czech Republic and Greece were especially named).

This strategy reduces the risk for counterfeiters by minimising transport, avoiding customs barriers and facilitating direct access to the illegal distribution networks inside the markets. A very recent example was the raid of a manufacturing facility in Salzburg, Austria, where the tax losses resulting from the production of counterfeit cigarettes in that facility were estimated at EUR 50 million (Voralberg Online, 2006).

This shift is also occurring in various countries in the Middle East (Iran, Iraq, UAE), where enforcements of IP rights are reportedly difficult to initiate.

Numerous counterfeiting factories have also been discovered in various countries throughout Latin America, and especially Paraguay, Venezuela, Uruguay and Brazil (Philip Morris International, 2004). For instance, illegal cigarettes (both counterfeit and smuggled genuine products) now represent 34% of all cigarettes sold in Brazil each year, having jumped from 5% of the market in 1991 and 20% in 1995 (Brazil – US Business Council, 2003).

Respondents also stated that the main target markets for counterfeit tobacco products are the EU and the US. As noted earlier, this is mainly due to the large potential profit margins for counterfeiters in these regions due to the high excise taxes imposed on tobacco products. However, apart from these main targets, it is likely that most countries and territories would to some degree be a target for counterfeited cigarettes.

13.9. Effects of counterfeiting in the tobacco products sector

With respect to financial losses due to the counterfeiting of cigarettes, the most important factor is lost sales, since cigarettes are generally deceptive goods and therefore each counterfeited item sold can be considered a lost sale for the genuine manufacturer. Also to be considered are the costs of anti-counterfeiting operations, development of new methods of manufacture to minimise opportunities for imitation and to provide secure product recognition, and associated personnel costs. One respondent estimated the cost to the company of anti-counterfeiting operations (not including personnel costs) to be around USD 8 million per year.

Another respondent estimated losses each year for his company due to counterfeiting, of around USD 200 million. Industry estimates for the loss in revenue by brand owners varied widely, with the lowest of these estimates being around USD 800 million.

As to market share, one firm indicated that it viewed counterfeit products as its 4th or 5th biggest competitor in the world market, while another estimated counterfeit cigarettes to represent approximately 2% to 3% of total global consumption. From a narrower perspective, a UK respondent estimated that counterfeit cigarettes accounted for around a 10% loss of market share in the UK.

As far as loss of company image is concerned, counterfeit cigarettes can have serious quality problems, and except in the appearance of the packaging, may bear little resemblance to genuine products. Because counterfeits are marketed under well-known brand names, the consumer who smokes a counterfeit product may be expected to associate this poor quality with the brand, and this could be extremely harmful to the image and reputation of genuine brands, as well as resulting in lost revenue if the consumer switches brands.

In extreme cases, these effects may lead to the closure or consolidation of manufacturing facilities, leading to job losses and downstream effects on local economies and government revenue.

At the government level, respondents estimated financial losses for governments worldwide (from loss of excise revenue) to be around USD 2 billion.

Finally, consumers suffer because they are deceived into buying an inferior copy of the legitimate product, which apart from anything else may also present additional serious and unforeseen health risks.

While there is no definitive evidence available, some researchers have detected signs that counterfeit cigarettes have higher (and sometimes considerably higher) levels of tar, nicotine and carbon monoxide emissions. Therefore, whatever the health implications associated with the use of tobacco, they are likely to be greater in the case of counterfeit cigarettes versus known brands. Further research into this aspect of the production of counterfeit tobacco products could yield more reliable data.

Further, the generally lower cost of counterfeit cigarettes is likely to encourage higher consumption, especially amongst financially disadvantaged sectors of society and the young. Apart from anything else, cheap counterfeit tobacco products cut across the efforts of health authorities to blunt the consumption of tobacco through high taxation.

In addition, research has shown that heavy metal concentrations (especially cadmium and lead) in the tobacco of counterfeit cigarettes are much higher than in the genuine counterparts. The research identified potential harmful consequences to human health from these heavy metals and concluded that the typical counterfeit product adds significantly to the risks normally associated with smoking.

However, the research also noted that while it is inconceivable that counterfeiters would deliberately add heavy metals to their products, since there is no obvious reason to do so, they nevertheless noted that these heavy metals, possibly derived from cheap, unsuitable fertilisers, may contaminate tobacco crops (Stephens *et al.*, 2005). From here, it is not too far off to speculate that since these contaminated crops would not be knowingly purchased by the major tobacco companies, they could become an attractive proposition for counterfeiters. In any event, whether intended or not, these impurities when present add to the health risks faced by smokers.

3.10. Countermeasures taken

Industry has reported that it has turned its efforts towards tracking down cigarette counterfeiters at the supply level, since at the distribution level it is becoming much harder to distinguish a fake packet from the genuine article, and amounts seized tend to be much smaller.

Some tobacco companies have introduced covert product-authentication devices in their products, and these have assisted their own personnel to identify counterfeit products at points of sale and during Customs and police operations. However, overt devices that would enable genuine sellers and buyers to readily identify fakes have proven much more difficult to implement. It is worth noting that in other industry sectors covered by this OECD study, the experience of those industry groups has been that even sophisticated overt devices (such as holograms) have been quickly reproduced by counterfeiters, so this remains a significant challenge to the tobacco industry.

Securing the legitimate distribution chain is regarded as another key issue. Some of the respondents noted that a significantly lower counterfeiting level was noticeable in countries and territories where distribution is controlled, and consumers can only buy cigarettes in regulated outlets. The reason for this might be that in case of strict regulation, consumers know that the cigarettes they buy in places other than authorised stores are likely to be illicit (including those that are counterfeit).

Therefore, in countries where strict regulations limit the possibilities for counterfeiters to infiltrate the supply chain, counterfeit cigarettes could be considered as being only partly deceptive, since consumers might consider the possibility that the illegal cigarettes they buy might be counterfeits rather than smuggled genuine items.

Also, as part of efforts to address counterfeiting, some tobacco companies have created a Brand Integrity group that provides training for Customs officials and assists Customs and law enforcement authorities around the world. These activities focus on tracking, seizing and destroying counterfeit products, identifying manufacturing sources and supporting the prosecution of those involved in counterfeiting activities. Industry reported excellent co-operation in this field by China, Russia, Canada, Germany, Belgium, the Netherlands, Spain, Italy and France.

Canada provides an explicit example of a government anti-counterfeiting initiative. There, the Canada Revenue Agency, together with tobacco companies, has developed a new packaging technology for cigarette packs that employs labelling and watermark technology similar to that used for banknotes.

However, despite reportedly good co-operation with governments, respondents also reported problems at the local government level in some countries that negatively affect anti-counterfeiting measures. This occurrence has also been reported by respondents in other industry sectors examined in the course of this study.

In general, it is difficult to quantify the success of the anti-counterfeiting measures. Seizure and destruction statistics alone do not indicate the level of success of those measures, as the quantity of counterfeit cigarettes that go undetected is unknown. Some tobacco companies conduct market surveys, but these only provide an indication of the level of counterfeit production in a specific area or market, and cannot be extrapolated to determine the overall consumption of counterfeit cigarettes, or the success of anti-counterfeiting strategies.

Nevertheless, an example can be given of the results achieved by operations organised and initiated by industry in co-operation with governments. One of the respondents reported that in 2004 and the first quarter of 2005, on a global basis, their anti-counterfeiting efforts resulted in over 1.8 billon counterfeit cigarettes being seized. In total, 428 printing and/or manufacturing facilities were raided in 23 countries. During the same time period, as part of an ongoing law enforcement training programme, this company conducted 93 law enforcement training sessions in 36 countries, with over 2 100 law enforcement officers trained.

However, these countermeasures come at a price, and respondents also reported that legal costs are significant in instances when tobacco companies are forced to take civil actions against counterfeiters. According to industry, a strictly objective assessment of these countermeasures would indicate that in the short term their cost can exceed the losses that would be incurred by taking no action. Despite this, fighting counterfeiting is considered a long-term investment, and companies report that they are continuing with their efforts to detect and prosecute counterfeiters.

Industry respondents also noted that law enforcement authorities would be involved wherever possible, as they can invoke criminal actions against the persons involved, which can result in heavy fines or jail terms, and these are considered to be much stronger deterrents than the court orders and civil damages available under private law. A similar point was made by respondents in other industry sectors surveyed during the course of this OECD study.

Some manufacturers have entered into MOUs (Memorandum of Understanding) with governments and Customs authorities in an effort to reduce smuggling and counterfeiting. Other intergovernmental and inter-regional co-operation (such as the Crocodile projects in the ASEAN region) has targeted the distribution and sale of illicit cigarettes (both genuine and counterfeit). As long as they can be sustained, these initiatives are likely to make it more difficult for counterfeiters to produce, distribute and market their products.

Table 13.1. **Propensity to produce or consume counterfeited tobacco products**

FOR PRODUCERS	EFFECTS ON PROPENSITIES TO CONSUME
Market characteristics	
Unit profitability	The potential profit margin can be quite large, due to the high excise and other taxes imposed on tobacco products, especially in the US and the EU.
Market size	Over 1.1 billion people smoke 5.5 trillion cigarettes per year. There is probably no other single product that is regularly consumed on such a large basis. Thus, the market opportunities are enormous.
Genuine brand power	Many tobacco brands (especially cigarettes) are widely advertised and promoted, and so are well-known throughout the world.
Production, distribution and technology	
Production investment	Once the investment has been made in cigarette manufacturing and packaging/labelling equipment, the cost of production is quite small (around USD 3.00 per carton). Manufacturing equipment is relatively compact, and thus the investment in production facilities is likely to be moderate.
Technology	Because of the simple nature of tobacco products, it is not necessary to invest in sophisticated technology.
Logistics	Tobacco products are small items that do not need special handling and can be transported using normal means. However, arrangements to either smuggle or bypass customs/excise attention would require special attention, and may require the participation of well-organised groups.
Marketing and sale	Branded products are well-known and have a ready market. Cigarettes can be sold in packets, or even individually, to increase their appeal in low-income markets. The use of the Internet is becoming increasingly important.
Ability to conceal operations	While some moderately bulky equipment is necessary for the production of counterfeit tobacco products, concealment would not be too difficult. Obtaining raw materials (especially tobacco), and moving stock in and out of premises are likely to be most difficult aspects to conceal.
Deception	For the average consumer it is practically impossible to detect counterfeit tobacco products, especially when the buyer is not familiar with the taste of the product. This is because it is very simple for counterfeiters to copy the look and packaging of the tobacco product. In some cases, counterfeiters can charge prices that are close to those of the original items.
Institutional characteristics	
Risk of discovery	Despite considerable customs/excise and industry efforts to apprehend smuggled and counterfeit tobacco products, in practice, the actual risk for counterfeiters seems to be acceptable to them, mainly due to the large volume of trafficking that takes place and the sophisticated methods used to avoid, or at least minimise, detection.
Enforcement	Given the illicit nature of the trade, and the fact that these are excisable goods, the likelihood of prosecution if apprehended would be very high.
Penalties	Penalties, including heavy fines and jail sentences, could be expected by those found guilty of counterfeiting and smuggling.
FOR CONSUMERS	**EFFECT ON PROPENSITIES TO CONSUME NON-DECEPTIVE ITEMS**
Product characteristics	
Price	Price may be a very strong contributing factor, and may encourage consumers to buy them, even if there is a suspicion that the cigarettes may not be genuine. This may be especially so in low-income markets where normally consumers would be excluded from smoking original brands at full prices.
Quality and nature of product	The appearance of counterfeit cigarettes can be very close to that of originals. While taste may differ, many consumers may not be able to make comparisons.
Ability to conceal status	Some consumers may buy counterfeit brands as status symbols, and the concealment of counterfeits could be relatively easy in unsophisticated markets. In such cases, the close outward appearance of the counterfeit items to the originals would certainly be a factor in consumption.

Consumer characteristics	
Health risks	Potentially very high, but this has not generally deterred smokers. However, for known counterfeit products, there may be strong reluctance to use them, unless other factors (such as image or price) override health concerns.
Safety risks	None obvious.
Personal values	Indications are that consuming counterfeit cigarettes is not considered to be a serious crime.
Institutional characteristics	
Risk of discovery	Very little, since detection of counterfeit cigarettes at the consumer level is ineffective, and reportedly companies and governments focus on manufacturers or the distribution/supply chain. Detection at the consumer level is generally not undertaken by either industry or governments.
Risk of prosecution	Little risk of prosecution, as the number of individuals would be very large, difficult to find, and the quantities involved are likely to be small. Overall, prosecuting consumers is likely to be quiet an ineffective way of dealing with counterfeiting in this sector.
Penalties	If at all existent, penalties would be limited to small fines, since consumers buy small quantities of cigarettes that do not justify large penalties. In addition, consumer could also claim to not having knowingly bought the counterfeits, especially if these were sold in regular outlets.
Availability and ease of acquisition	Freely available and easily acquired in many markets. Difficulty of smuggling in some jurisdictions may make availability uncertain. The Internet is a growing medium of sale.

References

Brazil-US Business Council (2003), "Counterfeiting and Piracy in Brazil: The Economy Impact", Brazil-US. Business Council, Washington D.C.

Chow, D., The Ohio State University College of Law (2003), "Organized crime, local protectionism, and the trade in counterfeit goods in China", China Economic Review 14, Elsevier Inc., Columbus, Ohio.

European Union, Taxation and Customs Unit (2005), "Community-wide statistics for 2004 and major changes 2003-2004", http://europa.eu.int/comm/taxation_customs/customs/customs_controls/counterfeit_piracy/statistics/index_en.htm.

European Union, Taxation and Customs Unit (2001), "Community-wide statistics for 2000", http://europa.eu.int/comm/taxation_customs/resources/documents/statistics_en_2000.pdf.

Federation of Tax Administrators (2006), "State Excise Tax Rates on Cigarettes as of January 1, 2006", www.taxadmin.org/FTA/rate/cigarett.html.

HM Treasury (2006), "New Responses to New Challenges: Reinforcing the Tackling Tobacco Smuggling Strategy", www.hm-treasury.gov.uk.

International Tax & Investment Center (2003), "Cigarette Taxation: Issues for EU Accession Countries, International Tax and Investment Center", Special Report, London.

National Center for Chronic Disease Prevention and Health Promotion (2006), "Tobacco Taxation - Fact Sheet", London, www.cdc.gov/tobacco/sgr/sgr_2000/factsheets/factsheets_taxation.htm

Phillip Morris International (2004), "The Illicit Trade in Cigarettes: The Phillip Morris International Perspective", Phillip Morris International, Lausanne.

Stephens W., Calder A. and J. Newton (2005), "Source and Health Implications of High Toxic Metal Concentrations in Illicit Tobacco Products", Environmental Science & Technology, Vol. 39 No. 2 2005, Fife, Scotland.

The Organized Crime Task Force (2006), "Illicit Tobacco – Statistics", www.octf.gov.uk/index.cfm/section/article/page/IllicitTobacco.

Voralberg Online (2006), Illegale Zigarettenfabrik entdeckt, http://www.vol.at/engine.aspx/page/vol-article-detail-page/cn/vol-news-chorn-20060607-111050/dc/tp%3Avol%3Aoesterreich/ag/tp-apa.

UK House of Commons (2002), "Tobacco Smuggling, Third Report of the Committee of Public Accounts", www.publications.parliament.uk.

US Customs and Border Protection and US Immigration and Customs Enforcement, Department of Homeland Security (2006), "Top IPR Commodities Seized", www.cbp.gov/linkhandler/cgov/import/commercial_enforcement/ipr/seizure/fy05_mid year_stats.ctt/fy05_ipr_midyear.pdf.

United States General Accounting Office (2004), "Cigarette Smuggling – Federal Law Enforcement Efforts and Seizures Increasing", US General Accounting Office, Washington D.C., USA.

VicHealth Centre for Tobacco Control, "Tobacco taxes and prices", at www.vctc.org.au/tc-res/latest.htm.

World Bank (2001), "Economics of Tobacco for the East Asian and Pacific (EAP Region)".

World Health Organization (2002), "The Tobacco Atlas", World Health Organization, Geneva, Switzerland.

OECD PUBLICATIONS, 2, rue André-Pascal, 75775 PARIS CEDEX 16
PRINTED IN FRANCE
(92 2008 04 1 P) ISBN 978-92-64-04551-4 – No. 56219 2008